THE GOSPEL OF MATTHEW

(VOLUME TWO—CHAPTERS XI to XXVIII)

The Rev. WILLIAM BARCLAY, B.D.

*Lecturer in New Testament Language and Literature
and in Hellenistic Greek in the University of Glasgow*

THE SAINT ANDREW PRESS
EDINBURGH

Published by The Saint Andrew Press,
121 George Street, Edinburgh 2
and printed in Scotland by
McCorquodale & Co., Ltd., Glasgow.

First Edition — June, 1957
Second Edition — June, 1958
Second Impression — November, 1959
Third Impression — November, 1960

GENERAL INTRODUCTION

IT may truly be said that this series of Daily Bible Studies began almost accidentally. A series which the Church of Scotland was using came to an end, and another series was immediately required. I was asked to write a volume on *Acts*, and, at the moment, had no intention beyond that. But one volume followed another, until the demand for one volume became a plan to write on the whole New Testament.

The translation which is given in each volume claims no special merit. It was included in order that the reader might be able to carry both the text of the New Testament and the comments on it wherever he went, and that he might be able to read it anywhere. While I was making the translation, the translations of Moffatt, Weymouth, and Knox were ever beside me. *The American Revised Standard Version, The Twentieth Century New Testament,* and *The New Testament in Plain English,* by Charles Kingsley Williams, have been in constant use. Since its publication, I have consistently consulted *The Authentic New Testament,* translated by Hugh J. Schonfield.

I cannot see another edition of these books going out to the public without expressing my very deep and sincere gratitude to the Church of Scotland Publications Committee for allowing me the privilege of first beginning, and then continuing, this series. And in particular I wish to express my very great gratitude to the convener, Rev. R. G. Macdonald, O.B.E., M.A., D.D., and to the committee's secretary and manager, Rev. Andrew McCosh, M.A., S.T.M., for constant encouragement and never-failing sympathy and help.

As these volumes went on, the idea of the whole series developed. The aim is to make the results of modern scholarship available to the non-technical reader in a form that does not require a theological education to understand; and then to seek to make the teaching of the New Testament books relevant to life and work to-day. The whole aim of these books is summed up in Richard of Chichester's famous prayer; they are meant to enable men and women to know Jesus Christ more clearly, to love Him more dearly, and to follow Him more nearly. It is my prayer that they may do something to make that possible.

CONTENTS

THE GOSPEL OF MATTHEW

CONTENTS

THE GOSPEL OF MATTHEW

CONTENTS

THE GOSPEL OF MATTHEW

CONTENTS

THE GOSPEL OF MATTHEW

CONTENTS

THE GOSPEL OF MATTHEW

CONTENTS

THE SIX ACCENTS IN THE VOICE OF JESUS

Matthew 11 is a chapter in which Jesus is speaking all the time; and, as He speaks to different people and about different things, we hear the accent of His voice vary and change. It will be of the greatest interest to look one by one at the six accents in the voice of Jesus.

THE ACCENT OF CONFIDENCE

Matthew 11: 1-6

> And when Jesus had completed His instructions to the twelve disciples, He left there to go on teaching and to go on making His proclamation in their towns.
>
> When John had heard in prison about the things that the Anointed One of God was doing, he sent to Him and asked Him through His disciples: " Are you the One who is to come, or, must we go on expecting another? " " Go back," said Jesus, " and give John the report of what you are hearing and seeing. The blind are having their sight restored, and the lame are walking; the lepers are being cleansed, and the deaf are hearing; the dead are being raised up, and the poor are receiving the good news. And blessed is the man who does not take offence at me."

THE career of John had ended in disaster. It was not John's habit to soften the truth for any man; and John was incapable of seeing evil without rebuking it. John had spoken too fearlessly and too definitely for his own safety. Herod of Antipas of Galilee had paid a visit to his brother in Rome. During that visit he seduced his brother's wife. He came home again, and dismissed his own wife, and married the sister-in-law whom he had lured away from her husband. Publicly and sternly John rebuked Herod. It was never safe to rebuke an eastern despot; Herod took his revenge; and John was thrown into the dungeons of the fortress of Machaerus down in the mountains near the Dead Sea.

For any man that would have been a terrible fate, but

I

for John the Baptist it was worse than for most men. He was the child of the desert; all his life he had lived in the wide open spaces, with the clean wind on his face and the spacious vault of the sky for his roof. And now he was confined within the four narrow walls of an underground dungeon. For a man like John, who had probably never lived in a house, this must have been an agony. In Carlisle Castle there is a little cell. Once long ago they had put a border chieftain in that cell and had left him for years. In that cell there is one little window, which is placed too high for a man to look out of it when he is standing on the floor. On the ledge of the window, in the stone, there are two depressions worn away. They are the marks of the hands of the border chieftain, the places where, day after day, he had lifted himself up by placing his hands on the ledge that he might look out on the green dales across which he would never ride again. John must have been like that; and there is nothing to wonder at and still less to criticize, in the fact that questions began to form themselves in John's mind. He had been so sure that Jesus was the One who was to come. That was one of the commonest titles for the Messiah for whom the Jews waited with such eager expectation (*Mark* 11: 9; *Luke* 13: 35; 19: 38; *Hebrews* 10: 37; *Psalm* 118: 26). A dying man cannot afford to have doubts; he must be sure; and so John sent his disciples to Jesus with the question: " Are you the One who was to come, or, must we go on wearily for someone else?" There are many possible things behind that question.

(i) Some people think that the question was asked, not for John's sake at all, but *for the sake of his disciples*. It may be that when John and his disciples talked in prison, the disciples may have questioned whether Jesus was really the One who was to come. And John's answer was: " If you have any doubts, and if you cannot be sure who Jesus really is, go and see what He is doing, and what He can do; and then your doubts will be at an end." If that is the case, it was a good answer. If anyone begins to argue with us about Jesus, and to question His supremacy, the best of all answers is not to counter argument with argument, but to say, " Give your life to Him; and see what He can do with it." The supreme argument for Christ is not intellectual debate, but experience of His changing power.

(ii) It may be that John's question was the question of *impatience*. John's message had been a message of doom (*Matthew* 3: 7-12). The axe was at the root of the tree; the winnowing process had begun; the divine fire of cleansing judgment had begun to burn. It may be that John was thinking: " When is Jesus going to start on action? When is He going to blast His enemies? When is He going to begin burning up the wicked? When is the day of God's holy destruction going to begin? " It may well be that John was impatient with Jesus because Jesus was not what he expected Him to be. One thing is certain that the man who waits for savage wrath will always be disappointed in Jesus, but the man who looks for love will never find his hopes defeated.

(iii) Some few have thought that this question of John was nothing less than the question of dawning *faith and hope*. He had seen Jesus at the Baptism; now in prison he had thought more and more about Him; and the more he thought the more certain he was that Jesus was the One who was to come; and now he puts all his hopes to the test in this one question. It may be that this is not the question of a despairing and an impatient man, but the question of one in whose eyes the light of hope shone, and who asked for nothing but confirmation of his hopes.

Then comes Jesus' answer; and in His answer we hear that *accent of confidence*. Jesus's answer to John's disciples was: " Go back, and don't tell John what I am saying; *tell him what I am doing*. Don't tell John what I am claiming; *tell him what is happening*." Jesus demanded that there

3

should be applied to Him the most acid of tests, the test of deeds and of results. Jesus was the only person who could ever demand without qualification and without condition to be judged, not by what He said, but by what He did. The challenge of Jesus is still the same. He does not so much say, " Listen to what I have to tell you." He says, " Look what I can do for you; and see what I have done for others."

The things that Jesus claimed to do in Galilee He still does. In Him those who were blind to the truth about themselves, about their fellow-men and about God, have their eyes opened; in Him those whose feet were never strong enough to remain in the right way are strengthened; in Him those who were tainted with the disease of sin are cleansed; in Him those who were deaf to the voice of conscience and of God begin to listen; in Him those who were dead and powerless in sin are raised to newness and loveliness of life; in Him the poorest man inherits and possesses the riches of the love of God.

And finally there comes the warning, " Blessed is the man who does not take offence at me." This was spoken to John; and it was spoken because John had only grasped half the truth. John preached the gospel of divine holiness with divine destruction; Jesus preached the gospel of divine holiness with divine love. So Jesus says to John, " Maybe I am not doing the things you expected me to do. But the powers of evil are being defeated; yet they are not being defeated by irresistible power, but by unanswerable love." Sometimes a man can be offended at Jesus because Jesus cuts across *his* ideas of what religion should be. We will always be offended at Jesus, if we think that *we* know best.

THE ACCENT OF ADMIRATION

Matthew II: 7-II

When they were going away, Jesus began to speak to the crowds about John. " What did you go out

4

to the desert to see?" He said. "Was it a reed shaken by the wind? If it was not that, what did you go out to see? Was it to see a man clothed in luxurious clothes? Look you, the people who wear luxurious clothes are in kings' houses. If it was not that, what did you go out to see? Was it to see a prophet? Indeed it was, I tell you, and something beyond a prophet. This is he of whom it stands written: ' Look you, I am sending before you my messenger, who will prepare your way before you.' This is the truth I tell you—amongst those born of women no greater figure than John the Baptizer has ever emerged in history. But the least in the Kingdom of Heaven is greater than he is."

THERE are few men to whom Jesus paid so tremendous a tribute as He did to John the Baptizer. He begins by asking the people what it was that they flocked out into the desert to see, when they streamed out to see John.

(i) Did they go out to see a reed shaken by the wind? That can mean one of two things. (a) Down by the banks of the Jordan the long cane grass grew; and the phrase *a shaken reed* was a kind of proverb for *the commonest of sights*. When the people flocked out to see John, were they going out to see something ordinary, as ordinary as the reeds swaying in the wind on Jordan's banks? (b) A *shaken reed* can mean *a weak vacillator*, one who could no more stand foursquare to the winds of peril and of danger than a reed by the river's bank could stand straight when the wind blew. Whatever else the people flocked out to the desert to see, they certainly did not go out to see an ordinary person. The very fact that they did go out in their crowds showed how extraordinary John was, for no one would cross the street, let alone tramp out into the desert, to see a commonplace kind of person, the like of whom they could meet any day. Whatever else they went out to see, they did not go out to see a weak vacillator. Mr. Pliables do not end in prison as martyrs for the truth. John was neither as ordinary as a shaken reed, nor as spineless as the reed which sways with every breeze.

(ii) Did they go out to see a man clothed in soft and luxurious garments? Such a man would be a courtier; and very certainly whatever else John was he was not a courtier. John knew nothing of the courtier's art of the flattery of kings; he followed the dangerous occupation of telling the truth to kings. John was the ambassador of God, not the courtier of Herod.

(iii) Did they go out to see a prophet? The prophet is the *forthteller* of the truth of God. The prophet is the man in the confidence of God. " Surely the Lord God will do nothing, but He revealeth His secret unto His servants the prophets " (*Amos* 3: 7). The prophet is two things—he is the man with a message from God, and he is the man with the courage to deliver that message. The prophet is the man with God's wisdom in his mind, God's truth on his lips, and God's courage in his heart. That most certainly John was.

(iv) But John was something more than and beyond a prophet. The Jews had, and still have, one settled belief. They believed that before the Messiah came, Elijah would return to herald his coming. To this day when the Jews celebrate the Passover Feast a vacant chair is left for Elijah to occupy. " Behold I will send you Elijah the prophet, before the coming of the great and terrible day of the Lord " (*Malachi* 4: 5). So Jesus declared that John was nothing less than the divine herald, the divine fore-runner whose duty and privilege it was to announce and to hail the coming of the Messiah. John was nothing less than the herald of God, and no man could have a greater task than that.

(v) Such was the tremendous tribute of Jesus to John, spoken with the accent of admiration for such a man as that. There had never been a greater figure born of women in all history; and then there comes the startling sentence: " But the least in the Kingdom of Heaven is greater than he is." Here there is one quite general truth. With Jesus there came into the world something which was totally and absolutely new. The prophets were great; their message was precious; but with Jesus there emerged something still greater, and a message still more wonderful. C. G. Montefiore, himself a Jew and not a Christian, writes: " Christianity does mark a new era in religious history and in human civilization. What the world owes to Jesus and to Paul is immense; things can never be, and men can never think, the same as things were, and as men thought, before these two great men lived." Even a non-Christian freely admits that things could never be the same now that Jesus had come.

But what was it that John had lacked? What is it that the Christian has that John could never have? The answer to that is very simple and very fundamental. *John had never seen the Cross.* And therefore one thing John could never know—the full revelation of the love of God. The holiness of God he might know; the justice of God he might declare; but the love of God in all its fulness he could never know. We have only to listen to the message of John and the message of Jesus. No one could call John's message a *gospel*, good news; it was basically and fundamentally a threat of destruction; it took Jesus and His Cross to show to men the length, breadth, depth and height of the love of God. It is a most amazing thing that it is possible for the humblest Christian to know more about God than the greatest of the Old Testament prophets. It is possible for us to know more about the heart of God than Isaiah or Jeremiah or any other of that goodly company. The man who has seen the Cross has seen the heart of God in a way that no man who lived before the Cross could ever see it; only in the Cross of Christ do we see the full revelation of the heart of God. Indeed the least in the Kingdom of Heaven is greater than any man who went before.

So it happened that John had the destiny which some-times falls to men; he had the task of pointing men to a greatness into which he himself did not enter. It is given

7

to some men to be the signposts of God. They point to a new ideal and a new greatness which others will enter into, but into which they will not come. It is very seldom that any great reformer is the first man to labour and to toil for the reform with which his name is connected in history. Before he ever emerged on the scene of history there were many who went before him who glimpsed the glory, who often laboured for it, and who sometimes died for it. Someone tells of a scene which he used to see from the windows of his house every evening. Every evening he used to watch the lamp-lighter go along the streets lighting the lamps—*and the lamp-lighter was himself a blind man.* He was bringing to others the light which he himself would never see. Let a man never be discouraged in the Church or in any other walk of life, if the dream he has dreamed and for which he has toiled is never worked out before the end of the day. God needed John; God needs his signposts who can point men on the way, although they themselves cannot ever reach the goal. It is no small function in life to point others to a goal, even if one never reaches the goal oneself.

VIOLENCE AND THE KINGDOM

Matthew 11: 12-15

> " From the days of John the Baptist until now, the Kingdom of Heaven is taken by storm, and the violent take it by force. For up to John all the prophets and the Law spoke with the voice of prophecy; and, if you are willing to accept the fact, this is Elijah who was destined to come. He who has ears to hear let him hear."

IN verse 12 there is a very difficult saying, " The kingdom of heaven is taken by storm, and the violent take it by force." *Luke* has this saying in another form (*Luke* 16: 16): " From that time the kingdom of heaven is preached, and everyone storms his way into it." It is quite clear that at some time Jesus said something in which *violence* and the *kingdom* were connected, something which was a dark and a difficult saying, which no one at the time fully understood. Certainly Luke and Matthew understood it in different ways.

Luke says that every man storms his way into the Kingdom; he means, as Denney said, that the " Kingdom of heaven is not for the well-meaning but for the desperate," that no one drifts into the Kingdom, that the Kingdom only opens its doors to those who are prepared to make as great an effort to get into it as men do when they storm a city.

Matthew says that from the time of John until now the Kingdom of heaven suffers violence and the violent take it by force. The very form of that expression seems to look back over a considerable time. It indeed sounds much more like a comment of Matthew than like a saying of Jesus. It sounds as if Matthew was saying: " From the days of John, who was thrown into prison, right down to our own times the Kingdom of heaven has suffered violence and persecution at the hands of violent men."

In point of fact, it is likely that we will get the full meaning of this difficult saying by putting together the recollection of Luke and Matthew. What Jesus may well have said is: " Always my Kingdom will suffer violence; always savage men will try to break it up, and snatch it away and destroy it; and therefore only the man who is desperately in earnest, only the man in whom the violence of devotion matches and defeats the violence of persecution will in the end enter into it." It may well be that this saying of Jesus was originally at one and the same time a warning of violence to come and a challenge to produce a devotion which would be even stronger than the violence.

It seems strange to find in verse 13 that the Law is said to speak with the voice of prophecy; but it was the Law itself which confidently declared that the voice of prophesy would not die. " The Lord thy God will raise up unto thee a Prophet, from the midst of thee, of thy brethren." " I will raise them up a Prophet from among their brethren, like unto thee, and will put my words in his mouth " (*Deuteronomy* 18: 15, 18). It was because He broke the Law, as they saw it, that the orthodox Jews hated Jesus; but, if they had only had eyes to see it, both the Law and the prophets pointed to Him.

Once again Jesus tells the people that John is the herald and the forerunner whom they have awaited for so long— *if they are willing to accept the fact.* There is all the tragedy of the human situation in that last phrase. The old proverb has it that you can take a horse to the water, but you cannot make him drink. God can send His messenger, but men can refuse to recognize him, and God can send His truth, and men can refuse to see it. God's revelation is powerless without man's response. That is why Jesus ends with the appeal that he who has ears should use them to hear.

THE ACCENT OF SORROWFUL REBUKE
Matthew 11: 16-19

> " To what will I compare this generation? It is like children in the market-place, calling to their companions, and saying, ' We piped to you and you did not dance; we wailed and you did not mourn.' For John came neither eating nor drinking, and they say, ' The man is mad.' The Son of Man came eating and drinking, and they say, ' Look you, a gluttonous man and a wine-drinker, the friend of tax-collectors and sinners.' But wisdom is shown to be right by her deeds."

JESUS was saddened by the sheer perversity of human nature. To him men seemed to be like children playing in the village square. One group said to the other: " Come on and let's play at weddings," and the others said, " We don't feel like being happy today." Then the first group said, " All right; come on and let's play at funerals," and the others said, " We don't feel like being sad today." They were what the Scots call *contrary*. No matter what was suggested, they did not want to do it; and no matter what was offered, they could find a fault in it.

John had come, living in the desert, fasting and despising food, isolated and divorced from the society of men; and they said of him, " The man is mad to cut himself off from human society and human pleasures like that." Jesus came, mixing with all kinds of people, sharing in their sorrows and their joys, companying with them in their times of joy; and they said of Him, " He is a socialite; He is a party-goer; He is the friend of outsiders with whom no decent person would have anything to do." They called John's asceticism madness; and they called Jesus' sociability laxness of morals. They could find a ground of criticism either way.

The plain fact is that when people do not want to listen to the truth, they will easily enough find an excuse for not listening to it. They do not even try to be consistent in their criticisms; they will criticize the same person, and the same institution, from quite opposite grounds and reasons. If people are determined to make no response, they will remain stubbornly and sullenly unresponsive no matter what invitation is made to them. Grown men and women can be very like spoiled children who refuse to play no matter what the game is.

Then comes Jesus' final sentence in this section: " Wisdom is shown to be right by her deeds." The ultimate verdict lies not with the cantankerous and perverse critics. but with events. The Jews might criticize John for his lonely isolation, but John had moved men's hearts to God as they had not been moved for centuries; the Jews might criticize Jesus for mixing too much in ordinary life and with ordinary people, but in Him people were finding a new life and a new goodness and a new power to live as they ought and a new access to God.

It would be well if we were to stop judging people and Churches by our own prejudices and our perversities; and if we were to begin giving thanks for any person and any Church who can bring people nearer to God, even if their methods are not the methods which suit us.

THE ACCENT OF HEARTBROKEN
CONDEMNATION

Matthew 11: 20-24

> Then He began to reproach the cities in which the most numerous of His deeds of power had been done, because they did not repent. "Alas for you Chorazin! Alas for you Bethsaida! For, if the deeds of power which happened in you had happened in Tyre and Sidon, they would have repented in sackcloth and ashes long ago. But I tell you, it will be easier for Tyre and Sidon in the day of judgment than for you! And you Capernaum, is it not true that you have been lifted up to heaven? You will go down to Hell, for, if the deeds of power which happened in you had happened amongst the men of Sodom, they would have survived to this day. But I tell you—it will be easier for the land of the men of Sodom in the day of judgment than for you."

WHEN John came to the end of his gospel, he wrote a sentence in which he indicated how impossible it was ever to write a full and complete account of the life of Jesus: "And there are also many other things which Jesus did, the which, if they should be written every one, I suppose that even the world itself could not contain the books that should be written" (*John* 21: 25). This passage of *Matthew* is one of the proofs of that saying in *John*. Chorazin was probably on a site an hour's journey north of Capernaum; Bethsaida was a fishing village on the west bank of Jordan, just as the river entered the northern end of the lake. Clearly the most tremendous things happened in these towns, and yet we have no account of them whatever. There is no record in the gospels of the work that Jesus did, and of the wonders He performed in these places, and yet they must have been amongst His greatest. A passage like this shows us how little we know of Jesus; it shows us—and we must always remember it—that in the gospels we have only the barest selection of Jesus' works. The things we do not know about Jesus far outnumber the things we do know.

We must be careful to catch the accent in Jesus' voice as He said this. The Authorized Version has it: " Woe unto thee, Chorazin! Woe unto thee, Bethsaida! " The Greek word for *woe* which we have translated *alas* is *ouai*; and it must be remembered that *ouai* expresses *sorrowful pity* as least as much as it does anger. This is not the accent of one who is in a temper because his self-esteem has been touched; it is not the accent of one who is blazingly angry because he has been insulted; it is not the accent of one in a passion of hatred at men; it is the accent of sorrow, the accent of one who offered men the most precious thing in the world, and who saw it completely disregarded; the accent of one who is watching a tragedy being played out, and who is powerless to stop men rushing on ruin. We must always remember that Jesus' condemnation of sin is holy anger, but the anger comes, not from outraged pride, but from a broken heart. What then was the sin of Chorazin, of Bethsaida, of Capernaum, the sin which was worse than the sin of Tyre and Sidon, and of Sodom and Gomorrah? It must have been very serious for again and again Tyre and Sidon are denounced for their wickedness (*Isaiah* 23; *Jeremiah* 25: 22; 47: 4; *Ezekiel* 26: 3-7; 28: 12-22), and Sodom and Gomorrah were and are a byword for iniquity.

(i) It was the sin of the people who forgot the responsibilities of privilege. To the cities of Galilee there had been given a privilege, a chance, an opportunity, which had never come to Tyre and Sidon, or to Sodom and Gomorrah, for the cities of Galilee had actually seen and heard Jesus Himself. We do not and cannot condemn a man who has gone wrong through ignorance, and because he never had the chance to know any better; but if a man who has had every chance to know the right does the wrong, then he does stand condemned. We do not condemn a child for that for which we would condemn an adult; we would not condemn a savage for conduct which we would condemn in a civilized man; we do not expect the person brought up in the handicaps of a city slum to live the life of a person brought up from birth in a good and a comfortable home. A man is judged by that which he had the chance to know. We must remember that the greater our privileges have been, the greater is our condemnation if we have failed to shoulder the responsibilities and accept the obligations which these privileges bring with them.

(ii) It was the sin of indifference. These cities did not attack Jesus Christ; they did not drive Him from their gates; they did not seek to crucify Him; they simply disregarded Him. Neglect can kill as much as persecution can. An author writes a book; it is sent out for review; some reviewers may praise it, others may damn it; it does not matter so long as it is noticed; the one thing which will kill a book stone dead is if it is never noticed at all for either praise or blame. An artist drew a picture of Christ standing on one of London's famous bridges. He is holding out his hands in appeal to the crowds, and they are drifting past without a second look; only one girl, a nurse, gives him any response. Here we have the modern situation in so many countries today. There is no hostility to Christianity; there is no desire to destroy it; there is blank indifference. Christ is relegated to the ranks of those who do not matter. We must remember that indifference too is a sin, and the worst of all sins, for indifference kills. Indifference does not burn a religion to death; it freezes it to death. It does not behead it; it slowly suffocates the life out of it.

(iii) And so we are face to face with one great threatening truth—*it is also a sin to do nothing*. There are sins of action, sins of deed; but there is also a sin of inaction, and of absence of deeds. The sin of Chorazin, of Bethsaida, and of Capernaum was the sin of doing nothing. Many a man's defence is: " But I never did anything." That defence may be in fact his condemnation.

THE ACCENT OF AUTHORITY

Matthew 11: 25-27

> At that time Jesus said: " I thank you, Father, Lord
> of heaven and earth, that you have hidden these
> things from the wise and the clever, and have revealed
> them to babes. Even so, Father, for thus it was your
> will in your sight. All things have been delivered to
> me by my Father; and no one really knows the Son
> except the Father, and no one really knows the Father
> except the Son, and he to whom the Son wishes to
> reveal His knowledge."

HERE Jesus is speaking out of experience. The experience
He had was that the Rabbis and the wise men rejected
Him; and the simple people accepted Him. The intel-
lectuals had no use for Him; but the humble welcomed
Him. We must be careful to see clearly what Jesus meant
here. He is very far from condemning intellectual power;
what He is condemning is *intellectual pride.* As Plummer
has it, " The heart, not the head, is the home of the
gospel." It is not cleverness which shuts out; it is pride.
It is not stupidity which admits; it is humility. Jesus
is not connecting ignorance and faith; He is connecting
lowliness and faith. A man may be as wise as Solomon,
but if he has not the simplicity, the trust, the innocence
of the childlike heart, he has shut himself out.

The Rabbis themselves saw the danger of this intellectual
pride; they did recognize that often simple people were
nearer God than the wisest Rabbi. The Rabbis had
a parable like this. Once Rabbi Berokah of Chuza was
in the market of Lapet, and Elijah appeared to him. The
Rabbi asked, " Is there among the people in this market-
place anyone who is destined to share in the life of the
world to come? " At first Elijah said there was none.
Then he pointed at one man, and said that that man would
share in the life of the world to come. Rabbi Berokah
went to the man and asked him what he did. " I am a
jailer," said the man, " and I keep men and women separate.
At night I place my bed between the men and the women

so that no wrong will be committed." Elijah pointed at two other men, and said that they too would share in the life to come. Rabbi Berokah asked them what they did. " We are merry-makers," they said. " When we see a man who is downcast, we cheer him up. Also when we see two people quarrelling with one another, we try to make peace between them." The men who did the simple things, the jailer who kept his charges in the right way, the men who brought a smile and peace, were in the kingdom. Again the Rabbis had a story like this: " An epidemic once broke out in Sura, but in the neighbourhood of Rab's residence (a famous Rabbi) it did not appear. The people thought that this was due to Rab's merits, but in a dream they were told . . . that it happened because of the merits of a man who willingly lent hoe and shovel to someone who wished to dig a grave. A fire once broke out in Drokeret, but the neighbourhood of Rabbi Huna was spared. The people thought it was due to the merits of Rabbi Huna, . . . but they were told in a dream that it was due to the merits of a certain woman, who used to heat her oven and place it at the disposal of her neighbours." The man who lent his tools to someone in need, the woman who helped her neighbours as she could had no intellectual standing, but their simple deeds of human love had won them the approval of God. Academic distinctions are not necessarily distinctions in the sight of God.

> " Still to the lowly soul
> He doth Himself impart,
> And for His dwelling and His throne
> Chooseth the pure in heart."

This passage closes with the greatest claim that Jesus ever made, the claim which is the centre of the Christian faith. It is Jesus' claim that He alone can reveal God to men. Other men may be sons of God; He is *The Son*. John put this in a different way, when he tells us that Jesus said, " He who has seen me has seen the Father " (*John* 14: 9). What Jesus says is this: " If you want to see what God is like, if you want to see the mind of God, the heart of God, the nature of God, if you want to see God's whole attitude to men—look at me! " It is the Christian conviction that in Jesus Christ alone we see what God is like; and it is also the Christian conviction that Jesus can give that knowledge to anyone who is humble enough and trustful enough to receive it.

THE ACCENT OF COMPASSION

Matthew II: 28-30

> " Come to me, all you who are exhausted and weighted down beneath your burdens, and I will give you rest. Take my yoke upon you, and learn of me, for I am gentle and lowly in heart, and you will find rest for your souls; for my yoke is easy and my burden is light."

JESUS spoke to men who were desperately trying to find God, and who were desperately trying to be good, and who were finding the tasks impossible, and who were driven to weariness and to despair.

He says, " Come unto me all you who are exhausted." His invitation to men is to those who are exhausted with the search for the truth. The Greeks had said, " It is very difficult to find God, and, when you have found Him, it is impossible to tell anyone else about Him." Zophar demanded of Job: " Canst thou by searching find out God? " (*Job* II: 7). It is Jesus' claim that the weary search for God ends in Himself. W. B. Yeats, the great Irish poet and mystic, wrote: " Can one reach God by toil? He gives Himself to the pure in heart. He asks nothing but our attention." The way to know God is not by mental search, but by giving attention to Jesus Christ. The search for God can end in the contemplation of Jesus Christ, for in Him we see what God is like.

He says, " Come unto me all you who are weighted down beneath your burdens." For the religious orthodox

Jew religion was a thing of burdens. Jesus said of the Scribes and Pharisees: " They bind heavy burdens and grievous to be borne, and lay them on men's shoulders " (*Matthew* 23: 4). To the Jew religion was a thing of endless rules and regulations, all of which had to be observed. A man lived his life in a forest of rules and regulations which dictated every action of his life. He must listen for ever to the voice which continually said, " Thou shalt not."

Even the Rabbis saw this. There is a kind of rueful parable put into the mouth of Korah, which shows just how binding and constricting and burdensome and impossible the demands of the Law could be. " There was a poor widow in my neighbourhood who had two daughters and a field. When she began to plough, Moses (i.e. the Law of Moses) said, ' You must not plough with an ox and an ass together.' When she began to sow, he said, ' You must not sow your field with mingled seed.' When she began to reap and to make stacks of corn, he said, Take not the gleaning, or what you forget (*Deuteronomy* 24: 19), or the corners ' (*Leviticus* 19: 9). She began to thresh, and he said, ' Give me the heave-offering, and the first and second tithe.' She accepted the ordinance and gave them all to him. What did the poor woman then do? She sold her field, and bought two sheep, to clothe herself from their fleece, and to have profit from their young. When they bore their young, Aaron (i.e. the demands of the priesthood) came and said, ' Give me the first-born.' So she accepted the decision, and gave them to him. When the shearing time came, and she sheared them, Aaron came and said, ' Give me the first fruit of the fleece ' (*Deuteronomy* 18: 4). Then she thought: ' I cannot stand up against this man. I will slaughter the sheep and eat them.' Then Aaron came and said, ' Give me the shoulder and the two cheeks and the maw ' (*Deuteronomy* 18: 3). Then she said, ' Even when I have killed them I am not safe from you. Behold they shall be *devoted*.'

Then Aaron said, ' In that case they belong entirely to me ' (*Numbers* 18: 14). He took them and went away and left her weeping with her two daughters." The story is a parable of the continuous demands that the Law made upon men in every action and activity of life. The demands of the Law were indeed a burden.

It is Jesus' invitation to take His yoke upon our shoulders. The Jews used the phrase *the yoke* for *entering into submission to.* They spoke of the yoke of the Law, the yoke of the commandments, the yoke of the Kingdom, the yoke of God. But it may well be that Jesus took the words of His invitation from something much nearer home than that. He says, " My yoke is *easy*." The word *easy* is in Greek *chrēstos*, which can mean *well-fitting*. In Palestine ox-yokes were made of wood; the ox was brought, and the measurements were taken. The yoke was then roughed out, and the ox was brought back to have the yoke tried on. The yoke was then carefully adjusted, so that it would fit well, and would not gall the neck of the patient beast. The yoke was tailor-made to fit the ox. Now there is a legend that Jesus made the best ox-yokes in all Galilee, and that from all over the country men came to Him to the carpenter's shop to buy the best yokes that skill could make. In those days, as now, shops had their signs above the door; and it has been suggested that the sign above the door of the carpenter's shop in Nazareth may well have been: " My yokes fit well." It may well be that Jesus is here using a picture from the carpenter's shop in Nazareth where He had worked throughout the silent years.

So Jesus says, " My yoke fits well." What He says is: " The life I give you to live is not a burden to gall you; your task, your life, is made to measure to fit you." Whatever God sends to us is made to fit our needs and our abilities exactly; God has a task for every one of us, which is made to measure for us. Jesus says, " My burden is light." As a Rabbi had it: " My burden is become my song." It is not that the burden is easy to carry; but it is laid on us in love; it is meant to be carried in love; and love makes even the heaviest burden light. When we remember the love of God, when we know that our burden is to love God and to love men, then the burden becomes a song. There is an old story which tells how a man came upon a little boy carrying a still smaller boy, who was lame, upon his back. " That's a heavy burden for you to carry," said the man. " That's no' a burden," came the answer. " That's my wee brother." The burden which is given in love and carried in love is always light.

CRISIS

In *Matthew* 12 we read the history of a series of crucial events in the life of Jesus. In every man's life there are decisive moments, times and events on which the whole of his life hinges. This chapter presents us with the story of such a period in the life of Jesus. In this chapter we see the orthodox Jewish religious leaders of the day coming to their final decision regarding Jesus—and that decision was rejection. It was not only rejection in the sense that they would have nothing to do with Him; it was rejection in the sense that they came to the conclusion that nothing less than His complete elimination would be enough. Here in this chapter we see the first definite steps, the end of which could be nothing other than the Cross. The characters are painted clear before us. On the one hand there are the Scribes and the Pharisees, the representatives of orthodox religion. We can see four stages in their increasing attitude of malignant hostility to Jesus.

(i) In verses 1-8, the story of how the disciples plucked the ears of corn on the Sabbath day, we see growing *suspicion*. The Scribes and Pharisees regarded with growing suspicion any teacher who was prepared to allow His followers to disregard the minutiæ of the Sabbath Law. This was the kind of thing which could not be allowed to develop and spread unchecked.

(ii) In verses 9-14, the story of the healing of the man with the paralysed hand, in the synagogue, on the Sabbath day, we see active and hostile *investigation*. It was not by chance that the Scribes and Pharisees were in the synagogue on that Sabbath. Luke says that they were there to watch Jesus (*Luke* 6: 7). From that time on Jesus would have to work always under the malignant eye of the orthodox leaders. They would dog His steps, like private detectives, seeking the evidence on which they could level a charge against Him.

(iii) In verses 22-32, the story of how the orthodox leaders charged Jesus with healing by the power of the devil, and of how He spoke to them of the sin which has no forgiveness, we see the story of deliberate and prejudiced *blindness*. From that time on nothing that Jesus could ever do would be right in the eyes of these men. They had so shut their eyes to God that they were completely incapable of ever seeing His beauty and His truth. Their prejudiced blindness had launched them on a path from which they were quite incapable of ever turning back.

(iv) In verse 14 we see evil *determination*. The orthodox were not now simply prepared to watch and to criticize; they were preparing to *act*. They had gone into council to find a way in which to put an end to this disturbing Galilaean. Suspicion, investigation, blindness were on the way to open and hostile action.

In face of all this the answer of Jesus is clearly delineated. We can see five ways in which Jesus met this growing opposition.

(i) He met it with courageous *defiance*. In the story of the healing of the man with the paralysed hand (verses 9-14) we see Him openly and deliberately defying the Scribes and Pharisees. This thing was not done in a corner; it was done in a crowded synagogue. It was not done in their absence; it was done when they were there with deliberate intent to formulate a charge against Jesus.

So far from avoiding or evading the challenge, Jesus is about to meet it head on.

(ii) He met it with *warning*. In verses 22-32 we see Jesus giving the most terrible of warnings. He is warning those men that, if they persist in shutting their eyes to the truth and the revelation of God, they are on the way to a situation where, by their own act, they will have shut themselves out from the grace of God. Here Jesus is not so much on the defence as He is on the attack. He makes quite clear where their attitude is taking them.

(iii) He met it with a staggering series of *claims*. He is greater than the Temple (verse 6), and the Temple was the most sacred place in all the world. He is greater than Jonah, and no preacher ever produced repentance so amazingly as Jonah did (verse 41). He is greater than Solomon, and Solomon was the very acme and incarnation of wisdom (verse 42). His claim is that there is nothing in spiritual history than which He is not greater. There are no apologies here; there is the statement of the claims of Christ at their highest.

(iv) He met it with the statement that His teaching is *essential*. The point of the strange parable of the Empty House (verses 43-45) is that the Law may negatively empty a man of evil, but only the gospel can fill him with good. The Law therefore simply leaves a man an empty invitation for all evil to take up its residence within his heart; the gospel so fills him with positive goodness that evil cannot enter in. Here is Jesus' claim that the gospel can do for men what the Law can never do.

(v) Finally, He met it with an *invitation*. Verses 46-50 are in essence an invitation. They are in the invitation to enter into kinship with Him through obedience to the will of God. These verses are not so much a disowning of Jesus' own kith and kin as an invitation to all men to enter into kinship with Him, through the acceptance of the will of God, as that will has come to men in His invitation and command. These verses are an invitation

to abandon our own prejudices and self-will and to accept
Jesus Christ as Master and Lord. If we refuse, we drift
farther and farther away from God; if we accept, we
enter into the very family and heart of God.

BREAKING THE SABBATH LAW

Matthew 12: 1-8

> At that time Jesus went through the cornfields on
> the Sabbath day. His disciples were hungry, and
> they began to pluck the ears of corn and to eat them.
> When the Pharisees saw this, they said to Him,
> " Look you, your disciples are doing that which it
> is not permitted to do on the Sabbath day." He
> said to them, " Have you not read what David
> and his friends did, when he was hungry—how he
> went into the house of God and ate the shewbread,
> which it was not permissible for him, nor for his
> friends to eat, but which the priests alone may eat?
> Or, have you not read in the Law that the priests
> profane the Sabbath, and yet remain blameless?
> I tell you that something greater than the Temple
> is here. But, if you had known the meaning of the
> saying, ' It is mercy that I wish, and not sacrifice,'
> you would not have condemned those who are blame-
> less. For the Son of Man is Lord of the Sabbath."
> (The last phrase should perhaps be translated:
> " For man is master of the Sabbath.")

In Palestine in the time of Jesus the cornfields and the
cultivated lands were laid out in long narrow strips;
and the ground between the strips was always a right of
way, along which the paths ran. It was on one of these
strips between the cornfields that the disciples and Jesus
were walking when this incident happened.

There is no suggestion whatever that the disciples were
stealing. The Law expressly laid it down that the hungry
traveller was entitled to do just what the disciples were
doing, so long as he only used his hands to pluck the
ears of corn, and did not use a sickle: " When thou comest
into the standing corn of thy neighbour, then thou mayest

pluck the ears of corn with thine hand; but thou shalt not move a sickle unto thy neighbour's standing corn " (*Deuteronomy* 23: 25). W. M. Thomson in *The Land and the Book* tells how, when he was travelling in Palestine, the same custom still existed. One of the favourite evening dishes for the traveller is parched corn. " When travelling in harvest time," Thomson writes, " my muleteers have very often prepared parched corn in the evenings after the tent has been pitched. Nor is the gathering of these green ears for parching ever regarded as stealing. . . . So, also, I have seen my muleteers, as we passed along the wheat fields, pluck off the ears, rub them in their hands, and eat the grains unroasted, just as the apostles are said to have done."

In the eyes of the Scribes and Pharisees, the fault of the disciples was not that they had plucked and eaten the grains of corn, but that they had done so *on the Sabbath*. The Sabbath Law was very complicated and very detailed. The commandment forbids work on the Sabbath day; but the interpreters of the Law were not satisfied with that simple prohibition. Work had to be defined. So thirty-nine basic actions were laid down, which were forbidden on the Sabbath, and amongst them were reaping, winnowing and threshing, and preparing a meal. But the interpreters were not even prepared to leave the matter there. Each item in the list of forbidden works had to be carefully defined. For instance, it was forbidden to carry a *burden*. But what is a burden? A burden is anything which weighs as much as two dried figs. Even the suggestion of work was forbidden; even anything which might symbolically be regarded as work was prohibited. Later the great Jewish teacher, Maimonides, was to say, " To pluck ears is a kind of reaping." By their conduct the disciples were guilty of far more than one breach of the Law. By plucking the corn they were guilty of *reaping*; by rubbing it in their hands they were guilty of *threshing*; by separating the grain and the chaff they were guilty of *winnowing*; and by the whole process they were guilty of *preparing a meal* on the Sabbath day, for everything which was to be eaten on the Sabbath had to be prepared the day before.

The orthodox Jews took this Sabbath Law with intense seriousness. *The Book of Jubilee* has a chapter (chapter 50) about the keeping of the Sabbath. Whoever lies with his wife, or plans to do anything on the Sabbath, or plans to set out on a journey (even the contemplation of work is forbidden), or plans to buy or sell, whoever draws water, whoever lifts a burden is condemned. Any man who does any work on the Sabbath, who goes a journey, who tills a farm, whether the work is in his house or in any other place, any man who lights a fire or rides any beast, or travels by ship at sea, any man who strikes or kills anything, or slaughters a beast or a bird, anyone who catches an animal, a bird, or a fish, any one who fasts or who makes war on a Sabbath—the man who does these things shall die. To keep these commandments was to keep the Law of God; to break them was to break the Law of God.

There is no doubt whatever that, from their own point of view, the Scribes and Pharisees were entirely justified in finding fault with the disciples for breaking the Law, and with Jesus for allowing them, if not encouraging them, to do so.

THE CLAIM OF HUMAN NEED

Matthew 12: 1-8 (*continued*)

To meet the criticism of the Scribes and Pharisees Jesus put forward three arguments.

(i) He quoted the action of David (I *Samuel* 21: 1-6) on the occasion when David and his young men were so hungry that they went into the tabernacle—not the Temple, because this happened in the days before the Temple was built—and ate the shewbread, which only the priests could eat. The shewbread is described in *Leviticus* 24: 5-9. It consisted of twelve loaves of bread, which were placed every week in two rows of six in the Holy Place. No doubt they were a symbolic offering to God in which God was thanked for His gift of sustaining food. These loaves were changed every week, and the old loaves became the perquisite of the priests and could only be eaten by them. On this occasion, in their hunger, David and his young men took and ate those sacred loaves, and no blame attached to them. The claims of human need and human hunger took precedence over any ritual custom and practice.

(ii) He quoted the Sabbath work of the Temple. The Temple ritual always involved work—the kindling of fires, the slaughter and the preparation of animals, the lifting of them on to the altar, and a host of other things. This work was actually doubled on the Sabbath, for on the Sabbath the offerings were doubled (cp. e.g. *Numbers* 28: 9). Any one of these actions would have been illegal for any ordinary person to perform on the Sabbath day. To light a fire, to slaughter an animal, to lift it up on to the altar would have been to break the Law, and hence to profane the Sabbath. But for the priests it was perfectly legal to do these things, for the Temple worship must go on. That is to say, worship offered to God took precedence of all the Sabbath rules and regulations.

(iii) He quoted God's word to Hosea the prophet: " It is mercy that I wish, and not sacrifice " (*Hosea* 6: 6). What God desires far more than ritual sacrifice is kindness, the spirit which knows no law other than that it must answer the call of human need.

In this incident Jesus lays it down that the claim of human need must take precedence of all other claims. The claims of worship, the claims of ritual, the claims of liturgy are important and have their place, but prior to any of them is the claim of human need.

One of the modern saints of God is Father George Potter

who, out of the derelict Church of St. Chrysostom's in Peckham, made a shining light of Christian worship and Christian service. To further the work he founded the Brotherhood of the Order of the Holy Cross, whose badge is the towel which Jesus Christ wore when He washed His disciples' feet. There was no service too menial for the brothers to render; their work for the outcast and for homeless boys with a criminal record or criminal potentialities is beyond all praise. Father Potter holds the highest possible ideas of worship; and yet when he is explaining the work of the Brotherhood he writes of anyone who wishes to enter into its triple vow of poverty, chastity and obedience: " He mustn't sulk if he cannot get to Vespers on the Feast of St. Thermogene. He may be sitting in a police court waiting for a ' client'. . . . He mustn't be the type who goes into the kitchen and sobs just because we run short of incense. . . . We put prayer and sacraments first. We know we cannot do our best otherwise, but the fact is that we have to spend more time at the bottom of the Mount of Transfiguration than at the top." He tells about one candidate who arrived, when he was just about to give his boys a cup of cocoa and put them to bed. " So I said, ' Just clean round the bath, will you, while it's wet? ' He stood aghast and stuttered, ' I didn't expect to clean up after dirty boys! ' Well, well! His life of devoted service to the Blessed Master lasted about seven minutes. He did not unpack." Florence Allshorn, the great principal of a women's missionary college, tells of the problem of the candidate who always discovers that her time for quiet prayer has come just when there are greasy dishes to be washed in not very warm water.

Jesus insisted that the greatest ritual service is the service of human need. It is an odd thing to think that, with the possible exception of the day in the Synagogue at Nazareth, we have no evidence that Jesus ever conducted a church service in all His life on earth, but we have abundance of evidence that He fed the hungry, and comforted the sad and cared for the sick. Christian service is not the service of any liturgy or ritual; it is the service of human need. Christian service is not monastic retiral; it is involvement in all the tragedies and problems and demands of the human situation. Whittier had it rightly:

" O brother man, fold to thy heart thy brother!
    Where pity dwells, the peace of God is there;
To worship rightly is to love each other,
    Each smile a hymn, each kindly deed a prayer.

For he whom Jesus loved hath truly spoken;
    The holier worship which he deigns to bless
Restores the lost, and binds the spirit broken,
    And feeds the widow and the fatherless.

Follow with reverent steps the great example
    Of Him whose holy work was doing good;
So shall the wide earth seem our Father's temple,
    Each loving life a psalm of gratitude."

That is what we mean—or ought to mean—when we say, " Let us worship God! "

MASTER OF THE SABBATH

Matthew 12: 1-8 (*continued*)

THERE remains in this passage one difficulty which it is not possible to solve with absolute certainty. The difficulty lies in the last phrase, the phrase which the Authorized Version translates: " For the Son of Man is Lord even of the Sabbath day." We may note to begin with that there is no *even* in the Greek; and by inserting an *even* which should not be there the Authorized Version has at least to some extent prejudged the case. This phrase can have two meanings.

(i) It may mean that Jesus is claiming to be Lord of the Sabbath, in the sense that He is entitled to use the Sabbath as He thinks fit. We have seen that the sanctity of the work of the Temple surpassed and over-rode the Sabbath rules and regulations; Jesus has just claimed that something greater than the Temple is here in Him; there, it can be argued, He all the more has the right to dispense with the Sabbath regulations and to do as He thinks best on the Sabbath day. That may be said to be the traditional interpretation of this sentence, but there are real difficulties in it.

(ii) It is to be noted that on this occasion Jesus is not defending *Himself* for anything that He did on the Sabbath; He is defending His *disciples*; and it is to be noted that the authority which He is stressing here is not so much His own authority as the authority of human need. And it is to be noted that when Mark tells of this incident he introduces another saying of Jesus as part of the climax of it: " The Sabbath was made for man, and not man for the Sabbath " (*Mark* 2: 27).

To this we must add the fact that in Hebrew and Aramaic the phrase *son of man* is not a title at all, but simply a way of saying *a man*. When the Rabbis began a parable, they often began it: " There was a son of man who . . . "; when we would simply say, " There was a man who . . . " The Psalmist writes, " What is *man* that Thou art mindful of him? and the *son of man* that Thou visitest him? " (*Psalm* 8: 4). Again and again the *Ezekiel* God addresses Ezekiel as *son of man*. " And He said unto me: ' Son of man, stand upon thy feet and I will speak unto thee ' " (*Ezekiel* 2: 1; cp. 2: 6; 2: 8; 3: 1, 4, 17, 25). In all these cases *son of man*, spelled without the capital letters, simply means *man*. In the Greek manuscripts of the New Testament in the early and the best day all the words were written completely in capital letters; these manuscripts are called *uncials*, which means that they are written entirely in capitals; in such a manuscript it would not be possible to tell where special capitals are necessary. Therefore, in *Matthew* 12: 8, it may well be that *son of man* should be written without capital letters, and that the phrase does not refer to Jesus but simply to *man*. If we consider that what Jesus is pressing is the claims of human need; if we remember that it is not Himself but His disciples that He is defending; if we remember that Mark tells us that He said that the Sabbath was made for man and not man for the Sabbath; then we may well conclude that what Jesus said here is: " Man is not the slave of the Sabbath; He is the master of it, to use it for his own good." Jesus may well be rebuking the Scribes and Pharisees for enslaving themselves and their fellow-men with a host of tyrannical regulations; and He may well be here laying down the great principle of Christian freedom, which applies to the Sabbath as it does to all other things in life.

LOVE AND LAW

Matthew 12: 9-14

> He left there and went into their Synagogue. And, look you, there was a man there with a withered hand. So they asked Him, " Is it permitted to heal on the Sabbath? " They asked this question in order that they might find an accusation against Him. " What man will there be of you," He said, " who will have a sheep, and, if the sheep falls into a pit on the Sabbath day, will not take a grip of it, and lift it out? How much more valuable is a man than a sheep? So, then, it is permitted to do a good thing on the Sabbath day." Then He said to the man, " Stretch forth your hand! " He stretched it out, and it was restored, sound as the other. So the Pharisees went away and conferred against Him, to find a way to destroy Him.

THIS incident is a crucial moment in the life of Jesus; on it Jesus deliberately and publicly broke the Sabbath Law; and the result was a deliberate conference of the orthodox leaders to search out a way to eliminate Him.

We will not understand the attitude of the orthodox unless we understand the amazing seriousness with which they took the Sabbath Law. The Sabbath Law forbade all work on the Sabbath day, and so seriously did the orthodox Jews take that Law that they would literally die rather than break it.

In the time of the rising under Judas Maccabaeus there were certain Jews who sought refuge in the caves in the wilderness. Antiochus sent a detachment of men to attack them; the attack was made on the Sabbath day; and these insurgent Jews died without even a gesture of defiance or defence, because to fight would have been to break the Sabbath. I *Maccabees* tells how the forces of Antiochus " gave them battle with all speed. Howbeit they answered them not, neither cast they a stone at them, nor stopped the places where they lay hid; but said: ' Let us die in our innocency: heaven and earth shall testify for us, that ye put us to death wrongfully.' So they rose up against them in battle on the Sabbath, and they slew them with their wives and children and cattle, to the number of a thousand people " (I *Maccabees* 2: 31-38). Even in a national crisis, even to save their lives, even to protect their nearest and their dearest, the Jews would not fight on the Sabbath. It was because the Jews insisted on keeping the Sabbath Law that Pompey was able to take Jerusalem. In ancient warfare it was the custom for the attacker to erect a huge mound which overlooked the battlements of the besieged city and from the height of the mound to bombard the defences. So Pompey built his mound, and he built it on the Sabbath days when the Jews simply looked on and refused to lift a hand to stop him. Josephus says, " And had it not been for the practice, from the days of our forefathers, to rest on the seventh day, this bank could never have been perfected, by reason of the opposition the Jews would have made; for though our Law gave us leave then to defend ourselves against those that begin to fight with us and assault us (this was a concession), yet it does not permit us to meddle with our enemies while they do anything else " (Josephus, *Antiquities*,

14. 4. 2.). Josephus recalls the amazement of the Greek historian Agatharchides at the way in which Ptolemy Lagos was allowed to capture Jerusalem: Agatharchides wrote: "There are a people called Jews, who dwell in a city the strongest of all cities, which the inhabitants call Jerusalem, and are accustomed to rest on every seventh day; at which time they make no use of their arms, nor meddle with husbandry, nor take care of any of the affairs of life, but spread out their hands in their holy places, and pray till evening time. Now it came to pass that when Ptolemy the son of Lagos came into this city with his army, these men, in observing this mad custom of theirs, instead of guarding the city, suffered their country to submit itself to a bitter lord; and their Law was openly proved to have commanded a foolish practice. This accident taught all other men but the Jews to disregard such dreams as these were, and not to follow the like idle suggestions delivered as a Law, when in such uncertainty of human reasonings they are at a loss what they should do" (Josephus, *Against Apion*, I: 22). The rigorous Jewish observance of the Sabbath seemed to other nations nothing short of insanity, since it could lead to such amazing national defeats and disasters.

It was that absolutely immovable frame of mind that Jesus was up against. The Law quite definitely and in so many words forbade healing on the Sabbath. It was true that the Law clearly laid it down that "every case when life is in danger supersedes the Sabbath Law." This was particularly the case in diseases of the ear, the nose, the throat and the eyes. But even then it was equally clearly laid down that steps could be taken to keep a man from getting worse, but not to make him better. So a plain bandage might be put on a wound, but not a medicated bandage, and so on. In this case there was no question of the paralysed man's life being in danger; as far as danger went, he would be in no worse condition the next day. Jesus knew the Law; He knew what He was doing;

He knew that the Pharisees were waiting and watching; *and yet He healed the man.* Jesus would accept no law which insisted that a man should suffer, even without danger to life, one moment longer than necessary. His love for humanity far surpassed His respect for ritual Law.

THE CHALLENGE ACCEPTED

Matthew 12: 9-14 (continued)

JESUS went into the synagogue, and in it there was a man with a paralysed hand. Our gospels tell us nothing more about this man, but the *Gospel according to the Hebrews*, which was one of the early gospels which did not succeed in gaining an entry to the New Testament, tells us something more about him. It tells us that he came to Jesus with the appeal: " I was a stone mason, seeking my living with my hands. I pray you, Jesus, to give me back my health, so that I shall not need to beg for food in shame."

But the Scribes and Pharisees were there too. They were not concerned with the man with the paralysed hand; they were concerned only with the minutiæ of their rules and regulations. So they asked Jesus a question: " Is it permitted to heal on the Sabbath day? " Jesus knew the answer to that question perfectly well; He knew that, as we have seen, unless there was actual danger to life, healing was forbidden, because it was regarded as an act of work. But Jesus was wise. If they wished to argue about the Law, He had the skill to meet them on their own ground. " Tell me," He said, " suppose a man has a sheep, and that sheep falls into a pit on the Sabbath day, will he not go and haul the sheep out of the pit? " That was, in fact, a case for which the Law provided. If an animal fell into a pit on the Sabbath, then it was within the Law to carry food, which in any other case would have been a burden, to it, and to render it all assistance. " So," said Jesus, " it is permitted to do a good thing on the Sabbath; and, if it is permitted to do a good thing to a sheep, how much more must it be lawful to do it for a man, who is of so much more value than any animal." Jesus reversed the argument. " If," He argued, " it is right to do good on the Sabbath, then to refuse to do good is evil." It was Jesus' basic principle that there is no time so sacred that it cannot be used for helping a fellow-man who is in need. We will not be judged by the number of church services which we attended, or by the number of chapters of the Bible we have read, or even by the number of the hours we have spent in prayer, but by the number of people we have helped, when their need came crying to us. To this, at the moment, the Scribes and Pharisees had nothing to answer, for their own argument had recoiled on their own head.

So Jesus healed this man, and in healing him He gave him three things.

(i) He gave him back his *health*. Jesus is vitally interested in the bodies of men. Paul Tournier, in his book *A Doctor's Case Book*, has some great things to pass on about healing and God. Professor Courvoisier writes that the vocation of medicine is " a service to which those are called, who, through their studies and the natural gifts with which the Creator has endowed them . . . are specially fitted to tend the sick and to heal them. Whether or not they are aware of it, whether or not they are believers, this is from the Christian point of view fundamental, that doctors are, by their profession, fellow-workers with God." " Sickness and healing," said Dr. Pouyanne, " are acts of grace." " The doctor is an instrument of God's patience," writes Pastor Alain Perrot. " Medicine is a dispensation of the grace of God, who in His goodness takes pity on men and provides remedies for the evil consequences of their sin." Calvin described medicine as a gift from God. He who heals men is helping God. The cure of men's bodies is just as much a God-given task as the cure of men's souls; and the doctor in his practice is just as much a servant of God as the minister in his parish.

(ii) Because Jesus gave this man back his health, He also gave him back his *work*. Without work to do a man is half a man; it is in his work that he finds himself and his satisfaction. Over the years idleness is harder than even pain to bear; and, if there is work to do, even sorrow loses at least something of its bitterness. One of the greatest things that any human being can do for any other human being is to give him work to do.

(iii) Because Jesus gave this man back his health and his work, He gave him back his *self-respect*. We might well add a new beatitude: Blessed are those who give us back our self-respect. A man becomes a man again when, on his two feet, and with his own two hands, he can face life, and can with independence provide for his own needs and for the needs of those who are dependent on him.

We have already said that this incident was crisis. At the end of it the Scribes and Pharisees went out and began to plot the death of Jesus. This man was dangerous. In a sense the highest compliment that you can pay a man is to persecute him. It shows that that man can only be regarded, not only as a dangerous, but as an effective force. The action of the Scribes and Pharisees is the measure of the power of Jesus Christ. True Christianity may be hated, but as an effective force it can never be disregarded.

THE CHARACTERISTICS OF THE SERVANT OF THE LORD

Matthew 12: 15-21

> Because Jesus knew this, He withdrew from there: and many followed Him and He healed them all; and He strictly enjoined them not to surround Him with publicity. All this happened that there might be fulfilled the word which came through Isaiah

and which says: " Look you, my servant, whom I have chosen! My beloved one in whom my soul finds delight! I will put my Spirit upon him, and He will tell the nations what justice is. He will not strive, nor will he cry aloud, nor will anyone hear his voice in the streets. He will not break the crushed reed, and he will not quench the smoking wick, till he sends forth his conquering judgment, and in his name shall the Gentiles hope."

WE must begin by noting two things about Jesus, both of which show that Jesus never confounded recklessness with courage. First, for the time being, He withdrew. The time for the head-on clash had not yet come. He had work to do before the Cross took Him to its arms. Second, He forbade men to surround Him with publicity. He knew only too well how many false Messiahs had arisen; He knew only too well how inflammable the people were. If the idea got around that someone with marvellous powers had emerged, then very certainly a political rebellion would have arisen, and lives would have been needlessly and cruelly lost. He had to teach them what Messiahship meant, that it meant, not crushing power, but sacrificial service, not a throne, but a cross, before men could spread the true story of Him abroad.

The quotation which Matthew uses to sum up the work of Jesus is from *Isaiah* 42: 1-4. In a sense it is a curious quotation, because in the first instance, and when it was first uttered, it referred to Cyrus, the Persian king (cp. *Isaiah* 45: 1). The original point of the quotation was this. Cyrus was sweeping onwards in his conquests; and the prophet saw those conquests as within the deliberate and definite plan of God. Although he did not know it, Cyrus, the Persian, was the instrument of God. Further, the prophet saw Cyrus as the gentle conqueror, as indeed he was. But although the original words referred to Cyrus, the full fulfilment of the prophecy undoubtedly came in Jesus Christ. In his day the Persian king mastered the eastern world, but the true Master of all the world is

Jesus Christ. Let us then see how wonderfully Jesus satisfied this forecast of Isaiah.

(i) The Authorized Version has it that He will bring *judgment* to the nations. The Authorized Version very commonly uses the word *judgment* where we would more naturally speak of *justice*. For instance *Amos 5: 24* would be better translated: " Let *justice* run down as waters, and righteousness as a mighty stream." So Jesus came to bring men *justice*. The Greeks defined *justice* as *giving to God and to men that which is their due*. Jesus showed men how to live in such a way that both God and men receive their proper place in our lives. He showed us how to behave both towards God and towards men.

(ii) He will not strive, nor cry aloud, nor will anyone hear his voice in the streets. The word that is used for to *cry aloud* is the word that is used for the barking of a dog, the croaking of a raven, the bawling of a drunken man, the uproar of a discontented audience in a theatre. It means that Jesus would not brawl with men. We know all about the quarrels of conflicting parties, in which each tries to shout the other down. The hatred of theologians, the *odium theoligicum* is one of the tragedies of the Christian Church. We know all about the oppositions of politicians and of ideologies. In Jesus there is the quiet, strong serenity of one who seeks to conquer by love, and not by strife of words.

(iii) He will not break the crushed reed or quench the smoking flax. The reed may be bruised and hardly able to stand erect; the wick may be weak and the light may be but a flicker. A man's witness may be shaky and weak; the light of his life may be but a flicker and not a flame; but Jesus did not come to discourage, but to encourage. He did not come to treat the weak with contempt, but with understanding; He did not come to extinguish the weak flame, but to nurse it back to a clearer and a stronger light. The most precious thing about Jesus is the fact that he is not the great discourager, but the great encourager.

(iv) In Him the Gentiles will hope. With Jesus there came into the world the invitation, not to a nation, but to all men, to share in and to accept the love of God. In Him God was reaching out to all men in every nation with the offer of His love.

SATAN'S DEFENCES ARE BREACHED

Matthew 12: 22-29

Then there was brought to Him a man possessed by a devil, blind and dumb; and He cured him, so that the dumb man spoke and saw. The crowds were beside themselves with amazement. "Surely," they said, "this cannot be the Son of David?" But, when they heard it, the Pharisees said, "The only way in which this fellow casts out devils, is by the help of Beelzeboul, the prince of the devils." When He saw what they were thinking, Jesus said to them, "Every kingdom which has reached a state of division against itself is laid waste; and any city or region which has reached a state of division against itself will not stand. If Satan is casting out Satan, he is in a state of division against himself. How then shall his kingdom stand? Further, if I cast out devils by the power of Beelzeboul, by whose power do your sons cast them out? They do cast them out, and therefore they convict you of hypocrisy in the charge which you level against me. But, if I cast out devils by the Spirit of God, then the Kingdom of God has come upon you. Or, how can anyone enter into the house of a strong man, and seize his goods, unless he first bind the strong man? Then he will be able to seize his house."

IN the eastern world it was not only mental and psychological illness which was ascribed to the influence of demons and devils; all illness was ascribed to their malignant power. Exorcism was therefore very commonly practised; and it was in fact frequently completely effective. There is nothing in that to be surprised at. When people believe in demon-possession, it is easy for them to convince themselves that they are so possessed; when they come under that delusion, the symptoms of demon-possession immediately arise in them. Even amongst ourselves anyone can think himself into having a headache, or can convince himself that he has the symptoms of an illness. When a person under such a delusion was confronted with an exorcist in whom he had faith and confidence, often the delusion was dispelled, and a cure resulted. In such cases if a man was convinced he was cured, he was cured.

In this case Jesus cured a man who was deaf and dumb and whose infirmity was attributed to demon-possession. The people were amazed. They began to wonder if this man Jesus could be the Son of David, so long promised, and so long expected, the great Saviour and Liberator, who was to come. Their doubt was due to the fact that Jesus was so unlike the picture of the Son of David in which they had been brought up to believe. Here was no glorious prince with pomp and circumstance; here was no rattle of swords and army with banners; here was no fiery cross calling men to war; here was a simple carpenter from Galilee, in whose words there was wisdom gentle and serene, in whose eyes there was compassion, and on whose hands there was mysterious power. The crowds could not understand Jesus because His compassionate gentleness was so unlike the pomp and panoply and power which they were expecting.

All the time the Scribes and Pharisees were looking grimly on. They had their own solution of the problem. Jesus was casting out devils because He was in league with the prince of devils. Jesus had three unanswerable replies to that charge.

(i) If He was casting out devils by the help of the prince of devils, it could only mean that in the demonic kingdom there was breach and disagreement and schism. If the prince of devils was actually lending his power to the destruction of his own demonic agents, then there was civil war in the kingdom of evil, and that kingdom was doomed. Neither a house nor a city nor a district can remain strong when it is divided against itself. Dissension within is the end of power. Even if the Scribes and Pharisees were right, Satan's days were numbered on this argument.

(ii) We shall take Jesus' third argument second, because there is so much to be said about the second that we wish to take it separately. Jesus said, " If I am casting out devils—and that you have not, and cannot, deny—it means that I have invaded the territory of Satan, and that I am actually like a burglar who is despoiling his house. Now clearly no one can get into a strong man's house until the strong man is bound and rendered helpless. Therefore the very fact that I have been able so successfully to invade Satan's territory is the proof that he is bound and powerless to resist." The picture of the binding of the strong man is taken from *Isaiah* 49: 24-26.

There is one question which this argument makes us wish to ask; it is not a question to which there can be any undoubted answer, but nonetheless we almost instinctively ask it. When was the strong man bound? When was the prince of the devils fettered in such a way that Jesus could make this breach in his defences? Maybe there is no answer to that question; but if there is an answer, the answer is that Satan was bound during Jesus' temptations in the wilderness. It sometimes happens that, although an army is not completely put out of action, it suffers such a defeat that its fighting potential is never quite the same again. Its losses are so great, its confidence is so shaken, that it will never be quite the force it was. When Jesus faced the Tempter in the wilderness and conquered him, something happened. For the first time Satan found someone whom not all his wiles could seduce, and whom not all his attacks could conquer. From that time henceforward the power of Satan has never been quite the same. He is no longer the all-conquering power of darkness; he is the defeated power of sin. The defences are breached; the enemy is not yet conquered; but his power can never be the same again, for Jesus can help others to win the victory which He Himself won.

THE JEWISH EXORCISTS

Matthew 12: 22-29 (continued)

(iii) Jesus' second argument, to which we now come, was that the Jews themselves practised exorcism; there were Jews themselves who expelled demons and who wrought cures. If He was practising exorcism by the power of the prince of devils, then they must be doing the same, for they were dealing with the same diseases and they had at least sometimes the same effect. Let us then look at the customs and the methods of the Jewish exorcists, for they were indeed a remarkable contrast to the methods of Jesus. Josephus, who was a perfectly reputable historian, says that the power to cast out demons was part of the wisdom of Solomon, and he describes a case which he himself saw (Josephus, *Antiquities* 8. 2. 5.): " God also enabled Solomon to learn that skill which expels demons, which is a science useful and health-bringing to men. He composed such incantations also, by which distempers are alleviated. And he left behind him also the manner of using exorcisms, by which they drive away demons so that they never return, and this method of cure is of great force unto this day; for I have seen a certain man of my own country, whose name was Eleazar, releasing people who were demoniacal in the presence of Vespasian, and his sons, and his captains, and the whole multitude of his soldiers. The manner of the cure was this. He put a ring that had a root which was one of those sorts mentioned by Solomon in the nostrils of the demoniac, after which he drew out the demon through his nostrils; and when the man fell down immediately, he adjured the demon to return into him no more, making still mention

of Solomon, and reciting the incantations which he composed. And when Eleazar would persuade and demonstrate
to the spectators that he had such a power, he set a little
way off a cup or basin full of water, and commanded
the demon, as he went out of the man, to overturn it,
and thereby to let the spectators know that he had left
the man; and when this was done, the skill and wisdom
of Solomon was shown very manifestly." Here was the
Jewish method; here was the whole paraphernalia of
magic. How different the calm serene word of power
which Jesus uttered!

Josephus has still further information about how the
Jewish exorcists worked. A certain root was much used
in exorcism. Josephus tells about it: " In the valley of
Macherus there is a certain root called by the same name.
Its colour is like to that of flame, and towards evening
it sends out a certain ray like lightning. It is not easily
taken by such as would do so, but recedes from their
hands, nor will it yield itself to be taken quietly until
either the urine of a woman, or her menstrual blood,
be poured upon it; nay, even then it is certain death
to those who touch it, unless anyone take and hang the
root itself down from his hand, and so carry it away.
It may also be taken another way without danger, which
is this: they dig a trench all round about it, till the hidden
part of the root be very small; they then tie a dog to it,
and when the dog tries hard to follow him that tied him,
this root is easily plucked up, but the dog dies immediately,
as if it were instead of the man that would take the plant
away; nor after this need anyone be afraid of taking
it into their hands. Yet after all these pains in getting it,
it is only valuable on account of one virtue which it
possesses, that if it be brought to sick persons, it drives
away those called demons " (Josephus, *Wars of the Jews*
7. 6. 3.). What a difference between Jesus' word of power,
and this witch-doctoring which the Jewish exorcist used!

We may add still one more illustration of this Jewish

exorcism. It comes from the apocryphal book of *Tobit*. Tobit is told by the angel that he is to marry Sara, the daughter of Raguel. She is a beautiful maiden with a great dowry, and she herself is good. She has been in turn married to seven different men, all of whom perished on their wedding night, because Sara was loved by a wicked demon, who would allow none to approach her. Tobit is afraid, but the angel tells him, " On the night when thou shalt come into the marriage chamber, thou shalt take the ashes of perfume, and shalt lay them upon some of the heart and liver of the fish, and shalt make a smoke with it; and the devil shall smell it and flee away, and never come again any more " (*Tobit* 6: 16). So Tobit did and the devil was banished for ever (*Tobit* 8: 1-4).

These were the things the Jewish exorcists did, and, as so often, these things were a parable and symbol. Men sought their deliverance from the evils and the sorrows of humanity in their magic and their incantations and their spells. Maybe even these things for a little while, in the mercy of God, brought some relief; but in Jesus there came the word of God with its serene power to bring to men the perfect deliverance which they had wistfully and even desperately sought, and which, until He came, they had never been able to find.

One of the most interesting things in the whole passage is Jesus' saying, " If I cast out devils by the finger of God, then the Kingdom of God has come upon you " (verse 27). It is very significant to note that the sign of the coming of the Kingdom was not full churches and great revivalistic meetings, but *the defeat of pain*.

THE IMPOSSIBILITY OF NEUTRALITY

Matthew 12: 30

> " He who is not with me is against me, and he who does not gather with me scatters abroad."

THE picture of *gathering* and *scattering* in this saying of Jesus may come from either of two backgrounds. It may come from *harvesting*; he who is not sharing in gathering the harvest is scattering the grain abroad, and is therefore losing it to the wind. It may come from *shepherding*; he who is not helping to keep the flock safe is exposing the flock to danger; he who is not bringing it into the fold is driving it out to the dangerous and the comfortless hills.

In this one piercing sentence Jesus lays down the impossibility of neutrality. W. C. Allen writes: "In this war against Satan's strongholds there are only two sides, for Christ or against Him, gathering with Him or scattering with Satan." We may take a very simple analogy. We may take this saying and apply it to ourselves and to the Church. *If our presence does not strengthen the Church, then our absence is weakening it*. There is no halfway house. If a nation is at war, then a neutral nation is helping the enemy by withholding the help it might have given. In all things in this world a man has to choose his side; abstention from choice, suspended action, is no way out, because the mere refusal to give one side assistance is in fact the giving of support to the other.

There are three things which make a man seek this impossible neutrality.

(i) There is the sheer *inertia of human nature*. It is true of so many people that the only thing they desire is to be left alone. They automatically shrink away from anything which is disturbing, and even choice is a disturbance.

(ii) There is the natural *cowardice of human nature*. Many a man refuses the way of Christ, because in his heart of hearts he is afraid to take the stand which Christinity demands. The basic thing that stops him is the thought of what other people will think and say. The voice of his neighbours is louder in his ears than the voice of God.

(iii) There is the sheer *flabbiness of human nature*. Most people would rather have security than adventure, and the older they grow the more that is so. A challenge always involves an adventure; Christ comes to us with a challenge, and so often we would rather have the comfort of selfish inaction than the adventure of action for Christ.

This saying of Jesus—" He who is not with me is against me "—presents us with a certain problem, for both Mark and Luke have a saying which is the very reverse of this: " He that is not against us is for us " (*Mark* 9: 40; *Luke* 9: 50). But these two sayings are not so contradictory as they seem. It is to be noted that Jesus spoke the second of them when His disciples came to Him and told Him that they had sought to stop a man from casting out devils in His name, because he was not one of their company. So a wise suggestion has been made. " He that is not with me is against me," is a test that we ought to apply to *ourselves*. Am I truly on the Lord's side, or, am I trying to shuffle through life in a state of cowardly neutrality? " He that is not against us is for us," is a test that we ought to apply to *others*. Am I intolerant? Am I given to condemning everyone who does not speak with my theology and worship with my liturgy and share my ideas? Am I limiting the Kingdom of God to those who think as I do? The saying in this present passage is a challenge and a test to apply to ourselves; the saying in *Mark* and *Luke* is a saying to apply to others; for we must ever judge ourselves with sternness and other people with tolerance.

THE SIN BEYOND FORGIVENESS

Matthew 12: 31-33

" That is why I tell you that every sin and every blasphemy will be forgiven to men; but blasphemy against the Holy Spirit will not be forgiven. If anyone speaks a word against the Son of Man, it will be forgiven him; but if anyone speaks a word against the Holy Spirit, it will not be forgiven him, either in this world or in the world to come. Either assume that the tree is good and the fruit is good, or assume that the tree is rotten and the fruit is rotten. For the tree is known by its fruits."

It is a startling thing to find words about an unforgivable sin on the lips of Jesus the Saviour of men. So startling is this that there have been some who wished to take away the sharp definiteness of the meaning. There are some who argue that this is only another example of that vivid Eastern way of saying things, as, for example, when Jesus said that a man must *hate* father and mother truly to be His disciple, and that this is not to be understood in all its terrible literalness, but simply means that the sin against the Holy Spirit is a supremely terrible sin. In support of that view certain Old Testament passages are quoted. " But the soul that doeth aught presumptuously, whether he be born in the land, or a stranger, the same reproacheth the Lord; and that soul *shall be cut off* from among the people. Because he hath despised the word of the Lord, and hath broken His commandment, that soul *shall be utterly cut off* " (*Numbers* 16: 30, 31). " And therefore I have sworn unto the house of Eli, that the iniquity of Eli's house *shall not be purged* with sacrifice nor offering *for ever* " (1 *Samuel* 3: 14). " And it was revealed in mine ears by the Lord of hosts, ' Surely this iniquity *shall not be purged from you till ye die,*' saith the Lord God of hosts " (*Isaiah* 22: 14). It is claimed that these texts say much the same thing as Jesus said, and that they are only insisting on the grave and terrible nature of the sin in question. We can only say that these Old Testament texts do not have the same air upon them, nor do they produce the same impression. There is something very much more alarming in hearing words about a sin which has no forgiveness on the lips of Him who was the incarnate love of God.

There is one section in this saying of Jesus which is

undoubtedly puzzling. In the Authorized Version Jesus is made to say that a sin against the Son of Man is forgivable, whereas a sin against the Holy Spirit is not forgivable. If that is to be taken as it stands, it is indeed a hard saying. Matthew has already said that Jesus is the touchstone of all truth (*Matthew* 10: 32, 33); and it is difficult to see what the difference between the two sins is. But it may well be that at the back of this there is a misunderstanding of what Jesus said. We have already seen (cp. notes on *Matthew* 12: 1-8) that the Hebrew phrase *a son of man* means simply *a man*, and that the Jews used this phrase when they desired to speak of *any man*. When we would say, " There was a man . . .," the Jewish Rabbi would say, " There was a son of man. . . . " It may well be that what Jesus said was this: " If any man speaks a word against *a man*, it will be forgiven; but if any man speaks a word against the Holy Spirit is will not be forgiven." It is quite possible that we may misunderstand a merely human messenger from God; but we cannot misunderstand—except deliberately—when God speaks to us through His own Holy Spirit. A human messenger is always open to misconstruction; but the divine messenger speaks so plainly that He can only be wilfully misunderstood. A man may disobey or disregard the prophet in the market place or the preacher in the pulpit; but he can never disobey or disregard the Holy Spirit speaking in his heart. It certainly makes this passage easier to understand, if we regard the difference between the two sins as a sin against God's human messenger, which is serious, but not unforgivable, and a sin against God's divine messenger, which is completely wilful, and which, as we shall see, can end by becoming unforgivable.

THE LOST AWARENESS

Matthew 12: 31-33 (*continued*)

LET us then try to understand what Jesus meant by the

sin against the Holy Spirit. To understand what Jesus was saying one thing is completely necessary. We must grasp the fact that Jesus was not speaking about the Holy Spirit *in the full Christian sense of the term*. He could not have been, for He was speaking to Jewish Scribes and Rabbis who knew nothing of the doctrine of the Holy Spirit, and, in any event, Pentecost had to come before the Holy Spirit came upon men in all His power and light and fulness. This must be interpreted in light of the *Jewish* conception of the Holy Spirit. What then was the Jewish conception of the Holy Spirit?

According to Jewish teaching the Holy Spirit had two supreme functions. First, the Holy Spirit brought God's truth to men; the Holy Spirit was God's instrument in revelation. Second, the Holy Spirit enabled men to recognize and to understand that truth when they saw it; the Holy Spirit was God's illuminator of men's minds. So then a man, as the Jews saw it, needed the Holy Spirit, both to receive and to recognise God's truth. In view of this Jewish conception of the Holy Spirit we may now express this in another way. *There is in man a Spirit-given faculty which enables him to recognize goodness and truth when he sees them.*

Now we must take the next step in our attempt to understand what Jesus meant. *A man can lose any faculty if he refuses to use it.* This is true in any sphere of life. It is true physically; if a man ceases to use and exercise certain muscles, they will atrophy and become unusable. It is true mentally; many a man at school or in his youth has acquired some slight knowledge of, for example French or Latin or music; but any knowledge that he had is long since gone, because he did not exercise it and use it. It is true of all kinds of perception and awareness. A man may lose all appreciation of good music, if he listens to nothing but cheap music; he may lose the ability to read a great book, if he reads nothing but ephemeral productions; he may lose the faculty of enjoying clean and healthy and pure pleasure, if he for long enough finds his pleasure in things which are degraded and soiled. *Therefore a man can lose the ability to recognize goodness and truth when he sees them.* If he for long enough shuts his eyes and ears to God's way, and takes his own way, if he for long enough refuses to listen to the guidance God is offering him, if he for long enough turns his back upon the messages which God is sending him, if he for long enough prefers his own human ideas to the ideas which God is seeking to put into his mind, then in the end he comes to a stage when he cannot recognize God's truth and God's beauty and God's goodness when he sees them. He comes to a stage when his own evil seems to him good, and when God's good seems to him evil. That is the stage to which these Scribes and Pharisees had come. They had so long been blind and deaf to the guidance of God's hand and the promptings of God's Spirit, they had insisted on their own way so long, that they had come to a stage when they could not recognize God's truth and goodness when they saw them. They were able to look on incarnate goodness and call it incarnate evil; they were able to look on the Son of God and call Him the ally of the devil. The sin against the Holy Spirit is the sin of so often and so consistently refusing God's will that in the end it cannot be recognized when it comes even full-displayed.

But why should that sin be *unforgivable?* What differentiates it so terribly from all other sins? The answer to that is simple. *When a man reaches that stage, repentance is impossible.* If a man cannot recognize the good when he sees it, he cannot desire the good. If a man does not recognize the evil as being evil, he cannot be sorry for it, and hate it, and wish to depart from it. And if he cannot, in spite of failures, love the good and hate the evil, then he cannot repent; and if he cannot repent, he cannot be forgiven, for repentance is the only condition of forgiveness. It would save much heartbreak if people would realise that

49

the one man who cannot have committed the sin against the Holy Spirit is the man who fears he has, for the sin against the Holy Spirit can be truly described as the loss of all sense of sin.

It was to that stage that the Scribes and Pharisees had come. They had so long been deliberately blind and deliberately deaf to God that they had lost the faculty of recognizing God when they were confronted with Him. It was not God who had shut them out, or banished them beyond the pale of forgiveness; they had shut themselves out, for years of resistance to God had made them what they were.

There is a dreadful warning here. We must so heed God all our days that our sensitivity is never blunted, that our awareness is never dimmed, that our spiritual hearing never becomes spiritual deafness. It is a law of life that we will only hear what we are listening for, and that we will only hear what we have fitted ourselves to hear. There is a story of a country man who was in the office of a city friend, with the roar of the traffic coming through the windows. Suddenly he said, " Listen! " " What is it? " asked the city man. " A grasshopper," said the country man. Years of listening to the country sounds had attuned his ears to the country sounds, sounds that a city man's ear could not hear at all. On the other hand, let a silver coin drop, and the chink of the silver would have immediately reached the ears of the money-maker, while the country man might never have heard it at all. Only the expert, the man who has made himself able to hear it, will pick out the note of each individual bird in the chorus of the birds. Only the expert, the man who has made himself able to hear it, will distinguish the different instruments in the orchestra and catch a lonely wrong note from the second violins. It is the law of life that we hear what we have trained ourselves to hear; day by day we must listen to God, so that day by day God's voice may become, not fainter and fainter until we cannot hear it at all, but clearer and clearer until it becomes the one sound to which above all our ears are attuned.

So Jesus finishes with the challenge: " If I have done a good deed, you must admit that I am a good man; if I have done a bad deed, then you may think me a bad man. You can only tell a tree's quality by its fruits, and a man's character by his deeds." But what if a man has become so blind to God that he cannot recognize goodness when he sees it?

HEARTS AND WORDS

Matthew 12: 34-37

> " You brood of vipers, how can you who are evil speak good things? For it is from the overflow of the heart that the mouth speaks. The good man brings out good things from his good treasure house; and the evil man brings out evil things out of his evil treasure house. I tell you that every idle word which men shall speak, of that word shall they render account in the day of judgment; for by your words you will be acquitted, and by your words you will be condemned."

It is little wonder that Jesus chose to speak here about the terrible responsibility of words. The Scribes and Pharisees had just spoken the most terrible words. They had looked on the Son of God and had called Him the ally of the devil. Such words were dreadful words indeed. So Jesus laid down two laws.

(i) The state of a man's heart can be seen through the words which he speaks. Long ago Menander the Greek dramatist, had said: " A man's character can be known from his words." That which is in the heart can only come to the surface through the lips. A man can only produce through his lips what he has in his heart. It is an obvious fact that there is nothing so revealing as words. We do not need to talk to a man long before we discover whether he has a mind that is pure or a mind that is dirty;

we do not need to listen to him long before we discover whether he has a mind that is kind and sympathetic or a mind that is cruel, callous, critical; we do not need to listen for long to a man who is preaching or teaching or lecturing to find out whether his mind is clear and lucid, or whether it is muddled and involved. We are continually revealing what we are by what we say.

(ii) Jesus laid it down that a man would specially render account for his *idle* words. The word that is used for idle is *aergos*; *ergon* is the Greek for a *deed*; and the prefix *a*—means *without*; *aergos* described that which was *not meant to produce anything*. It is used, for instance of a barren tree, of fallow land, of the Sabbath day when no work could be done, of an idle man. Jesus was saying something which is profoundly true. There are in fact two great truths here.

(*a*) It is the words which a man speaks in his unguarded moments, the words which he speaks without thinking, the words which he utters when the conventional restraints are removed, which really show what he is like. As Plummer puts it, " The carefully spoken word may be a calculated hypocrisy." When a man is consciously on his guard, he will be careful what he says and how he says it; but when he is off his guard, and when he is not watching what he says, then his words reveal his character. It is quite possible for a man's public utterances to be fine and noble, and for his private conversation to be coarse and salacious. In public he carefully chooses what he says; in private he takes the sentinels away, and any word leaves the gateway of his lips. It is so with anger; a man will say in anger what he really thinks, and what he has often wanted to say, but which the cool control of prudence has kept him from saying. Many a man is a model of charm and courtesy in public, when he knows that he is being watched, and when he is deliberately careful about his words; while in his own house and home he is a dreadful example of irritability, sarcasm, temper, criticism, querulous complaint because he thinks that he does not need to keep up his guard, because there is no one to hear and to see. It is a humbling thing—and a warning thing—to remember that the words which show what we are are the words we speak when our guard is down.

(b) It is often these words which cause the greatest damage. A man may say in anger things he would never have said if he was in control of himself. He may say afterwards that he never meant what he said; but that does not free him from the responsibility of having said it; and the fact that he has said it often leaves a wound that nothing will cure, and erects a barrier that nothing will take away. A man may say in his relaxed moment a coarse and questionable thing that he would never have said in public—and that very thing may lodge in someone's memory and stay there unforgotten. Pythagoras, the Greek philosopher, said, " Choose rather to fling a chance stone than to speak a chance word." Once the hurting word or the soiling word is spoken nothing will bring it back; and it pursues a course of damage wherever it goes.

Let a man examine himself. Let him examine his own words that he may discover the state of his own heart. And let him remember that God does not judge him by the words he speaks with care and deliberation, but by the words he speaks, when the conventional restraints are gone, and the real feelings of his heart come bubbling to the surface.

THE ONLY SIGN

Matthew 12: 38-42

> Then the Scribes and Pharisees answered Him: " Teacher," they said, " we wish to see a sign from you." He answered, " It is an evil and apostate generation which seeks a sign. No sign will be given to it, except the sign of Jonah the prophet. For, as Jonah was in the belly of the whale three days and three nights, so the Son of Man will be in the heart of the earth for three days and three nights.

> At the judgment the men of Nineveh will be witnesses against this generation, and they will condemn it, because they repented at the preaching of Jonah, and, look you, something more than Jonah is here. The Queen of the South will rise in judgment with this generation, and will condemn it, because she came from the ends of the earth to listen to the wisdom of Solomon and, look you, something more than Solomon is here! "

" THE Jews," said Paul, " require a sign " (I *Corinthians* I: 22). It was characteristic of the Jews that they asked signs and wonders from those who claimed to be the messengers of God. It was as if they said, " Prove your claims, and produce your credentials by doing something extraordinary." Edersheim quotes a passage from the Rabbinic stories to illustrate the kind of thing that popular opinion expected from the Messiah: " When a certain Rabbi was asked by his disciples about the time of the Messiah's coming, he said, ' I am afraid you will also ask me for a sign.' When they promised that they would not do so, he told them that the gate of Rome would fall and be rebuilt, and fall again, when there would not be time to restore it before the Son of David came. On this they pressed him in spite of his remonstrance for a sign. A sign was given him, that the waters which issued from the cave of Banias were turned into blood. Again, when the teaching of Rabbi Eliezer was challenged, he appealed to certain signs. First, a locust bean tree moved at his bidding, one hundred, or according to some, four hundred cubits. Next the channels of water were made to flow backwards. The walls of the academy leaned forward, and were only arrested at the bidding of another Rabbi. Lastly Eliezer exclaimed: ' If the Law is as I teach, let it be proved from heaven.' A voice came from the sky saying, ' What have you to do with Rabbi Eliezer, for the instruction is as he teaches? ' " That is the kind of sign that the Jews desired. They did so because they were guilty of one basic and fundamental mistake. They desired to see God in the *abnormal*; they forgot that we are never nearer God, and God never shows Himself to us so much and so continually as in the ordinary things of everyday.

Jesus calls them an evil and an *adulterous* generation. The word *adulterous* is not to be taken literally; it means *apostate*. Behind it there is a favourite Old Testament prophetic picture. The relationship between Israel and God was conceived of as a marriage bond. God was the husband of Israel, and Israel was the bride of God. When therefore Israel was unfaithful and gave her love to other gods, the nation was said to be adulterous and to go awhoring after strange gods. *Jeremiah* 3: 6-11 is a typical passage. There the nation is said to have gone up into every high mountain, and under every green tree, and to have played the harlot. Even when Israel had been put away and divorced for infidelity by God, Judah did not take the warning and still played the harlot. Her whoredoms have defiled the land, and she has committed adultery with stones and stocks. The word describes something worse than physical adultery; it describes that infidelity to God from which all sin, physical and spiritual, springs.

Jesus says that the only sign which will be given to this nation is the sign of *Jonah the prophet*. Now here we have a problem. Matthew says that the sign is that, as Jonah was in the belly of the whale three days and three nights, the Son of Man will be in the heart of the earth for three days and three nights. It is to be noted that these are not the words of Jesus, but the explanation of Matthew. When Luke reports this incident (*Luke* 11: 29-32) he makes no mention at all of Jonah being in the belly of the whale. He simply says that Jesus said, " For as Jonah was a sign unto the Ninevites, so shall also the Son of Man be to this generation " (*Luke* 11: 30). The fact is that Matthew understood wrongly the point of what Jesus said; and in so doing he made a strange mistake; for Jesus was not in the heart of the earth for three nights, but only for two nights. He was laid in the earth on the night of the first Good Friday, and rose on the morning of the first Easter Sunday. The point is that to the Ninevites *Jonah himself* was God's sign, and Jonah's words were God's message.

Jesus is saying, " You are asking for a sign—*I am God's sign.* You have failed to recognize me. The Ninevites recognized God's warning in Jonah; the Queen of Sheba recognized God's wisdom in Solomon. In me there has come to you a greater wisdom than Solomon ever had, and a greater message than Jonah ever brought—but you are so blind that you cannot see the truth and so deaf that you cannot hear the warning. And for that very reason the day will come when these people of old time who recognized God when they saw Him will be witnesses against you, who had so much better a chance, and failed to recognize God, because you refused to do so."

Here is a tremendous truth—*Jesus is God's sign,* just as Jonah was God's message to the Ninevites and Solomon God's wisdom to the Queen of Sheba. In Jesus we are confronted with God; and the one real question in life is: " What is our reaction when we are confronted with God in Jesus Christ? " Is that reaction bleak hostility, as it was in the case of the Scribes and Pharisees? Or, is it humble acceptance of God's warning and God's truth as it was in the case of the people of Nineveh, and of the Queen of Sheba? The all-important question in life is: " What think ye of Christ? "

THE PERIL OF THE EMPTY HEART

Matthew 12: 43-45

" When an unclean spirit goes out of a man, it goes through waterless places, seeking for rest, and does not find it. Then it says, ' I will go back to my house, from which I came out,' and when it comes, it finds it empty, swept and in perfect order. Then it goes and brings with it seven other spirits more evil than itself, and they go in and take up their residence there. So the last state of that man becomes worse than the first; so it will be with this evil generation."

THERE is a whole world of the most practical truth in this compact and eerie little parable about the haunted house.

(i) We have to note that the evil spirit is banished from the man, not destroyed. That is to say that, in this present age, evil can be conquered, and evil can be repulsed, and evil can be driven away—but evil cannot be destroyed. Evil is always looking for the opportunity to make a counter-attack, and to regain the ground that is lost. Evil is a force which is at bay, but which is not eliminated.

(ii) That is bound to mean that a negative religion can never be enough. A religion which consists in *thou shalt nots* is bound to end in failure. The trouble about such a religion is that it may be able to cleanse a man, by prohibiting all his evil habits, and forbidding all his evil actions, but *it cannot keep him cleansed*. Let us think of this in actual practice. A drunkard may be reformed; he may decide that he will no longer spend his time in the public house; but he must find something else to do; he must find something to fill up his now empty time, or he will simply slip back into his evil ways. A man whose constant pursuit has been pleasure, may decide that he must stop; but he must find something else to do to fill up his life and his time, or he will simply, through the very emptiness of his life, drift back to his old pursuits. A man's life must not only be sterilized from evil; it must be fructified to good. It will always remain true that "Satan finds some mischief still for idle hands to do." And if one kind of action is banished from life, another kind of action must be substituted for it, for life cannot remain empty.

(iii) It therefore follows that the only real and permanent cure for evil action is Christian action. Any teaching which stops at telling a man what he must not do is bound to be a failure; it must go on to tell him what he must do. The

57

one fatal disease is idleness; even a sterilized idleness will soon be infected. The easiest way to conquer the weeds in a garden is to fill it with useful things, even if it be potatoes. The easiest way to keep a life from sin is to fill it with healthy action. To put it quite simply, the Church will most easily keep her converts when she gives them Christian work to do. Our aim is not the mere negative absence of evil action; it is the positive presence of life and work for Christ. If we are finding the temptations of evil very threatening, one of the best ways to conquer them is to forget them by plunging into activity for God and for our fellow-men.

TRUE KINSHIP

Matthew 12: 46-50

> While He was still speaking to the crowds, look you, His mother and His brothers stood outside, for they were seeking an opportunity to speak to Him. Someone said to Him: " Look you, your mother and your brothers are standing outside, seeking an opportunity to speak to you." He answered the man who had spoken to Him: " Who is my mother? And who are my brothers?" And He stretched out His hand towards His disciples. " See," He said, " my mother and my brothers! Whoever does the will of my Father in heaven is my brother and sister and mother."

IT was one of the great human tragedies of Jesus' life that, during His lifetime, His nearest and dearest never understood Him. " Neither," says John, " did His brothers believe in Him " (*John* 7: 5). Mark tells us that when Jesus set out on His public mission, His friends tried to restrain Him, for they said that He was mad (*Mark* 3: 21). He seemed to them to be busily engaged in throwing His life away in a kind of insanity.

It has often been the case that, when a man embarked on the way of Jesus Christ, his nearest and his dearest could not understand him, and were even hostile to him.

" A Christian's only relatives," said one of the early martyrs, " are the saints." Many of the early Quakers had this bitter experience. When Edward Burrough was moved to the new way, " his parents resenting his ' fanatical spirit ' drove him forth from his home." He pleaded humbly with his father: " Let me stay and be your servant. I will do the work of the hired lad for thee. Let me stay! " But, as his biographer says, " His father was adamant, and much as the boy loved his home and its familiar surroundings, he was to know it no more."

True friendship and true love are founded on certain things and without these things they cannot exist.

(i) Friendship is founded on a common ideal. People who are very different in their background, their mental equipment, and even their methods, can be firm friends, if they have before them a common ideal, for which they work, and towards which they press. The ideal is the bond which unites them.

(ii) Friendship is founded on a common experience, and on the memories which come from that experience. It is when two people have together passed through some great experience, and when they can together look back on it, that real friendship begins.

(iii) True love is founded on obedience, and on nothing else. " You are my friends," said Jesus, " *if you do what I command you* " (*John* 15: 14). There is no way of showing the reality of love unless by the spirit of obedience.

It is for all these reasons that true kinship is not always a matter of a flesh and blood relationship. It remains true that blood is a tie that nothing can break; and it remains true that many a man finds his delight and his peace in the circle of his family; but it is also true that sometimes a man's nearest and dearest are the people who understand him least, and he finds his true fellowship with those who work for a common ideal and who share a common experience. This certainly is true—even if a Christian finds that those who should be closest to him are those who are most out of sympathy with him, there remains for him the fellowship of Jesus Christ and the friendship of all those who love the Lord.

MANY THINGS IN PARABLES

Matthew 13 is a very important chapter in the pattern of the gospel.

(i) It shows a definite turning-point in the ministry of Jesus. At the beginning of His ministry we find Him teaching in the *synagogues*; but now we find Him teaching on the *seashore*. The change is very significant. It is not that the door of the synagogue is as yet finally shut to Him, but it is closing. Even yet in the synagogue He would find a welcome from the common people; but the official leaders of Jewish orthodoxy were now in open opposition to Him. When He entered a synagogue now, it would not be to find only an eager crowd of listeners; it would be also to find a bleak-eyed company of Scribes and Pharisees and elders weighing and sifting every word to find a charge against Him, and watching every action in order to turn it into a condemnation and an accusation. It is one of the supreme tragedies that Jesus was banished from the Church of His day; but that could not stop Him from bringing His invitation to men; for when the doors of the synagogue were closed against Him, He took to the temple of the open air, and taught men in the village streets, and on the roads, and by the lake-side, and in their own homes. The man who has a real message to deliver, and a real desire to deliver it, will always find a way of giving it to men.

(ii) The great interest of this chapter is that here we see Jesus beginning to use to the full His characteristic method of teaching, His way of *teaching in parables*. Even before this He had used a way of teaching which had the germ of the parable in it. The simile of the salt and the light (5: 13-16), the picture of the birds and the lilies (6: 26-30), the story of the wise and the foolish builder (7: 24-27), the illustration of the garments and the wine-skins (9: 16, 17), the picture of the children playing in the market-place (11: 16, 17) are all embryo parables. They are truth in pictures; but it is in this chapter that we find Jesus' way of using parables fully developed, and at its most vivid. As someone has said, " Whatever else is true of Jesus, it is certainly true that He was one of the world's supreme masters of the short story." Before we begin to study these parables in detail, let us ask why Jesus used this method, and what are the great teaching advantages which it offers.

(a) The parable always *makes truth concrete*. There are very few people who can grasp and understand abstract ideas; most people think in pictures. We could for long enough try to put into words what *beauty* is, and at the end of it no one would be very much the wiser; but if we can point at someone and say, " That is a beautiful person," then no more description is needed. We might try for long enough to define *goodness*, and in the end we might leave no clear idea of goodness in peoples' minds, but everyone recognizes a good person and good deed when he sees one. In order to be understood, every great word must become flesh. Every great idea must take form and shape in a person; and the first great quality of a parable is that it makes truth into a picture which all men can see and understand.

(b) It has been said that all great teaching *begins from the here and now, in order to get to the there and then*. If a man wishes to teach people about things which they do not understand, he must begin from things which they do understand. The parable begins with material which lies ready to hand, and which every man under-stands, because it is within his own experience, and from that it leads him on to things which he does not understand, and opens his eyes to things which he has failed to see.

The parable opens a man's mind and opens a man's eyes by beginning from where he is, and by leading him on to where he ought to be.

(c) The great teaching virtue of the parable is that it compels *interest*. The surest way to interest people is to tell them stories. The story-teller has always been the person to whom simple people will listen. The parable puts truth in the form of a story; the simplest definition of a parable is in fact to say that it is " an earthly story with a heavenly meaning." People will not listen, and their attention cannot be retained, unless they are interested; with simple people it is stories which awaken and maintain interest, and the parable is a story.

(d) The parable has the great virtue that it enables and compels a man *to discover truth for himself*. It does not do a man's thinking for him; it says, " Here is a story. What is the truth in it? What does it mean *for you*? Think it out for yourself." There are some things which a man cannot be told; he must discover them for himself. Walter Pater once said that you cannot tell a man the truth; you can only put him into a position in which he can discover it for himself. Unless we discover truth for ourselves, it remains a second-hand and external thing; and still further, unless we discover truth for ourselves, we will almost certainly forget it quickly. The parable, by compelling a man to draw his own conclusions and to do his own thinking, at one and the same time makes truth real to him and fixes it in his memory.

(e) The other side of that is that the parable *conceals truth from those who are either too lazy to think or too blind through prejudice to see*. The parable puts the responsibility fairly and squarely on the individual. The parable *reveals* truth to him who desires truth; it *conceals* truth from him who does not wish to see the truth.

(f) One final thing must be remembered. The parable, as Jesus used it, was *spoken*; it was not read. Its impact had to be immediate, not the result of long study with commentaries and dictionaries. It made truth flash upon a man as the lightning suddenly illumines a pitch-dark night. In our study of the parables that means two things for us. First, it means that we must amass every possible detail about the background of life in Palestine, so that the parable will strike us as it did those who heard it for the first time. We must think and study and imagine ourselves back into the minds of those who were listening to Jesus. Second, it means that generally speaking a parable *will only have one point*. A parable is not an allegory; an allegory is a story in which every possible detail has an inner meaning; but an allegory has to be *read and studied*; a parable is *heard*. We must be very careful not to make allegories of the parables, but to remember that they were designed to make one stabbing truth flash out at a man the moment he heard it.

THE SOWER WENT OUT TO SOW

Matthew 13: 1-9, 18-23

On that day, when He had gone out from the house, Jesus sat on the seashore; and such great crowds gathered to hear Him that He went into a boat, and sat there; and the whole crowd took their stand on the seashore; and He spoke many things in parables to them. " Look! " He said, " the sower went out to sow; and, as he sowed, some seed fell by the wayside: and the birds came and devoured it. But some seed fell upon stony ground, where it had not much earth; and, because it had no depth of earth, it sprang up immediately; but when the sun rose it was scorched, and it withered away because it had no root. Other seed fell upon thorns, and the thorns came up, and choked the life out of it. But others fell on good ground, and yielded fruit, some a hundredfold, some sixtyfold, some thirtyfold. Who has ears, let him hear."

. . . .

" Listen then to the meaning of the parable of the sower. When anyone hears the word of the kingdom, and does not understand it, the evil one comes, and snatches away that which was sown in his heart.

This is represented by the picture of the seed which was sown by the wayside. The picture of the seed which was sown on the stony ground represents the man who hears the word, and immediately receives it with joy. But he has no root in himself, and is at the mercy of the moment, and so, when affliction and persecution come, because of the word, he at once stumbles. The picture of the seed which is sown among the thorns represents the man who hears the word, but the cares of this world and the seduction of riches choke the word, and it bears no crop. The picture of the seed which was sown on the good ground represents the man who hears the word and understands it. He indeed bears fruit and produces some a hundredfold, some sixtyfold, some thirtyfold."

HERE is a picture which anyone in Palestine would understand. Here we actually see Jesus using the here and now to get to the there and then. There is a point which the Authorized Version obscures. The Authorized Version has: " Behold *a* sower went forth to sow." The Greek is not *a* sower, but: " Behold *the* sower went forth to sow." What in all likelihood happened was that Jesus was using the boat by the lakeside as a pulpit, and in one of the fields near the shore a sower was actually sowing; and then and there Jesus took that sower, which they could all see, as a text, and began: " Look at the sower there sowing his seed in that field! " Jesus began from something which at the moment they could actually see to open their minds to truth which as yet they had never seen.

In Palestine there were two ways of sowing seed. It could be sown as it is sown in this country by the sower scattering it broadcast as he walked up and down the field. Of course, if the wind was blowing, in that case some of the seed would be caught by the wind and blown into all kinds of places, and sometimes out of the field altogether. The second way was a lazy way, but it was not uncommonly used. It was to put a sack of seed on the back of an ass, to tear or cut a hole in the corner of the sack, and then to walk the animal up and down the field while the seed ran out. In such a case some of the seed might well dribble out while the animal was crossing the pathway and before it reached the field at all.

In Palestine the fields were in long narrow strips; and the ground between the strips was always a right of way. It was used as a common path; and therefore it was beaten as hard as a pavement by the feet of countless passers-by. That is what Jeaus means by the wayside. If seed fell there, and some was bound to fall there in whatever way it was sown, there was no more chance of its penetrating into the earth than if it had fallen on the road.

The stony ground was not ground that was filled with stones; it was, what was very common in Palestine, a thin skin of earth on the top of an underlying shelf of limestone rock. The earth might be only a very few inches deep before the rock was reached. On such ground the seed would certainly germinate; and it would germinate quickly, because such ground grew speedily warm with the heat of the sun, but there was no depth of earth and when it sent down its roots in search for nourishment and moisture, it would meet only the rock, and would be starved to death, and quite unable to withstand the heat of the sun.

The thorny ground was deceptive ground. When the sower was sowing the ground would look clean enough. It is easy to make a garden look clean by simply turning it over; but in the ground there still lay the fibrous roots of the couch grass and the bishop weed and all the perennial pests, ready to spring to life again. Every gardener knows that the weeds grow with a speed and a strength that few good seeds can equal. The result was that the good seed and the dormant weeds grew together; but the weeds were so strong that they throttled the life out of the seed, and it died, while the weeds flourished.

The good ground was deep and clean and soft; the seed could gain an entry; it could find nourishment; it could grow unchecked; and in the good ground it brought forth an abundant harvest.

THE WORD AND THE HEARER

Matthew 13: 1-9, 18-23 (*continued*)

THIS parable has really a double impact; it is aimed at two sets of people.

(*a*) It is aimed at the *hearers of the word*. It is fairly frequently held by scholars that the interpretation of the parable in verses 18-23 is not the interpretation of Jesus Himself, but the interpretation of the preachers of the early Church, and that it is not in fact the correct interpretation. It is said that it transgresses the law that a parable is not an allegory, and that it is too detailed to be grasped by listeners at the first hearing. If Jesus was really pointing at an actual sower sowing seed that does not seem a valid objection; and in any event the interpretation which identifies the different kinds of soil with different kinds of hearers has always held its place in the Church's thought, and must have come from some authoritative source; and if so, why not from Jesus Himself?

If we take this parable as a warning to hearers, then it means that there are different ways of accepting the word of God, and the fruit which it produces depends on the heart of him who accepts it. The fate of any spoken word depends on the hearer. As it has been said, " A jest's prosperity lies not in the tongue of him who tells it, but in the ear of him who hears it." A jest will succeed when it is told to a man who has a sense of humour, and who is prepared to smile. A jest will fail when it is told to a humourless creature, or to a man who is grimly determined not to be amused. Who then are the hearers who are described and warned in this parable?

(i) There is the hearer *with the shut mind*. There are people into whose minds the word has no more chance of gaining an entry than the seed has of settling into the ground that has been beaten hard by many feet. There are many things which can shut a man's mind. Prejudice can make a man blind to everything he does not wish to see. The unteachable spirit can erect a barrier which cannot easily be broken down. The unteachable spirit can result from one of two things. It can be the result of pride which does not know that it needs to know; and it can be the result of the fear of new truth, and the refusal to adventure on the ways of thought. Sometimes an immoral character and a man's way of life can shut his mind. There may be truth which condemns the things he loves and which accuses the way he takes and the things he does; and many a man refuses to listen to or to recognize the truth which condemns him, for there are none so blind as those who deliberately will not see.

(ii) There is the hearer with the mind like the shallow ground. He is the man who *fails to think things out and to think them through.* There are people who are at the mercy of every new craze. They take a thing up quickly, and just as quickly drop it. They must always be in the fashion. They begin some new hobby, or begin to acquire some new accomplishment with enthusiasm, and the thing becomes difficult and they abandon it, or the enthusiasm wanes and they lay it aside. Some people's lives are littered with things they began and never finished. A man can be like that with the word. When he hears it he may be swept off his feet with an emotional reaction; but no man can live on an emotion. A man has a mind and it is a moral obligation to have an intelligent faith. Christianity has its demands, and these demands must be faced before it can be accepted. The Christian offer is not only a privilege, it is also a responsibility. A sudden enthusiasm can always so quickly become a dying fire.

(iii) There is the hearer who has *so many interests in life that certain things, and often the most important things, get crowded out.* It is characteristic of modern life that it becomes increasingly crowded and increasingly fast. A man becomes too busy to pray; he becomes so preoccupied with many things that he forgets to study the word of God: he can become so involved in committees and good works and charitable services that he has left himself no time for Him from whom all love and service come. His business can take such a grip of him that he is too tired to think of anything else. It is not the things which are obviously bad which are dangerous. It is the things which are good, for the " second best is always the worst enemy of the best." It is not even that a man deliberately banishes prayer and the Bible and the Church from life; it can be that he often thinks of them, and wishes he had time for them, and intends to make time for them, but somehow in his crowded life never gets round to it. We must be very careful to see that Christ is not shouldered out of the topmost niche in life.

(iv) There is the man who is like the good ground. In his reception of the word there are four stages. Like the good ground, *his mind is open.* He is at all times willing to learn. He is prepared *to hear.* He is never either too proud or too busy to listen. Many a man would have been saved all kinds of heartbreak, if he had simply stopped to listen to the voice of a wise friend, or to the voice of God. *He understands.* He has thought the thing out and knows what this means for him, and is prepared to accept it. *He translates his hearing into action.* He produces the good fruit of the good seed. The real hearer is the man who listens, who understands, and who obeys.

NO DESPAIR

Matthew 13: 1-9, 18-23 (*continued*)

(b) We said at the beginning of our study of this parable that it had a double impact. We have now looked at the impact it was designed to have on *those who heard the word.* But it was equally designed to have an impact on *those who preach the word.* Not only was it meant to say something to the listening crowds; it was also meant to say something to the inner circle of the disciples.

It is not difficult to see that in the hearts of the disciples there must have sometimes been a certain discouragement. To them Jesus was everything, the wisest and the most wonderful of all. But, humanly speaking, He had very little success. The doors of the synagogue were shutting against Him. The leaders of orthodox religion were His bitterest critics and were obviously out to destroy Him. True, the crowds came to hear Him, but there were so few who were really changed, and there were so many who came to reap the benefit of His healing power, and, who, when they had received it, went away and forgot. There were so many who came to Jesus only for what they could get. The disciples were faced with a situation in which Jesus seemed to rouse nothing but hostility in the leaders of the Church, and nothing but a very evanescent response in the crowd. It is nothing surprising if in the hearts of the disciples there was sometimes a deep discouragement and disappointment. What then does the parable say to the preacher who is discouraged?

To those in discouragement the lesson of the parable is clear—the lesson is that *the harvest is sure*. For them the lesson is in the climax of the parable, in the picture of the seed of the word which brought forth abundant fruit. Some seed may fall by the wayside and be snatched away by the birds; some seed may fall on the shallow ground and never come to maturity; some seed may fall among the thorns and be choked to death; but in spite of all that *the harvest does come, the harvest is sure*. No farmer ever expects every single seed he sows to generate and to bring forth fruit; he knows quite well that some will be blown away by the wind, and some will fall in places where it cannot grow; but that does not stop him sowing; and that does not make him give up hope of the harvest; the farmer sows in the confidence that, even if some of the seed is wasted, none the less the harvest will certainly come.

So then this parable is a parable of encouragement to those who sow the seed of the word.

(i) When any man sows the seed of the word, he does not know what he is doing, and what effect the seed is having. H. L. Gee in one of his books tells a story. In the church where he worshipped there was a lonely old man, old Thomas. Thomas had outlived all his friends and hardly anyone knew him. Thomas died. H. L. Gee had the feeling that there would be no one to go to the funeral so he decided to go, so that someone might follow old Thomas to his last resting-place. There was no one; and it was a wild, wet day. The funeral reached the cemetery; it was during the war; and at the gate there was a soldier waiting. He was an officer, but on his raincoat there were no rank badges. The soldier came to the graveside for the ceremony; when it was over he stepped forward and standing before the open grave he swept his hand to a salute that might have been given to a king. H. L. Gee walked away with this soldier, and as they walked the wind blew the soldier's raincoat open; and now H. L. Gee saw the shoulder badges of rank; the soldier was nothing less than a brigadier. The soldier said to H. L. Gee: " You will perhaps be wondering what I am doing here. Years ago Thomas was my Sunday School teacher; I was a wild lad and a sore trial to him; he never knew what he did for me; but I owe everything I am or will be to old Thomas; and today I had to come to salute him at the end." Thomas did not know what he was doing. No preacher or teacher ever does. It is our task to sow the seed, and, without discouragement, to leave the rest to God.

(ii) When any man sows the seed, he cannot and he must not look for quick results. There is never any haste in nature's growth. It takes a long, long time before an acorn becomes an oak; and it may take a long, long time before the seed germinates in the heart of a man. But often a word dropped into a man's heart in his boyhood lies dormant and asleep until some day it awakens and saves him from some great temptation and preserves his soul from death. We live in an age which looks for quick results, but in the sowing of the seed we must sow in patience and sow in hope, and sometimes we must leave the harvest to the years.

THE TRUTH AND THE LISTENER

Matthew 13: 10-17, 34, 35

The disciples came and said to Him: " Why do you speak to them in parables? " " To you," He answered them, " it has been given to know the secrets of the Kingdom, which only a disciple can understand, but to them it has not been so given. For it will be given to him who already has, and he will have an over-flowing knowledge. But what he has will be taken away from him who has not. It is for that reason that I speak to them in parables, for although they can see, they do not see; and although they can hear, they do not hear or understand. There is being fulfilled in them Isaiah's prophecy which says, ' You will certainly hear, but you will not understand; and you will certainly look, but you will not see; for the heart of this people has grown fat, and they hear dully with their ears, and their eyes are smeared, lest at any time they should see with their eyes, and hear with their ears, and understand with their heart, and turn, and I will heal them. But blessed are your eyes for they see, and your ears because they hear.' This is the truth I tell you—many prophets and righteous men longed to see things that you are seeing, and did not see them, and to hear the things that you are hearing, and did not hear them."

. . . .

Jesus spake all these things to the crowds in parables, and it was not His custom to speak to them without a parable. He did this that that which was spoken through the prophet might be fulfilled: " I will open my mouth in parables: I will utter things which have been hidden since the foundation of the world."

THIS is a passage which is full of difficult things; and we must take some time to try to seek out its meaning. First of all there are two general things at the beginning of it, and, if we understand them, it will go far to light up the whole passage.

The Authorized Version in verse 14 has: " It is given to
you to know the *mysteries* of the Kingdom of Heaven,
but to them it is not given." In New Testament times the
word *mystery* (*mustērion*) was used in a special and a
technical way. To us a *mystery* means simply something
which is dark and difficult and impossible to understand,
something which is *mysterious*. But in New Testament
times a *mystery* was the technical name for something
which was dark and unintelligible to the outsider, but
which was crystal clear to the man who had been initiated
and who therefore had learned to understand its meaning.
In the time of Jesus in both Greece and Rome the most
intense and real religion was to be found in what were
known as the *Mystery Religions*. These religions had all
a common character. They were in essence passion plays
in which there was told in drama the story of some god
or goddess who had lived and suffered and toiled and died
and who had risen again to blessedness. The initiate was
given a long course of instruction in which the inner
meaning of the drama was explained to him; that course
of instruction extended over months and even years.
Before he was allowed finally to see the drama he had to
undergo a period of fasting and abstinence. Everything
was done to work him up to a state of emotion and of
excitement and expectation. He was then taken to see
the play; the atmosphere was carefully constructed;
there was cunning lighting; there were incenses and
perfumes; there was sensuous music; there was in many
cases a most noble liturgy. The drama was then played
out; and it was intended to produce in the worshipper a
complete identification with the god or the goddess whose
story was told on the stage. The worshipper was intended
literally to share in the divinity's life and sufferings and
death and resurrection; he was supposed to live with
the god and die with the god and rise with the god. It
was the intention that he should become so one with the
god that he shared in the god's death and resurrection,

and therefore shared in the god's risen life and immortality. The cry of the worshipper in the end was: " I am Thou, and Thou art I."

We take an actual example of the kind of story that was dramatized and thus presented. One of the most famous of all the mysteries was the mystery of Isis. Osiris was a wise and good king. Seth, his wicked brother, hated him, and with seventy-two conspirators persuaded him to come to a banquet. There he persuaded him to enter a cunningly wrought coffin which exactly fitted him. When Osiris was in the coffin, the lid was snapped down and the coffin was flung into the Nile. After long and weary search, Isis, the faithful wife of Osiris, found the coffin and brought it home in mourning. But when she was absent from home, the wicked Seth came again, stole the body of Osiris, cut it into fourteen pieces, and scattered it throughout all Egypt. Once again Isis set out on her weary and sorrowful quest. After long search she found all the pieces; by a wondrous power the pieces were fitted together and Osiris rose from the dead; and he became for ever afterwards the immortal king of the living and the dead. It is easy to see how moving a story that could be made to one who had undergone a long instruction, to one who saw it in the most carefully calculated setting. There is the story of the good king; there is the attack of sin; there is the sorrowing search of love; there is the triumphant finding of love; there is the raising to a life which has conquered death. It was with that experience that the worshipper was meant to identify himself, and he was supposed to emerge from it, in the famous phrase of the Mystery Religions, " reborn for eternity".

That is a mystery; a mystery was something meaningless to the outsider, but supremely precious to the initiate. In point of fact the Lord's Supper is like that. To an outsider, to one who came in and who had never seen such a thing before, it would look like a company of men eating little cubes of bread and drinking little glasses of wine, and it would seem to him even a ridiculous thing; but to the man who knows what he is doing, and for what these elements stand, to the man who is initiated into the meaning, it is the most precious and the most moving service in the Church.

So Jesus says to His disciples: " Outsiders cannot understand what I say; but you know me; you are my disciples; you can understand." The great fact of Christianity is that *it can only be understood from the inside.* It is only after the personal encounter with Jesus Christ that a man can understand. No one can understand Christianity until he has tried to be a Christian. To criticize from outside is to criticize in ignorance. It is only the man who is prepared to become a disciple who can enter into the most precious things of the Christian faith.

LIFE'S STERN LAW

Matthew 13: 10-17, 34, 35 (*continued*)

THE second general thing at which we may look is the saying in verse 12 that still more will be given to the man who has, and even what he has will be taken away from the man who has not. At first sight this looks like a saying which is nothing less than cruel; but so far from being cruel, it simply states a truth which is an inevitable and inescapable law of life.

In every sphere of life more is given to the man who has, and that which he has is taken away from the man who has not. In the world of scholarship the student who works and toils and labours to amass knowledge is capable of acquiring more knowledge. It is to him that the research, the advanced courses, the deeper things are given; and that is so because by his diligence and fidelity he has made himself fit to receive them. On the other hand, the student who is lazy and who refuses to work inevitably loses even the knowledge which he has. There is many a person who in childhood and schooldays has had a smattering of Latin or of French or of some other language, and who in later life has lost every word of them, because he never made any attempt to develop or use them. Many a person has had some skill in a craft or game or accomplishment and has lost it, because he neglected it and failed to use it. The diligent and the faithful and the hard-working and hard-studying and hard-practising person is in a position to be given more and more; the lazy person is not in a position to receive more, and may well lose even what he has. Any gift can be developed; and, since there is nothing in life which stands still, if any gift is not developed, it is lost.

It is so with goodness. Every temptation we conquer makes us more able to conquer the next temptation; and every temptation to which we fall makes us less able to withstand the next attack. Every good thing we do, every act of self-discipline and of service, makes us better able for the next; and every time we fail to seize such an opportunity we make ourselves less able to seize the next opportunity when it comes. Life is always a process of gaining more or losing more. Jesus laid down the truth that the nearer a man lives to Him, the nearer to the Christian ideal he can live; more strength comes to him in his living. And the more a man drifts away from Christ, the less he is able to reach to goodness; for weakness, like strength, is an increasing thing.

MAN'S BLINDNESS AND GOD'S PURPOSE

Matthew 13: 10-17, 34, 35 (*continued*)

VERSES 13-17 of this passage are among the most difficult verses in the whole gospel narrative. And the fact that they appear differently in the different gospels shows how much that difficulty was felt in the early Church. *Mark* is the earliest gospel, and therefore we would expect

Mark to be nearest to the actual words of Jesus. *Mark* (4: 11, 12) has:

> Unto them that are without, all these things are done in parables, that seeing they may see, and not perceive; and hearing they may hear, and not understand; lest at any time they should be converted, and their sins should be forgiven them.

If these verses be taken at their superficial value, and with no attempt to understand their real meaning, they make the extraordinary statement that Jesus spoke to men in parables in order that they might not understand, and in order to prevent them turning to God and finding forgiveness. *Matthew* is later than *Mark*, and *Matthew* makes one significant change:

> Therefore I speak unto them in parables, *because* seeing they see not; and hearing they heard not, neither do they understand.

As *Matthew* has it Jesus spoke in parables because men were too blind and deaf to glimpse the truth in any other way.

Now it is to be noted that this saying of Jesus leads into a quotation from *Isaiah* 6: 9, 10. That saying of Isaiah was another passage which caused those who thought of it a great deal of heart-searching. In the Authorized Version, which is a literal translation of the Hebrew, it runs:

> Go, and tell this people, hear ye indeed, but understand not; and see ye indeed, but perceive not. Make the heart of this people fat, and make their ears heavy and shut their eyes; lest they see with their eyes, and hear with their ears, and understand with their heart, and convert, and be healed.

There again it sounds as if God had deliberately blinded the eyes, and deafened the ears and hardened the hearts of the people, so that they would be unable to understand. The nation's lack of understanding is made to seem nothing other than a deliberate act of God.

Just as *Matthew* toned down *Mark*, so the *Septuagint* the Greek translation of the Hebrew scriptures, and the version which most Jews used in the time of Jesus, toned down the original Hebrew:

> Go, say to this people: " Ye shall hear indeed, but ye shall not understand; and seeing ye shall see and not perceive. For the heart of this people has become gross, and with their ears they hear heavily, and their eyes they have closed, lest at any time they should see with their eyes, and hear with their ears, and understand with their heart, and should be converted, and I should heal them."

The *Septuagint*, so to speak, removes the responsibility from God and lays it fairly and squarely upon the people.

What then is the explanation of all this? We may surely be certain of one thing—whatever else this passage means, it cannot mean that Jesus deliberately delivered His message in such a way that people would necessarily fail to understand it. Jesus did not come to hide the truth from men; He came to reveal the truth to men. And beyond a doubt there were times when men grasped that truth. When the orthodox Jewish leaders heard the threat of the Parable of the Wicked Husbandmen, they understood all right, and their reaction was to recoil in horror from the message of the parable, and to say: " God forbid! " (*Luke* 20: 16). And in verses 34 and 35 of this present passage Jesus quotes a saying of the Psalmist:

> Give ear, O people, to my law; incline your ears to the words of my mouth. I will open my mouth in a parable; I will utter dark sayings of old, which we have heard and known, and our fathers have told us.

That is a quotation from *Psalm* 78: 1-3, and in it the Psalmist knows that what he is saying will be understood, and that he is recalling men to truth that both they and their fathers have known.

The truth is that the words of Isaiah, and the use that Jesus made of them, must be read with insight and with an attempt to put ourselves in the position both of Isaiah and of Jesus. These words tell of three things.

(i) They tell of a prophet's *bewilderment*. The prophet brought a message to people which to him was crystal clear; and he was bewildered that they could not understand it. That is repeatedly the experience of both the preacher and the teacher. Often when we preach or teach or discuss things with people, we try to tell them something which to us is relevant, vivid, compelling, of absorbing interest and of paramount importance, and they hear it with a complete lack of interest, understanding, and urgency. And then we are amazed and bewildered that that which means so much to us apparently means nothing at all to them, that that which kindles a fire in our bones leaves them stone cold, that that which thrills and moves our hearts leaves them stonily and icily indifferent. That is the experience of every teacher and preacher and evangelist.

(ii) They tell of a prophet's *despair*. It was Isaiah's feeling that his preaching was actually doing more harm than good, that he might as well speak to a brick wall, that there was no way into the mind and the heart of this deaf and blind people, that, as far as any effects went, they seemed to be getting worse instead of better. Again that is the experience of every teacher and preacher. There are times when those whom we seek to win seem, in spite of all our efforts, to be getting further away from, instead of nearer to, the Christian ideal. Our words go whistling down the wind; our message meets the impenetrable barrier of men's indifference; the result of all our work seems less than nothing, for at the end of it men seem further away from God than they were at the beginning of it.

(iii) But these words tell of something more than a prophet's bewilderment and a prophet's despair; they also tell of a prophet's *ultimate faith*. Here we find ourselves face to face with a Jewish conviction apart from which much of what the prophet, and of what Jesus, and of what the early Church said is not fully intelligible. To put it simply, it was a primary article of Jewish belief that *nothing in this world happens outside the will of God*; and when they said *nothing* they meant *literally nothing*. It was just as much God's will when men did not listen as when they did listen; it was just as much God's will when men refused to understand the truth as when they welcomed the truth. The Jew clung fast to the belief that everything had its place in the purpose and in the scheme of God, that somehow God was weaving together success and failure, good and evil in a web of His designing. The ultimate purpose of everything was good. It is exactly this thought that Paul plays on in *Romans* 9: 11. These are the chapters which tell how the Jews, the chosen people of God, actually refused God's truth and crucified God's Son when He came to them. That sounds an inexplicable thing. But what was the result of it? The result was that the gospel went out to the Gentiles; and the ultimate result is that the Gentiles will some day gather in the Jews. The apparent evil is gathered up in a larger good, for all is within the plan and the scheme of God. That is what Isaiah was feeling. At first he was bewildered and in despair; then the light comes; and in effect he says, " I cannot understand the conduct of this people; but I know that all this failure is somehow in the ultimate purpose of God, and He will use it for His own ultimate glory and for the ultimate good of men." So Jesus took these words of Isaiah and used them to encourage His disciples; He said in effect, " I know that this looks disappointing; I know how you are feeling when men's minds and hearts refuse to receive the truth and when their eyes refuse to recognize it; but in this too there is purpose—and some day you will see it."

Here is our own great encouragement. Sometimes we see our harvest and we are glad; sometimes there seems to be nothing but barren ground, nothing but total lack of response, nothing but failure. That may be so to human eyes and human minds, but at the back of it there is a God who is fitting even that failure into the divine plan of His omniscient mind and His omnipotent power. There are no failures and there are no loose ends in the ultimate plan of God.

THE ACT OF AN ENEMY

Matthew 13: 24-30, 36-43

Jesus put forward another parable. " The Kingdom of Heaven," He said to them, " is like what happened when a man sowed good seed in his field. When men slept, his enemy came and sowed darnel in the middle of the corn, and went away. When the green grain grew, and when it began to produce its crop, then the darnel appeared. The servants of the master of the house came to him and said, ' Sir, did we not sow good seed in your field? From where, then, did it get the darnel? ' ' An enemy has done this,' he said to them. The servants said to him, ' Do you wish us to go and collect the darnel? ' But he said, ' No; for if you gather the darnel the danger is that you may root up the corn at the same time. Let them both grow together until the harvest time; and at the time of the harvest I will say to the reapers, " First gather the darnel and bind them into burdens for burning. But gather the corn into my storehouse." ' "

. . . .

When He had sent the crowds away, He went into the house. His disciples came to him. " Explain to us," they said, " the parable of the darnel in the field." He answered: " He who sows the good seed is the Son of Man. The field is the world. The good seed stands for the sons of the Kingdom; the darnel is the sons of the evil one. The enemy who sowed it is the devil. The harvest is the end of this age; the reapers are the angels. Just as the darnel is gathered and burned with fire, so it will be at the end of this age. The Son of Man will send His angels, and they will gather all the stumbling-blocks, and all those who act lawlessly, out of the Kingdom, and will cast them into the furnace of fire; and weeping and gnashing of teeth will be there. Then the righteous will shine as the sun in the Kingdom of their Father. Who has ears let him hear."

THE pictures in this parable would be quite clear and familiar to a Palestinian audience. Tares were one of the curses against which the farmer had to labour. The tares were a weed called bearded darnel (*lolium temulentum*). In their early stages the tares so closely resembled the wheat that it was impossible to distinguish the one from the other. When both had headed out it was easy to distinguish them; but by that time the roots of the wheat and the tares were so intertwined that the tares could not be pulled up and weeded out without tearing the wheat out with them. Thomson in *The Land and the Book* tells how he saw the tares in the Wady Hamam: " The grain is just in the proper stage of development to illustrate the parable. In those parts where the grain has headed out, the tares have done the same, and there a child cannot mistake them for wheat or barley; but when both are less developed, the closest scrutiny will often fail to detect them. I cannot do it at all with any confidence. Even the farmers, who in this country generally weed their fields, do not attempt to separate the one from the other. They would not only mistake good grain for them, but very commonly the roots of the two are so intertwined that it is impossible to separate them without plucking up both. Both, therefore, must be left to grow together until the time of harvest."

The tares and the wheat are so like each other that the Jews called the tares *bastard wheat*. The Hebrew for tares is *zunim*, whence comes the Greek *zizanion*; *zunim* is said to be connected with the word *zanah*, which means *to commit fornication*; and the popular story is that the tares took their origin in the time of wickedness which preceded the flood, for at that time the whole creation, men, animals and plants, all went astray, and committed fornication and brought forth contrary to nature. In their early stages the wheat and the tares so closely resembled each other that the popular idea was that the tares were a kind of degenerated wheat which had gone wrong.

The wheat and tares could not be safely separated when both were growing, but in the end they had to be separated. The separation had to be made because the grain of the bearded darnel is slightly poisonous. It causes dizziness and sickness and is narcotic in its effects, and even a small amount of it has a bitter and unpleasant taste. In the end it is usually separated by hand. Levison describes the process: " Women have to be hired to pick the darnel grain out of the seed which is to be milled. . . . As a rule the separation of the darnel from the wheat is done after the threshing. By spreading the grain out on a large tray which is set before the women, they are able to pick out the darnel, which is a seed similar in shape and size to wheat, but slate-grey in colour."

So then the darnel in its early stages is indistinguishable from the wheat, but in the end it has to be laboriously separated from the wheat, or the consequences are serious.

The picture of a man deliberately sowing darnel in someone else's field is by no means only imagination. That was actually sometimes done. To this day in India one of the direst threats which a man can make to his enemy is " I will sow bad seed in your field." And in codified Roman law this crime is mentioned and forbidden and its punishment laid down.

The whole series of pictures within this parable were familiar to the people of Galilee who heard it for the first time.

THE TIME FOR JUDGMENT

Matthew 13: 24-30, 36-43 (*continued*)

It may well be said that in its lessons this is one of the most practical parables which Jesus ever told.

(i) It teaches us that there is always a hostile power

in the world, seeking and waiting to destroy the good seed. Our experience of life is that both kinds of influence act upon our lives, the influence which will help the seed of the word to flourish and to grow, and the influence which will seek to destroy the good seed, before it can produce fruit at all. It is the lesson of life that we must be for ever on our guard.

(ii) It teaches us how hard it is to distinguish between those who are in the Kingdom and those who are not. A man may appear to be a good man, and may in fact be a bad man; and a man may appear to be a bad man, and may yet be a good man. It may well be—in fact it certainly is—that we are much too quick to classify people and to label them good or bad without knowing all the facts, and without the necessary knowledge.

(iii) It teaches us not to be so quick with our judgments. If the reapers had had their way, they would have tried to tear out the darnel, and the only result would have been that they would have torn out the wheat as well. Judgment had to wait until the harvest came. A man in the end will be judged, not by any single act or stage in his life, but by his whole life. Judgment cannot come until the end. A man may make a great mistake, and then redeem himself and, by the grace of God, atone for it by making the rest of life a lovely thing. A man may live an honourable life and then in the end wreck it all by a sudden collapse into sin. No one who only sees the part of a thing can judge the whole thing; and no one who knows only a part of a man's life can judge the whole man.

(iv) It teaches us that judgment does come in the end. Judgment is not hasty, but judgment does come. The separation of the good and the bad does come in the end. It may be that, humanly speaking, in this life the sinner seems to escape the consequences, but there is a life to come. It may be that, humanly speaking, goodness never seems to enter into its reward, but there is a new world to redress the balance of the old.

(v) It teaches us that the only person with the right to judge is God. It is God alone who can discern the good and the bad; it is God alone who sees all of a man and all of a man's life. It is God alone who can judge.

So, then, ultimately this parable is two things—it is a warning to us not to judge other people at all, and it is a warning to us that in the end there comes the judgment of God.

THE SMALL BEGINNING

Matthew 13: 31, 32

> Jesus put forward another parable to them: " The Kingdom of Heaven is like a grain of mustard seed, which a man took and sowed in his field. It is the smallest of all seeds, and, when it has grown, it is the greatest of herbs, and it becomes a tree, so that the birds of the air come and lodge in its branches."

THE mustard plant of Palestine is very different from the mustard plant which we know in this country. To be strictly accurate the mustard seed is not the smallest of seeds; the seed of the cypress tree, for instance, is still smaller; but in the east it was proverbial for smallness. For instance, the Jews talked of a drop of blood as small as a mustard seed; or, if they were talking of some small breach of the ceremonial law, they would speak of a defilement as small as a mustard seed; and Jesus Himself used the phrase in this way when He spoke of faith as a grain of mustard seed (*Matthew* 17: 20). In Palestine this little grain of mustard seed did grow into something very like a tree. Thomson in *The Land and the Book* writes: " I have seen this plant on the rich plain of Akkar as tall as the horse and his rider." He says, " With the help of my guide, I uprooted a veritable mustard-tree which was more than twelve feet high." In this parable there is no exaggeration at all. Further, it was a common sight to see such mustard bushes or trees surrounded with a cloud of birds, for the birds love the little black seeds of the tree, and settle on the tree to eat them. So Jesus said that His Kingdom was like the mustard seed and its growth into a tree. The point of this parable is crystal clear. The Kingdom of Heaven starts from the smallest beginnings, but no man knows where it will end. In eastern language and in the Old Testament itself one of the commonest pictures of a great empire is the picture of a great tree, and the subject nations are depicted as birds finding rest and shelter within its branches (*Ezekiel* 31: 6). So, then, this parable tells us that the Kingdom of Heaven begins from the smallest of beginnings, but that in the end many nations will be gathered within it. It is the fact of history that the greatest things must always begin with the smallest beginnings.

(i) An idea which may well change civilization begins with one man. In the British Empire it was William Wilberforce who was responsible for the freeing of the slaves. The idea of that liberation came to him when he read an exposure of the slave trade by Thomas Clarkson. He was a close friend of Pitt, the great Prime Minister. One day he was sitting with Pitt and George Grenville in Pitt's garden at Holwood. It was a scene of beauty with the Vale of Keston opening out before them, but the thoughts of Wilberforce were not on the beauty but on the blots of the world. Suddenly Pitt turned to him: " Wilberforce," he said, " why don't you give a notice of a motion on the slave-trade? " The idea was sown in the mind of the one man, and the idea changed life for hundreds of thousands of people. An idea must find a man in order that the idea may possess the man; but when an idea finds such a man an unstoppable tide begins to flow.

(ii) A witness must begin with one man. Cecil Northcott tells in one of his books of how a group of young people from many nations were discussing how the Christian gospel might be spread. They talked of propaganda, of literature, of all the ways of disseminating the gospel in the twentieth century. Then the girl from Africa spoke. " When we want to take Christianity to one of our villages," she said, " we don't send them books. We take a Christian family and send them to live in the village and they make the village Christian by living there." In any group or society, in any school or factory, or shop or office, again and again it is the witness of one individual which has brought the coming of Christianity to the group. The one man or woman who is set on fire for Christ is the person who kindles others.

(iii) A reformation begins with one person. One of the great stories of the Christian Church is the story of Telemachus. He was a hermit of the desert, but something told him—the call of God—that he must go to Rome. He went. Rome was nominally Christian, but even in Christian Rome the gladiatorial games went on, in which men fought with each other, and crowds roared with the lust for blood. Telemachus found his way to the games. Eighty thousand people were there to spectate. He was horrified. Were these men who were slaughtering each other not also children of God? He leaped from his seat, right into the arena, and stood between the gladiators. He was tossed aside. He came back. The crowd were angry; they began to stone him. Still he struggled back between the gladiators. The prefect's command rang out; a sword flashed in the sunlight, and Telemachus was dead. And then suddenly there was a hush; suddenly the crowd realized what had happened, a holy man lay dead. Something happened that day to Rome, for there were never any gladiatorial games any more. The one man had let loose something by his death that cleansed an empire of a sin. Someone must begin a reformation; he need not begin it in a nation; he can begin it in his home or where he works every day. If he begins it no man knows where it will end.

(iv) But this was one of the most personal parables which Jesus ever spoke. Sometimes his disciples must have despaired. Their little band was so small and the world was so wide. How could they ever win and change a world? Yet with Jesus something entered into this world. Hugh Martin quotes H. G. Wells as saying, " His is easily the dominant figure in history. . . . A historian without any theological bias whatever should find that he simply cannot portray the progress of humanity honestly without giving a foremost place to a penniless teacher from Nazareth." In this parable Jesus is saying to His disciples, and He is saying to His followers to this day, that there must be no discouragement, that they must serve and witness each in his place, that each one of us must be the small beginning from which the Kingdom grows until the kingdoms of the earth finally become the Kingdom of God

> " Though few and small and weak your bands,
>   Strong in your Captain's strength,
> Go to the conquest of all lands;
>   All must be His at length."

THE TRANSFORMING POWER OF CHRIST

Matthew 13: 33

> He spoke another parable to them: " The Kingdom of Heaven is like leaven, which a woman took and hid in three measures of meal, until the whole was leavened."

IN this chapter there is nothing more significant than the sources from which Jesus drew His parables. In every case He drew them from the scenes and the activities of everyday life. He began with things which were entirely familiar to His hearers in order to lead them to things which had never yet entered into their minds. He takes the parable of the sower from the farmer's field and the parable of the mustard seed from the husbandman's garden; He takes the parable of the wheat and the tares from the perennial problem which confronts the farmer in his struggle with the weeds, and the parable of the drag-net from the seashore of the Sea of Galilee. He takes the parable of the hidden treasure from the everyday task of digging in a field, and the parable of the pearl of great price from the world of commerce and trade. But in this parable of the leaven Jesus comes nearer home than in any other parable, because He takes it from the kitchen of an ordinary home.

In Palestine bread was baked at home; three measures of meal was, as Levison points out, just the average amount which would be needed for a baking for a fairly large family, like the family at Nazareth. Jesus took His parable of the Kingdom from something that He had often seen His mother, Mary, do. Leaven was a little piece of dough which had been kept over from a previous baking; in the keeping it fermented; and leaven was simply a piece of fermented dough. It is quite true that in Jewish language and thought leaven is almost always connected with an *evil* influence; the Jews connected fermentation with putrefaction and rottenness, and leaven stood for that which is evil (cp. *Matthew* 16: 6; I *Corinthians* 5: 6-8; *Galatians* 5: 9). One of the ceremonies of preparation for the Passover Feast was that every scrap of leaven had to be sought out from the house and burned and destroyed. It may well be that Jesus chose this illustration of the Kingdom deliberately. There would be a certain shock in hearing the Kingdom of God compared to leaven; and the shock would arouse interest and rivet attention, as an illustration from an unusual and unexpected source always does.

The whole point of the parable lies in one thing—*the transforming power of the leaven*. Leaven changed the character of a whole baking. Unleavened bread, bread baked without leaven, is like a water biscuit, hard, dry, unappetising and uninteresting; bread baked with leaven is soft and porous and spongy, and tasty and good to eat. The introduction of the leaven causes a transformation in the dough; and the coming of the Kingdom causes a transformation in life. We have often, in our study of the New Testament, seen this transformation, as it were, piecemeal and in the passing. At the risk of repetition let us gather together the characteristics of this transformation.

(i) Christianity transforms life for *the individual man.* In I *Corinthians* 6: 9, 10, Paul gathers together a list of the most terrible and disgusting and loathsome kinds of sinners, and then, in the next verse, there comes the tremendous statement: "And such were some of you." As Denney had it, we must never forget that the function and the power of Christ is to make bad men good. The transformation of Christianity begins in the individual life, for through Christ the victim of temptation can become the victor over temptation.

(ii) There are four great social directions in which Christianity transformed life. Christianity transformed life for *women.* The Jew in his morning prayer thanked God that God had not made him a Gentile, a slave or a woman. In Greek civilization the woman lived a life of utter seclusion, with nothing to do beyond the household tasks. K. J. Freeman writes of Athens even in her greatest days when he is speaking of the life of the Greek child or young man: "When he came home, there was no home life. His father was hardly ever in the house. His mother was a nonentity, living in the women's apartments; he probably saw little of her." In the eastern lands it was often possible to see a family on a journey. The father would be mounted on an ass; the mother would be walking, and often bent beneath a burden. One demonstrable historical truth is that Christianity transformed life for women.

(iii) Christianity transformed life for *the weak and the ill.* In heathen life the weak and the ill were considered a nuisance. In Sparta a child, when he was born, was submitted to the examiners; if he was fit, he was allowed to live; if he was weakly or deformed, he was exposed to death on the mountain side. Dr. A. Rendle Short points out that the first blind asylum was founded by Thalasius, a Christian monk; the first free dispensary was founded by Apollonius, a Christian merchant; the first hospital of which there is any record was founded by Fabiola, a Christian lady. Christianity was the first faith to be interested in the broken things of life.

(iv) Christianity transformed life for *the aged*. Like the weak, the aged were a nuisance. Cato, the Roman writer on agriculture, gives advice to anyone who is taking over a farm: " Look over the livestock and hold a sale. Sell your oil, if the price is satisfactory, and sell the surplus of your wine and grain. Sell worn-out oxen, blemished cattle, blemished sheep, wool, hides, an old wagon, old tools, *an old slave, a sickly slave*, and whatever else is superfluous." The old, whose day's work was done, were fit for nothing else than to be discarded on the rubbish heaps of life. Christianity was the first faith to regard men as persons and not instruments capable of doing so much work.

(v) Christianity transformed life for *the child*. In the immediate background of Christianity, the marriage relationship had broken down, and the home was in peril. Divorce was so common that it was neither unusual nor particularly blameworthy for a woman to have a new husband every year. In such circumstances children were a disaster; and the custom of simply exposing children to death was tragically common. There is a well-known letter from a man Hilarion, who was gone off to Alexandria, to his wife Alis, whom he has left at home. He writes to her: " If—good luck to you—you bear a child, if it is a boy, let it live; if it is a girl, throw it out." In modern civilization life is almost built round the child; in ancient civilization the child had a very good chance of dying before it had begun to live.

Anyone who asks the question: " What has Christianity done for the world? " has delivered himself into a Christian debater's hands. There is nothing in history so unanswerably demonstrable as the transforming power of Christianity and of Christ on the individual life and on the life of society

THE WORKING OF THE LEAVEN

Matthew 13: 33 (*continued*)

THERE remains only one question in regard to this parable of the leaven. Almost all scholars would agree that it speaks of the transforming power of Christ and of His Kingdom in the life of the individual and of the world; but there is a difference of opinion as to how that transforming power works and operates.

(i) It is sometimes said that the lesson of this parable is that the Kingdom works unseen. It is said that we cannot see the leaven working in the dough, any more than we can see a flower growing, but that the work of the leaven is always going on. Just so, it is said, we cannot see the work of the Kingdom, but always in history and life the Kingdom is working and drawing men and the world ever nearer to God. This, then, would be a message of encouragement. It would mean that at all times we must take the long view of things, that we must not compare things of the present day with last week, or last month, or even last year, but that we must look back down the centuries, and then we will see the steady progress of the Kingdom. As A. H. Clough had it:

" Say not, ' The struggle nought availeth;
    The labour and the wounds are vain;
The enemy faints not nor faileth,
    And as things have been they remain.'

If hopes were dupes, fears may be liars;
    It may be, in yon smoke concealed,
Your comrades chase even now the fliers,
    And, but for you, possess the field.

For while the tired waves, vainly breaking,
    Seem here no painful inch to gain,
Far back, through creeks and inlets making,
    Comes silent, flooding in, the main.

And, not by eastern windows only,
    When daylight comes, comes in the light;
In front the sun climbs slow, how slowly!
    But westward, look! the land is bright."

On this view this parable teaches that with Jesus Christ and His gospel a new force has been let loose in the world, and that, silently but inevitably, that force is working for righteousness in this world, that God indeed is working His purpose out as year succeeds to year.

(ii) But it has sometimes been said, as for instance by C. H. Dodd, that the lesson of this parable is indeed the very opposite of this, and that, so far from being unseen, the working of the Kingdom can be plainly seen. It is said that the working of the leaven is plain for all to see. Put the leaven into the dough, and the leaven changes the dough from a passive lump into a seething, bubbling, heaving mass. Just so the influence and the working of the Kingdom is a violent and a disturbing force plain for all to see. When Christianity came to Thessalonica the cry was: " These that have turned the world upside down are come hither also " (*Acts* 17: 6). The action of Christianity is disruptive, disturbing, violent in its effect. There is an undeniable truth there. It is true that men crucified Jesus Christ because He disturbed all their orthodox habits and conventions; again and again it has been true that Christianity has been persecuted because it desired to take both men and society and to remake them. It is abundantly true that there is nothing in this world so disturbing as Christianity; that is, in fact, the reason why so many people hate it and resent it, and refuse it, and would wish to eliminate it.

But when we come to think of it, we do not need to choose between these two views of this parable, because they are both true. There is a sense in which the Kingdom, the power of Christ, the Spirit of God are always working, whether or not we see that work; and there is a sense in which the power of the Kingdom and the work of Christ are plainly manifest. Many an individual life is manifestly and violently changed by Christ; and at the same time there is the silent operation of the purposes of God in the long road of history. We may put it in a picture like this. The Kingdom, the power of Christ, the purpose of God is like a great river, which for much of its course glides on beneath the ground unseen, but which ever and again comes to the surface in all its power and its greatness, plain for all to see in its action. This parable teaches both that the Kingdom is for ever working unseen, and that there are times in every individual life and in history when the work of the Kingdom is so obvious, and so manifestly powerful, that all can see it.

ALL IN THE DAY'S WORK

Matthew 13: 44

> " The Kingdom of Heaven is like a treasure which lay hidden in a field. A man found it, and hid it; and, as a result of his joy, away he goes, and sells everything that he has, and buys the field."

ALTHOUGH this parable sounds strange and unusual to us, it would sound perfectly natural to people in Palestine in the days of Jesus, and even to this day it would paint a picture which people in the East would know well.

In the ancient world there were banks, but not banks such as ordinary people could use. People in ordinary everyday practice used the ground as the safest place to keep their most cherished belonging. In the parable of the talents the unprofitable servant hid his talent in the ground, lest he should lose it (*Matthew* 25: 25). There was a rabbinic saying that there was only one safe repository for money—the earth. This was still more the case in a land where any man's garden might at any time become a battlefield. Palestine is probably the most fought over country in the world; and, when the tide of war threatened to flow over them and engulf them, it was common practice for people to hide their valuables in the ground, before they took to flight, in the hope that the day would come when they could return and regain them. Josephus speaks of " the gold and the silver and the rest of that most precious furniture which the Jews had, and which the

93

owners treasured up underground against the uncertain fortunes of war."

Thomson in *The Land and the Book*, which was first published in 1876, tells of a case of treasure discovery which he himself found out in Sidon. There is in that city a famous avenue of acacia trees. Certain workmen, digging in a garden, on that avenue, uncovered several copper pots full of gold coins. They had every intention of keeping the discovery to themselves; but there were so many of them, and they were so wild with excitement, that their treasure trove was discovered and claimed by the local government. The coins were all coins of Alexander the Great and his father Philip. Thomson suggests that, when Alexander unexpectedly died in Babylon, news came through to Sidon, and some Macedonian officer or government official buried these coins with the intention of appropriating them in the chaos which was bound to follow Alexander's death. Thomson goes on to tell how there are even people who make it their life's business to search for hidden treasure, and that they get into such a state of excitement that they have been known to faint at the discovery of one single coin. There are people who spend their last farthing in this gambler's search for hidden treasure. When Jesus told this story, He told the kind of story that anyone would recognize in Palestine and in the east generally.

It may be thought that in this parable Jesus glorifies a man who was guilty of very sharp practice in that he hid the treasure, and then took steps to possess himself of it. There are two things to be said about that. First, although Palestine in the time of Jesus was under the Romans and under Roman law, in the ordinary, small, day to day things it was traditional Jewish law which was used; and in regard to hidden treasure Jewish Rabbinic law is quite clear: "What finds belong to the finder, and what finds must one cause to be proclaimed? These finds belong to the finder—if a man finds scattered fruit,

scattered money . . . these belong to the finder." In point
of fact this man had a prior right to what he had found.
Second, even apart from that, when we are dealing with
any parable, the details are never meant to be stressed;
the parable has one main point, and to that point everything else is subservient, and beside it nothing really
matters. In this parable the two great points are the joy
of the discovery, and the willingness of the man to give
up everything to make the treasure indubitably his own.
Everything else in the parable is beside the point.

(i) The lesson of this parable is, first, that the man
found the precious thing, not so much by chance, a *ins
his day's work*. It is true to say that he stumbled all
unexpectedly upon it, but he did so *when he was going
about his daily business*. And it is legitimate to infer that
he must have been going about his daily business with
diligence and efficiency, because he must have been digging
deep, and not merely scraping the surface, in order to
strike against the treasure. It would be a sad thing, if it
were only in churches, in so-called holy places, and on
so-called religious occasions that we found God, and felt
close to Him. There is an unwritten saying of Jesus, a
saying which never found its way into any of the gospels,
but which rings true: " Raise the stone and thou shalt
find me; cleave the wood and I am there." When the
mason is working on the stone, when the carpenter is
working with the wood, Jesus Christ is there. True happiness, true satisfaction, the sense of God, the presence of
Christ Himself are all to be found in the day's work, when
that day's work is honestly and conscientiously done.
Brother Lawrence, the great saint and mystic, spent much
of his working life in the monastery kitchen amidst the
dirty dishes, and he could say, " I felt Jesus Christ as
close to me in the kitchen as ever I did at the blessed
sacrament."

(ii) The lesson of this parable is, second, that it is worth
any sacrifice to enter the Kingdom. What does it mean

to enter the Kingdom? Let us remember that when we were studying the Lord's Prayer (*Matthew* 6: 10) we found that we could say that the Kingdom of God is a state of society upon earth where God's will is as perfectly done as it is in heaven. Therefore to be in the Kingdom, to enter the Kingdom, is to accept and to do God's will. So, then, it is worth anything to do God's will. Suddenly, as the man discovered the treasure, there may flash upon us in some moment of illumination the conviction of what God's will is for us. To accept it may be to give up certain aims and ambitions which were very dear, to abandon certain habits and ways of life which are very difficult to lay down, to accept a discipline and a self-denial which are by no means easy, in a word, to take up our cross and follow after Jesus. But there is no other way to peace of mind and heart in this life and to glory in the life to come. It is indeed worth giving up everything to accept and to do the will of God.

THE PRECIOUS PEARL

Matthew 13: 45, 46

> " Again, the Kingdom of Heaven is like a merchant who was seeking goodly pearls. When he had found a very valuable pearl, he went away and sold everything he had, and bought it."

IN the ancient world pearls had a very special place in men's hearts. People desired to possess a lovely pearl, not only for its money value, but for its beauty. They found a pleasure in simply handling it and contemplating it. They found an aesthetic joy in simply possessing and looking at a pearl. The main sources of pearls in those days were the shores of the Red Sea and far off Britain itself; but a merchant would scour the markets of the world to find a pearl which was of surpassing beauty. There are certain most suggestive truths hidden in this parable.

(i) It is suggestive to find the Kingdom of Heaven compared to a pearl. To the ancient peoples, as we have just seen, a pearl was the loveliest of all possessions, a joy to contemplate and to admire. That means that the Kingdom of Heaven is the loveliest thing in the world. Let us remember what the Kingdom is. To be in the Kingdom is to accept and to do the will of God. That is to say, to do the will of God is no grim, gray, agonizing thing; it is a lovely thing. Beyond the discipline, beyond the sacrifice, beyond the self-denial, beyond the cross, there lies the supreme loveliness which is nowhere else. There is only one way to bring peace to the heart, joy to the mind, beauty to the life, and that is to accept and to do the will of God.

(ii) It is suggestive to find that there are other pearls, but there is only one pearl of great price. That is to say, there are many fine things in this world, and there are many things in which a man can find loveliness. He can find loveliness in knowledge and in the reaches of the human mind, in art and music and literature and all the triumphs of the human spirit; he can find loveliness in serving his fellow-men, even if that service springs from humanitarian rather than from purely Christian motives; he can find loveliness in human relationships. These are all lovely, but they are all lesser lovelinesses. The supreme beauty lies in the acceptance of the will of God. This is not to belittle the other things; they too are pearls; but the supreme pearl is the willing obedience which makes us friends of God.

(iii) Once again we find in this parable the same point as in the previous one. There is a difference. The man who was digging the field was not searching for treasure; it came on him all unaware and all unexpectedly. The man who was searching for pearls was spending his life in the search. But no matter whether the discovery was the result of a moment or the result of a life-time's search, the reaction was the same—everything had to be sold and sacrificed to gain the precious thing. Once again we are left with the same truth—that, however a man discovers the will of God for himself, whether it be in the lightning flash of a moment's illumination, or at the end of a long and conscious search, it is worth anything unquestioningly and unhesitatingly to accept it.

THE CATCH AND THE SEPARATION

Matthew 13: 47-50

" Again, the Kingdom of Heaven is like a net which was cast into the sea, and which gathered all kinds of things. When it was full, they hauled it up on to the shore, and sat down, and collected the good contents into containers, but threw the useless contents away. So it will be at the end of the age. The angels will come, and they will separate the evil from the righteous, and they will cast them into the furnace of fire. There will be weeping and gnashing of teeth there."

IT was the most natural thing in the world that Jesus should use illustrations from fishing when he was speaking to fishermen. It was as if He said to them: " Look how your daily work speaks to you of the things of heaven."

In Palestine there were two main ways of fishing. One was with the casting-net, the *amphiblēstron*. It was a hand-net which was cast from the shore. Thomson describes the process: " The net is in shape like the top of a bell-tent, with a long cord fastened to the apex. This is tied to the arm, and the net so folded that, when it is thrown, it expands to its utmost circumference, around which are strung beads of lead to make it drop suddenly to the bottom. Now, see the actor; half bent, and more than half naked, he keenly watches the playful surf, and there he spies his game tumbling in carelessly toward him. Forward he leaps to meet it. Away goes the net, expanding as it flies, and its leaded circumference strikes the bottom ere the silly fish is aware that its meshes have closed around him. By the aid of the cord the fishermen leisurely draws up the net and the fish with it. This requires a keen eye, an active frame, and great skill in throwing the net. He, too, must be patient, watchful, wide awake, and prompt to seize the exact moment to throw."

The second way of fishing was with the drag-net, the *sagēnē*, what we would call the seine net, or the trawl. This is the way which is referred to in this parable. The seine net was a great square net with cords at each corner, and weighted so that, at rest, it hung, as it were, upright in the water. Then when the boat began to move the net was drawn into the shape of a great cone and into the cone all kinds of fish were swept.

The net was then drawn to land, and the catch was separated. The useless material was flung away; the good material was put into containers. It is interesting to note that sometimes the fish were put alive into containers filled with water. There was no other way to transport them in freshness over any time or any distance.

There are two great lessons in this parable.

(i) It is in the nature of the drag-net that it does not and cannot select and discriminate. It is bound to draw in all kinds of things in its course through the water. Its contents are bound to be a mixture. If we apply that to the Church, which is the instrument of God's Kingdom upon earth, it must mean that the Church cannot be selective and discriminative, that the earthly Church is bound to be a mixture, that it will contain all kinds of people, good and bad, useless and useful, and that it is not ours to judge. There have always been two views of the Church—the exclusive and the inclusive view. The exclusive view holds that the Church is for people who are good, people who, as it is said, are really and fully committed, people who are quite different from the world. There is an attraction in that view, but it is not the New Testament view, because, apart from anything else, *who is to do the judging*, when we are told that we must not judge? (*Matthew* 7: 1). It is not man's place to judge any man, nor is it any man's place to say who is committed to Christ and who is not. The inclusive view feels instinctively that the Church must be open to all, and that, like the drag-net, so long as it is a human institution it is bound to be a mixture. And that is exactly what this parable teaches.

(ii) But equally this parable teaches that the time of separation will come, that the time when the good and the bad are sent to their respective destinations will come. But that separation, certain as it is, is not man's work but God's. Therefore it is our duty to gather in all who will come, and not to judge and not to separate, but to leave the final judgment to God who alone can judge.

OLD GIFTS USED IN A NEW WAY

Matthew 13: 51, 52

> Jesus said, " Have you understood all these things? " They said to Him: " Yes." He said to them: " That is why every scribe, who has been instructed in the Kingdom of Heaven, is like a householder who brings out of his treasure-house things new and old."

WHEN Jesus had finished speaking about the Kingdom, He asked His disciples if they had understood. And they had understood, at least in part. Then Jesus goes on to speak about the scribe, instructed in the Kingdom of Heaven, bringing out of his treasure-house things old and new. What Jesus is in effect saying is this: " You are able to understand, because you came to me with a fine heritage. You came with all the teaching of the law and the prophets. A scribe comes to me with a lifetime of study of the law and of all its commandments. That background helps you to understand. But after you have been instructed by me, you have the knowledge, not only of the things you used to know, but of things you never knew before, and even the knowledge which you had before is lit up and illuminated by what I have told to you."

There is something very suggestive here. For this means that Jesus never desired or intended that any man should forget all he knew when he comes to Him;

but that he should see that knowledge in a new light, and that he should use it in a new service; and when he does that, what he knew before becomes a greater treasure than ever it was.

Every man comes to Jesus Christ with some gift and with some ability. Jesus does not ask that that man should give up his gift. So many people think that when a man declares for Christ he must give things up, and concentrate upon what are the so-called religious things. But a scholar does not give up his scholarship when he becomes a Christian; rather he uses it for Christ. A business men need not give up his business; rather he should run it as a Christian would run it. One who can sing, or dance, or act, or paint need not give up his art, but must use his art as a Christian would use it. The sportsman need not give up his sport, but must play as a Christian would play. Jesus did not come to empty life, but to fill it, not to impoverish life, but to enrich it. Here we see Jesus telling men, not to abandon their gifts, but to use them even more wonderfully because they are using them in the light of the knowledge which He has given them.

THE BARRIER OF UNBELIEF

Matthew 13: 53-58

When Jesus had concluded these parables, He left there. He went into His native place and He taught them in their synagogue. His teaching was such that they were astonished and said, " Where did this man get this wisdom and these powers? Is not this the son of the carpenter? Is not His mother called Mary? And are James and Joseph and Simon and Juda not His brothers? Where did He get all these things? " And they were offended at Him. Jesus said to them, " A prophet is not without honour except in his own native place and in his own family." And He did not do many deeds of power there because of their unbelief.

IT was natural that at some time Jesus should pay a visit to Nazareth where He had been brought up. And yet it was a brave thing to do. The hardest place for a preacher to preach is the church where he was a boy; the hardest place for a doctor to practise is the place where people knew him when he was young. But to Nazareth Jesus went. In the synagogue there was no definite person to give the address. Any distinguished stranger who was present might be asked by the ruler of the synagogue to speak, or anyone who had a message might venture to give it. There was no danger that Jesus would not be given the opportunity to speak. But when He did speak, all that He encountered was hostility and incredulity. They would not listen to Him because they knew His father and His mother and His brothers and His sisters. They could not conceive that anyone who had lived among them and whom they had known had any right to speak as Jesus was speaking. The prophet, as so often happens, had no honour in his own country; and their attitude to Him raised a barrier which made it impossible for Jesus to have any effect upon them.

There is a great lesson here. In any service where people meet together the congregation preaches more than half the sermon. The congregation brings an atmosphere with it. That atmosphere is either a barrier through which the preacher's word cannot penetrate; or else it is such an expectancy that even the poorest sermon becomes a living flame.

Again, we should not judge a man by his background and his family connections; we should judge a man by what he is. Many a message has been killed stone dead, not because there was anything wrong with the message, but because the minds of the people were so prejudiced against the messenger that the message never had a chance.

When we meet together to worship God and to listen to the word of God, we must come with eager expectancy, and we must think, not of the man who speaks, but of the Spirit who speaks through Him.

THE TRAGIC DRAMA OF JOHN THE BAPTIST

Matthew 14: 1-12

> At that time Herod the tetrarch heard the report about Jesus, and said to his servants, " This is John the Baptizer. He has been raised from the dead, and, because of this, these deeds of power work in him." For Herod had seized John the Baptizer, and had bound him and put him in prison, because of Herodias, his brother Philip's wife, for John insisted to him: " It is not right for you to have her." So he wished to kill him, but he was afraid of the crowd, for they regarded him as a prophet. On the occasion of Herod's birthday celebrations the daughter of Herodias danced in public and delighted Herod. Hence he affirmed with an oath that he would give her whatsoever she might ask. Urged on by her mother, she said, " Give me here and now the head of John the Baptizer on a dish." The king was distressed, but, because of his oath, and because of those who sat at table with him, he ordered the request to be granted. So he sent and had John beheaded in the prison. And his head was brought on a dish and given to the maiden; and she brought it to her mother. His disciples came and took away the body and buried him. And they came and told Jesus about it.

HERE is the story of the tragic drama of the death of John the Baptist; and, as Matthew tells it, the *dramatis personae*, the characters in the drama, stand clearly delineated and vividly displayed.

(i) There is John himself. As far as Herod was concerned John had two faults. (*a*) He was too popular with the people. Josephus also tells the story of the death of John, and it is from this point of view that he tells it. Josephus writes (*Antiquities of the Jews*, 18. 5. 2): " Now when many others came in crowds about him, for they were greatly moved by hearing his words, Herod, who feared lest the great influence John had over the people might put it into his power and inclination to raise a rebellion (for they seemed ready to do anything he should advise) thought it best, by putting him to death, to prevent any mischief he might cause, and not bring himself into difficulties by sparing a man who might make him repent of it when it was too late. Accordingly he was sent a prisoner out of Herod's suspicious temper to Machaerus . . . and was there put to death." As Josephus read the facts, it was Herod's suspicious jealousy of John which made him kill John. Herod, like every weak and suspicious and frightened tyrant, could think of no way of dealing with a possible rival other than killing him. (b) But the gospel writers see the story differently; it is not a different story, it is the same story told from a different point of view. As they saw it, Herod killed John because John was a man who told the truth. It is always dangerous to rebuke a tyrant, and that is precisely what John did. The facts were quite simple. Herod Antipas was married to a daughter of the king of the Nabatean Arabs. He had a brother in Rome also called Herod; the gospel writers call this Roman Herod Philip; his full name may have been Herod Philip, or they may simply have got mixed up in the complicated marriage relationships of the Herods. This Herod who stayed in Rome was a wealthy private individual, who had no kingdom of his own. On a visit to Rome Herod Antipas seduced his brother's wife, and persuaded her to leave his brother and to marry him. In order to do so he had to put away his own wife, with, as we shall see, disastrous consequences to himself. In doing this, apart altogether from the moral aspect of the question, Herod had broken two laws. He had divorced his own wife without cause, and he had married his sister-in-law, which was a marriage, under Jewish law, within the prohibited relationships. Without hesitation John rebuked him; it is always dangerous to rebuke an eastern despot, and by his rebuke John signed his own death warrant. John was the man who fearlessly rebuked evil wherever he saw it. When John Knox was standing for his principles against Queen Mary, she demanded whether he thought it right that the authority of rulers should be resisted. His answer was: " If princes exceed their bounds, madam, they may be resisted and even deposed." The world owes much to the great men who took their lives in their hands, and who had the courage to tell even kings and queens that there is a moral law which they break at their peril.

(ii) There was Herodias. As we shall see, she was the ruination of Herod in every possible sense, although she was a woman not without a sense of greatness. At the moment we simply note this, Herodias was stained by a triple guilt. She was a woman of loose morals and of infidelity. She was a vindictive woman, who nursed her wrath to keep it warm, and who was out for revenge, even when she was justly condemned. And—perhaps worst of all—she was a woman who did not hesitate to stoop to use even her own daughter to realize her own vindictive ends. It would have been bad enough if she herself had sought for ways of taking vengeance on the man of God who confronted her with her shame. It was infinitely worse that she used her daughter for her nefarious purposes, and made her daughter as great a sinner herself. There is little to be said for a parent who stains a child with guilt in order to achieve some evil personal end.

(iii) There was Herodias' daughter, Salome. Salome must have been young, perhaps sixteen or seventeen years of age. Whatever she may later have become, in this instance she is surely more sinned against than sinning. There must have been in her an element of shamelessness. Here was a royal princess who acted as a dancing-girl. The dances which these girls danced were suggestive and immoral. For a royal princess to dance in public at all was an amazing thing. Herodias thought nothing of outraging modesty and demeaning her daughter, if only she could gain her revenge on a man who had justly rebuked her.

THE FALL OF HEROD

Matthew 14: 1-12 (*continued*)

(iv) Fourth in the list of *dramatis personae* comes Herod himself. He is called the *tetrarch*. *Tetrarch* literally means *the ruler of a fourth part*; but it came to be used quite generally, as here, of any subordinate ruler of a section of a country. Herod the Great had had many sons. When he died, he divided his territory into three, and, with the consent of the Romans, willed it to three of them. To Archelaus he left Judaea and Samaria; to Philip he left the northern territory of Trachonitis and Ituraea. To Herod Antipas—the Herod of this story—he left Galilee and Peraea. Herod Antipas was by no means an exceptionally bad king. But on this occasion Herod began on the road that led to his own complete ruin. We may note three things about Herod.

(*a*) He was a man with a guilty conscience. When Jesus became prominent Herod immediately leaped to the conclusion that this was John come back to life again. Origen has a most interesting suggestion about this. Origen points out that Mary, the mother of Jesus, and Elisabeth, the mother of John, were in fact closely related (*Luke* 1: 36). That is to say, Jesus and John were blood relations. And Origen speaks of a tradition which says that Jesus and John closely resembled each other in appearance, as might well be the case. If that was the case, then Herod's guilty conscience might appear to him to have even more grounds for its fears. Herod is the great proof that no man can rid himself of a sin by eliminating the man who confronted him with it. There is such a thing as conscience, and, even if a man's human accuser is eliminated, his divine accuser is still not silenced.

(*b*) Herod's action was typical of a weak man. Herod kept a foolish oath and broke a great law. He had promised Salome to give her anything she might ask, little thinking what she was about to ask. He knew well that to grant her request, and to keep that oath, was to break a far greater law; and yet he chose to keep his oath, because he was too weak to admit his error. Herod was more frightened of a woman's tantrums than he was of the moral law. He was more frightened of the criticism, and perhaps the amusement, of his guests, than he was of the voice of conscience. Herod was a man who could take a firm stand on the wrong things, when he knew very well what was right; and such a stand is the sign, not of strength, but of weakness.

(c) We have already said that Herod's action in this case was the beginning of his ruin, and so it was. The result of Herod's seduction of Herodias and his divorce of his own wife, was that Aretas, the father of his wife, and the ruler of the Nabateans, very naturally bitterly resented the insult Herod had perpetrated against his daughter. He made war against Herod, and heavily defeated him. The comment of Josephus is: " Some of the Jews thought that the destruction of Herod's army came from God, and that very justly, as a punishment for what he did against John, who was called the Baptist " (*Antiquities of the Jews*, 18. 5. 2). Herod was in fact only rescued by calling in the power of the Romans to clear things up for him. From the very beginning Herod's illegal and immoral alliance with Herodias brought him nothing but trouble. But the influence of Herodias was not to stop there. The years went by and Caligula came to the Roman throne. The Philip who had been tetrarch of Trachonitis and Ituraea died, and Caligula gave the province to another of the Herod family named Agrippa; and with the province he gave him the title of king. The fact that Agrippa was called king moved Herodias to bitter envy. Josephus says, " She was not able to conceal how miserable she was, by reason of the envy she had towards him " (*Antiquities of the Jews*, 18. 7. 1). The consequence of her envy was that she incited Herod to go to Rome and to ask Caligula that he too should be granted the title of king, for Herodias was determined to be a queen. " Let us go to Rome," she said, " and let us spare no pains or expenses, either of silver or gold, since they cannot be kept for any better use than for the obtaining of a kingdom." Herod was very unwilling to take action; he was naturally lazy, and he also foresaw serious trouble. But this persistent woman had her way. Herod prepared to set out to Rome; but Agrippa sent messengers to forestall him, with accusations that Herod was preparing treacherously to rebel from Rome. The result was that Caligula believed Agrippa's accusations, and took Herod's province from him, with all his money, and gave it to Agrippa, and banished Herod to far off Gaul to languish there in exile until he died. So in the end it was through Herodias that Herod lost his fortune and his kingdom, and dragged out a weary existence in the far away places of Gaul. It is just here that Herodias showed her one flash of greatness and of magnanimity. She was in fact Agrippa's sister, and Caligula told her that he did not intend to take her private fortune from her, and that or Agrippa's sake he intended to spare her, and that therefore she need not accompany her husband into exile. Herodias answered, " Thou indeed, O Emperor, actest after a magnificent manner, and as becomes thyself, in what thou offerest me; but the love which I have for my husband hinders me from partaking of the favour of thy gift; for it is not just that I, who have been a partner in his prosperity, should forsake him in his misfortune " (*Antiquities of the Jews*, 18. 7. 2). And so Herodias accompanied Herod to his exile.

If ever there was a proof that sin brings its own punishment, that proof lies in the story of Herod. It was an ill day when Herod first seduced Herodias. From that act of infidelity there came the murder of John, and in the end there came to him disaster, in which he lost all, except the woman who loved him and ruined him.

COMPASSION AND POWER

Matthew 14: 13-21

> When Jesus heard the news (of the death of John),
> He withdrew from there in a boat, into a deserted
> place alone. When the crowds heard of it, they
> followed Him on foot from the towns. When He had
> disembarked, He saw a great crowd, and He was
> moved with compassion for them to the depths of
> His being, and He healed their sick. When it had
> become late, His disciples came to Him: " The place
> is deserted," they said, " and the hour for the evening
> meal has already passed. Send the crowds away,
> in order that they may go into the villages, and buy
> themselves food." But Jesus said to them, " Give
> them food to eat yourselves." They said to Him,
> " We have nothing except five loaves and two fishes."
> He said, " Bring them here to me." So He ordered
> the crowds to sit down on the green grass. He took
> the five loaves and the two fishes, and looked up to
> heaven, and said a blessing, and broke the loaves and
> gave them to the disciples, and the disciples gave
> them to the crowds; and they all ate and were satisfied.
> They took up what was left over, twelve baskets
> full of the fragments. The number of those who ate
> was about five thousand men, apart from women and
> children.

GALILEE itself must have been a place where it was very
difficult to be alone, and to get away any distance from
the crowds. Galilee is a small country; it is only 50 miles
from north to south and 25 miles from east to west; and
Josephus tells us that in his time within that small area
there were 204 towns and villages, none with a population
of less than 15,000 people. In such a thickly populated
area it was not easy to get away from people for any
length of time. But it was quiet on the other side of the
lake, and at its widest the lake was only 8 miles wide.
Jesus' friends were fisherfolk; and it was not difficult to
embark on one of their boats and to seek retirement on
the east side of the lake. That is what Jesus did when He
heard of the death of John.

There were three perfectly simple and natural reasons why Jesus should seek to be alone. He was human and He needed rest. He never recklessly ran into danger, and it was well to withdraw, lest too early He should share the fate of John. And, most of all, with the Cross coming nearer and nearer, Jesus knew that He must meet with God before He met with men. Jesus was seeking rest for His body and strength for His soul in the lonely places. But He was not to get it. It would be easy to see the boat set sail and to deduce where it was going; and the crowds flocked round the top of the lake, and they were waiting for Him at the other side when He arrived there. So Jesus healed them, and when the evening came, He fed them, before they took the long road home. There are few of Jesus' miracles which are so revealing as this.

(i) It tells us of the compassion of Jesus. When Jesus saw the crowds He was moved with compassion to the depths of His being. That is a very wonderful thing. Jesus had come to find peace and quiet and loneliness; instead of that He found a vast crowd eagerly demanding what He could give to them. He might so easily have resented the crowd; He might so easily have found them a nuisance, and might have showed that it was so. What right had they to invade His privacy with their continual demands? Was He to have no rest and quiet and time to Himself at all? But Jesus was not like that. So far from finding them a nuisance, He was moved with compassion for them. Premanand, the great Christian who was once a wealthy and high-caste Indian, says in his autobiography: " As in the days of old, so now our message to the non-Christian world has to be the same, that *God cares*." If that be so, we must never be too busy for people, and we must never even seem to find them a trouble and a nuisance. Premanand writes: " My own experience has been that when I or any other missionary or Indian priest showed signs of restlessness or impatience towards any educated and thoughtful Christian or non-Christian visitors, and gave them to understand that we were hard-pressed for time, or that it was our lunch- or tea-time and that we could not wait, then at once such enquirers were lost, and never returned again." We must never deal with people with one eye on the clock, and as if we were anxious to be rid of them as soon as we decently could be. Premanand goes on to relate an incident which, it is not too much to say, may quite possibly have changed the whole course of the spread of Christianity in Bengal. " There is an account somewhere of how the first Metropolitan Bishop of India failed to meet the late Pandit Iswar Chandar Vidyasagar of Bengal through official formality. The Pandit had been sent as spokesman of the Hindu community in Calcutta, to establish friendly relations with the Bishop and with the Church. Vidyasagar, who was the founder of a Hindu College in Calcutta and a social reformer, author and educationalist of repute, returned disappointed without an interview, and formed a strong party of educated and wealthy citizens of Calcutta to oppose the Church and the Bishop, and to guard against the spread of Christianity. . . . The formality observed by one known to be an official of the Christian Church turned a friend into a foe." What an opportunity for Christ was lost because someone's privacy could not be invaded, except through official channels. Jesus never found any man a nuisance, even when His whole being was crying out for rest and quiet—and neither must His followers.

(ii) In this story we see Jesus witnessing that all gifts are from God. He took the food and He said a blessing. The Jewish grace before meals was very simple: " Blessed art Thou, Jehovah our God, King of the universe, who bringest forth bread from the earth." That would be the grace which Jesus said, for that was the grace which every Jewish family used. Here we see Jesus showing that it is God's gifts which He brings to men. The grace of gratitude is rare enough towards men; it is rarer still towards God.

THE PLACE OF THE DISCIPLE IN THE WORK OF CHRIST

Matthew 14: 13-21 (*continued*)

(iii) This miracle tells us very clearly of the place of the disciple in the work of Christ. The story tells that Jesus gave to the disciples, and the disciples gave to the crowd. Jesus worked through the hands of His disciples that day, and He still does. Again and again we come face to face with the truth which is at the heart of the Church. It is true that the disciple is helpless without his Lord, but it is also true that the Lord is helpless without His disciple. If Jesus wants something done, if He wants a child taught or a person helped, He has to get a man to do it. Jesus needs people through whom He can act, and through whom He can speak. Very early in the days of his enquiring Premanand came into contact with Bishop Whitley at Ranchi. He writes: " The Bishop read the Bible with me daily, and sometimes I read Bengali with him, and we talked together in Bengali. The longer I lived with the Bishop the closer I came to him, and found that his life revealed Christ to me, and his deeds and words made it easier for me to understand the mind and teaching of Christ about which I read daily in the Bible. I had a new vision of Christ, when I actually saw Christ's life of love, sacrifice and self-denial in the everyday life of the Bishop. He became actually the epistle of Christ to me." Jesus Christ needs disciples through whom He can work, and through whom His truth and His love can enter into the lives of others. He needs men to whom He can give in order that they may give to others. Without such men He cannot work, and it is our task to be such men for Him.

It would be easy to be daunted and discouraged by a task of such height and magnitude. But there is another thing in this story to lift up our hearts. When Jesus told the disciples to feed the crowd, they told him that all that they had was five loaves and two fishes; and yet with what they brought to Him, Jesus wrought His miracle. Jesus sets every one of us the tremendous task of communicating Himself to men; but He does not demand from us splendours, and qualities and magnificences that we do not possess. He says to us, " Come to me as you are, however ill-equipped; bring to me what you have, however little, and I will use it greatly in my service." Little is always much in the hands of Christ.

(iv) At the end of the miracle there is that strange little touch that the fragments were gathered up. Even when a miracle could feed men sumptuously there was no waste. There is something to note here. God gives to men with munificence, but it is never right to waste God's gifts. God gives generously but a wasteful extravagance is never right. God's generous giving and our wise using must go hand in hand.

THE MAKING OF A MIRACLE

Matthew 14: 13-21 (*continued*)

THERE are some people who read the miracles of Jesus, and who feel no need to understand. Let them remain for ever undisturbed in the sweet simplicity of their faith. There are others who read and whose minds question and who feel that they must understand. Let them take no shame of it, for God comes far more than half way to meet the questing mind. But in whatever way we approach the miracles of Jesus, one thing is certain. We must never regard them as something which *happened*; we must always regard them as something which *happens*. They are not isolated events in history; they are demonstrations of the always and forever operative power of Jesus Christ. There are three ways in which we can look at this miracle.

(i) We may look at it as a simple multiplication of loaves and fishes. That would be very difficult to understand;

and it would be something which happened once, and which never in this world repeated itself; but if we regard it that way, then let us be content, but let us also not be critical and condemnatory of anyone who feels that he must find another way.

(ii) Many people have seen in this miracle a sacrament. They have felt that those who were present received only the smallest morsel of food, and yet with that food were strengthened for their journey and were content. They have felt that this was not a meal where people sat and glutted their physical appetite; but that it was a meal where they ate the spiritual food of Christ. If that be so, this is a miracle which is re-enacted every time that we sit at the table of our Lord; for there there comes to us the spiritual food which sends us out to walk with firmer feet and greater strength the way of life which leads to God.

(iii) There are those who have seen in this miracle something which in a sense is perfectly natural, and yet which in another sense is a real miracle, and which in any sense is very precious. Picture the scene. There is the crowd; it is late; and they are hungry. But was it really likely that the vast majority of that crowd would set out across the lake without any food at all? Would they not take something with them, however little? Now it was evening and they were hungry. *But they were also selfish.* And no one would produce what he had lest he had to share it and he himself had not enough. Rather than share their scanty provisions they kept them in their wallets. Then Jesus took the lead. Such as He and His disciples had He began to share with a blessing and an invitation and a smile. And thereupon all began to share, and before they knew what was happening, there was enough and more than enough for all.

If that happened, this was not the miracle of the multiplication of loaves and fishes; it was the miracle of the changing of selfish people into generous people at the touch of Christ. It was the miracle of the birth of love in grudging hearts. It was the miracle of changed men and women with something of Christ in them to banish the selfishness of their hearts. If that be so, then in the realest sense Christ fed them with Himself, and sent His Spirit to dwell within their hearts.

It does not matter how we understand this miracle. One thing is sure—when Christ is there the weary find rest and the hungry soul is fed.

IN THE HOUR OF TROUBLE

Matthew 14: 22-27

> Immediately He compelled His disciples to embark in the boat and to go on ahead to the other side, until He should send away the crowds. When He had sent away the crowds, He went up into a mountain by Himself to pray. When it was late, He was there alone. The boat was by this time in the middle of the sea, battered by the waves, for the wind was contrary. About three o'clock in the morning, He came to them walking on the sea. When the disciples saw Him walking on the sea they were alarmed. " This is an apparition," they said, and they cried out from fear. Immediately Jesus spoke to them. " Courage! " He said. " It is I. Do not be afraid."

THE lesson of this passage is abundantly and preciously clear; what actually happened is far from being clear. First of all, let us set this incident in its scene.

After the feeding of the multitude Jesus sent His disciples away. Matthew says that He *compelled* them to embark on the boat and to go on ahead. At first sight the word *compelled* sounds strange; but if we turn to John's account of the incident we will most likely find the explanation. John tells us that after the feeding of the multitude, the crowd wished to come and to make Him a king by force (*John* 6: 15). There was a surge of popular acclamation, and in the excited state of Palestine a revolution might well have there and then begun. It was a dangerous situation, and the disciples might well have complicated it, for they too were still thinking of Jesus in terms of earthly power. Jesus sent away His disciples because a situation had arisen with which He could best deal alone, and in which He did not wish them to become involved.

When He was alone, He went up into a mountain to pray; and by this time the night had come. The disciples had set out back across the lake; one of the sudden storms, for which the lake was notorious, had come down, and they were struggling against the winds and the waves, and were making little progress. As the night wore on Jesus began to walk round the head of the lake to reach the other side. Matthew has already told us that, when Jesus fed the crowds, He made them sit down on *the green grass*. By that we know it must have been the springtime. Very likely it was near the Passover time, which was in the middle of April. If that is so, the moon would be full. In ancient times the night was divided into four *watches*— 6 p.m. to 9 p.m., 9 p.m. to 12 midnight, 12 midnight to 3 a.m., and 3 a.m. to 6 a.m. So at three o'clock in the morning, Jesus walking on the high ground at the north of the lake, clearly saw the boat fighting with the waves, and came down to the shore to help.

It is then that there is a real difficulty in knowing what happened. In verses 25 and 26 we read twice about Jesus walking *on the water*, and the curious thing is that the two phrases in the Greek for *on the water* are different. In verse 25 it is *epi tēn thalassan*, which can equally mean *over* the water, and *towards* the water. In verse 26 it is *epi tēs thalassēs*, which can mean *on* the water, and which is actually the very same phrase which is used in *John* 21: 1 for *at the sea*, that is by the sea-shore, of Tiberias. Still further, the word which is used for *walking* in both verses 25 and 26 is *peripatein*, which means *to walk about*. The truth is that there are two perfectly possible interpretations of this passage, so far as the actual Greek goes. It may describe a miracle in which Jesus actually walked

on the water. Or, it may equally mean that the disciples'
boat was driven by the wind to the northern shore of
the lake, that Jesus came down from the mountain to
help them when He saw them struggling in the moonlight,
and that He came walking through the surf of the shore
and the waves towards the boat, and came so suddenly
upon them that they were terrified when they saw Him.
Both of these interpretations are equally valid. Some will
prefer one, and some the other.

But, whatever interpretation of the Greek we choose,
it does not matter. The meaning and the significance
is perfectly clear. *In the hour of the disciples' need Jesus
came to them.* When the wind was contrary, and when life
was a struggle, Jesus was there to help. No sooner had a
need arisen, then Jesus was there to help and to save.

In life the wind is often contrary. There are times
when we are up against it, and when life is a desperate
struggle with ourselves, with our circumstances, with
our temptations, with our sorrows, with our decisions.
At such a time no man has to struggle alone, for Jesus
comes to him across the storms of life, with hand stretched
out to save, and with His calm clear voice bidding us to
be of good courage, and not to be afraid.

It does not matter how we take this incident; it is
in any event far more than the story of what Jesus once
did in a storm in far-off Palestine; it is the sign and the
symbol of what He always does for His people, when the
wind is contrary, and when we are in danger of being
overwhelmed by the storms of life.

COLLAPSE AND RECOVERY

Matthew 14: 28-33

> Peter got down from the boat and walked on the
> water to come to Jesus. But, when he saw the wind,
> he was afraid; and, when he began to sink below
> the water, he cried out, " Lord, save me! " Immed-
> iately Jesus stretched out His hand and grasped him.

" O man of little faith! " He said. " Why did you begin to have doubts? " And when they got into the boat, the wind sank. And those in the boat knelt in reverence before Him, saying, " Truly you are the Son of God."

THERE is no passage in the New Testament in which Peter's character is more fully revealed than in this. It tells us three things about Peter.

(i) Peter was given to acting upon impulse, and without thinking of what he was doing. It was Peter's mistake that again and again he acted without fully facing the situation and without counting the cost. He was to do exactly the same when he affirmed eternal and undying and unshakable loyalty to Jesus (*Matthew* 26: 33-35), and then denied his Lord's name. And yet there are worse sins than that, because Peter's whole trouble was that he was ruled by his heart; and, however he might sometimes fail, his heart was always in the right, and the instinct of his heart was always love.

(ii) As we have seen, because Peter acted on impulse he often failed and came to grief. It was always Jesus' insistence that a man should look at a situation in all its bleak grimness before he acted (*Luke* 9: 57, 58; *Matthew* 16: 24, 25). Jesus was completely honest with men; He always bade them to see how difficult it was to follow Him before they set out upon the Christian way. A great deal of Christian failure is due to acting upon an emotional moment without counting the cost.

(iii) But Peter never finally failed, for always in the moment of his failure he clutched at Christ. The wonderful thing about Peter is that every time he fell, he rose again; and that it must have been true that even his failures brought him closer and closer to Jesus Christ. As it has been well said, a saint is not a man who never falls; a saint is a man who gets up and goes on again every time he falls. Peter's failures only made him love Jesus Christ the more.

These verses finish with another great and permanent truth. When Jesus got into the boat the wind sank. The great truth there is that, wherever Jesus Christ is, the wildest storm becomes a calm. Olive Wyon, in her book *Consider Him*, quotes a thing from the letters of St. Francis of Sales. St. Francis had noticed a custom of the country districts in which he lived. He had often noticed a farm servant going across a farmyard to draw water at the well; he also noticed that, before she lifted the brimming pail, the girl always put a piece of wood into it. One day he went out to the girl and asked her, " Why do you do that? " She looked surprised and answered, as if it were a matter of course, . " Why? to keep the water from spilling . . . to keep it steady! " Writing to a friend later on the bishop told this story and then added: " So when your heart is distressed and agitated, put the Cross into the centre of your heart, to keep it steady! " In every time of storm and stress the presence of Jesus and the love which flows from the Cross bring peace and serenity and calm.

THE MINISTRY OF CHRIST

Matthew 14: 34-36

> When they had crossed over, they came to land at Gennesaret. When the men of that place recognized Him, they sent the news that He had come to the whole surrounding countryside, and they brought to Him all those who were ill, and besought Him to be allowed only to touch the fringe of His robe; and all who touched Him were restored to health.

THIS is just one of Matthew's almost colourless little connecting passages. It is a sentence or two of the gospel story that the eye might easily pass over, as quite unimportant; and yet it is very revealing of Jesus.

(i) There is beauty in it. No sooner did Jesus appear anywhere than men were crowding and clamouring for His help; and He never refused it. He healed them all.

There is no word here that He preached or taught at any length; there is simply the record that He healed. The most tremendous thing about Jesus was that He taught men what God was like by showing men what God was like. He did not *tell* men that God cared; He *showed* men that God cared. There is little use in preaching the love of God in words without showing the love of God in action.

(ii) But there is also pathos here. No one can read this passage without seeing in it the grim fact that there were hundreds and thousands of people who desired Jesus only for what they could get out of Him. Once they had received the healing which they sought, they were not really prepared to go any further. It has always been the case that people have wanted the privilege of Christianity without the responsibilities of Christianity. It has always been the case that so many of us only remember God when we need Him. Ingratitude is the ugliest of all sins; and towards God and towards Jesus Christ there is no sin of which men are more often and more consistently guilty.

CLEAN AND UNCLEAN

Matthew 15: 1-9

> Then the Pharisees and Scribes from Jerusalem approached Jesus. " Why," they said, " do your disciples transgress the tradition of the elders? They do so transgress, because they do not wash their hands before they eat bread." Jesus answered them: " Why do you too transgress God's commandment, because of your tradition? For God said, ' Honour your father and your mother,' and, ' He who curses his father and mother, let him die '; but, as for you, you say, ' Whoever says to his father or his mother: " That by which you might have been helped by me is a dedicated gift," will certainly not honour his father and his mother, and is yet guiltless.' You have annulled the commandment of God through your tradition. Hypocrites, Isaiah in his prophecy

described you well: ' This people honour me with their lips, but their heart is far away from me. It is in vain that they reverence me; for it is man-made commandments that they teach as their teaching.' "

IT is not too much to say that, however difficult and obscure this passage may seem to us, it is none the less one of the most important passages in the whole gospel story. It represents a head-on clash between Jesus and the leaders of orthodox Jewish religion. Its opening sentence makes it clear that the Scribes and Pharisees had come all the way from Jerusalem to Galilee to put their questions to Jesus. On this occasion it need not be thought that the questions are malicious. The Scribes and Pharisees are not on this occasion ill-naturedly seeking to entangle Jesus. They were genuinely bewildered; and in a very short time they were going to be genuinely outraged and shocked; for the basic importance of this passage is that it is not so much a clash between Jesus and the Pharisees in a personal way; it is something far more—it is the collision of two views of religion, and two views of the demands of God. Nor was there any possibility of a compromise, or even a working agreement, between these two views of religion. Inevitably the one had to destroy the other or perish. Here, then, embedded in this passage, there is one of the supreme religious contests in history. To understand it we must try to understand the background of Jewish Pharisaic and Scribal religion.

In this passage there meets us the whole conception of *clean* and *unclean*. We must be quite clear that this idea of cleanness and uncleanness has nothing to do with physical cleanness, or, except distantly, with hygiene. It is entirely a ceremonial matter. For a man to be clean was for him to be in a state when he might worship and approach God; for him to be unclean was for him to be in a state when such a worship and such an approach were impossible for him. This uncleanness was contracted by touching or eating certain persons or things. For instance a woman was unclean if she had an issue of blood, even if that issue of blood was that of the normal monthly period; she was unclean for a stated time after she had had a child; every dead body was unclean, and to touch a dead body was to become unclean; every Gentile was unclean.

This uncleanness was transferable; it was, so to speak, infectious. For instance, if a mouse touched an earthenware vessel, that vessel was unclean. Unless that vessel was ritually washed and cleansed, everything that was put into it was unclean; the consequence was that anyone who touched that vessel, or who ate or drank from its contents became unclean; and in turn anyone who touched the person who had so become unclean then became unclean. This is not only a Jewish idea; it occurs in other religions. To a high-caste Indian anyone not belonging to his own caste is unclean; if that person becomes a Christian, he is still more seriously unclean. Premanand, the great Indian Christian, tells us in his autobiography what happened to himself. He became a Christian; his family ejected him. Sometimes he used to come back to see his mother, who was broken-hearted at what she considered his apostasy, but who still loved him dearly. Premanand tells us: " As soon as my father came to know that I was visiting my mother in the daytime while he was away at the office, he ordered the door-keeper, a stalwart up-country man, Ram Rup . . . . not to allow me to enter the house." Ram Rup was persuaded to slacken his vigilance. " At last my mother won over Ram Rup, the door-keeper, and I was allowed to enter her presence. The prejudice was so great that even the menial Hindu servants of the house would not wash the plates on which I was fed by my mother. Sometimes my aunt would purify the place and the seat on which I had sat by sprinkling Ganges water, or water mixed with cow dung." Premanand was unclean, and everything he touched became unclean.

We must note that there was nothing moral about this at all. The touching of certain things produced this uncleanness; and this uncleanness debarred from the society of men and the presence of God. It was as if some special virtue or infection hung like an aura about certain persons and things. We may understand this a little better, if we remember that even in western civilization this idea is not completely dead, although it works, in this case, mainly in reverse. There are still those who will find in a four-leafed clover, or in some metal or wooden charm, or in a black cat, something which brings good or bad fortune.

So, then, here is an idea of religion which sees in religion something which consists in avoiding contact with certain things and people because they are unclean; and, then, if that contact should have been made, in taking the necessary ritual cleansing measures to rid oneself of the contracted uncleanness. But we must pursue this even a little further.

THE FOODS WHICH ENTER INTO A MAN

Matthew 15: 1-9 (*continued*)

THESE laws of cleanness and uncleanness had a further wide area of application. They laid down what a man might eat, and what he might not eat. Broadly speaking, all food and vegetables were unclean. But, in regard to living creatures, the laws were strict. These laws are in *Leviticus* 11. We may briefly summarize them. Of beasts, only those could be eaten who part the hoof and chew the cud. That is why no Jew can eat the flesh of the pig, the rabbit, or the hare. In no case might the flesh of an animal which had died a natural death be eaten (*Deuteronomy* 14: 21). In all cases the blood must be drained from the carcase; the orthodox Jew still buys his meat from a *kosher* butcher, where only meat so treated is sold. Ordinary fat upon the flesh might be eaten, but the fat on the kidneys and on the entrails of the abdomen, which we call suet, might not be eaten. In regard to sea food, only sea creatures which have both fins and scales may be eaten. This means that shellfish, such as lobsters, are unclean. All insects are unclean, with one exception; locusts might be, and still are, eaten in the east. In the case of animals and fish there is a standard test, as we have seen, of what might be eaten, and what might not be eaten. In the case of birds there is no such test; and the list of unclean and forbidden birds is in *Leviticus* 11: 13-21. There were certain identifiable reasons for all this.

(i) The refusal to touch dead bodies, or to eat the flesh of an animal which had died from natural causes, may well have something to do with the belief in evil spirits. It would be easy to think of a demon as taking up residence in such a body, and gaining an entry into the body of the eater.

(ii) Certain animals were sacred in other religions; for instance, the cat and the crocodile were sacred in Egyptian religion; and it would be very natural for the Jews to regard as unclean any animal which another nation worshipped. The animal would then be reckoned to be a kind of idol, sacred to a heathen god, and therefore dangerously unclean.

(iii) As Dr. Rendle Short points out in his most helpful book, *The Bible and Modern Medicine*, certain of the regulations were in fact wise from the point of view of health and hygiene. Dr. Short writes: " True, we eat the pig, the rabbit and the hare, but these animals are liable to parasitic infections and are safe only if the food is well-cooked. The pig is an unclean feeder, and harbours two worms, trichina and a tape worm, which may be passed on to man. The danger is minimal under present conditions in this country, but it would have been far otherwise in Palestine of old, and such food was better avoided." The prohibition of eating anything with blood in it comes from the fact that the blood is the life in Jewish thought. This is a natural thought for as blood flows away, life ebbs away. And the life belongs to God, and to God alone. The same idea explains the prohibition of eating the fat. The fat is the richest part of the carcase, and the richest part must be given to God. In some cases, although they are few, there was sound sense behind the prohibitions and the food laws.

(iv) But there remain a large number of cases in which things and beasts and animals were unclean for no reason at all, except that they were. Taboos are always inexplicable; they are simply unexplained superstitions, by which certain living things came to be connected with good or with bad fortune, with cleanness or uncleanness.

These things would not in themselves matter very much, but the trouble and the tragedy was that they had become to the Scribes and Pharisees matters of life and death. To serve God, to be religious, was to observe these good laws. If we put it in the following way, we will see the result of this. To the Pharisaic mind the prohibition of eating rabbit's or pig's flesh was just as much a command-ment of God as the prohibition of adultery; it was therefore just as much a sin to eat pork or rabbit as it was to seduce a woman and to enjoy illegal sexual intercourse. Religion had got itself mixed up with all kinds of external rules and regulations; and, since it is much easier both to observe rules and regulations, and to check up on those who do not, these rules and regulations had *become* religion to the orthodox Jews.

THE WAYS OF CLEANSING

Matthew 15: 1-9 (*continued*)

Now we come to the particular impact of this on this passage which we are studying. It was clearly impossible to avoid all kinds of ceremonial uncleanness. A man might himself avoid them, but how could he possibly know when on the street he had touched someone who was unclean? Such a touch would make him unclean, for, as we have seen, uncleanness was infectious. This was further complicated by the fact that there were Gentiles in Palestine, and the very dust touched by a Gentile foot became unclean.

To combat this uncleanness an elaborate system of washings was worked out. These washings became ever more elaborate. At first there was a hand-washing on rising in the morning. Then there grew up an elaborate system of hand-washing which was at first confined to the priests in the Temple. Before they ate the part of the sacrifice which was their perquisite they had to use these washings. Then these complicated washings came to be used and demanded by the strictest of the orthodox Jews for themselves, and for all who claimed to be truly religious.

Edersheim in *The Life and Times of Jesus the Messiah* outlines the most elaborate of these washings. Water jars were kept ready to be used before a meal. The minimum amount of water to be used was a quarter of a log, which is defined as enough to fill one and a half egg-shells. The water was first poured on both hands, held with the fingers pointed upwards, and must run up the arm as far as the wrist. It must drop off from the wrist, for the water was now itself unclean, having touched the unclean hands, and if it ran down the fingers again, it would again render the fingers unclean. The process was repeated with the hands held in the opposite direction, with the fingers pointing down; and then finally each hand was cleansed by being rubbed with the fist of the other. A really strict Jew would do all this, not only before a meal, but also between each of the courses.

So the question of the Jewish orthodox leaders to Jesus is: " Why do your disciples not observe the laws of washing which our tradition lays down? "

They speak of *the tradition of the elders*. To the Jew the Law had two sections. There was *the written Law* which was contained in scripture itself; and there was *the oral Law*, which consisted of the developments, such as those in hand-washing, which the Scribes and the experts had worked out through the generations; and all these developments were the tradition of the elders, and were regarded as just as much, if not more, binding than the written Law. Again we must stop to remember the salient point—to the orthodox Jew all this ritual ceremony *was* religion; this is what, as they believed, God demanded. To do these things was to please God, and to be a good man. To put it in another way, all this business of ritual washing was regarded as just as important and just as binding as the Ten Commandments themselves. Religion had become identified with a host of external regulations. It was more important to wash the hands in a certain way than to obey the commandment: " Thou shalt not covet."

BREAKING GOD'S LAW TO KEEP MAN'S LAW

Matthew 15: 1-9 (*continued*)

JESUS did not answer the question of the Pharisees directly. What He did was to take an example of the operation of the oral and ceremonial law to show how the observance of that law, so far from being obedience to the law of God, could become actual contradiction of the Law of God.

Jesus says that the Law of God lays it down that a man shall honour his father and his mother; then he goes on to say that if a man says, " It is a gift," then he is free from the duty of honouring his father and his mother. If we look at the parallel passage in *Mark*, we see that the phrase is: " It is *Corban*." What is the meaning of this obscure passage to us? In point of fact it can have two meanings, because *Corban* has two meanings.

(i) *Corban* can mean *that which is offered or dedicated* to God. Now suppose that a man had a father or mother in poverty and in need; and suppose that that poor and aged parent came to him with a request for help. There was a way in which the man could avoid helping his parents. He could, as it were, *officially* dedicate all his money and all his property to God and to the Temple; his property would then be *Corban*, God-offered, God-dedicated; then he would say to his father or mother: " I'm very sorry, I can give you nothing; all my belongings are dedicated to God." The man could use a ritual and ceremonial practice and regulation to evade the basic duty of helping and honouring his father and mother. He could take a scribal regulation to wipe out one of the Ten Commandments.

(ii) But *Corban* has another meaning, and it may well be that it is this second meaning which is in question here. *Corban* was used as an oath. A man might say to his father or mother: " *Corban*, if anything I have will ever be used to help you." Now suppose this man to have remorse of conscience ; suppose him to have made the refusal in a moment of anger, or temper, or even of irritation; suppose him to have second and kinder and more filial thoughts, and to feel that after all there was a duty and an obligation to help his parents. In such a case any reasonable person would say that that man had undergone a genuine repentance, and that his change of mind was a good thing, and that he was now prepared to do the right thing, and to obey the Law of God. The strict Scribe said, " No." The Scribe would say, " Our Law says that no oath can ever be broken." He would quote *Numbers* 30: 2: " If a man vow a vow unto the Lord, or swear an oath to bind his soul with a bond, he shall not break his word, he shall do all that proceedeth out of his mouth." The Scribe would legalistically argue: " You took an oath; and for no reason can you ever break it." That is to say, the Scribe would hold a man to a reckless oath, taken in a moment of passion, an oath which actually compelled a man to break the higher law of humanity and of God. That is what Jesus meant. He meant: " You are using your scribal interpretations, your traditions, to compel a man to dishonour his father and mother, even when he himself has repented and has seen the better way." The strange and tragic thing was that the Scribes and Pharisees of the day of Jesus were actually going against what the greatest Jewish teachers had said. Rabbi Eliezer said, " The door is opened for a man on account of his father and his mother," and he meant that, if any man had sworn an oath which dishonoured his father and his mother, and had then repented of it, the door was open to him to change his mind and to take a different way, even if an oath had been sworn. As so often, Jesus was not presenting men with unknown truth; He was reminding them of things that God had already told them, and that they had already known, but which they had forgotten, because they had come to prefer their own man-made ingenuities to the great simplicities of the Law of God.

Here is the clash and the collision; here is the contest between two kinds of religion, and two kinds of worship. To the Scribes and Pharisees religion was the observance of certain outward rules and regulations and rituals, such as the correct way to wash the hands before eating; it was the strict observance of a legalistic outlook on all life. To Jesus religion was a thing which had its seat in the heart; it was a thing which issued in compassion and kindness, which are above and beyond the law.

To the Scribes and Pharisees worship was ritual, ceremony law; to Jesus worship was the clean heart and the loving life. Here is the clash. And that clash still exists. What is worship? Even today there are many who would say that worship is not worship unless it is carried out by a priest ordained in a certain succession, in a building conse-crated in a certain way, and from a liturgy laid down by a certain Church. And all these things are externals. One of the greatest definitions of worship ever laid down was laid down by William Temple: " To worship is to quicken the conscience by the holiness of God, to feed the mind with the truth of God, to purge the imagination by the beauty of God, to open the heart to the love of God, to devote the will to the purpose of God." We must have a care lest we stand aghast at the apparent blindness of the Scribes and the Pharisees, lest we are shocked by their insistence on outward ceremonial, and lest we ourselves are guilty of the same fault in our own way. Religion can never be founded on any ceremonies or any ritual; religion must always be founded on personal relationships between man and man.

THE REAL GOODNESS AND THE REAL EVIL
Matthew 15: 10-20

Jesus called the crowd and said to them: " Listen and understand. It is not that which goes into the mouth which defiles a man; but what comes out of the mouth, *that* defiles a man." Then His disciples came to Him and said, " Do you know that when the Pharisees heard your saying, they were shocked by it? " He answered: " Every plant which my heavenly Father did not plant will be rooted up. Let them be. They are blind guides. If the blind lead the blind, both of them will fall into the ditch." Peter said to Him, " Tell us what this dark saying means." He said, " Are you even yet without understanding? Do you not know that everything which goes into a man's mouth goes down into the stomach, and is evacuated out into the drain? But that which comes out of the mouth comes from the heart, and it is these things which defile a man. For from the heart come pernicious thoughts, acts of murder, adultery, theft, false witness, slander. It is these things which defile a man. To eat with unwashed hands does not defile a man."

IT may well be held that for a Jew this was the most startling thing that Jesus ever said. For in this saying

He does not only condemn Scribal and Pharisaic ritual and ceremonial religion; He actually wipes out large sections of the book of *Leviticus*. This is not a contradiction of the tradition of the elders alone. This is a contradiction of scripture itself. This saying of Jesus cancels all the food laws of the Old Testament. Quite possibly these food laws might still stand as matters of health and hygiene and common-sense and medical wisdom; but they could never again stand as matters of religion. Once and for all Jesus lays it down that what matters is not the state of a man's ritual observance, but the state of a man's heart.

No wonder the Scribes and Pharisees were shocked. The very ground of their religion was cut from beneath their feet. This statement was not simply alarming; it was revolutionary. If Jesus was right, their whole theory of religion was wrong. They identified religion and pleasing God with the observing of rules and regulations which had to do with cleanness and with uncleanness, with what a man ate, with how he washed his hands before he ate it; Jesus identified religion with the state of a man's heart, and said bluntly that these Pharisaic and Scribal regulations had nothing to do with religion. Jesus said that the Pharisees were blind guides who had no idea of the way to God, and that if people followed them all they could expect was to stray off the road and to fall into the ditch. And Jesus was profoundly right.

(i) If religion consists in external regulations and observances it is two things. It is far *too easy*. It is very much easier to abstain from certain foods, and to wash the hands in a certain way than it is to love and to forgive the unlovely and the unlovable, and to help the needy at the cost of one's own time and money, and comfort and pleasure. We have still not fully learned this lesson. To go to Church regularly, to give liberally to the Church, to be a member of a Bible reading circle are all external things. They are means towards religion; but they are not religion; for we can never too often remind ourselves that religion consists in personal relationships and in an attitude to God and to our fellow-men. Further, if religion consists in external observances, it is quite *misleading*. Many a man has a faultless life in externals, but has the bitterest and the most evil thoughts within his heart, and the teaching of Jesus is that not all the outward observances in the world can atone for a heart where pride and bitterness and lust hold sway.

(ii) It is Jesus' teaching that the part of a man that matters is his heart. " Blessed are the pure in heart, for they shall see God " (*Matthew* 5: 8). As Burns had it in the *Epistle to Davie* :

> " The heart aye's the part aye
> That makes us right or wrang."

What matters to God is not so much *how* we act, but *why* we act; not so much what we *actually do,* but what we *wish in our heart of hearts to do.* " Man," as Aquinas had it, " sees the deed, but God sees the intention."

It is Jesus' teaching—and it is a teaching which condemns every one of us—that no man can call himself a good man because he observes external rules and regulations; he can only call himself a good man when his heart is pure. And that very fact is the end of pride, and the reason why every one of us can only say, " God be merciful to me a sinner."

FAITH TESTED AND FAITH ANSWERED

Matthew 15: 21-28

> And Jesus left there, and withdrew to the districts of Tyre and Sidon. And, look you, a Canaanite woman from these parts came and cried, " Have pity upon me, Sir, Son of David! My daughter is grievously afflicted by a demon." But He answered her not a word. His disciples came and asked Him, " Send her away, for she is shrieking behind us." Jesus answered, " I was sent only to the lost sheep of

Israel." She came and knelt in entreaty before Him. " Lord," she said, " help me! " Jesus answered, " It is not right to take the children's bread, and to throw it to the pet dogs." She said, " True, Lord, but even the dogs eat of the pieces which fall from their master's table." Then Jesus answered her, " Woman, great is your faith! Let it be done for you as you wish." And her daughter was restored to health from that hour.

THERE are tremendous implications in this passage. Apart from anything else, it has this unique interest, that it describes the only occasion on which Jesus was ever outside of Palestine and outside of Jewish territory. The supreme significance of this passage is that it fore-shadows the going out of the gospel to the whole world; it shows us the beginning of the end of all the barriers.

For Jesus this was a time of deliberate withdrawal. The end was coming near; and before the end Jesus wished some time of quiet when He could prepare for the end. It was not so much that He wished to prepare Himself, although that purpose was also in His mind, but rather that He wished some time in which He could teach and prepare His disciples against the day of the Cross. There were things which He must tell them, and which He must compel them to understand. There was no place in Palestine where He could be sure of privacy; wherever He went, the crowds would find Him. So He went right north through Galilee until He came to the land of Tyre and Sidon where the Phoenicians dwelt. There, at least for a time, He would be safe from the malignant hostility of the Scribes and Pharisees, and from the dangerous popularity of the people, for no Jew would be likely to follow Him into Gentile territory. This passage shows us Jesus seeking a time of quiet before the turmoil of the end. This is not in any sense a picture of Jesus running away; it is a picture of Jesus nerving and preparing Himself and His disciples for the final and the decisive battle which lay so close ahead.

But even in these foreign parts Jesus was not to be free from the clamant demand of human need. There was a woman who had a daughter who was grievously afflicted. This woman must have heard somehow of the wonderful things which Jesus could do; and she followed Him and His disciples crying desperately for help. At first Jesus seemed to pay no attention to her. The disciples were embarrassed. " Give her what she wants," they said, " and be rid of her." The reaction of the disciples was not really compassion at all; it was the reverse; to them the woman was a nuisance, and all they wanted was to be rid of her as quickly as possible. To grant a request to get rid of a person who is, or may become, a nuisance is a common enough reaction, but it is very different from the response of Christian love and pity and compassion.

But to Jesus there was a problem here. That He was moved with compassion for this woman we cannot for a moment doubt. But she was a Gentile. Not only was she a Gentile; she belonged to the old Canaanite stock, and the Canaanites were the ancestral enemies of the Jews. Even at that very time, or not so very much later, Josephus could write: " Of the Phoenicians, the Tyrians have the most ill-feeling towards us." We have already seen that, if Jesus was to have any effect, He had to limit His objectives like a wise general. He had to begin with the Jews and here was a Gentile crying for mercy. There was only one thing for Jesus to do; He must awaken true faith in the heart of this woman.

So Jesus at last turned to her: " It is not right to take the children's bread and to throw it to the pet dogs." To call a person a dog was a deadly and a contemptuous insult. The Jew spoke with arrogant insolence about " Gentile dogs," " infidel dogs," and later " Christian dogs." In those days the dogs were the unclean scavengers of the street—lean, savage, often diseased curs. But there are two things to remember. The tone and the look with which a thing is said make all the difference. Even a thing which seems hard can be said with a disarming smile. We can call a friend " an old villain ", or " a rascal ", with a smile and a tone which takes all the sting out of it and which fills it with affection. We can be quite sure that the smile on Jesus' face and the compassion in his eyes robbed the words of all insult and bitterness. And second, it is the diminutive word for *dogs* (*kunaria*) which is used, and the *kunaria* were not the street dogs, but the little household pets, very different from the pariah dogs who roamed the streets and probed in the refuse heaps. The woman was a Greek; she was quick to see, and she had all a Greek's ready wit. " True," she said, " but even the dogs get their share of the crumbs which fall from their master's table." And Jesus' eyes lit up with joy at such an indomitable faith; and He granted her the blessing and the healing which she so much desired.

THE FAITH WHICH WON THE BLESSING

Matthew 15: 21-28 (*continued*)

THERE are certain things about this woman which we must note.

(i) First and foremost, she had *love.* As Bengel said of her, " She made the misery of her child her own." Heathen she might be, but in her heart there was that love for her child which is always the reflection of God's love for His children. It was love which made her approach this stranger; it was love which made her accept His silence and yet still appeal; it was love which made her suffer the apparent rebuffs; it was love which made her able to see the compassion beyond and behind the words of Jesus. The driving force of this woman's heart was love; and there is nothing stronger and nothing nearer God than love.

(ii) This woman had *faith.* (*a*) It was a *faith which grew* in contact with Jesus. She begins by calling Him *Son o*. *David*; that was a popular title, a political title. It was a title which looked on Jesus as a great and powerful wonder worker, but it was a title which looked on Jesus in terms of *earthly* power and glory. She came asking a boon of one whom she took to be a great and powerful *man*. She came with a kind of superstition as she might have come to any magician. She ends by calling Jesus *Lord*. Jesus, as it were compelled her to look at Himself, and in Him she saw something that was not expressible in earthly terms at all, but which was nothing less than divine. That is precisely what Jesus wanted to awaken in her before He granted her request. He wanted her to see that *a request to a great man* must be turned into *a prayer to the living God*. We can see this woman's faith growing as she is confronted with Christ, until she glimpsed Him, however distantly, for what He was. (*b*) It was a faith which *worshipped*. She began by following; she ends upon her knees. She begins with a request; she ends in prayer. Whenever we come to Jesus, we must come first with adoration of His majesty, and only then with the statement of our own need.

(iii) This woman had *indomitable persistence*. She was undiscourageable. So many people, as it has been said, pray really because they do not wish to miss a chance. They do not really believe in prayer; they have only the feeling that something might just possibly happen, and they do not wish to miss a chance. This woman came because Jesus was not just a possible helper; He was her only hope. She came with a passionate hope, a clamant sense of need, and a refusal to be discouraged. This woman had the one supremely effective quality in prayer—*she was in deadly earnest*. Prayer for her was no ritual form; it was the outpouring of the passionate desire of her soul, which somehow felt that she could not—and must not— and need not—take no for an answer.

(iv) This woman had *the gift of cheerfulness*. She was in the midst of trouble; she was passionately in earnest; and yet she could smile. She had a certain sunny-heartedness about her. God loves the cheerful faith, the faith in whose eyes there is always the light of hope, the faith with a smile which can light the gloom.

This woman brought to Christ a gallant and an audacious love, a faith which grew until it worshipped at the feet of the divine, an indomitable persistence springing from an unconquerable hope, a cheerfulness which would not be dismayed. That is the faith which cannot help finding an answer to its prayers.

THE BREAD OF LIFE

Matthew 15: 29-39

And Jesus left there, and went to the Sea of Galilee; and He went up into a mountain, and He was sitting there; and great crowds came to Him, bringing with them people who were lame and blind and deaf and maimed, and laid them at His feet, and He healed them, so that the crowd were amazed when they saw the dumb speaking, the maimed restored to soundness, and the lame walking, and the blind seeing; and they praised the God of Israel.

Jesus called His disciples to Him. " My heart is sorry for the crowd," He said, " because they have stayed with me now for three days, and they have nothing to eat. I do not wish to send them away hungry in case they collapse on the road." The disciples said to Him, " Where could we find enough loaves in a desert place to satisfy such a crowd? " Jesus said to them, " How many loaves have you? " They said, " Seven, and a few little fishes." He gave orders to the crowd to sit down on the ground, and He took the seven loaves and the fishes, and, when He had given thanks, He broke them and gave them to the disciples, and the disciples gave them to the crowds. And they gathered what remained of the fragments, seven hampers full. Those who ate were four thousand men, apart from women and children. When He had sent the crowds away, He embarked on the boat, and went to the district of Magadan.

WE nave already seen that when Jesus set out on His journey to the districts of the Phoenicians, He was entering upon a period of deliberate withdrawal and retirement that He might prepare Himself and His disciples for the last days which lay ahead. One of the difficulties about the gospels is that they do not give us any definite indication of times and dates; these we have to work out for ourselves, using such hints as the story may give us. When we do use these hints we find that Jesus' period of retiral with His disciples was very much longer than we might think from a casual reading of the story.

When Jesus fed the five thousand (*Matthew* 14: 15-21; *Mark* 6: 31-44) we read that they sat down on the *green grass* (*Matthew* 14: 19; *Mark* 6: 39). It was therefore the spring time, for at no other time would the grass be green in that hot land. After His discussions with the Scribes and Pharisees He withdrew to the districts of Tyre and Sidon (*Mark* 7: 24; *Matthew* 15: 21). That in itself was no small journey to take on foot. For the next note of time and place we must go back to *Mark*. In *Mark* 7: 31 the correct translation of the Greek is: "Departing from Tyre, He came by way of Sidon unto the Sea of Galilee, through the coasts of Decapolis." That was a strange way of travelling. Sidon is *north* of Tyre; the Sea of Galilee is *south* of Tyre; and the Decapolis was a confederation of ten Greek cities on the *east* of the Sea of Galilee. That is to say Jesus went *north* in order to go *south*. It is as if to get from one end of the base of a triangle to the other He went right round by the apex. It is as if He went from Edinburgh to Glasgow by way of Perth, or from Bristol to London by way of Manchester. It is clear that Jesus deliberately lengthened out this journey to have as long as possible with His disciples before the last journey to Jerusalem. Finally He came to the Decapolis, where, as we learn from Mark (*Mark* 7: 31; 8: 9), the incidents of our passage happened. Here we get our next hint. On this occasion when the crowd are bidden to sit down, they sit on the ground (*epi tēn gēn*), on the earth; it is by this time high summer, and the grass is scorched leaving only the bare earth. That is to say, this northern journey to Jesus took *almost six months*. We know nothing about what happened in the course of these six months; but we can be perfectly sure that they were the most important six months through which the disciples ever lived; for in them Jesus deliberately taught and instructed them, and opened their minds to the truth. It is a thing to remember that the disciples had six months apart with Jesus before the testing time came.

There are many scholars who think that the feeding of the five thousand and the feeding of the four thousand are different versions of the same incident; but that is not so. As we have seen, the date is different; the first took place in the spring, the second in the summer. The people and the place are different. The feeding of the four thousand in this passage took place in Decapolis; *Decapolis* literally means *ten cities*, and the Decapolis was a loose federation of ten free Greek cities. On this occasion there would be many Gentiles present, perhaps more Gentiles than Jews. It is that fact that explains the curious phrase in verse 31, " They glorified *the God of Israel.*" To the Gentile crowds this was a demonstration of the power of the God of Israel. There is another curious little hint of difference. In the feeding of the five thousand the baskets which were used to take up the fragments are called *kophinoi*; in the feeding of the four thousand they are called *sphurides*. The *kophinos* was a narrow-necked, flask-shaped basket which Jews often carried with them, for a Jew often carried his own food, lest he should be compelled to eat food which had been touched by Gentile hands and which was therefore unclean. The *sphuris* was much more like a hamper; it could be big enough to carry a man, and it was a kind of basket that a Gentile would use.

The wonder of this story is that in these healings, and
in this feeding of the hungry, we in fact see the mercy
and the compassion of Jesus going out to the Gentiles.
Here is a kind of symbol and foretaste that the bread of
God is not confined to the Jews; that the Gentiles were
also to have their share of Him who is the living bread.

THE GRACIOUSNESS OF JESUS

Matthew 15: 29-39 (*continued*)

IN this passage we see fully displayed the graciousness
and the sheer kindness of Jesus Christ. We see Him relieving
every kind of human need.

(i) We see Him curing physical *disability*. The lame, the
maimed, the blind and the dumb are laid at His feet and
cured. Jesus is infinitely concerned with the bodily pain
of the world; and those who bring men health and healing
are still doing the work of Jesus Christ.

(ii) We see Him concerned for the *tired*. The people
were tired and He wanted to strengthen their feet for
a long, hard road. Jesus is infinitely concerned for the
world's wayfarers, for the world's toilers, for those whose
eyes are weary and whose hands are tired.

(iii) We see Him feeding the *hungry*. We see Him giving
all He had to relieve physical hunger and physical need.
Jesus was infinitely concerned for men's bodies as He was
for their souls.

Here we see the power and the compassion of God
going out to meet the many needs of the human situation.

In writing of this passage Edersheim has a lovely thought.
He points out that at three successive stages in His ministry,
Jesus ended each stage by setting a meal before His people.
First, there was the feeding of the five thousand; that
comes at the end of His ministry in Galilee, for after
that Jesus was never to teach and preach and heal in
Galilee again. Second, there was this feeding of the four

thousand. This comes at the end of His brief ministry to the Gentiles, beyond the bounds of Palestine—first in the districts of Tyre and Sidon and then in the Decapolis. And third and last, there was the Last Supper in Jerusalem, when Jesus came to the final stage of the days of His flesh among men.

Here indeed is a lovely thought. Jesus always left men with strength for the way; always He gathered men to Him to feed them with the living bread. Always He gave them Himself before He moved on. And still He comes to us offering to us also the bread which will satisfy the immortal hunger of the human soul, and in the strength of which we shall be able to go all the days of our life.

BLIND TO THE SIGNS

Matthew 16: 1-4

> The Pharisees and Sadducees came to Him, trying to put Him to the test, and asked Him to show them a sign from Heaven. He answered them: " When evening comes, you say, ' It will be fine weather, because the sky is red.' And early in the morning you say, ' It will be stormy today, because the sky is red and threatening.' You know how to discern the face of the sky, but you cannot discern the signs of the times. An evil and apostate generation seeks for a sign. No sign will be given to it except the sign of Jonah." And He left them and went away.

HOSTILITY, like necessity, makes strange bedfellows. It is an extraordinary phenomenon to find a combination of the Pharisees and Sadducees. They stood for both beliefs and policies which were diametrically opposed. The Pharisees lived life according to the minutiae and the details of the oral and the scribal law; the Sadducees rejected the oral and the scribal law completely, and accepted only the written words of the Bible as their law of life. The Pharisees believed in angels and in the resurrection of the body and the Sadducees did not, an opposition which Paul made use of when he was on trial before the Sanhedrin (*Acts* 23: 6-10). And—in this case, most important of all—the Pharisees were not a political party; they were prepared to live under any government which would allow them to observe their own religious principles; the Sadducees were the small, wealthy aristocracy, who were the collaborationist party, and who were quite prepared to serve and co-operate with the Roman government, in order to retain their wealth and their privileges. Still further, the Pharisees looked for and longed for the Messiah; the Sadducees did not. It would have been well-nigh impossible to find two more different sects and parties; and yet they came together in their envenomed desire to eliminate Jesus. All error has this in common—that it is hostile to Christ.

The demand of the Pharisees and the Sadducees was for a sign. As we have already seen, the Jews had a way of wishing a prophet or a leader to authenticate his message by some abnormal and extraordinary sign (*Matthew* 12: 38-40). It is Jesus' reply that the sign is there, if they could only see it. They were weather-wise. They knew the same weather saying as we ourselves know:

> "A red sky at night is the shepherd's delight;
> A red sky in the morning is the shepherd's warning."

They knew very well that a red sky in the evening presaged fine weather; and that a red sky in the morning was the warning of a storm to come. But they were blind to the signs of the times.

So Jesus told them that the only sign they would receive was *the sign of Jonah*. We have already seen what the sign of Jonah was (*Matthew* 12: 38-40). Jonah was the prophet who converted the people of Nineveh, and who turned them from their evil ways towards God. Now the sign which turned the people of Nineveh to God was not the fact that Jonah was swallowed by the great sea monster. Of that they knew nothing; and Jonah never used that as a means of appeal. The sign of Jonah was

Jonah himself and his message from God. It was the emergence of the prophet and the message which he brought which changed life for the people of Nineveh.

So what Jesus is saying is that God's sign is *Jesus Himself and His message.* It is as if He said to them: " In me you are confronted with God and with the truth of God. What more could you possibly need? But you are so blind that you cannot see it." There is truth and there is warning here. Jesus Christ is God's last word. Beyond Jesus Christ the revelation of God cannot go. Here is God plain for all to see. Here is God's message plain for all to hear. Here is God's sign to man. It is the warning truth that, if Jesus cannot appeal to men, nothing can. If Jesus cannot convince men, no one can. If men cannot see God in Jesus, they cannot see God in anything or anyone. When we are confronted with Jesus Christ, we are confronted with God's last and final word, and God's ultimate appeal. And, if that is so, what can be left for the man who throws away that last chance, who refuses to listen to that last word, and who rejects that last appeal?

THE DANGEROUS LEAVEN

Matthew 16: 5-12

When the disciples came to the other side, they had forgotten to take loaves with them. Jesus said to them, " See that you beware of the leaven of the Pharisees and Sadducees." They argued amongst themselves: " He must be saying this because we did not bring loaves." Jesus knew what they were thinking. " Why," He said, " are you arguing among yourselves, you of little faith, because you have no loaves? Do you not yet understand, and do you not remember the five loaves of the five thousand, and how many baskets you took up? And do you not remember the seven loaves of the four thousand, and how many hampers you took up? How is it that you do not understand that it was not about loaves that I spoke to you? Beware of the leaven of the Pharisees

and Sadducees!" Then they understood that He
did not tell them to beware of the leaven that is in
loaves, but of the teaching of the Pharisees and
Sadducees.

WE are presented here with a passage of very great difficulty.
In fact, it is true to say that we can only guess at its meaning.

Jesus and His disciples had set out for the other side of
the lake, and the disciples had forgotten to take any
bread with them. For some reason they were quite dispro-
portionately worried and disturbed by this omission.
Jesus said to them: " See that you beware of the leaven
of the Pharisees and Sadducees." Now the word *leaven*
has two meanings. It has a physical and literal meaning.
Leaven was a little piece of fermented dough, and without
leaven in the ingredients bread cannot be baked. It was
in that sense that the disciples understood Jesus to speak
about leaven. With their minds fixed on the forgotten
loaves, all that they could think of was that He was warning
them against a certain kind of dangerous leaven. It is
quite possible that their minds ran in this way—they had
forgotten to bring bread; that meant that if they were
to obtain bread, they must buy it from the Gentiles on
the other side of the lake. Now no Jew, who was strictly
orthodox, could eat any bread which had been baked or
touched or handled by a Gentile. Therefore the problem
of getting bread on the other side of the lake was insoluble.
The disciples had forgotten to take bread; and they may
well have thought that Jesus was saying, " You have
forgotten the bread which is clean because it is Jewish
bread; take care when you get to the other side of the
lake that you do not pollute yourselves by buying bread
with defiling leaven in it."

In any event the disciples' minds were running on nothing
but bread. So Jesus asked them to remember. " Remember," He said, " the feeding of the five thousand and
of the four thousand; and remember the plenty there
was to eat, and the abundance which was left over. And

when you remember about these things, surely you will stop fussing and worrying about trifles. You have surely seen that in My presence these trifling problems have already been solved, and can be solved again. Stop worrying and trust Me."

That was put so bluntly and so clearly that the disciples were bound to understand. Then Jesus repeated His warning: " Beware of the leaven of the Pharisees and Sadducees! " Now *leaven* has a second meaning, a meaning which is metaphorical and not literal and physical. *Leaven* was the Jewish metaphorical expression for an *evil influence*. To the Jewish mind leaven was always symbolic of evil. It is fermented dough; the Jew identified fermentation with putrefaction; leaven stood for all that was rotten and evil and bad. Leaven has the power to permeate any mass of dough into which it is inserted. Therefore leaven stood for an evil influence, liable to spread through life and to corrupt it. Now the disciples understood. They knew that Jesus was not talking about bread at all; but that He was warning them against the evil influence of the teaching and the beliefs of the Pharisees and Sadducees. What would that evil influence be? What would be in Jesus' mind when He warned against the evil influence of the teaching of the Pharisees and Sadducees? That is something which we can only surmise; but we do know the characteristics of the minds of the Pharisees and Sadducees.

(i) The Pharisees saw religion in terms of laws and commandments and rules and regulations. They saw religion in terms of outward ritual and outward purity. So Jesus is saying, " Take care lest you make your religion a series of ' thou shalt nots ' in the way the Pharisees do. Take care that you do not identify religion with a series of outward actions, and forget that what matters is the state of a man's heart." This is a warning against living in legalism and calling it religion; it is a warning against a religion of externalism; to put it in modern terms, it is a warning against a religion of outward respectability, which looks on a man's outward actions and forgets the inner state of his heart.

(ii) The Sadducees had two characteristics, which are closely connected. They were wealthy and aristocratic, and they were deeply involved in politics. So Jesus may well have been saying, " Take care that you never identify the kingdom of heaven with outward goods, and that you never pin your hopes of bringing it in to political action." This may well be a warning against giving material things too high a place in our scheme of values, and against thinking that men can be reformed by political action. Jesus may well have been reminding men that material prosperity is far from being the highest good, and that political action is far from producing the most important results. The true blessings are the blessings of the heart; and the true change is not the change of outward circumstances but the change of the hearts of men.

THE SCENE OF THE GREAT DISCOVERY

Matthew 16: 13-16

> When Jesus had come into the districts of Caesarea Philippi, He asked His disciples, " Who do men say that the Son of Man is? " They said, " Some say John the Baptist, others Elijah, others Jeremiah, or one of the prophets." He said to them, " And you— who do you say that I am? " Simon Peter answered, " You are the Anointed One, the Son of the living God."

HERE we have the story of another withdrawal which Jesus made. The end was coming very near, and Jesus needed all the time alone with His disciples that He could gain. He had so much to say to them, and so much to teach them, although there were many things which then they could not bear and could not understand. To that end He withdrew to the districts of Caesarea Philippi. Caesarea Philippi lies about twenty-five miles north-east of the Sea of Galilee. It was outside the domain of Herod Antipas, who was the ruler of Galilee, and within the area of Philip the Tetrarch. The population was mainly non-Jewish, and there Jesus would have peace to teach the Twelve.

Confronting Jesus at this time was one clamant and demanding problem. His time was short; His days in the flesh were numbered. The problem was—was there anyone who understood Him? Was there anyone who had recognized Him for who and what He was? Were there any who, when He was gone from the flesh, would carry on His work, and labour for His kingdom? Obviously that was a crucial problem. To put it bluntly, it involved the very survival of the Christian faith. If there were none who had grasped the truth, or even glimpsed it, then all His work was undone; if there were some few who realized the truth, His work was safe. So Jesus was determined to put all to the test and to ask His followers who they believed Him to be.

It is of the most dramatic interest to see *where* Jesus chose to ask this question. There can have been few areas with more religious associations than Caesarea Philippi.

(i) The area was scattered with temples of the ancient Syrian Baal worship. Thomson in *The Land and the Book* enumerates no fewer than fourteen such temples in the near neighbourhood. Here was an area where the very breath of ancient religion breathed in the very air and atmosphere. Here was a place beneath the shadow of the ancient gods.

(ii) Not only the Syrian gods had their worship here. Hard by Caesarea Philippi there rose a great hill, and in it was a deep cavern; and that cavern was said to be the birthplace of the great god Pan, the god of nature. So much was Caesarea Philippi identified with that god that its original name was Panias, and to this day the place is known as Banias. The legends of the gods of Greece gathered around Caesarea Philippi.

(iii) Still further, that cave was said to be the place where the sources of the Jordan sprang to life. Josephus writes: "This is a very fine cave in a mountain, under which there is a great cavity in the earth; and the cavern is abrupt, and prodigiously deep, and full of still water. Over it hangs a vast mountain, and under the cavern arise the springs of the River Jordan." The very idea that this was the place where the River Jordan took its rise would make it redolent of all the history and the memories of Jewish story. The ancient faith of Judaism would be in the air for anyone who was a devout and pious Jew.

(iv) But there was something more. In Caesarea Philippi there was a great temple of white marble built to the godhead of Ceasar. It had been built by Herod the Great. Josephus says: "Herod adorned the place, which was already a very remarkable one, still further by the erection of this temple, which he dedicated to Caesar." In another place Josephus describes the cave and the temple: "And when Ceasar had further bestowed on Herod another country, he built there also a temple of white marble, hard by the fountains of Jordan. The place is called Panium, where there is the top of a mountain which is raised to an immense height, and at its side, beneath, or at its bottom, a dark cave opens itself; within which there is a horrible precipice that descends abruptly to a vast depth. It contains a mighty quantity of water, which is immovable; and when anyone lets down anything to measure the depth of the earth beneath the water, no length of cord is sufficient to reach it." So Herod had built the great white temple to the godhead of Caesar. Later it was Philip, Herod's son, who still further beautified and enriched the temple, and changed the name of Panias to Caesarea—Caesar's town—and added his own name— *Philippi*, which means *of Philip*—to distinguish it from the Caesarea on the coasts of the Mediterranean. Still later, in days still to come, Herod Agrippa was to call the place

Neroneas in honour of the Emperor Nero. No one could look at Caesarea Philippi, even from the distance, without seeing that pile of glistening marble, and thinking of the might and of the divinity of Rome.

Here then indeed is a dramatic picture. Here is a homeless, penniless Galilaean carpenter, with twelve very ordinary men around Him. At the moment the orthodox people of His day are actually plotting and planning to eliminate and to destroy Him as a dangerous heretic. He stands in an area littered with the temples of the Syrian gods; in a place where the ancient Greek gods looked down; in a place where the history of Israel crowded in upon the minds of men; where the white marble splendour of the home of Caesar-worship dominated the landscape and compelled the eye. And there—of all places—this amazing carpenter stands, and asks men who they believe Him to be, and expects the answer, The Son of God. It is as if Jesus deliberately set Himself against the background of the world's religions in all their history and their splendour, and demanded to be compared with them, and to have the verdict given in His favour. There are few scenes where Jesus' consciousness of His own divinity shines out with a more dazzling light.

THE INADEQUACY OF HUMAN CATEGORIES

Matthew 16: 13-16 (*continued*)

So then at Caesarea Philippi Jesus determined to demand a verdict from His disciples. He must know before He sets out for Jerusalem and for the Cross if anyone has even dimly grasped who and what He is. He did not ask the question directly; He led up to it. He began by asking what people were saying about Him, and who they took Him to be.

Some said that He was John the Baptist. Herod Antipas was not the only man who felt that John the Baptist was so great a figure that it might well be that he had come back from the dead.

Others said that He was Elijah. In doing so, they were saying two things about Jesus. They were saying that He was as great as the greatest of the prophets, for Elijah had always been looked on as the summit and the peak and the prince of the prophetic line. They were also saying that Jesus was the forerunner of the Messiah. As *Malachi* had it, the promise of God was: " Behold, I will send you Elijah the prophet before the coming of the great and dreadful day of the Lord " (*Malachi* 4: 5). To this day the Jews expect the return of Elijah before the coming of the Messiah, and to this day they leave a chair vacant for Elijah when they celebrate the Passover, for when Elijah comes, the Messiah will not be far away. So the people looked on Jesus as the herald of the Messiah and the forerunner of the direct intervention of God.

Some said that Jesus was Jeremiah. Jeremiah had a curious place in the expectations of the people of Israel. It was believed that, before the people went into exile, Jeremiah had taken the ark and the altar of incense out of the Temple, and had hidden them away in a lonely cave on Mount Nebo, and that, before the coming of the Messiah, he would return and produce them, and the glory of God would come to the people again (2 *Maccabees* 2: 1-12). In 2 *Esdras* 2: 18 the promise of God is: " For thy help I will send my servants Isaiah and Jeremiah." There is a strange legend of the days of the Maccabaean wars. Before the battle with Nicanor, in which the Jewish commander was the great Judas Maccabaeus, Onias, the good man who had been high priest, had a vision. He prayed for victory in the battle. " This done, in like manner there appeared a man with grey hairs, and exceeding glorious, who was of a wonderful and excellent majesty. Then Onias answered saying: ' This is a lover of the brethren, who prayeth much for the people, and for the holy city, to wit, Jeremiah, the prophet of God.' Whereupon

Jeremiah, holding forth his right hand, gave to Judas a sword of gold, and, in giving it to him, spake thus: ' Take this holy sword, a gift from God, with which thou shalt wound the adversaries of my people Israel ' " (2 *Maccabees* 15: 1-14). Jeremiah also was to be the forerunner of the coming of the Messiah, and his country's help in time of trouble.

When the people identified Jesus with Elijah and with Jeremiah they were, according to their lights, paying Him a great compliment, and setting Him in a high place, for Jeremiah and Elijah were none other than the expected forerunners of the Anointed One of God. When they arrived the Kingdom would be very near indeed.

So then, when Jesus has heard the verdicts of the crowd, He asks the all-important question: " And *you*—who do you say that I am? " At that question there may well have been a moment's silence, while into the minds of the disciples there came thoughts which they were almost afraid to express in words; and then Peter makes his great discovery and his great confession; and Jesus knows that His work is safe because there is at least someone who understands.

It is interesting to note that each of the three gospels has its own version of the saying of Peter. *Matthew* has:

Thou art the Christ, the Son of the living God.

Mark is briefest of all (*Mark* 8: 29):

Thou art the Christ.

Luke is clearest of all (*Luke* 9: 20):

Thou art the Christ of God.

Jesus knew now that there was at least someone who had recognized Him for the Messiah, the Anointed One of God, the Son of the living God. The word *Messiah* and the word *Christ* are the same word; the one is the Hebrew and the other is the Greek for *The Anointed One*. Kings were ordained to office by anointing, as they still are. The Messiah, the Christ, the Anointed One is God's Divine King over men.

Within this passage there are two great truths.

(i) Essentially Peter's discovery was that human categories, even the highest human categories, are inadequate to describe Jesus Christ. When the people described Jesus as Elijah or Jeremiah or one of the prophets they thought that they were setting Jesus in the highest category that they could find. Elijah was the forerunner whom all men expected; Jeremiah also had his place in the divine kingdom, and was the destined helper of God's people in the day of trouble. It was the belief of the Jews that for four hundred years the voice of prophecy had been silent; and they were saying that in Jesus men heard again the direct and authentic voice of God. These are great tributes; but they are not great enough; for there are no human categories and descriptions and classifications which are adequate to describe Jesus Christ. Once Napoleon gave his verdict on Jesus. " I know men," said Napoleon, " and Jesus Christ is more than a man." Doubtless Peter could not have given a theological account and a philosophic expression of what he meant when he said that Jesus was the Son of the living God; the one thing of which Peter was quite certain was that no merely human description was adequate to describe Jesus Christ.

(ii) This passage teaches us that our discovery of Jesus Christ must be a *personal discovery*. Jesus' question is: " *You*—what do *you* think of Me? " When Pilate asked Jesus if He was the king of the Jews, Jesus' answer was: " Sayest thou this thing of thyself, or did others tell it thee of Me? " (*John* 18: 33, 34). Our knowledge of Jesus can never be at second hand. A man might know every verdict that had ever been passed on Jesus; he might know every Christology that the mind of man had ever thought out; he might be able to give a competent summary of the teaching about Jesus of every great thinker and theologian—and still not be a Christian. Christianity never consists in *knowing about* Jesus; it always consists in *knowing Jesus*. Jesus Christ demands a personal verdict.

He did not only ask Peter, He asks every man: " *You*—
what do *you* think of Me? "

THE GREAT PROMISE

Matthew 16: 17-19

> Jesus answered him, " Blessed are you, Simon son
> of Jonah, because flesh and blood has not revealed
> this unto you, but my Father who is in Heaven.
> And I tell you, that you are Peter, and on this rock
> I will build my Church, and the gates of Hades will
> not prevail against it. I will give you the keys of the
> Kingdom of Heaven; and whatever you bind on
> earth will remain bound in heaven; and whatever
> you loose on earth will remain loosed in heaven."

THIS passage is one of the storm-centres of New Testament
interpretation. It has always been difficult to approach
it calmly and without prejudice, for this passage is the
Roman Catholic foundation of the position of the Pope
and of the Church. It is taken by the Roman Catholic
Church to mean that to Peter were given the keys which
admit or exclude a man from heaven, and that to Peter
was given the power to absolve or not to absolve a man
from his sins. It is further argued by the Roman Catholic
Church that Peter, with these tremendous rights, became
the bishop of Rome; and that this power descended to all
the bishops of Rome; and exists today in the Pope, who
is the head of the Church and the Bishop of Rome. It is
easy to see how impossible any such doctrine is for a
Protestant believer; and it is also easy to see how both
Protestant and Roman Catholic alike will approach this
passage, not with the single-hearted desire to discover its
meaning, but with the determination to yield nothing of
their own position, and, if possible, to destroy the position
of the other. Let us then try to find the meaning of this
passage.

In it there is a play on words. In Greek *Peter* is *Petros*
and a *rock* is *petra*. Peter's Aramaic name was *Kephas,*

and that also is the Aramaic for a *rock*. In either language there is here a play upon words. Immediately Peter had made his great discovery and confession, Jesus said to him: " You are *Petros*, and on this *petra* I will build my Church."

We must begin by noting that, whatever else this is, it is a word of tremendous praise. Nor is it a metaphor which is by any means strange or unusual to Jewish thought. The Rabbis applied the word *rock* to Abraham. They had a saying: " When the Holy One saw Abraham who was going to arise, He said, ' Lo, I have discovered a rock (*petra*) to found the world upon.' Therefore he called Abraham *rock* (*sur*), as it is said: ' Look unto the rock whence ye are hewn.' " Abraham was the rock on which the nation and the purpose of God were founded. Even more the word *rock* (*sur*) is again and again applied to God Himself. " He is the Rock; His work is perfect " (*Deuteronomy* 32: 4). " For their rock is not as our Rock " (*Deuteronomy* 32: 31). " Neither is there any rock like our God " (1 *Samuel* 2: 2). " The Lord is my rock, and my fortress, and my deliverer " (2 *Samuel* 22: 2). The same phrase occurs in *Psalm* 18: 2. " Who is a rock save our God? " (*Psalm* 18: 31). The same phrase is in 2 *Samuel* 22: 32. One thing is clear. That to call anyone a *rock* is the greatest of compliments; and it is also clear that no Jew, who knew his Old Testament, could ever use the phrase without his thoughts turning to God, who alone was the true rock of his defence and salvation. What then did Jesus mean when in this passage He used the word *rock*? To that question at least four answers have been given.

(i) Augustine took the *rock* to mean *Jesus Himself*. It is as if Jesus said: " You are Peter; and on myself as rock I will found my Church; and the day will come when, as the reward of your faith, you will be great in the Church."

(ii) The second explanation is that the rock is the truth that Jesus Christ is the Son of the living God. To Peter that great truth had been divinely revealed. It was God

Himself who had opened Peter's eyes to that great discovery. The fact that Jesus Christ is the Son of God is indeed the foundation stone of the Church's faith and belief. On that great truth the Church is founded for ever and for ever. This explanation holds that the divinely revealed truth that Jesus is the Son of God is the only foundation on which the Church is founded. That is undoubtedly true but it hardly seems to bring out the play on words which is here.

(iii) The third explanation is that the rock is Peter's faith. On the faith of Peter the Church is founded. It was that faith of Peter which was the spark which was to kindle the faith of the whole world-wide Church. Peter's faith was the initial impetus which was one day to bring the universal Church into being.

(iv) We come to the last interpretation, and it is still the best. It is that Peter himself is the rock, but in a special sense. He is not the rock on which the Church is founded; that rock is God. He is the first initial foundation stone of the whole Church. Peter was the first man on earth to discover who Jesus was; he was the first man to make the leap of faith which saw in Jesus Christ the Son of the living God. In other words, Peter was the first member of the Church, and, in that sense, the whole Church is built on him. Here is the meaning. It is as if Jesus said to Peter: " Peter, you are the first man to grasp who I am; you are therefore the first stone, the foundation stone, the very beginning of the Church which I am founding." And in ages to come, everyone who makes the same discovery as Peter is another and another stone added into the edifice of the Church of Christ.

Let us note two things which help to make this clear.

(i) Often the Bible uses pictures for the sake of one definite point. The details of the picture are not to be stressed; it is one point which is being made. Now in connection with the Church the New Testament repeatedly uses the picture of *building*, but it uses that picture for many purposes and from many points of view. Here Peter is the foundation, in the sense that he is the one person on whom the whole Church is built, for he was the first man to discover who Jesus was. In *Ephesians* 2: 20 the prophets and the apostles are said to be the foundation of the Church. It is on their work and on their witness and on their fidelity that the Church on earth, humanly speaking, depends. In the same passage, Jesus Christ is the chief *corner-stone*; He is the power and the force who holds the Church together. Without Him the whole edifice would disintegrate and collapse. In I *Peter* 2: 4-8 all Christians are living stones who are to be built into the fabric of the Church. In I *Corinthians* 3: 11 Jesus is the only foundation, and no man can lay any other. It is clear to see that the New Testament writers took the picture of *building* and used it in many ways. But at the back of it all there is always the idea that Jesus Christ is the real foundation of the Church, and the only power who holds the Church together. When Jesus said to Peter that on him He would found His Church, He did not mean that the Church *depended* on Peter, as it depended on Himself, and on God the Rock, alone. He did mean that the Church *began* with Peter; in that sense Peter is the foundation of the Church; and that is an honour that no man can take from him.

(ii) The second point to be made is that the very word *Church* (*ekklēsia*) in this passage conveys something of a wrong impression. When we hear the word Church we are apt to think of our own Church; or at least we are apt to think of the Church as an institution and an organization with buildings and offices, and services and meetings, and organizations and all kinds of activities. Now the word that Jesus almost certainly used was *quahal*, which is the word which the Old Testament uses for *the congregation of Israel*, the gathering of the people of the Lord. What Jesus said to Peter was: " Peter, you are the beginning of the new Israel, the new people of the Lord, the new fellowship of those who believe in my name." Peter was the first of the fellowship of believers in Christ. It is not a Church in the human sense, still less a Church in an denominational sense, that began with Peter. What began with Peter was the fellowship of all believers in Jesus Christ, which is not identified with any Church, and which is not limited to any Church, but which embraces all those in all Churches who love the Lord.

So then we may say that the first part of this so controversial passage means that Peter is the foundation stone of the Church in the sense that he was the first of that great fellowship who joyfully declare their own discovery that Jesus Christ is Lord; but that in the ultimate sense, it is God Himself who is the rock on which the Church is built.

THE GATES OF HELL

Matthew 16: 17-19 (continued)

JESUS goes on to say that the gates of hell shall not prevail against His Church. What does that mean? The idea of *gates prevailing* is not by any means a natural or an easily understood picture. Again there is more than one explanation.

(i) It may be that the picture is the picture of a *fortress*. That picture might be helped by the fact that on the top of the mountain overlooking Caesarea Philippi there stand today the ruins of a great castle which may well have stood there in all its glory in the time of Jesus. It may be that Jesus is thinking of His Church as a fortress, and the forces of evil as an opposing fortress; and is saying that the embattled might of evil will never prevail against the Church.

(ii) Richard Glover has an interesting explanation of this phrase. In the ancient east the *Gate* was always the place, especially in the little towns and villages, where the elders and the rulers met and dispensed counsel and justice. For instance, the law is laid down that, if a man has a rebellious and disobedient son, he must bring him " unto the elders of the city, and unto the *gate* of his place " (*Deuteronomy* 21: 19), and there judgment will be given and justice done. In *Deuteronomy* 25: 7 the man with a certain problem is told to " go up unto the gate to the elders." The gate was the scene of simple justice where the elders met. So it came to be that the expression *the gate* may have come to mean *the place of government*. For long, for instance, the government of Turkey was called the *Sublime Porte* (*Porte* is the French for *gate*). So then the phrase would mean: The powers, the government of Hades will never prevail against the Church.

(iii) There is a third possibility. Suppose we go back to the idea that the rock on which the Church is founded is the belief and the faith and the conviction that Jesus is none other than the Son of the living God. Now in any event this phrase is *not* the gates of *hell*; it is the gates of *Hades*; and Hades was not the place of punishment, but the place where, in primitive Jewish belief, all the dead went. Obviously, the function of gates is *to keep things in*, to confine them, shut them up, control them. There was one person whom the gates of Hades could not shut in; and that one person was Jesus Christ. He burst the bonds of death. As the writer of *Acts* has it, " It was not possible that He should be holden of death. . . . Thou wilt not leave my soul in Hades, nor suffer Thine Holy One to see corruption " (*Acts* 2: 24, 27). So then this may be a triumphant reference to nothing less than the coming Resurrection. Jesus may be saying: " You have discovered that I am the Son of the living God. The time will soon come when I will be crucified, and the gates of Hades will close behind me. But they are powerless to shut me in. The gates of Hades have no power against me the Son of the living God."

However we take it, this phrase triumphantly expresses the indestructibility of Christ and His Church.

THE PLACE OF PETER

Matthew 16: 17-19 (*continued*)

WE now come to two phrases in which Jesus describes certain privileges which were given to, and certain duties which were laid on Peter.

(i) Jesus says that He will give to Peter *the keys of the Kingdom.* This is an obviously difficult phrase; and we will do well to begin by setting down the things about it of which we can be sure.

(*a*) The phrase always signified some kind of very special power. For instance, the Rabbis had a saying: " The keys of birth, of the rain, and of the resurrection of the dead belong to God." That is to say, only God has the power to create life, to send the rain, and to raise the dead to life again. The phrase always indicates a special and unique power.

(*b*) In actual usage in the New Testament, this phrase is regularly attached to Jesus. It is in His hands, and in no one else's, that the keys are. In *Revelation* 1: 8 the risen Christ says: " I am He that liveth and was dead; and, behold, I am alive for evermore, Amen; and have *the keys* of Hades and of death." Again in *Revelation* 3: 7 the Risen Christ is described as, " He that is holy, He that is true, He that hath *the key of David*, He that openeth and no man shutteth; and shutteth and no man openeth." It is clear that this phrase must be interpreted as indicating a certain divine right, and whatever the promise made to Peter was, that promise cannot be taken as annulling, or infringing, a right which belongs alone to God and to the Son of God.

(*c*) All these New Testament pictures and usages go back to a picture in *Isaiah* (*Isaiah* 22: 22). In that picture

Isaiah describes Eliakim, who will have the key of the house of David on his shoulder, and who alone will open and shut. Now the duty of Eliakim was to be *the faithful steward of the house*. It is the steward who carries the keys of the house, who in the morning opens the door, and in the evening shuts it, and through whom visitors gain access to the royal presence. So then what Jesus is saying to Peter is that in the days to come, Peter will be *the steward of the Kingdom*. And in the case of Peter the whole idea is that of *opening*, not shutting, the door of the Kingdom. And indeed that came abundantly true. At Pentecost, Peter, the steward of the Kingdom, opened the door to three thousand souls (*Acts* 2: 41). He opened the door to the Gentile centurion Cornelius, so that the door of the Kingdom was swinging on its hinges to admit the great Gentile world (*Acts* 10). *Acts* 15 tells how the Council of Jerusalem opened wide the door for the Gentiles, and how it was Peter's witness which made that possible (*Acts* 15: 14; *Simeon* is *Peter*). The promise that Peter would have the keys to the Kingdom was the promise that Peter would be the means of opening the door to God for thousands upon thousands of people in the days to come. The plain fact is that it is not only Peter who has the keys of the Kingdom; every Christian has; for it is open to every one of us to open the door of the Kingdom to some one, and to enter into the great promise of Jesus Christ.

(ii) Jesus further promised Peter that what he *bound* would remain *bound*, and what he *loosed* would remain *loosed*. Richard Glover takes it to mean that Peter would lay men's sins, bind them, to men's consciences, and that then he would loose them from their sins by telling them of the divine love and the divine forgiveness of God. That is a lovely thought, and no doubt true, for such is the duty of every Christian preacher and teacher, but there is more to it than that. *To loose* and *to bind* were very common Jewish phrases. They were used especially of the decisions of the great teachers and the great Rabbis.

Their regular sense, which any Jew would recognize was *to allow* and *to forbid*; to *bind* something was *to declare it forbidden* ; to *loose something* was *to declare it allowed*. These were the regular phrases for taking decisions in regard to the law. That is in fact the only thing these phrases in such a context would mean. So what Jesus is saying to Peter is: " Peter, you are going to have grave and heavy responsibilities laid upon you. You are going to have to take decisions which will affect the welfare of the whole Church. In the days to come the administration of the Church will fall upon you. You will be the guide and the director of the infant Church. And the decisions you give will be so important, that they will affect the souls of men in time and in eternity." The privilege of the keys meant that Peter would be the steward of the household of God, opening the door for men to enter into the Kingdom. The duty of binding and loosing meant that Peter would have to take decisions about the Church's life and practice which would have the most far-reaching consequences. And indeed, when we read the early chapters of *Acts*, we see that in Jerusalem that is precisely what Peter did, for Peter was true to the duty and the task and the privilege that were laid upon him.

So now let us paraphrase this passage which has caused so much argument and controversy, and when we do, we will see that it deals, not with ecclesiastical forms and with the things of Churches, but with the things of salvation. Jesus said to Peter: " Peter, your name means a rock, and your destiny is to be a rock. You are the first man to recognize me for what I am, and therefore you are the first stone in the edifice of the fellowship of those who are mine. Against that fellowship the embattled powers of evil will no more prevail than they will be able to hold me captive in death. And in the days to come, you must be the steward who will unlock the doors of the Kingdom that Jew and Gentile may come in; and you must be the wise administrator and guide who will solve the problems and

direct the work of the infant and the growing fellowship."
Peter had made the great discovery; and Peter was given
the great privilege and the great responsibility. It is a
discovery which everyone must make for himself; and,
when he has made it, the same privilege and the same
responsibility are laid upon him.

THE GREAT REBUKE

Matthew 16: 20-23

> He gave orders to His disciples to tell no one that He
> was God's Anointed One. From that time Jesus
> began to show His disciples that He must go to Jeru-
> salem, and suffer many things from the elders and
> chief priests and scribes, and be killed and be raised
> on the third day. Peter caught hold of Him, and began
> to urge upon Him: " God forbid that this should
> happen to you! This must never come to you! "
> He turned and said to Peter, " Get behind me, Satan!
> You are putting a stumbling-block in my way. Your
> ideas are not God's but men's."

ALTHOUGH the disciples had grasped the fact that Jesus
was God's Messiah, they still had not grasped what that
great fact meant. To them it meant something totally
different from what it meant to Jesus. They were still
thinking in terms of a conquering Messiah, a warrior
king, who would sweep the Romans from Palestine and
lead Israel to power. That is why Jesus commanded them
to silence. If they had gone out to the people and had
preached their own ideas, all that they would have succeeded
in doing would have been to raise a tragic rebellion and
revolution; they could only have produced another out-
break of violence, doomed to disaster. Before they could
preach that Jesus was the Messiah, they had to learn what
that great fact meant. In point of fact, Peter's reaction
shows just how far the disciples were from realizing just
what Jesus meant when He claimed to be the Messiah and
the Son of God.

So Jesus began to seek to open their eyes to the fact that for Him there was no way but the way of the Cross. He said that He must go to Jerusalem and suffer at the hands of the " elders and chief priests and scribes." These three groups of men were in fact the three groups of which the Sanhedrin was composed. The elders were the respected men of the people; the chief priests were predominantly Sadducees; and the scribes were Pharisees. In effect, Jesus is saying that He must suffer at the hands of the Sanhedrin and of the orthodox religious leaders of the country. No sooner had Jesus said that than Peter reacted with violence. Peter had been brought up and nurtured on the idea of a Messiah of power and glory and conquest. To him the idea of a suffering Messiah, the connection of a cross with the work of the Messiah, were incredible. He " caught hold " of Jesus. Almost certainly the meaning is that he flung a protecting arm round Jesus, as if to hold Him back from a suicidal course. " This," said Peter, " must not and cannot happen to you." And then there came the great rebuke which makes us catch our breath when we hear it—" Get behind me, Satan! " There are certain things which we must understand to understand this tragic and dramatic scene.

We must try to catch the tone of voice in which Jesus said this. He certainly did not say it with a snarl of anger in His voice and a blaze of indignant passion in His eyes. He said it like a man wounded to the heart, with a poignant grief, with a kind of shuddering horror. Why should Jesus react like that?

Jesus reacted like that because in that moment there came back to Him with cruel force the temptations which He had already faced in the wilderness at the beginning of His ministry. Right at the beginning, He had been tempted to take the way of power. " Give them bread, give them material things," said the tempter, " and they will follow you." " Give them sensations," said the tempter, " give them wonders, and they will follow you."

" Compromise with the world," said the tempter. " Reduce your standards, and meet the world half way, and they will follow you." It was precisely the same temptations with which Peter was confronting Jesus all over again. Nor were these temptations ever wholly absent from the mind of Jesus. Luke sees far into the heart of the Master. At the end of the temptation story, Luke writes: " And when the devil had ended all the temptation, he departed from Him *for a season* " (*Luke* 4: 13). Again and again the tempter launched this attack. No one wants a cross; no one wants to die in agony; even in the Garden that same temptation came to Jesus, the temptation to take another way; and here Peter is offering it to Him now. The sharpness, and the poignancy of Jesus' answer is due to the fact that Peter was urging upon Him the very things which the tempter was always whispering to Him, the very things against which He had to steel Himself; Peter was confronting Jesus with that way of escape from the Cross which to the end beckoned to Him.

That is why Peter was *Satan*. *Satan* literally means *the Adversary*. That is why Peter's ideas were not God's but men's. Satan is any force which seeks to deflect us from the way of God; Satan is any influence which seeks to make us turn back from the hard way that God has set before us; Satan is any power who seeks to make human desires take the place of the divine imperative.

And what made the temptation more acute and severe was the fact that it came from one who loved Him. Peter spoke as he did speak only because he loved Jesus so much that he could not bear to think of Jesus treading that dreadful path and dying that awful death. The hardest temptation of all is the temptation which comes from protecting love. There are times when fond love seeks to deflect us from the perils of the path of God; but the real love is not the love which holds the knight at home, when he should go out to battle, but the love which sends him out to obey the commandments of the chivalry which is given, not to make life easy, but to make life great. It is quite possible for love to be so protecting that it seeks to protect those it loves from the adventure of the warfare of the soldier of Christ, and from the strenuousness of the pathway of the pilgrim of God. That which really wounded Jesus' heart, and that which made Him speak as He did speak, was that the tempter spoke to Him that day through the fond but mistaken love of Peter's hot heart.

THE CHALLENGE BEHIND THE REBUKE

Matthew 16: 20-23 (continued)

BEFORE we leave this passage, it is interesting to look at two very early interpretations of the phrase: " Get behind me, Satan! " Origen suggested that, when Jesus said this, He was saying to Peter: " Peter, your place is *behind* me, not *in front* of me. It is your place *to follow* me in the way I choose, not to try *to lead* me in the way in which you would like me to go." If the phrase can be interpreted in that way, something at least of its sting is removed, for it does not banish Peter from Christ's presence; rather it recalls him to his proper place, as a follower walking in the footsteps of Jesus. It is true for all of us that we must ever take the way of Christ, and we must never seek to compel Christ to take the way of ourselves.

A further development of that comes when we closely examine this saying of Jesus in the light of His saying to Satan at the end of the temptations as Matthew tells it in *Matthew* 4: 10. Although in the English translations the two passages sound different they are almost, but not quite, the same. In *Matthew* 4: 10 the Authorized Version translates: " Get thee hence, Satan! " which in Greek is: " *Hupage Satana.*" (The final e of *hupage* is pronounced as the e in *the*, and the g is hard as in *get*). In the Authorized Version translation, Jesus says to Peter: " Get thee behind me, Satan," which in Greek is: " *Hupage opiso mou, Satana.*" Now the point is that Jesus' command to Satan is simply: " Begone! " while His command to Peter is: " Begone *behind me!* " that is to say, " Become my follower again." Satan is banished from the presence of Christ; Peter is recalled to be Christ's follower. The one thing that Satan could never become is a follower of Christ; in his diabolical pride he could never submit to that; that is why he is Satan. On the other hand, Peter might be mistaken and might fall and migh. sin, but for him there was always the challenge and the chance to become a follower again. It is as if Jesus said to Peter: " At the moment you have spoken as Satan would. But that is not the real Peter speaking. You can redeem yourself. Come behind me, and be my follower again, and even yet, all will be well." The basic difference between Peter and Satan is precisely the fact that Satan would never get behind Jesus. So long as man is prepared to try to follow, even after he has fallen, there is still for him the hope of glory here and hereafter.

THE GREAT CHALLENGE

Matthew 16: 24-26

> Then Jesus said to His disciples: " If anyone wishes to come after me, let him deny himself, and take up his cross, and let him follow me. For whoever wishes to keep his life safe, will lose it; and whoever loses his life for my sake, will find it. For what shall a man be profited if he shall gain the whole world at the penalty of the price of his life? Or what will a man give in exchange for his life? "

HERE we have one of the dominant and ever-recurring themes of Jesus' teaching. These are things which Jesus said to men again and again (*Matthew* 10: 37-39; *Mark* 8: 34-37; *Luke* 9: 23-27; 14: 25-27; 17: 33; *John* 12: 25). Again and again Jesus confronted men with the challenge of the Christian life. There are three things which a man must be prepared to do, if he is to live the Christian life.

(i) He must *deny himself.* Ordinarily we use the word *self-denial* in a restricted sense. We use it to mean doing without something, giving up something. For instance, a week of self-denial is a week when we do without certain pleasures or luxuries, usually in order to contribute to some good cause. But that is only a very small part of what Jesus meant by self-denial. To deny oneself means in every moment of life to say no to self, and to say yes to God. To deny oneself means once, finally and for all to dethrone self and to enthrone God. To deny oneself means to obliterate self as the dominant principle of life, and to make God the ruling principle, more, the ruling passion, of life. The life of constant self-denial is the life of constant assent to God.

(ii) He must *take up his cross.* That is to say, he must take up the burden of sacrifice. The Christian life is the life of sacrificial service. The Christian may have to abandon personal ambition to serve Christ; it may be that he will discover that the place where he can render the greatest service to Jesus Christ is somewhere where the reward will be small and where the prestige will be non-existent. He will certainly have to sacrifice time and leisure and pleasure in order to serve God through the service of his fellow-men. To put it quite simply, the comfort of the fireside, the pleasure of a visit to a place of entertainment, may well have to be sacrificed for the duties of the eldership, the calls of the youth club, the visit to the home of some sad or lonely soul. He may well have to sacrifice certain things he could well afford to possess in order to give more away. The Christian life is the sacrificial life. Luke, with a flash of sheer insight, adds one word to this command of Jesus: " Let him take up his cross *daily.*" The really important thing is not the great moments of sacrifice, but a life lived in the constant hourly awareness of the demands of God and the needs of others. The Christian life is a life which is always concerned with others more than it is concerned with itself.

(iii) He must *follow Jesus Christ*. That is to say, he must render to Jesus Christ a perfect obedience. When we were young we used to play a game called " Follow my Leader." Everything the leader did, however difficult, and, in the case of the game, however ridiculous, we had to copy. The Christian life is a constant following of our leader, a constant obedience, in thought and word and action to Jesus Christ. The Christian walks in the footsteps of Christ, wherever Christ may lead.

LOSING AND FINDING LIFE
Matthew 16: 24-26 (continued)

THERE is in this world all the difference in the world between *existing* and *living*. To exist is simply to have the lungs breathing and the heart beating; to live is to live in a world where everything is worth while, where there is peace in the soul, joy in the heart, and a thrill in every moment. Jesus here gives us the recipe for *life* as distinct from *existence*.

(i) The man who plays for safety loses life. Matthew was writing somewhere between A.D. 80 and 90. He was therefore writing in some of the bitterest days of persecution. He was saying: " The time may well come when you can save your life by abandoning your faith; but if you do, so far from saving life in the real sense of the term you are losing life." The man who is faithful may die but he dies to live; the man who abandons his faith for safety may live, but he lives to die. In our day and generation it is not a question of martyrdom, but it still remains a fact that, if we meet life with the constant search for safety, security, ease and comfort, if every decision is taken from worldly-wise and prudential motives, we are losing all that makes life worth while. Life becomes a soft and flabby thing, when it might have been an adventure. Life becomes a selfish thing, when it might have been radiant with service. Life becomes an earthbound thing, when it might have been for ever reaching for the stars. Someone once wrote a bitter epitaph on a man: " He was born a man and died a grocer." Any trade or profession might be substituted for the word grocer. The man who plays for safety ceases to be a man, for man is made in the image of God.

(ii) The man who risks all—and maybe looks as if he had lost all—for Christ finds life. It is the simple lesson of all history that it has always been the adventurous souls who bade farewell to security and safety who wrote their names on history and who greatly helped the world of men. Unless there were those who had been prepared to take risks, many a medical cure would not exist. Unless there were those who had been prepared to take risks many of the machines which make life easier would never have been invented. Unless there were mothers who were prepared to take risks, no child would ever be born. It is the man who is prepared " to bet his life that there is a God " who in the end finds life.

(iii) Then Jesus speaks with warning: " Suppose a man plays for safety; suppose he gains the whole world; then suppose that he finds that life is not worth living, what can he give to get life back again? " And the grim truth is that we cannot get life back again. In every decision of life we are doing something to ourselves; we are making ourselves a certain kind of person; we are building up steadily and inevitably a certain kind of self and character; we are making ourselves able to do certain things and quite unable to do others. It is perfectly possible for a man to gain all the things he set his heart upon, and then to awaken one morning to find that he has missed the most important things of all. The *world* stands for material things as opposed to God. And of all material things there are three things to be said. (*a*) No one can take them with him at the end; he can only take himself; and if he degraded himself in order to get them, then his regret will be bitter. (b) They cannot help a man in the shattering days of life. Material things will never mend a broken heart or cheer a lonely soul. (c) If by any chance a man gained his material possessions in a way that is dishonourable, there will come a day when conscience will speak, and a man will know his hell on this side of the grave.

The world is full of voices crying out that that man is a fool who sells real life for material things.

(iv) Finally Jesus asks: " What will a man give in exchange for his soul? " The Greek is, " What *antallagma* will a man give for his soul? " This word *antallagma* is an interesting word. In the book of *Ecclesiasticus* we read: " There is no *antallagma* for a faithful friend," and, " There is no *antallagma* for a disciplined soul " (*Ecclesiasticus* 6: 15; 26: 14). It means that there is no price which will buy a faithful friend or a disciplined soul. So then this final saying of Jesus can mean two things.

(a) It can mean: Once a man has lost his real life, because of his desire for security and for material things, there is no price that he can pay to get it back again. He has done something to himself which cannot ever be fully obliterated.

(b) It can mean: A man owes himself and everything else to Jesus Christ; and there is nothing that a man can give to Christ in place of his life. It is quite possible for a man to try to give his money to Christ, and yet to withhold his life. It is still more possible for a man to give lip-service to Christ, and to withhold his life. Many a person gives his weekly freewill offering to the Church, but does not go to Church; obviously that does not satisfy the demands of Church membership. The only possible gift to the Church is ourselves; and the only possible gift to Christ is our whole life. There is no substitute for it, and nothing less will do.

THE WARNING AND THE PROMISE

Matthew 16: 27, 28

" For the Son of Man will come with the glory of His Father, with His angels, and then He will render to each man in accordance with his way of action. This is the truth I tell you—there are some of those who are standing here who will not taste death, until they see the Son of Man coming in His Kingdom."

THIS passage falls into two quite distinct sayings.

(i) The first saying is a *warning*. It is the warning of inevitable judgment. Life is going somewhere—and life is going to judgment. In any sphere of life there inevitably comes the day of reckoning. There is no escape from the fact that Christianity teaches that after life there comes the judgment; and when we take this passage in conjunction with the passage which goes before, we see at once what the standard of judgment is. The man who selfishly hugs life to himself, the man whose first concern is his own safety, his own security and his own comfort, is in heaven's eyes the failure, however rich and successful and prosperous he may seem to be. The man who spends himself for others, and who lives life as a gallant adventure is the man who receives heaven's praise and God's reward.

(ii) The second saying is a *promise*. As Matthew records this phrase, it reads as if Jesus spoke as if He expected His own visible return in the lifetime of some of those who were listening to Him. If Jesus said that He was mistaken. But we see the real meaning of what Jesus said when we turn to Mark's record of this saying. Mark has: " And He said unto them: ' Verily I say unto you, that there be some of them that stand here, which shall not taste of death, till they have seen the Kingdom of God come with power " (*Mark* 9: 1). It is of the mighty working of His Kingdom that Jesus is speaking; and what He said came most divinely true. There were those standing there who saw the coming of Jesus in the coming of the Spirit at the day of Pentecost. There were those who were to see Gentile and Jew swept into the Kingdom; they were to see the tide of the Christian message sweep across Asia Minor and cover Europe until it reached Rome. Well within the lifetime of those who heard Jesus speak the Kingdom came with power.

Again, this is to be taken closely with what goes before. Jesus warned His disciples that He must go to Jerusalem, and that there He must suffer many things and die. That was the shame; but the shame was not the end. After the Cross there came the Resurrection. The Cross was not to be the end; it was to be the beginning of the unleashing of that power which was to surge throughout the whole world. This is a promise to the disciples of Jesus Christ that nothing that men can do can hinder the expansion of the Kingdom of God.

THE MOUNT OF TRANSFIGURATION

Matthew 17: 1-8

> Six days after, Jesus took Peter, and James, and John his brother, and brought them by themselves to a high mountain, and His appearance was changed in their presence. His face shone like the sun, and His garments became as white as the light. And, look you, Moses and Elijah appeared to them, talking with Him. Peter said to Jesus, " Lord, it is a fine thing for us to be here. I will make three booths, one for you, one for Moses, and one for Elijah." While he was still speaking, look you, a shining cloud overshadowed them; and, look you, there came a voice out of the cloud saying, " This is my beloved Son, in whom I am well pleased. Hear Him! " When the disciples heard that, they fell on their faces and were exceedingly afraid. Jesus came and touched them and said, " Rise, and do not be afraid." They lifted up their eyes, and saw no one, except Jesus alone.

THE great moment of Caesarea Philippi was followed by the great hour on the Mount of Transfiguration. Let us first look at the scene where this time of glory came to Jesus and to His three chosen disciples. There is a tradition which connects the Transfiguration with Mount Tabor, but that is entirely unlikely. The top of Mount Tabor was an armed fortress, and a great castle; it seems almost impossible that the Transfiguration could have happened on a mountain which was a fortress. Much more likely the scene of the Transfiguration is Mount Hermon. Hermon was fourteen miles from Caesarea Philippi. It is a very high mountain, so high that it can actually be seen from the Dead Sea, at the other end of Palestine, more than one hundred miles away. Hermon is 9,400 feet high, 11,000 feet above the level of the Jordan valley. It cannot have been on the very summit of the mountain that this happened. The mountain is too high for that. Canon Tristram tells how he and his party ascended it. They were able to ride practically to the top, and the ride took five hours. Activity is not easy on so high a summit. Tristram says, " We spent a great part of the day on the summit, but were before long painfully affected by the rarity of the atmosphere." It was somewhere on the slopes of the beautiful and stately Mount Hermon that the Transfiguration happened. It must have happened in the night. Luke tells us that the disciples were weighted down with sleep (*Luke* 9: 32). It was the next day when Jesus and His disciples came back to the plain to find the father of the epileptic boy waiting for them (*Luke* 9: 37). It was some time in the sunset, or the late evening, or the night, that this amazing vision took place.

We must ask, Why did Jesus go there? Why did He make this expedition to these lonely mountain slopes? It is Luke who gives us the clue. For Luke tells us that Jesus was praying (*Luke* 9: 29). We must put ourselves, as far as we can, in Jesus' place. By this time He was on the way to the Cross. Of that He was quite sure; again and again He told His disciples that it was so. At Caesarea Philippi we have seen Him facing one problem and dealing with one question. We have seen Him seeking to find out if there was anyone who had recognized Him for who and what He was. We have seen that question triumphantly answered, for Peter had grasped the great fact that Jesus could only be described as the Son of God. But there was an even greater question than that that Jesus had to solve before He set out on the last journey. He had to make quite sure, sure beyond all doubt, that He was doing what God wished Him to do. He had to make certain that it was indeed God's will that He should go to Jerusalem to the Cross. Jesus went up Mount Hermon to ask God the question: " Am I doing your will in setting my face to go to Jerusalem? " Jesus went up Mount Hermon to listen to the commands of God, and to listen for the voice of God. Jesus would take no step without consulting God. How then could He take the biggest step He ever took, or ever could take, without consulting God? Of everything Jesus asked one question, and only one question: " Is it God's will for me? " And that is the question which He was asking in the loneliness of the slopes of Hermon.

It is one of the supreme differences between Jesus and us, it is one of the great facts which made Jesus what He was, that Jesus always asked: " What does *God* wish me to do? "; we nearly always ask: " What do *I* wish to do? " We often say that the unique characteristic of Jesus was that He was *sinless*. What do we mean by that? We mean precisely this, that Jesus had no will, but the will of God. The hymn of the Christian must always be:

> " Thy way, not mine, O Lord,
>   However dark it be!
> Lead me by Thine own hand;
>   Choose out the path for me.
>
> I dare not choose my lot,
>   I would not if I might:
> Choose Thou for me, my God,
>   So shall I walk aright.

Not mine, not mine the choice
In things or great or small;
Be Thou my Guide, my Strength,
My Wisdom and my All."

When Jesus had a problem, He did not seek to solve it
only by the power of His own thought; He did not take
it to others for human advice; He took it to the lonely
place and to God.

THE BENEDICTION OF THE PAST

Matthew 17: 1-8 (*continued*)

THERE on the mountain slopes two great figures appeared
to Jesus, Moses and Elijah. It is fascinating to see in
how many respects the experience of these two great
leaders of the people and servants of God matched the
experience of Jesus. When Moses came down from the
mountain of Sinai, he wist not that the skin of his face
shone (*Exodus* 34: 29). Both Moses and Elijah had their
most intimate experiences of God on a mountain top.
It was into Mount Sinai that Moses went to receive the
tables of the law (*Exodus* 31: 18). It was on Mount Horeb
that Elijah found God, not in the wind, and not in the
earthquake, but in the still small voice (I *Kings* 19: 9-12).
It is a strange thing that there was something awesome
about the deaths of both Moses and Elijah. *Deuteronomy*
34: 5, 6 tells of the lonely death of Moses on Mount Nebo.
It reads as if God Himself was the burier of the great
leader of the people: " And he buried him in a valley
in the land of Moab, over against Beth-peor; but no man
knoweth of his sepulchre unto this day." As for Elijah,
as the old story has it, he took his departure from the
astonished Elisha in a chariot and horses of fire (2 *Kings*
2: 11). The two great figures who appeared to Jesus as
He was setting out for Jerusalem were men who seemed
too great to die.

Still further, as we have already seen, it was the consistent Jewish belief that Elijah was to be forerunner and herald of the Messiah, and it was also believed by at least some Jewish teachers that, when the Messiah came, he would be accompanied by Moses as his companion. It is easy to see how appropriate and fitting this vision of Moses and Elijah was. But none of these reasons is the real reason why the vision of Moses and Elijah came to Jesus.

Once again we must turn to Luke's account of the Transfiguration. Luke tells us that Moses and Elijah spoke with Jesus, as the Authorized Version has it, " of His decease which He should accomplish at Jerusalem " (*Luke* 9: 31). The word which is used for *decease* in the Greek is very significant. It is the word *exodos,* which is exactly the same word as the English word *exodus.* These two great figures of the past spoke with Jesus about His *exodus.* Now the word *exodus* has one special connection; it is the word which is always used of the departure of the people of Israel out of the land of Egypt, into the unknown way of the desert, which in the end was going to lead them to the Promised Land. The word *exodus* is the word which describes what we might well call the most adventurous journey in human history, a journey in which a whole people in utter trust in God went out into the unknown. *That is precisely what Jesus was going to do.* In utter trust in God He was going to set out on the tremendous adventure of that journey to Jerusalem, a journey beset with perils, a journey involving a cross, but a journey issuing in glory. Now in Jewish thought these two figures, Moses and Elijah, always inevitably stood for certain things. Moses was the greatest of all the *law-givers*; he was supremely and uniquely the man who brought God's law to men. Elijah was the greatest of all the *prophets*; in him the voice of God spoke to men with unique directness. These two men were the twin peaks of Israel's religious history and achievement. It is as if the greatest figures in Israel's history came to Jesus, as He was setting out on the last and greatest adventure into the unknown, and told Him to go on. In them all history rose up and pointed Jesus on His way. In them all history recognized Jesus as its own consummation. The greatest of the law-givers and the greatest of the prophets recognized Jesus as the one of whom they had dreamed, as the one whom they had foretold. Their appearance was the signal for Jesus to go on. So, then, the greatest human figures witnessed to Jesus that He was on the right way, and bade Him go out on His adventurous *exodus* to Jerusalem and to Calvary.

But there was more than that; not only did the greatest law-giver and the greatest prophet assure Jesus that He was right; the very voice of God came to Him telling Him that He was on the right way, that He was on God's way, that He must go on. All the gospel writers speak of the luminous cloud which overshadowed them. That cloud was part of Israel's history. All through the history of Israel the luminous cloud stood for the *shechinah,* which was nothing less than the glory of Almighty God. Let us see that cloud in the history of Israel. In *Exodus* we read of *the pillar of cloud* which was to lead the people on their way (*Exodus* 13: 21, 22). Again in *Exodus* we read of the building and the completing of the Tabernacle; and at the end of the story there come the words: " Then a *cloud* covered the tent of the congregation, and the glory of the Lord filled the tabernacle " (*Exodus* 40: 34). It was in the *cloud* that the Lord descended to give the tables of the law to Moses (*Exodus* 34: 5). Once again we meet this mysterious, luminous cloud at the dedication of Solomon's Temple: " And it came to pass, when the priests were come out of the holy place, that the *cloud* filled the house of the Lord " (I *Kings* 8: 10, 11; cp. 2 *Chronicles* 5: 13, 14; 7: 2). All through the Old Testament there is this picture of the cloud, in which was the mysterious glory of God.

It so happens that we are able to add another vivid
fact to this. Travellers tell us of a curious and characteristic
phenomenon connected with Mount Hermon. Edersheim
writes: " A strange peculiarity has been noticed about
Hermon in ' the extreme rapidity of the formation of
cloud upon the summit. In a few minutes a thick cap
forms over the top of the mountain, and as quickly disperses,
and entirely disappears.' " No doubt on this occasion
there came a cloud on the slopes of Hermon; and no
doubt at first the disciples thought little enough of it,
for Hermon was notorious for the clouds which came and
went. But something happened; it is not for us to guess
what happened; but the cloud became luminous and
mysterious, and out of it there came the voice of the divine
majesty, setting God's seal of approval on Jesus His Son.
And in that moment Jesus' prayer was answered; He
knew beyond a doubt that He was right to go on.

The Mount of Transfiguration was for Jesus indeed a
spiritual mountain peak. His *exodus* lay before Him.
Was He taking the right way? Was He right to adventure
out to Jerusalem and to the waiting arms of the Cross?
First, there came to Him the verdict of history, the greatest
of the law-givers and the greatest of the prophets, to
tell Him to go on. And then, greater by far than even that
greatness, there came the voice, which gave Him nothing
less than the approval of God. It was the experience
on the Mount of Transfiguration which enabled Jesus
inflexibly to walk the way to the Cross.

THE INSTRUCTION OF PETER

Matthew 17: 1-8 (*continued*)

BUT the episode of the Transfiguration did something,
not only for Jesus, but for the disciples also.

(i) It must have been that the minds of the disciples
were still hurt and bewildered by the insistence of Jesus

that He must go to Jerusalem to be humiliated, to be treated like a criminal, to suffer, to be crucified and to die. It must have looked to them as if there was nothing but black shame ahead. But the whole atmosphere of the Mountain of Transfiguration is *glory*. From start to finish the keynote of this whole incident is glory. Jesus' face shone like the sun, and His garments glistened and gleamed like the light. The Jews well knew the promise of God to the victorious righteous: " Their face shall shine as the sun " (2 *Esdras* 7: 97). No Jew could ever have seen that luminous cloud without thinking of the *shechinah*, the glory of God resting upon His people. There is one very revealing little touch in this passage. No fewer than three times in its eight brief verses there occurs the little interjection: " Behold! Look you! " It is as if Matthew could not even tell the story without a catch of the breath at the sheer staggering wonder of it. Here surely was something which would lift up the hearts of the disciples; it would enable them to see the glory through the shame; the triumph through the humiliation; the crown beyond the Cross. It is obvious that even yet they did not understand; but it must surely have given them some little glimmering that the Cross was not all humiliation, that somehow it was tinged with glory, that somehow glory was the very air and atmosphere of the exodus to Jerusalem and to death.

(ii) Still further, Peter must have learned two lessons that night. When Peter woke to what was going on, his first reaction was to build three tabernacles, one for Jesus, one for Moses and one for Elijah. Peter was always the man for action; Peter was always the man who must be doing something. But there is a time for stillness; there is a time for contemplation, for wonder, for adoration, for awed reverence in the presence of the supreme glory. " Be still, and know that I am God " (*Psalm* 46: 10). It may be that sometimes we are too busy trying to do something, when we would be better to be silent, to be listening, to be wondering, to be adoring in the presence of God. Before a man can fight and adventure upon his feet, he must wonder and pray upon his knees.

(iii) But there is a converse of that. It is quite clear that Peter wished to wait upon the mountain slopes. He wished that great moment to be prolonged. He did not want to go down to the everyday and the common things again; he wished to remain for ever in the sheen of glory. That is a feeling which everyone must know. There are moments of intimacy, of serenity, of peace, of nearness to God, which everyone has known, and which everyone would wish to prolong. As A. H. McNeile has it: " The Mountain of Transfiguration is always more enjoyable than the daily ministry or the way of the Cross." But the Mountain of Transfiguration is only given to us to give us strength for the daily ministry and to enable us to walk the way of the Cross. Susanna Wesley had a prayer: " Help me, Lord, to remember that religion is not to be confined to the church or closet, nor exercised only in prayer and meditation, but that everywhere I am in Thy presence." The moment of glory does not exist for its own sake; it exists to clothe the common things with a sheen and a radiance they never had before.

TEACHING THE WAY OF THE CROSS

Matthew 17: 9-13, 22, 23

> As they were coming down from the mountain, Jesus gave them strict injunctions: " Tell no man about the vision until the Son of Man has been raised from the dead." The disciples asked Him, " Why then do the Scribes say that Elijah must first come? " He answered, " It is true that they say that Elijah is to come and will restore all things; but I tell you that Elijah has already come, and they did not recognize him, but they did to him what they wished. So also the Son of Man is to suffer at their hands."

Then the disciples understood that He spoke to them about John the Baptizer.

. . . .

When they were gathering in Galilee, Jesus said to them, " The Son of Man is going to be delivered into the hands of men, and they will kill Him, and on the third day He will be raised." And they were exceedingly distressed.

HERE again we find Jesus' injunction to secrecy, and it was much needed. The great danger was that men should proclaim Jesus as Messiah without knowing who and what the Messiah was. Their whole conception both of the fore-runner and of the Messiah had to be radically and fundamentally changed.

It was going to take a long time for the idea of a conquering Messiah to be unlearned; it was so ingrained into the Jewish mind that it was difficult—almost impossible —to alter it. Verses 9-13 are a very difficult passage. Behind them there is this idea. The Jews were agreed that, before the Messiah came, Elijah would return to be His herald and His forerunner. " Behold I will send you Elijah the prophet before the coming of the great and dreadful day of the Lord." So writes Malachi, and then he goes on: " And he shall turn the heart of the fathers to the children, and the heart of the children to their fathers, lest I come and smite the earth with a curse " (*Malachi* 4: 5, 6). Bit by bit this idea of the coming of Elijah gathered detail, until the Jews came to believe that not only would Elijah come, but he would restore all things before the Messiah came, that he would, we might put it, make the world fit for the Messiah to enter into. The idea was that Elijah would be a great and terrible reformer, who would walk throughout the world destroying all evil and setting things to rights. The result was that both the forerunner and the Messiah were thought of in terms of *power*.

So Jesus corrects this. " The Scribes," He said, " say that Elijah will come like a blast of cleansing and avenging fire. *He has come*; but his way was the way of suffering and of sacrifice, as must also be the way of the Son of Man." Jesus has laid it down that the way of God's service is never the way which blasts men out of existence, but always the way which woos them with sacrificial love.

That is what the disciples had to learn; and that is why they had to be silent until they had learned. If they had gone out preaching a conquering Messiah there could have been nothing but tragedy. It has been computed that in the century previous to the Crucifixion no fewer than 200,000 Jews lost their lives in futile and useless revolutions and rebellions. Before men could preach Christ, they must know who and what Christ was; and until Jesus had taught His followers the necessity of the Cross, they had to be silent and to learn. It is not our ideas, it is Christ's message, that we must bring to men; and no man can teach others until Jesus Christ has taught him.

THE ESSENTIAL FAITH

Matthew 17: 14-20

> When they came to the crowd, a man came to Him and fell at His feet and said, " Sir, have pity on my son, for he is an epileptic, and he suffers severely; for often he falls into the fire, and often into the water; and I brought him to your disciples, and they were not able to cure him." Jesus answered, " O faithless and perverse generation, how long shall I be with you? How long shall I bear with you? Bring him to me! " And Jesus spoke sternly to him, and the demon came out of him, and the boy was cured from that hour. Then the disciples came to Jesus in private and said, " Why were we not able to cast out the demon? " Jesus said to them, " Because of the littleness of your faith. This is the truth I tell you—if you have faith as a grain of mustard seed, you will say to this mountain, ' Be removed from here,' and it will remove. So nothing will be impossible to you."

THE GOSPEL OF MATTHEW

No sooner had Jesus come down from the heavenly glory
than He was confronted with the earthly problem and
the practical demand. A man had brought his epileptic
boy to the disciples in the absence of Jesus. Matthew
describes the boy by the verb *selēniazesthai*, which literally
means *to be moonstruck*. As was inevitable in that age,
the father attributed the boy's condition to the malign
influence of evil spirits. So serious was the boy's condition
that he was a danger to himself and to everyone else.
We can almost hear the sigh of relief as Jesus appeared,
and we can see Him at once taking a grip of a situation
which had got completely out of hand. With one strong,
stern word He bade the demon be gone and the boy was
cured. This story is full of significant things.

(i) We cannot but be moved by the faith of the boy's
father. Even though the disciples had been given power
to cast out devils (*Matthew* 10: 1), here was a case in
which they had signally and publicly failed. And yet in
spite of the failure of the disciples, the father never doubted
the power of Jesus Himself. It is as if he said: " Only
let me get at Jesus Himself, and my problems will be
solved and my need will be met." There is something
very poignant about that; and there is something which
is very universal and very modern. There are many who
feel that the Church, the professed disciples of Jesus in
their own day and generation, have failed and are powerless
to deal with the ills of the human situation; and yet at
the back of their minds there is the feeling: " If we could
only get beyond His human followers, if we could only
get behind the facade of ecclesiasticism and the failure
of the Church, if we could only get at Jesus Himself,
we would receive the things we need." It is at once our
condemnation and our challenge that, even yet, though
men have lost their faith in the Church, they have never
lost a wistful faith in Jesus Christ Himself.

(ii) We see here the constant demands which were
made upon Jesus. Straight from the glory of the mountain

top, He came to be met by the demands of human need
and human suffering. Straight from hearing the voice
of God, He came to hear the clamant demand of human
need. The most precious and the most Christ-like person
in the world is the person who never finds his fellow-
men a nuisance. It is easy to feel Christian in the moment
of prayer and meditation; it is easy to feel close to God
when the world is shut out, and when heaven is very near.
But that is not religion—that is escapism. Real religion
is to rise from our knees before God to meet men and the
problems of the human situation. Real religion is to draw
strength from God *in order to give it to others*. Real religion
involves both meeting God in the secret place and men
in the market place. Real religion means taking our own
needs to God, not that we may have peace and quiet and
undisturbed comfort, but that we may be enabled graciously,
effectively and powerfully to meet the needs of others.
The wings of the dove are not for the Christian, who
would follow his Master in going about doing good.

(iii) We see here the grief of Jesus. It is not that Jesus
says that He wants to be quit for ever of His disciples.
It is that he says, " How long must I be with you, before
you will understand? " There is nothing more Christlike
than patience. When we are like to lose our patience
at the follies and the foolishness of men, let us call to mind
God's infinite patience with the wanderings and the
disloyalties and the unteachability of our own souls.

(iv) We see here the central need of faith, without
which nothing can happen. When Jesus spoke about
removing mountains He was using a phrase which the Jews
knew well. A great teacher, who could really expound
and interpret scripture, and who could explain and resolve
difficulties, was regularly known as an *uprooter* or, even
a *pulverizer*, of mountains. To tear up, to uproot, to
pulverize mountains were all regular phrases for removing
difficulties. Jesus never meant this to be taken physically
and literally. After all the ordinary man seldom finds

any necessity to remove a physical mountain. What He meant was: " If you have faith enough, all difficulties can be solved, and even the hardest task can be accomplished." Faith in God is the instrument which enables men to remove the hills of difficulty which block their path.

THE TEMPLE TAX

Matthew 17: 24-27

When they came to Capernaum, those who received the half-shekel Temple tax came to Peter and said, " Does your teacher not pay the tax? " Peter said, " He does pay it." When he had gone into the house, before he could speak, Jesus said to him, " What do you think, Simon? From whom do earthly kings take tax and tribute? From their sons or from strangers? " When he said, " From strangers," Jesus said to him, " So then the sons are free. But, so as not to set a stumbling-block in anyone's way, go to the sea, and cast a hook into it, and take the first fish which comes up; and when you have opened its mouth, you will find a shekel. Take it and give it to them for me and for you." ·

THE Temple at Jerusalem was a costly place to run. There was the daily morning and evening sacrifice which involved the offering of a year-old lamb, both in the morning and the evening. With the lamb there were offered the attendant offerings of wine and flour and oil. The incense which was burned every day had to be bought and prepared. The costly hangings and the robes of the priests constantly wore out; and the robe of the High Priest was itself worth a king's ransom. All this required money to pay for it. So, on the basis of Exodus 30: 13, it was laid down that every male Jew over twenty years of age must pay an annual Temple tax of one half-shekel. In the days of Nehemiah, when the people were poor, it was one-third of a shekel. One half-shekel was equal to two Greek drachmae; and the tax was commonly called the didrachm, as it is called in this passage. The value of the tax was about one shilling

and sixpence; and that sum must be evaluated in the
memory that a working man's wage in Palestine in the
time of Jesus was only eightpence. The tax was in fact
the equivalent of two days' pay. It brought into the
Temple treasury no less than about £76,000 a year. Theor-
etically the tax was obligatory, and the Temple authorities
had power to distrain upon a man's goods, if he failed to pay.

The method of collection was carefully organized.
On the first of the month Adar, which is March of our year,
announcement was made in all the towns and villages of
Palestine that the time to pay the tax had come. On the
fifteenth of the month booths were set up in each town and
village, and at the booths the tax was paid. If the tax
was not paid by the twenty-fifth of Adar, it could only
be paid direct to the Temple in Jerusalem.

In this passage we see Jesus paying this Temple tax.
The tax authorities came to Peter and asked him if his
Master paid His taxes. There is little doubt that that
question was asked with malicious intent, and that the
hope was that Jesus would refuse to pay the tax; for,
if He refused, the orthodox would have a ground of accusation against Him. Peter's immediate answer was that
Jesus did pay. So Peter went and told Jesus of the situation,
and Jesus used a kind of parable in verses 25 and 26.
The picture may be one of two pictures, but in either case
the meaning is the same. (i) In the ancient world conquering
and colonizing nations had little or no idea of governing
for the benefit of subject peoples. Rather, they considered
that the subject peoples existed to make things easy for
them. The result of this point of view was that a king's
own nation never paid tribute, if there were any nations
subject to it. It was the subject nations who bore the
burden and who paid the tax, while the king's own nation
was free and exempt. So Jesus may be saying, " God is
the King of Israel; but we are the true Israel, for we are
the citizens of the Kingdom of Heaven; outsiders may
have to pay; but we are free." (ii) The picture is more

likely a much simpler picture than that. If any king imposed taxes on a nation, he certainly did not impose them on his own family and household. It was indeed for the support of his own household that the taxes were imposed. Now the task in question was for the Temple, which was the house of God. Jesus was the Son of God. Did He not say—as it should be translated—when His parents sought Him in Jerusalem: " Did you not know that I must be in *my Father's house?* " (*Luke* 2: 49). How could the Son be under obligation to pay the tax which was for His own Father's house? None the less Jesus said that they must pay, not because of the compulsion of the law, but because of a higher duty. Jesus said that they must pay " lest we should offend them." The New Testament always uses the verb *to offend* (*skandalizein*) and the noun *offence* (*skandalon*) in a special way. The verb never means to insult or to annoy or to injure the pride of. It always means *to put a stumbling-block in someone's way*, to cause someone to trip up and to fall. In Greek *skandalon* is not a *scandal* or *offence* in our sense of the term; it is always something which makes someone trip, or slip, or fall. Therefore what Jesus is saying is: " We must pay so as not to set a bad example to others. We must not only do our duty, we must go beyond duty, in order that we may show others what they ought to do. Jesus would allow Himself nothing which might make someone else think less of the ordinary obligations of life. In life there may sometimes be exemptions and allowances which we could claim; there are things which, it may be, we could quite safely allow ourselves to do. But we must claim nothing and allow ourselves nothing which might possibly be a bad example to someone else.

But, we may well ask, why is it that this story was ever transmitted at all? Obviously, for reasons of space, the gospel writers had to select their material. Why select this story? Let us remember when Matthew's gospel was written. It was written between A.D. 80 and 90. Now just a little before that time Jews and Jewish Christians had been faced with a very real and a very disturbing problem. We saw that every male Jew over twenty had to pay the Temple tax; but the Temple was totally destroyed in A.D. 70, never to be rebuilt. After the destruction of the Temple, Vespasian, the Roman emperor, enacted that the half-shekel Temple tax should now be paid to the treasury of the Temple of Jupiter Capitolinus in Rome. Here indeed was a problem. Many of the Jews and of the Jewish Christians were violently inclined to rebel against this enactment. Any such widespread rebellion would have caused disastrous consequences, for it would have been utterly crushed at once, and it would have gained the Jews and the Christians the reputation of being bad and disloyal and rebellious and disaffected citizens. This story was put into the gospels to tell the Christians, especially the Jewish Christians, that, however unpleasant they might be, the duties of a citizen must be shouldered and accepted. This story is told to tell us that Christianity and good citizenship go hand in hand. The Christian who exempts himself from the duties of good citizenship is not only failing in citizenship, he is also failing in Christianity.

HOW TO PAY OUR DEBTS

Matthew 17: 24-27 (continued)

BUT now we must come to the story itself. If we take the story with a bald and crude literalism, it means that Jesus told Peter to go and catch a fish, and that he would find a *stater* in the fish's mouth, and that would be sufficient to pay the tax for both of them. It is not irrelevant to note that the gospel never tells us that Peter did so. The story ends with that saying. Before we begin to examine the story we must remember that all oriental people love to say a thing in the most dramatic and vivid way possible; and that they love to say a thing with the flash of a smile. This miracle is difficult on three grounds.

(i) It is a first truth that God does not send a miracle to enable us to do what we can quite well do for ourselves. To do so would be to harm us and not to help us. However poor the disciples were, they did not need a miracle to enable them to earn two half-shekels. It was not beyond human power to earn such a sum.

(ii) This miracle transgresses the great decision of Jesus that He would never use His miraculous power for His own ends and benefits. That was in fact His decision in the temptations in the wilderness. He could have turned stones into bread to satisfy His own hunger—but He refused. He could have used His power to enhance His own prestige as a wonder-worker—but He refused. In the wilderness Jesus decided once finally and for all that He would not and could not selfishly use His power. Beyond a doubt if this story is taken with a crude literalism, it does show Jesus using His divine power to satisfy His own personal needs—and that is what Jesus would never do.

(iii) If this miracle is taken literally, there is a sense in which it is even immoral. Life would become a chaotic thing, if a man could pay his debts by finding coins in fishes' mouths. Life was never meant to be arranged in such a way that men can meet their obligations in such a lazy and effortless way. " The gods," said one of the great Greeks, " have ordained that sweat should be the price of all things." That is just as true for the Christian thinker as it was for the Greek.

If all this is so, what then are we to say? Are we to say that this is a mere legendary story, that it is a mere imaginative fiction, with no truth behind it at all? Far from it. Beyond a doubt something happened. Let us remember again the Jewish love of dramatic vividness. Undoubtedly what happened was this. Jesus said to Peter: " Yes, Peter. You're right. We, too, must pay our just and lawful debts. Well, you know how to do it. Back you go to the fishing for a day. You'll get plenty money in the fishes' mouths to pay our dues! A day at the fishing will soon produce all we need." Jesus was saying, " Back to your job, Peter; that's the way to pay your debts." So the typist will find a new coat in the keys of her typewriter. The motor mechanic will find food for himself and his wife and family in the cylinder of the motor car. The teacher will find money to pay his way in the blackboard and the chalk. The clerk will find enough to support himself and his dear ones in the ledger and in the account sheets.

When Jesus said this, He said it with that swift smile of His and with His gift for dramatic language. He was not telling Peter to get literal coins in literal fishes' mouths. He was telling him that in his day's work he would get what he needed to pay his way.

PERSONAL RELATIONSHIPS

Matthew 18 is a most important chapter for Christian Ethics, because it deals with those qualities which should characterize the personal relationships of the Christian. We shall be dealing in detail with these relationships as we study the chapter section by section; but before we do so, it will be well to look at the chapter as a whole. It singles out seven qualities which should mark the personal relationships of the Christian.

(i) First and foremost, there is the quality of *humility* (verses 1-4). Only the person who has the humility of the child is a citizen of the Kingdom of Heaven. Personal ambition, personal prestige, personal publicity, personal profit are motives which can find no place in the life of the Christian. The Christian is the man who has forgotten self in his devotion to Jesus Christ, and in his service of his fellow-men.

(ii) Second, there comes the quality of *responsibility* (verses 5-7). The greatest of all sins is to teach another to sin, especially if that other should be a weaker, a younger, and a less-experienced brother. God's sternest judgment is reserved for those who put a stumbling-block in the way of others. The Christian is a man who is constantly aware that he is responsible for the effect of his life, his deeds, his words, his example on other people.

(iii) There follows the quality of *self-renunciation* (verses 8-10). The Christian is like an athlete for whom no training is too hard, if by it he may win the prize; he is like the student who will sacrifice pleasure and leisure to reach the crown. The Christian is the man who is ready surgically to excise from life everything which would keep him from rendering a perfect obedience to God.

(iv) There is *individual care* (verses 11-14). The Christian is a man who realizes that God cares for him individually, and that he must reflect that individual care of God in his care for others. The Christian never thinks in terms of crowds; he thinks in terms of persons. For God no man is unimportant, and no one is lost in the crowd; for the Christian every man is important, and every man is a child of God, who, if he is lost, must be found. The individual care of the Christian is in fact the motive and the dynamic of evangelism.

(v) There is the quality of *discipline* (verses 15-20). The Christian kindness and the Christian forgiveness do not mean that a man who is in error is to be allowed to do as he likes. Such a man must be guided and corrected and, if need be, disciplined back into the right way. But that discipline is always to be given in humble love, and not in self-righteous condemnation; it is always to be given with the desire for reconciliation and never with the desire for vengeance.

(vi) There is the quality of *fellowship* (verses 19, 20). It might even be said that Christians are people who pray together. Christians are people who in fellowship seek the will of God, who in fellowship listen and worship together. Individualism is the reverse of Christianity.

(vii) There is the *spirit of forgiveness* (verses 23-35); and the Christian's forgiveness of his fellow-men is founded on the fact that he himself is a forgiven man. He forgives others, even as God, for Christ's sake, has forgiven him.

THE MIND OF A CHILD

Matthew 18: 1-4

> On that day the disciples came to Jesus. " Who, then," they said, " is the greatest in the Kingdom of Heaven? " Jesus called a little child and made him stand in the middle of them, and said, " This is the truth I tell you—unless you turn and become as children, you will not enter into the Kingdom of Heaven. Whoever humbles himself as this little child, he is the greatest in the Kingdom of Heaven."

HERE is a very revealing question, followed by a very revealing answer. The disciples asked who was the greatest in the Kingdom of Heaven. Jesus took a child and said that unless they turned and became as this little child, they would not get into the Kingdom at all. The question of the disciples was: " Who will be the greatest in the Kingdom of Heaven? " and the very fact that they asked that question showed that they had no idea at all what the Kingdom of Heaven was. Jesus said, " Unless you turn." The very fact that He used that way of speaking means that He was warning them that they were going in completely the wrong direction, and unless they made a right-about turn they were going away from the Kingdom of Heaven, and not towards it. In life it is all a question of what a man is aiming at; and if a man is aiming at the fulfilment of personal ambition, the acquisition of personal power, the enjoyment of personal prestige, the exaltation of self, then he is aiming at precisely the opposite of the Kingdom of Heaven; for to be a citizen of the Kingdom means the complete forgetting of self, the obliteration and the abolition of self, the spending of self in a life which aims at service and not at power. So long as a man considers his own self as the most important thing in the world, his back is turned to the Kingdom, and if he wants ever to reach the Kingdom, he must turn round and face in the opposite direction.

So Jesus took a child. There is a tradition that the child grew to be Ignatius of Antioch, who in the later days became a great servant of the Church, a great writer, and finally a martyr for Christ. The tradition springs from the fact that Ignatius was surnamed *Theophoros*, which means *God-carried* or *God-borne*, and the tradition grew up that he had received that name because Jesus carried him on his knee. It may be so. Maybe it is even more likely that it was Peter who asked the question, and that it was Peter's little boy whom Jesus took and set in the midst, because we know that Peter was married (*Matthew* 8: 14; I *Corinthians* 9: 5). So Jesus said that in a child we see the characteristics which should mark the man of the Kingdom. There are many lovely characteristics in a child—the power to wonder, before he has become deadeningly used to the wonder of the world; the power to forgive and to forget, even when adults and parents treat him unjustly as they so often do; the innocence, which, as Richard Glover beautifully says, brings it about that the child has only to learn, not to unlearn; only to do, not to undo. No doubt Jesus was thinking of these things; but wonderful as these things are they are not the main things in His mind. The child has three great qualities which make him the symbol of those who are citizens of the Kingdom.

(i) First and foremost, there is the quality which is the keynote of the whole passage, the child's *humility*. A child does not wish to push himself forward; rather, he wishes to fade into the background. He does not wish for prominence; he would rather be left in obscurity.

It is only as he grows up, and begins to be initiated into a competitive world, with its fierce struggle and scramble for prizes and for first places that his instinctive humility s left behind.

(ii) There is the child's *dependence*. To the child a state of dependence is a perfectly natural state. He never thinks that he can face life by himself, and for himself. He is perfectly content to be utterly dependent on those who love him and care for him. If men would accept the fact of their dependence on God, a new strength and a new peace would enter into life.

(iii) There is the child's *trust*. The child is instinctively dependent, and just as instinctively he trusts his parents that his needs will be met. When we are children, we cannot buy our own food or our own clothes, or maintain our own home; yet we never doubt that we will be clothed and fed, and that there will be shelter and warmth and comfort waiting for us when we come home. When we are children we set out on a journey with no means of paying the fare, and with no idea of how to get to our journey's end, and yet it never enters our heads to doubt that our parents will bring us safely there.

The child's humility is the pattern of the Christian's behaviour to his fellow-men, and the child's dependence and trust are the pattern of the Christian's attitude towards God, the Father of all.

CHRIST AND THE CHILD

Matthew 18: 5-7, 10

" Whoever receives one such little child in my name, receives me. But whoever puts a stumbling-block in the way of one of these little ones, who believe in me, it is better for him that a great millstone should be hanged about his neck, and that he should be drowned far out in the open sea. Alas for the world because of stumbling-blocks! Stumbling-blocks are bound to come; but alas for the man by whom the stumbling-block comes!

. . . .

See that you do not despise one of these little ones; for, I tell you, their angels in heaven always look upon the face of my Father who is in heaven."

THERE is a certain difficulty of interpretation in reading this passage, which must be borne in mind. As we have often seen, it is Matthew's consistent custom to gather together the teaching of Jesus under certain great heads; he arranges Jesus' teaching systematically. In the early part of this chapter, as here, he is collecting Jesus' teaching about *children*; and the thing which we must remember is that the Jews used the word *child* in a double sense. They used it literally of the *young child*; but regularly a teacher's disciples were called his *sons* or his *children*. Therefore a child also means a *beginner in the faith*, one who has just begun to believe, one who is not yet mature and established in the faith, one who has just begun on the right way, and who can very easily be deflected from it. And in this passage very often the child means both the *young child* and the *beginner on the Christian way*.

Jesus says that whoever receives one such little child in His name receives Himself. The phrase *in my name* can mean one of two things. (i) It can mean *for my sake*. The care of children is something which is carried out for nothing less than the sake of Jesus Christ. To teach a child, to bring up a child in the way in which he ought to go, is something which is done not only for the sake of the child, but for the sake of Jesus Himself. (ii) It can mean *with a blessing*. It can mean receiving the child, and, as it were, naming the name of Jesus over the child. He who brings Jesus and the blessing of Jesus to a child is doing a Christlike work.

To receive the child is also a phrase which is capable of bearing more than one meaning. (i) It can mean, not so much to receive a child, as to receive a person who has this childlike quality of humility. In this highly competitive world it is very easy to pay most attention to the person who is pugnacious and aggressive and self-assertive and full of self-confidence. It is easy to pay most attention to the person who, in the worldly sense of the term, has made a success of life. Jesus may well be saying that the most important people are not the thrusters, and those who have climbed to the top of the tree by pushing everyone else out of the way, but the quiet, humble, simple people, who have the heart of a child. (ii) It can mean simply to welcome the child, to give him the care and the love and the teaching which he requires to make him into a good man. To help a child to live well and to know God better is to help Jesus Christ. (iii) But this phrase can have a very wonderful meaning. It can mean to see Christ in the child. To teach unruly, disobedient, restless little children can be a wearing job. To satisfy the physical needs of a child, to wash his clothes and bind his cuts and soothe his bruises and cook his meals may often seem a very unromantic task; the cooker and the sink and the work-basket have not much glamour; but there is no one in all this world who helps Jesus Christ more than the teacher of the little child and the harassed, hard-pressed mother in the home. All such will find a glory in the grey, if in the child they sometimes glimpse none other than Jesus Himself.

THE TERRIBLE RESPONSIBILITY

Matthew 18: 5-7, 10 *(continued)*

BUT the great keynote of this passage is the terrible weight of responsibility it leaves upon every one of us.

(i) It stresses the terror of teaching another to sin. It is true to say that no man sins uninvited; and the bearer of the invitation to sin is so often a human fellow-man. A man must always be confronted with his first temptation to sin; a man must always receive his first encouragement to do the wrong thing; a man must always experience his first push along the way to the forbidden things. The Jews took the view that the most unforgivable of all sins is to teach another to sin; and they took that view for this reason—a man's own sins can be forgiven, for in a sense they are limited in their consequences; but if we teach another to sin, he in his turn may teach still another to sin, and a train of sin is set in motion with no foreseeable end. There is nothing in this world more terrible than to destroy someone's innocence. And, if a man has any conscience left, there is nothing which will haunt him more. Someone tells of an old man who was dying; he was obviously sorely troubled. At last they got him to tell them why. "When we were boys at play," he said, "one day at a cross-roads we reversed a sign-post so that its arms were pointing in the wrong direction, and I've never ceased to wonder how many people were sent in the wrong direction by what we did." The sin of all sins is to teach another to sin.

(ii) This passage stresses the terror of the punishment of those who teach another to sin. When we see what it means, we see that it goes out of its way to do that. If a man teaches another to sin, it would be better for him that a millstone were hanged about his neck and he were drowned in the depths of the sea. The millstone in this case is a *mulos onikos*. The Jews ground corn by crushing it between two circular stones. This was done at home; and in any cottage such a mill could be seen. The upper stone, which turned round upon the lower was equipped with a handle, and it was commonly of such a size that the housewife could easily turn it, for it was she who did the grinding of the corn for the household needs. But a *mulos onikos* was a grinding-stone of such a size that it needed an ass pulling it (*onos* is the Greek for an *ass* and *mulos* is the Greek for a millstone) to turn it round at all. The very size of the millstone shows the awfulness of the condemnation. Further, in the Greek it is said, not so much that the man would be better to be drowned in the depths of the sea, but that it would be better if he were drowned far out in the open sea. The Jew feared the sea; for him Heaven was a place where there would be no more sea (*Revelation* 21: 1). The man who taught another to sin would be better to be drowned far out in the most lonely of all lonely and waste places. Still further, the very picture of drowning had for the Jew its terror. Drowning was sometimes a Roman punishment, but never a Jewish punishment. To the Jew it was the symbol of utter destruction. When the Rabbis taught that heathen and Gentile objects were to be utterly destroyed they said that they must be " cast into the salt sea." Josephus (*Antiquities of the Jews* 14.15.10) has a terrible account of a Galilaean revolt in which the Galilaeans took the supporters of Herod and drowned them in the depths of the Sea of Galilee. The very phrase to the Jew would paint a picture of utter destruction and annihilation. Jesus' words are carefully and deliberately chosen to show the fate that awaits a man who teaches another to sin.

(iii) This passage has a warning to silence all evasion This is a sin-stained world, and this is a tempting world; no one can go out into the world without being tempted and without meeting seductions to sin. That is specially true if the person goes out from a protected home where no evil influence was ever allowed to play upon him. Jesus says, " That is perfectly true; this world is full of temptations; it is quite true that that is inevitable in a world into which sin has entered; but that does not in the least lessen the responsibility of the man who actually is the cause of a stumbling-block being placed in the way of a younger person or of a beginner in the faith." We know that this is a tempting world; it is therefore the Christian duty to remove stumbling-blocks, never to be the cause of putting them in another's way. This means that it is not only a sin to put a stumbling-block in another's way; it is also a sin even to bring that person into any situation, or circumstance, or environment where he may meet with such a stumbling-block. No Christian can be satisfied to live complacently and lethargically in a civilization where there are conditions of living and housing and life in general where a young person has no chance of escaping the seductions of sin.

(iv) Finally this passage stresses the supreme importance of the child. " Their angels," said Jesus, " always behold the face of my Father who is in Heaven." In the time of Jesus the Jews believed in a very highly-developed angelology. Every nation had its angel; every natural force, such as the wind and the thunder and the lightning and the rain had its angel. They even went the length of saying very beautifully that every blade of grass has its angel. So, then, they believed that every child has his guardian angel. Further, to say that these angels behold the face of God in heaven means that these angels always have the right of direct access to God. The picture is the picture of a great royal court where only the most favoured courtiers and ministers and officials have direct access to the king. In the sight of God the children are so important that their guardian angels always have the right of direct access to the inner presence of God.

For us the great value of a child must always lie in the possibilities which are locked up within that child. Everything depends on how that child is taught and trained. The possibilities may never be realized; they may be stifled and stunted; that which might be used for good may be deflected to the purposes of evil; or they may be released and unleashed in such a way that a new tide of power floods the earth. Away back in the eleventh century Duke Robert of Burgundy was one of the great warrior and knightly figures. He was about to go off on a campaign. He had a little baby son who was his heir; and, before he departed, he made his great barons and nobles come and swear fealty to the little baby, in the event of anything happening to himself. They came with their waving plumes and their clanking armour and knelt before the little child. One great baron as he came smiled. Duke Robert asked him why he smiled. He said, " The child is so little." " Yes," said Duke Robert, " he's little—*but he'll grow.*" Indeed he grew, for that baby became William the Conqueror of England. In every child there are infinite possibilities for good and ill. It is the supreme responsibility of the parent, of the teacher, of the Christian Church, to see that these dynamic possibilities for good are realized. To stifle them, to leave them untapped, to twist them into evil powers, is sin.

THE SURGICAL EXCISION

Matthew 18: 8, 9

> " If your hand or your foot proves a stumbling-block to you, cut it off and throw it away from you. It is the fine thing for you to enter into life maimed or lame, rather than to be cast into everlasting fire with two hands or two feet. And if your eye proves a stumbling-block to you, pluck it out and throw it away from you. It is the fine thing for you to enter into life with one eye, rather than to be cast into the Gehenna of fire with two eyes."

THERE are two senses in which this passage can be taken. It can be taken purely *personally*. It may be saying that it is worth any sacrifice and any self-renunciation to escape the punishment of God.

We have to be clear what that punishment involves. It is here called *everlasting* punishment. This word *everlasting* occurs frequently in the Jewish ideas of punishment. The word is *aiōnios*. The Book of Enoch speaks about *eternal* judgment, about judgment *for ever*, about punishment and torture *for ever*, about the fire which burns *for ever*. Josephus calls hell an *everlasting* prison. The *Book of Jubilees* speaks about an *eternal* curse. *The Book of Baruch* says that "there will be no opportunity of returning, *nor a limit to the times*. There is a Rabbinic tale of Rabbi Jochanan ben Zaccai who wept bitterly at the prospect of death. On being asked why, he answered, "All the more I weep now that they are about to lead me before the King of kings, the Holy One, blessed is He, who lives and abides for ever and for ever and for ever; whose wrath, if He be wrathful, is an eternal wrath; and, if He bind me, His binding is an eternal binding; and if He kill me, His killing is an eternal killing; whom I cannot placate with words, nor bribe with wealth."

All these passages use the word *everlasting*; but we must be careful to remember what this word means. *Aiōnios* literally means *belonging to the ages*; there is only one person to whom the word *aiōnios* can properly be applied, and that one person is God. There is far more in *aiōnios* than simply a description of that which has no end. Punishment which is *aiōnios* is punishment which it befits God to give, and punishment which only God can give. When we think of punishment, we can only say, "Shall not the judge of all the earth do right?" Our human pictures, and our human time-scheme, fail; this is in the hands of God.

But there is one clue which we do have. This passage speaks of *the Gehenna of fire*. Gehenna is the valley of Hinnom. It was a valley below the mountain of Jerusalem. It was for ever accursèd, because it was the place where, in the days of the kingdom, the renegade Jews had sacrificed their children in the fire to the pagan god Moloch. Josiah had made it a place accursed. In later days it became the refuse dump of Jerusalem; it was a kind of vast incinerator. Always the refuse was burning there, and a pall of smoke and a glint of smouldering fire surrounded it. Now, what was this Gehenna, this Valley of Hinnom? It was the place into which everything that was useless was cast and there destroyed. That is to say, God's punishment is for those who are useless, for those who make no contribution to life, for those who hold life back instead of urging life on, for those who drag life down instead of lifting life up, for those who are the handicaps of others and not the inspirations. It is again and again New Testament teaching that *uselessness invites disaster*. The man who is useless, the man who is an evil influence on others, the man who cannot justify the simple fact of his existence, is in danger of the punishment of God, if he does not surgically excise from his life those things which make him the handicap he is.

But it is just possible that here this passage is not to be taken so much personally as *in connection with the Church*. Matthew has already used this saying of Jesus in a different context in *Matthew* 5: 30. Here there may be a difference. The whole passage is about children, and perhaps especially about children in the faith. This passage may be saying, " If in your Church there is someone who is an evil influence, if there is someone who is a bad example to those who are young in the faith, if there is someone whose life and conduct is damaging the body of the Church, he must be rooted out, excised, and cast away." In this context that may well be the meaning. The Church is the Body of Christ; then, if that body is to be healthy and health-giving, that which has the seeds of cancerous and poisonous infection in it must be even surgically removed.

One thing is certain, in any person and in any Church, that which is a seduction to sin must be removed, however painful the removal may be, for if we allow it to flourish a worse punishment will follow. In this passage there may well be stressed both the necessity of self-renunciation for the Christian individual, and discipline for the Christian Church.

THE SHEPHERD AND THE LOST SHEEP
Matthew 18: 12-14

" What do you think? If a man has a hundred sheep, and one of them wanders away, will he not leave the ninety-nine, and go out to the hills, and will he not seek the wandering one? And if he finds it— this is the truth I tell you—he rejoices more over it than over the ninety-nine who never wandered away. So it is not the will of your Father that one of these little ones should perish.''

THIS is surely the simplest of all the parables of Jesus, for it is the simple story of the lost sheep and the seeking shepherd. In Judaea it was tragically easy for sheep to go astray. The pasture land is on the hill country which runs like a backbone down the middle of the land. This ridge-like plateau is narrow, only a few miles across. There are no restraining walls. At its best, the pasture is sparse. And, therefore, the sheep are ever liable to wander; and, if they stray from the grass of the plateau into the gullies and the ravines at each side, they have every chance of finishing up on some ledge from which they cannot get up or down, and of being marooned there until they die.

The Palestinian shepherds were experts at tracking down their sheep. They could follow the track of the lost sheep for miles; and they would brave the cliffs and the precipice, to bring it back.

In Palestine, in the time of Jesus, the flocks were often communal flocks; they belonged, not to an individual, but to a village. There were, therefore, usually two or three shepherds with them. That is why the shepherd could leave the ninety-nine. If he had left them with no guardian and no watcher, he would have come back to find still more of them gone; but he could leave them in the care of his fellow-shepherds, while he sought the wanderer. The shepherds always made the most strenuous and the most sacrificial efforts to find a lost sheep. It was the rule that, if a sheep could not be brought back alive, then at least, if it was at all possible, its fleece or its bones must be brought back to prove how it had died, and that it was dead. We can imagine how the other shepherds would return with their flocks to the village fold at evening time, and how they would tell how one shepherd was still out on the mountain-side seeking the wanderer. We can imagine how the eyes of the people would turn ever and again to the hillside watching for the shepherd who had not come home; and we can imagine the shout of joy when they saw him coming striding along the pathway to the village with the weary wanderer slung across his shoulder, safe at last; and we can imagine how the whole village would welcome him, and gather round with gladness to hear the story of the sheep who was lost and found. Here in the shepherd we have what was Jesus' favourite picture of God, and of the love of God. This parable teaches us many things about the love of God.

(i) The love of God is an *individual love*. The ninety-and-nine were not enough; one sheep was out on the hillside and the shepherd could not rest until he had brought it home. However large a family a parent has, he cannot spare even one; there is not one who does not matter. God is like that; God cannot be happy until the last wanderer is gathered in.

(ii) The love of God is a *patient love*. Sheep are proverbially foolish creatures. The sheep had no one but itself to blame for the danger it had got itself into. Men are apt to have so little patience with the foolish ones. When they get into trouble, we are apt to say, " It's their own fault; they brought it on themselves; don't waste any sympathy on a fool." Thank God God is not like that. The sheep might be foolish, but the shepherd would still risk his life to save it. Men may be fools, but God in His love loves even the foolish man who has no one to blame but himself for his sin and his sorrow.

(iii) The love of God is a *seeking love*. The shepherd was not content to wait for the sheep to come back; he went out to search for it. That is what the Jew could not, and cannot, understand about the Christian idea of God. The Jew would gladly agree that, if the sinner comes crawling wretchedly home, God will forgive. But we know that God is far more wonderful than that, for in Jesus Christ, God came to seek and to search for those who wander away. God is not content to wait until men come home; He goes out to search for them, no matter what it costs Him.

(iv) The love of God is a *rejoicing love*. Here there is nothing but joy. There are no recriminations; there is no receiving back with a grudge and a sense of superior contempt; it is all joy. So often we accept a man who is penitent, but we accept him with a moral lecture, and a clear indication that he must regard himself as a contemptible creature, and the practical statement that we have no further use for him, and that we do not propose to trust him ever again. It is human never to forget a man's past, and always to remember his sins against him. God puts our sins behind His back; and when we come back to Him, it is all joy.

(v) The love of God is a *protecting love*. It is the love which seeks and *saves*. There can be a love which ruins; there can be a love which softens; but the love of God is the protecting love which saves a man for the service of his fellow-men, a love which makes the wanderer wise, the weak strong, the sinner pure, the captive of sin the free man of holiness, and the vanquished by temptation the conqueror of sin.

SEEKING THE STUBBORN

Matthew 18: 15-18

" If your brother sins against you, go, and try to convince him of his error between you and him alone. If he listens to you, you have gained your brother. If he will not listen to you, take with you one or two more, that the whole matter may be established in the mouth of two or three witnesses. If he refuses to listen to them, tell it to the Church. And if he refuses to listen to the Church, let him be to you as a Gentile and a tax-collector. This is the truth I tell you—

all that you bind upon earth will remain bound in
heaven; and all that you loose upon earth will remain
loosed in heaven."

IN many ways this is one of the most difficult passages
to interpret in the whole of Matthew's gospel. Its difficulty
lies in the undoubted fact that it does not ring true; it
does not sound like Jesus; it sounds much more like the
regulations of an ecclesiastical committee than it does
like the words of Jesus Christ.

We may go further. It is not possible that Jesus said
it in its present form. It is far too legalistic to be a saying
of Jesus; it might well be the saying of any Jewish Rabbi.
Jesus could not have told His disciples to take things to
the Church, for the Church did not exist, and the whole
tone of the passage implies a fully developed and organized
Church with a system of ecclesiastical discipline. The
passage speaks of tax-collectors and Gentiles as irreclaimable outsiders. Jesus was in fact accused of being the
friend of tax-gatherers and sinners, and He never spoke
of them as hopeless outsiders; He always spoke of them
with sympathy and love, and even with praise (cp. *Matthew*
9: 10ff; 11: 19; *Luke* 18: 10ff; and especially *Matthew*
21: 31ff), where it is actually said that the tax-gatherers
and harlots will go into the Kingdom before the orthodox
religious people of the time. And, finally, the whole tone
of the passage is that there is a limit to forgiveness, that
there comes a time when a man may be abandoned by his
fellow-men as beyond hope, a piece of advice which it is
impossible to think of Jesus as having given. And the
last verse, which deals with binding and loosing, actually
seems to give the Church the power to retain and to forgive
sins. There are many reasons which make us think that
this, *as it stands*, cannot be a correct report of the words
of Jesus, and that it must be an adaptation of something
which He said, made by the Church in later days, when
Church discipline was rather a thing of rules and regulations
than of charity and forgiveness.

But although this passage is certainly not a correct report of what Jesus said, it is equally certain that it goes back to something which Jesus did say. Can we then press behind it and come to the actual commandment of Jesus? At its widest what Jesus was saying was, " If anyone sins against you, spare no effort to make that man admit his fault, and to get things right again between you and him." Basically this passage means that we must never tolerate any situation in which there is a breach of personal relationships between us and another member of the Christian community. Suppose something does go wrong, what are we to do to put it right? This passage presents us with a whole scheme of action for the mending of broken relationships within the Christian fellowship.

(i) If we feel that anyone has wronged us, we should immediately put our complaint into words. The worst thing that we can do about a wrong is to brood about it. That is fatal. It can poison the whole mind and life, until we can think of nothing else but our sense of personal injury. Any such feeling should be brought out into the open, faced, and stated, and often the very stating of it will show how unimportant and trivial the whole thing is. There are times when to suffer in a brooding silence is the worst thing any man can do.

(ii) Second, if we feel that someone has wronged us we should go to see him personally. More trouble has been caused by the writing of letters than by almost anything else. A letter can be misread and misunderstood; it can quite unconsciously convey a tone which it was never meant to convey. If we have a difference with anyone, there is only one way to settle it—and that is face to face. The spoken word can often settle a difference which the written word would only have exacerbated.

(iii) If a private and personal meeting fails of its purpose, then we should take some wise person or persons with us. *Deuteronomy* 19: 15 has it: " One witness shall not rise up against a man for any iniquity, or for any sin, in any sin that he sinneth; at the mouth of two witnesses, or at the mouth of three witnesses, shall the matter be established." That is the saying which Matthew has in mind. But in this case the taking of the witnesses is not meant to be a way of proving to a man that he has sinned. The taking of two or three wise people is meant to help the process of reconciliation. It may well be that it is *we*, and not the other man, who are in the wrong. A man often hates those whom he has injured most of all; and it may well be that nothing we can say can win back the other man. But to talk matters over with some wise and kindly and gracious people present is to create a new atmosphere in which there is at least a chance that we should see ourselves " as others see us." The Rabbis had a wise saying, " Judge not alone, for none may judge alone save One (that is God)."

(iv) If that still fails, we must take our personal troubles to the Christian fellowship. Why? Because troubles are never settled by going to law, or by Christless argument. Legalism settles nothing; it merely produces further trouble. It is in an atmosphere of Christian prayer, Christian love and Christian fellowship that personal relationships may be righted. It is clear that that assumes that the Christian fellowship *is* Christian, and that it seeks to judge everything, not in the light of a book of practice and procedure, but in the light of love.

(v) It is now we come to the difficult part of this passage. Matthew says that if even that does not succeed then the man who has wronged us is to be regarded as a heathen man and a publican. We have seen that the first impression of that saying is that the man must be abandoned as hopeless and irreclaimable. That is precisely what Jesus did not and cannot have meant. He could never set limits to human forgiveness. What then did He mean? We have seen that when He speaks of tax-gatherers and sinners He always does so with sympathy and gentleness and an appreciation of their good qualities. It may be that what

Jesus said was something like this: "When you have done all this, when you have given the sinner every chance, and when he remains stubborn and obdurate, you may think that he is no better than a renegade tax-collector, or even a godless Gentile. Well, you may be right. But I have not found the tax-gatherers and the Gentiles and the sinners hopeless. My experience of them is that they, too, have a heart to be touched; and there are many of them, like Matthew and Zacchaeus, who have become my best friends. Even if the stubborn sinner is like a tax-collector and a Gentile, you can still win him, as I have done." This, in fact, is *not* an injunction to abandon a man; it is a challenge to win him with the love which can touch even the hardest heart. It is not a statement that some men are hopeless; it is a statement that Jesus Christ has found no man hopeless—and neither must we.

(vi) Finally, there is the saying about loosing and binding. That is a difficult saying. It cannot mean that the Church can remit or forgive sins, and so settle a man's destiny in time or in eternity. What it may well mean is that the relationships which we establish with our fellow-men last, not only through time, but enter into eternity—therefore we *must* get them right.

THE POWER OF THE PRESENCE

Matthew 18: 19, 20

> "Again, I tell you, that if two of you agree upon earth upon any matter for which you are praying, you will receive it from my Father who is in Heaven. Where two or three are assembled together in my name, there am I in the midst of them."

HERE is one of these sayings of Jesus, the meaning of which we need to probe and to understand, or we will be left with nothing but heartbreak and a great disappointment. Jesus says that, if two upon earth agree upon any matter for which they are praying, they will receive it from

God. If that is to be taken literally, and without any condition or qualification, it is manifestly untrue. Times without number two people have agreed to pray for the physical or the spiritual welfare of a loved one—and their prayer has not, in the literal sense, been answered. Times without number God's people have agreed to pray for the conversion of their own land or the conversion of the heathen and the coming of the Kingdom, and even yet that prayer is far from being fully answered. People do agree to pray—and they do pray desperately—and they do not receive that for which they pray. There is no point in refusing to face the facts of the situation, and nothing but harm can result from teaching people to expect that which does not happen. But when we come to see what this saying of Jesus means, there is a precious depth of meaning in it.

(i) First and foremost, it means that prayer must never be selfish, and that selfish prayer cannot find an answer. We are not meant to pray for our needs, thinking of nothing and no one but ourselves; we are meant to pray as members of a fellowship, in agreement, remembering that life and the world are not arranged for us as individuals, but for the fellowship as a whole. It would often happen that, if our prayers were answered, the prayers of someone else would be disappointed. Often our prayers for our success would necessarily involve someone else's failure. Effective prayer must be the prayer of agreement, from which the element of a selfish concentration on our own needs and desires has been quite cleansed away.

(ii) When prayer is unselfish, it is always answered. But here as everywhere we must remember the basic law of prayer; that law is that in prayer we receive, not the answer which we desire, but the answer which God in His wisdom and His love knows to be best. Simply because we are human beings, with human hearts and human fears and human hopes and human desires, most of our prayers are prayers for escape. We pray to be saved from some trial, some sorrow, some disappointment, some hurting and difficult situation. And always God's answer is not the offer of escape, but of victory. God does not give us escape from a human situation; He enables us to accept what we cannot understand; He enables us to endure what without Him would be unendurable; He enables us to face what without Him would be beyond all facing; He gives us a wisdom to deal with things which without Him we could not possess. The perfect example of all this is Jesus in Gethsemane. Jesus prayed to be released from the dread situation which confronted Him; He was not released from it; but He was given power to meet it, to endure it, and to conquer it. When we pray unselfishly, God sends His answer—but the answer is always His answer—not necessarily ours.

(iii) Jesus goes on to say that where two or three are gathered in His name, He is there in the midst of them. The Jews themselves had a saying, " Where two sit and are occupied with the study of the Law, the glory of God is among them." We may take this great promise of Jesus into two spheres with us.

(a) We may take it into the sphere of the *Church*. Jesus is just as much present in the little congregation as He is in the great mass meeting. He is just as much present at the Prayer Meeting or the Bible Study Circle with their handful of people as He is in the crowded arena. Jesus Christ is not the slave of numbers. He is there wherever faithful hearts meet, however few they may be, for He gives all of Himself to each individual person.

(b) We may take it into the sphere of the *home*. One of the earliest interpretations of this saying of Jesus was that *the two or three* are *father, mother, and child*, and that it means that Jesus is there, the unseen guest in every home.

There are those who never give of their best except on the so-called great occasion; but for Jesus Christ every occasion where even two or three are gathered in His name is a great occasion.

HOW TO FORGIVE

Matthew 18: 21-35

> Then Peter came and said to Him, "Lord, how
> often will my brother sin against me, and I forgive
> him? Up to seven times?" Jesus said to him, "I
> tell you not up to seven times, but up to seventy
> times seven. That is why the Kingdom of Heaven
> can be likened to what happened when a king wished
> to make a reckoning with his servants. When he
> began to make a reckoning one debtor was brought
> to him who owed him £2,400,000. Since he was quite
> unable to pay, his master ordered him to be sold,
> together with his wife and children, and all his posses-
> sions, and payment to be made. The servant fell
> on his face and besought him: 'Sir, have patience
> with me, and I will pay you in full.' The master of
> the servant was moved with compassion, and let
> him go, and forgave him the debt. When that servant
> went out, he found one of his fellow-servants, who
> owed him £5. He caught hold of him and seized
> him by the throat: 'Pay what you owe,' he said.
> The fellow-servant fell down and besought him,
> 'Have patience with me, and I will pay you in full.'
> But he refused. Rather, he went away and flung
> him into prison, until he should pay what was due.
> So, when his fellow-servants saw what had happened,
> they were very distressed; and they went and informed
> their master of all that had happened. Then the
> master summoned him, and said to him, 'You wicked
> servant! I forgave you all that debt when you besought
> me to do so. Ought you not to have had pity on your
> fellow-servant, as I had pity on you?' And his
> master was angry with him and handed him over
> to the torturers, until he should pay all that was due.
> Even so shall my heavenly Father do to you, if
> you do not each one forgive his brother from your
> hearts."

WE owe a very great deal to the fact that Peter had a
quick tongue. Again and again Peter rushed into speech,
and his impetuosity drew from Jesus teaching which is
immortal. On this occasion Peter thought that he was
being very generous and that he was doing well. He asked
Jesus how often he ought to forgive his brother, and then

he answered his own question by suggesting that he should forgive seven times. Peter was not without warrant for this suggestion. It was Rabbinic teaching that a man must forgive his brother *three* times. Rabbi Jose ben Hanina said, " He who begs forgiveness from his neighbour must not do so more than three times." Rabbi Jose ben Jehuda said, " If a man commits an offence once, they forgive him; if he commits an offence a second time, they forgive him; if he commits an offence a third time, they forgive him; the fourth time they do not forgive." The Biblical proof that this was correct was taken from *Amos*. In the opening chapters of *Amos* there is a series of condemnations on the various nations *for three transgressions and for four* (*Amos* 1: 3, 6, 9, 11, 13; 2: 1, 4, 6). From this it was deduced that God's forgiveness extends to three offences, and that He visits the sinner with punishment at the fourth. It was not to be thought that a man could be more gracious than God, so forgiveness was limited to three times. Peter thought that he was going very far, for he takes the Rabbinic three times, multiplies it by two, for good measure adds one; and suggests, with eager self-satisfaction, that it will be enough if he forgives seven times. Peter expected to be warmly commended; but Jesus' answer is that the Christian must forgive seventy times seven, that, in fact, there is no reckonable limit to forgiveness.

Then Jesus told the story of the servant who was himself forgiven a great debt; and who went out and dealt mercilessly with a fellow-servant who owed him a debt that was an infinitesimal fraction of what he himself had owed; and who for his mercilessness was utterly condemned. This parable teaches certain lessons which Jesus never tired of teaching.

(i) It teaches that lesson which runs through all the New Testament—a man must forgive in order to be forgiven. He who will not forgive his fellow-men cannot hope that God will forgive him. " Blessed are the merciful," said

Jesus, " for they will obtain mercy " (*Matthew* 5: 7). No sooner had Jesus taught His men His own prayer, than He went on to expand and explain one petition in it: " For if ye forgive men their trespasses, your heavenly Father will also forgive you; but if ye forgive not men their trespasses, neither will your heavenly Father forgive your trespasses " (*Matthew* 6: 14, 15). As James had it, " He shall have judgment without mercy that hath showed no mercy " (*James* 2: 13). Divine and human forgiveness must go hand in hand.

(ii) And why should that be so? One of the great points in this parable is the contrast between the two debts. The first servant owed his master 10,000 talents; a talent was the equivalent of £240; therefore 10,000 talents is £2,400,000. That is an incredible debt. It was more than the total budget of the ordinary province. The total revenue of the province which contained Idumaea, Judaea and Samaria was only 600 talents; the total revenue of even a wealthy province like Galilee was only 300 talents. Here was a debt which was greater than a king's ransom. It was this debt that the servant was forgiven. The debt which a fellow-servant owed him was a trifling thing; it was 100 *denarii*; a *denarius* was about 9d. in value; and therefore the total debt was less than £5. It was approximately one five-hundred-thousandth of his own debt. A. R. S. Kennedy drew this vivid picture to contrast the debts. Suppose the debts to be paid in sixpences. The 100 denarii debt could have been carried in one pocket. The ten thousand talent debt would have taken to carry it an army of about 8,600 carriers, each carrying a sack of sixpences 60 lbs. in weight; and they would have formed, at a distance of a yard apart, a line five miles long! The contrast between the debts is staggering. And the point is that nothing that men can do to us can in any way compare with what we have done to God; and if God has forgiven us the debt we owe to Him, we must forgive our fellow-men the debts they owe to us. Nothing that we have to forgive can even faintly or remotely compare with that which we have been forgiven.

> " Not the labours of my hands
>   Can fulfil Thy law's demands;
>   Could my zeal no respite know,
>   Could my tears for ever flow,
>   *All for sin could not atone.*"

We have been forgiven a debt which is beyond all paying— for the sin of man brought about the death of God's own Son—and, if that is so, we must forgive others as God has forgiven us, or we can hope to find no mercy.

JEWISH MARRIAGE AND DIVORCE

Matthew 19: 1-9

> When Jesus had finished these words, He left Galilee, and came into the districts of Judaea which are on the far side of the Jordan. Many crowds followed Him, and He healed them there.
>
> Pharisees came to Him, trying to test Him. " Is it lawful," they said, " for a man to divorce his wife for any cause? " He answered, " Have you not read that from the beginning the Creator made them male and female, and He said, ' For this cause a man shall leave his father and his mother, and shall cleave to his wife, and the two shall become one flesh '? They are therefore no longer two, but one flesh. What, then, God has joined together, let no man separate." They said to Him, " Why, then, did Moses lay it down to give her a bill of divorcement, and to divorce her? " He said to them, " It was to meet the hardness of your heart that Moses allowed you to divorce your wives; but in the beginning that was not the state of things which was intended. I tell you that whoever divorces his wife, except on the ground of fornication, and marries another, commits adultery; and he who marries her who has been divorced commits adultery."

HERE Jesus is dealing with what was in His day, as it is in our own, a vexed and burning question. The question of divorce was something about which there was no unanimity among the Jews; and the question of the Pharisees was deliberately designed to involve Jesus in controversy.

No nation has ever had a higher view of marriage than the Jews had. Marriage was a sacred duty. To remain unmarried after the age of twenty, except in order to concentrate upon the study of the Law, was to break a positive commandment, the commandment to " be fruitful and multiply." He who had no children " slew his own posterity," and " lessened the image of God upon earth." " When husband and wife are worthy, the glory of God is with them."

Marriage was not to be entered into carelessly or lightly. Josephus outlines the Jewish approach to marriage, based on the Mosaic teaching (*Antiquities of the Jews* 4. 8. 23). A man must marry a virgin of good parentage. He must never corrupt another man's wife; and he must not marry a woman who had been a slave or a harlot. If a man accused his wife of not being a virgin when he married her, he must bring proofs of his accusation. Her father or brother must defend her. If the girl was vindicated he must take her in marriage, and could never again put her away, except for the most flagrant sin. If the accusation was proved to have been rash and reckless and malicious, the man who made it must be beaten with forty stripes save one, and must pay fifty shekels to the girl's father. But if the charge was proved, and if the girl was found guilty, if she was one of the ordinary people, the law was that she must be stoned to death, and if she was the daughter of a priest, she must be burned alive.

If a man seduced a girl who was espoused to be married, if the seduction took place with her consent, both he and she must be put to death. If in a lonely place, or where there was no help present, the man forced the girl into sin, the man alone was put to death. If a man seduced an unespoused girl, he must marry her, or, if her father was unwilling for him to marry her, he must pay the father fifty shekels.

The Jewish laws of marriage and of purity aimed very high. Ideally divorce was hated. God had said, " I hate putting away " (*Malachi* 2: 16). It was said that the very altar wept tears when a man divorced the wife of his youth.

But ideal and actuality did not go hand in hand. In the situation there were two dangerous and damaging elements.

First, in the eyes of Jewish law a woman was a thing. She was the possession of her father, or of her husband as the case might be; and, therefore, she had, technically, no legal rights at all. Most Jewish marriages were arranged either by the parents or by professional match-makers. A girl might be engaged to be married in childhood, and was often engaged to be married to a man whom she had never seen. There was this safeguard—that when she came to the age of twelve she could repudiate her father's choice of husband. But in matters of divorce the general law was that the entire initiative must lie with the husband. The law ran: " A woman may be divorced with or without her consent, but a man can be divorced only with his consent." The woman could never initiate the process of divorce; she could not divorce, she had to be divorced. There were certain safeguards. If a man divorced his wife, on any other grounds than those of flagrant immorality, he must return her dowry, and this must have been a barrier to irresponsible divorce. The courts might put pressure on a man to divorce his wife, in the case, for instance, of refusal to consummate the marriage, of impotence, or of proved inability to support her properly. A wife could force her husband to divorce her, if he contracted a loathsome disease, such as leprosy, or if he was a tanner, which involved the gathering of dog's dung, or if he proposed to make her leave the Holy Land. But, by and large, the law was that the woman had no legal rights, and the right to divorce lay entirely with the husband.

Second, the ease of the process of divorce was fatal. That process was founded on the passage in the Mosaic Law to which Jesus' questioners referred: " When a man hath taken a wife, and married her, and it come to pass that she find no favour in his eyes, because he hath found some uncleanness in her, then let him write her a bill of divorcement, and give it in her hand, and send her out of his house " (*Deuteronomy* 24: 1). The bill of divorcement was a simple, one-sentence statement that the husband dismissed his wife. Josephus writes, " He that desires to be divorced from his wife for any cause whatsoever (and many such causes happen among men) let him, in writing, give assurance that he will never use her as his wife any more; for by this means she may be at liberty to marry another husband." The ease of the process of divorce was fatal. As we have said, the one safeguard was the fact that, unless the woman was a notorious sinner, her dowry must be returned.

JEWISH GROUNDS OF DIVORCE

Matthew 19: 1-9 (*continued*)

CLEARLY one of the great problems of Jewish divorce lies within the Mosaic enactment. That enactment states that a man may divorce his wife, " if she find no favour in his eyes, because he hath found *some uncleanness* in her." The question clearly is—how is that phrase *some uncleanness* to be interpreted? On this question the Jewish Rabbis were violently divided, and it was in this question that Jesus' questioners wished to involve him. The school of Shammai were quite clear that *a matter of uncleanness* meant fornication, and fornication alone, and that for no other cause could a wife be put away. Let a woman be as mischievous as Jezebel, so long as she did not commit adultery, she could not be put away. On the other hand, the school of Hillel interpreted this *matter of uncleanness* in the widest possible way. They said that it meant that a man could divorce his wife, if she spoiled his dinner, if she spun, or went with unbound hair, or spoke to men in the streets, if she spoke disrespectfully of his parents in his presence, if she was a brawling woman whose voice could be heard in the next house. Rabbi Akiba even went the length of saying that the phrase *if she find no favour in his eyes* meant that a man could divorce his wife, if he found a woman whom he liked better, and considered more beautiful.

The tragedy was that the obvious result followed— it was the school of Hillel whose teachings prevailed; and the marriage bond was often lightly held, and divorce on the most trivial ground was tragically common.

To complete this picture certain further facts must be added. It is relevant to note that under Rabbinic law divorce was *compulsory* for two reasons. It was compulsory for adultery. " A woman who has committed adultery must be divorced." Here there was no choice; divorce was inevitable. Second, divorce was compulsory for *sterility*. The object of marriage was the procreation of children; and if after ten years a couple were still childless, then divorce was compulsory. In this case the woman might remarry, but the same regulation governed the second marriage.

Two further interesting Jewish regulations in regard to divorce must be added. First, *desertion* was never a cause for divorce. If there was desertion, death must be proved. The only relaxation was that, whereas all other facts need the corroboration of two witnesses in Jewish law, one witness was enough to prove the death of a partner in marriage who had vanished and not come back.

Second, strangely enough, *insanity* was not a ground of divorce. If the wife became insane, the husband could not divorce her, for, if she was divorced, she would have no protector in her helplessness. There is a certain poignant mercy in that regulation. If the husband became insane, divorce was impossible, for in that case he was incapable of writing a bill of divorcement, and without such a bill, initiated by him, there could be no divorce.

When Jesus was asked this question, at the back of it there was a dispute, and at the back of it there was a situation which was vexed and troubled. He was to answer it in a way which came as a staggering surprise to both parties in the dispute, and which suggested a radical change in the whole situation.

THE ANSWER OF JESUS

Matthew 19: 1-9 (*continued*)

IT was with this situation that Jesus was faced, when He was asked for His views on divorce. In effect, the Pharisees were asking Him whether He favoured the strict views of Shammai, or the laxer view of Hillel, and thereby seeking to involve Him in controversy.

Jesus' answer was to take things back to the very beginning. He went back to the ideal of creation. In the beginning, He said, God created Adam and Eve, man and woman. Now inevitably, in the very circumstances of the creation story, Adam and Eve were created for each other and for no one else; their union was necessarily complete and unbreakable. Now, says Jesus, these two are the pattern and the symbol of all who were to come. As A. H. M'Neile puts it, " Each married couple is a reproduction of Adam and Eve, and their union is therefore no less indissoluble." The argument is quite clear. In the case of Adam and Eve divorce was not only inadvisable; it was not only wrong; it was completely impossible, for the very simple reason that there was no one else whom either of them could possibly marry. Therefore Jesus is laying down the principle that all divorce is wrong. Thus early we must note that that is not a *law*; it is a *principle*, which is a very different thing.

Here, at once, the Pharisees saw a point of attack. Moses (*Deuteronomy* 24: I) had said that, if a man wished to divorce his wife because she had found no favour in his eyes, nd because of some matter of uncleanness in her, then he could give her a bill of divorce, and the marriage was dissolved. Here is the very chance the Pharisees wanted. They can now say to Jesus, " Are you saying Moses was wrong? Are you seeking to abrogate the divine law which was given to Moses? Are you setting yourself above Moses as a law-giver? " Jesus' answer is that what Moses said was not in fact a *law*; that it was nothing more than a *concession*. Moses did not *command* divorce; at the best he only *permitted* it in order to regulate a situation which would have become chaotically promiscuous. The Mosaic regulation is only a concession to fallen human nature. In *Genesis* 2: 23, 24, we have the ideal which God intended, the ideal that two people who marry should become so indissolubly one that they are one flesh. Jesus' answer is: " True, Moses *permitted* divorce; but that was a *concession* in view of a lost ideal. The ideal of marriage is to be found in the unbreakable, perfect union of Adam and Eve. *That* is what God meant marriage to be."

It is now that we are face to face with one of the realest and acutest difficulties in the New Testament. What did Jesus mean? There is even a prior question—what did Jesus say? The difficulty is—and there is no escaping it—that Mark and Matthew report the words of Jesus differently.

Matthew has:

> I say unto you, whosoever shall put away his wife, *except it be for fornication,* and shall marry another, committeth adultery; and whosoever marrieth her that is put away doth commit adultery (*Matthew* 19: 9).

Mark has:

> Whosoever shall put away his wife, and marry another, committeth adultery against her; and, if a woman shall put away her husband, and be married to another she committeth adultery (*Mark* 10: 11, 12).

Luke has still another version of this saying:

> Whosoever putteth away his wife and marrieth another, committeth adultery; and whosoever marrieth her that is put away from her husband committeth adultery (*Luke* 16: 18).

There is the comparatively small difficulty that Mark implies that a woman can divorce her husband, a process which, as we have seen, was not possible under Jewish law. But the explanation of that difficulty is that Jesus must have well known that under Gentile law a woman could divorce her husband, and in that particular clause He was looking beyond the Jewish world. The great difficulty is that both Mark and Luke make the prohibition of divorce *absolute*; with them there are no exceptions whatsoever. But Matthew has one saving clause—divorce is permitted on the ground of adultery. In this case there is no real escape from a decision. The only possible way out would be to say that in point of fact, under Jewish law, divorce for adultery was in any event *compulsory*, as we have seen, and that therefore Mark and Luke did not think that they need mention it; but then so was divorce for sterility, as we have also seen.

In the last analysis we must choose Matthew's version of this saying, or that of Mark and Luke. We think that there is little doubt that the version of Mark and Luke is right. There are two reasons for that. Only the absolute prohibition of separation will satisfy the ideal of the Adam and Eve symbolic complete union. And the staggered words of the disciples imply this absolute prohibition, for, in effect, they say (verse 10) that if marriage is as binding as that, it is safer not to marry at all. There is little doubt that here we have Jesus laying down the *principle*—mark again, not, the *law*—that the ideal of marriage is a union which cannot be broken. There is much more than that to be said—but here the *ideal*, as God meant it, is laid down, and Matthew's saving clause is a later interpretation inserted in the light of the practice of the Church when he wrote.

THE HIGH IDEAL

Matthew 19: 1-9 (*continued*)

LET us now go on to see the high ideal of the married state which Jesus sets before those who are willing to accept His commands. In this we will see that the Jewish ideal gives us the basis of the Christian ideal. The Jewish term for marriage was *Kiddushin*. *Kiddushin* means *sanctification* or *consecration*. It is used to describe something which is dedicated to God as God's exclusive and peculiar possession. Anything which is absolutely given and totally surrendered to God is *kiddushin*. This means that in marriage the husband is dedicated and consecrated to the wife, and the wife is dedicated and consecrated to the husband. The one becomes the exclusive possession of the other, as much as an offering and a sacrifice become the exclusive possession of God. That is what Jesus meant when He said that for the sake of marriage a man would leave his father and his mother and cleave to his wife; and that is what He meant when He said that man and wife become so totally one that they can be called one flesh. That was God's ideal of marriage as the old *Genesis* story saw it (*Genesis* 2: 24), and that is the ideal which Jesus restates. Clearly that idea has certain consequences.

(i) This total unity means that marriage is not given for one act in life, however important that act may be, but for all acts in life. That is to say that, while sex is a supremely important part of marriage, it is not the whole of marriage. Any marriage which is entered into simply because an imperious physical desire can be satisfied in no other way is foredoomed to failure. Marriage is given, not that two people should do one thing together, but that they should do all things together.

(ii) Another way to put that is that marriage is the total union of two personalities. Two people can exist together in a variety of different ways. One can be the dominant partner to such an extent that nothing matters but his wishes and his desires and his convenience and his aims in life, while the other is totally subservient and exists only to serve the desires and the needs of the other. Again, two people can exist in a kind of armed neutrality, where there is continuous tension, and continuous opposition, and continuous collision between their wishes and desires. Life can be one long argument, and the relationship is based at best on an uneasy compromise. Again, two people can base their relationship on a more or less resigned acceptance of each other. To all intents and purposes, while they live together, each goes his or her own way, and each has his or her own life. They share the same house, but it would be an exaggeration to say that they share the same home. Clearly none of these relationships is the ideal. The ideal is that in the marriage state two people find the completing of their personalities. Plato had a strange idea. He has a kind of legend that originally human beings were double what they are now. Because their size and strength made them arrogant, the gods cut them in halves; and real happiness comes when the two halves find each other again, and marry, and so complete each other. Marriage should not narrow life; it should complete it. For both partners it must bring a new fulness, a new satisfaction, a new contentment into life. It is the union of two personalities in which the two complete each other. That does not mean that adjustments, and even sacrifices, have not be be made; but it does mean that the final relationship is fuller, more joyous, more satisfying than any life in singleness and in isolation could be.

(iii) We may put this even more practically—marriage must be a sharing of all the circumstances of life. There is a certain danger in the days of the delight of courtship. In such days it is almost inevitable that two people should see each other at their best. These are the days of what is called glamour. They see each other in their best clothes; usually they are bent on some pleasure together; often money has not yet become a problem. But in marriage two people must see each other when they are not at their best; when they are tired and weary; when children bring the upset to a house and home that children must bring; when money is tight, and food and clothes and bills become a problem; when the moonlight and roses become the kitchen sink and walking the floor at night with a crying baby. Unless two people are prepared to face the routine of life as well as the glamour of life together, marriage must of necessity be a failure.

(iv) From that there follows one thing, which is not necessarily universally true, but which is much more likely than not to be true. Marriage is most likely to be successful after a fairly long acquaintanceship, and when two people really know the background from which each of them comes. The better two people know each other, and the more circumstances in which they have seen each other, the more likely marriage is to succeed. Marriage means constantly living together. It is perfectly possible for ingrained habits, unconscious mannerisms, ways of upbringing to collide. The fuller the knowledge that people have of each other, before they decide indissolubly to link their lives together, the better. This is not to deny that there can be such a thing as love at first sight, and that love can conquer all things, but it is to say that the greater the mutual knowledge which people have of each other the more likely they are to succeed in making their marriage what it ought to be.

(v) All this leads us to a final practical conclusion—the basis of all marriage is *togetherness*, and the basis of togetherness is nothing other than *considerateness*. If marriage is to succeed, the partners in it must always be thinking more of each other than of themselves. Selfishness is the murderer of any personal relationship with other people; and that is truest of all when these people are so linked that they cannot get away from each other, but are bound together. Somerset Maughan tells of his own mother. She was lovely and charming and beloved by all. His father was not by any means handsome, and had few social and surface gifts and graces. Someone once said to his mother, " When everyone is in love with you, and when you could have anyone you liked, how can you remain faithful to that ugly little man you married? " She answered simply: " He never hurts my feelings." There could be no finer tribute. The true basis of marriage is not elaborate and complicated and recondite—it is simply the love which thinks more of the happiness of others than it thinks of its own, the love which is proud to serve, the love which is able to understand, and therefore always able to forgive. That is to say, it is the Christlike love, which knows that in forgetting self it will find self, and that in losing itself it will complete itself.

THE REALIZATION OF THE IDEAL

Matthew 19: 10-12

> His disciples said to Him, " If the only reason for divorce between a man and his wife stands thus, it is not expedient to marry." He said to them, " Not all can receive this saying, but only those to whom it has been granted to do so. There are eunuchs who were born so from their mothers' womb; and there are eunuchs who have been made eunuchs by men; and there are eunuchs who have made themselves eunuchs for the sake of the Kingdom of Heaven. Let him who is able to receive this saying, receive it."

HERE we come to the necessary amplification of what has gone before. When the disciples heard the ideal of Christian marriage which Jesus set before them, they were daunted. Many a rabbinic saying would come into the mind of the disciples. The Rabbis had many sayings about unhappy marriages. " Among those who will never behold the face of Gehinnom is he who has had a bad wife." Such a man is saved from hell because he has expiated his sins on earth! " Among those whose life is not life is the man who is ruled by his wife." " A bad wife is like leprosy to her husband. What is the remedy? Let him divorce her and be cured of his leprosy." It was even laid down: " If a man has a bad wife, it is a religious duty to divorce her." To men who had been brought up to listen to sayings like that the uncompromising demand of Jesus was an almost frightening thing. The reaction of the disciples was that, if marriage is so final and binding a relationship, and, if divorce is forbidden, it is better not to marry at all, for there is no escape route—as they understood it—from an evil situation. Jesus gives two answers.

(i) He says quite clearly that not everyone can in fact accept this situation, that only those to whom it has been granted to do so can accept this saying. What Jesus is really saying is this—*Only the Christian can accept the Christian ethic*. Only the man who has the continual help of Jesus Christ and the continual guidance of the Holy Spirit can build up the personal relationship which the ideal of marriage demands. Only by the help of Jesus Christ can a man develop the sympathy, the understanding, the forgiving spirit, the considerate love, which true marriage requires. Without the help of Jesus Christ these things are plainly impossible. The Christian ideal of marriage involves the prerequisite that the partners to marriage are Christian. Here is a truth which goes far beyond this particular application of it. We continually hear people say, " We accept the ethics of the Sermon on the Mount; but why bother about the idea of the divinity of Jesus, and His Resurrection, and His risen presence, and His Holy Spirit, and all that kind of thing? We accept the fact that He was a good man, and that His teaching is the highest teaching that was ever given. Why not leave it at that, and get on with the living out of that teaching and never mind the theology?" The answer to that is quite simple. No one can live out Jesus Christ's teaching without Jesus Christ. To do so is impossible. And if Jesus was only a great and good man, even if He was the greatest and the best of man, then at best He is only a great example; He is not a great power. On the assumption that Jesus lived and died His teaching is impossible; His teaching only becomes possible in the conviction that He is not dead, but that He is present here to help us to carry it out. The teaching of Christ demands the presence of Christ; otherwise it is only an impossible—and a torturing—ideal. So, then, we have to face the fact that Christian marriage is only possible for Christians.

(ii) The passage finishes with a very puzzling verse about eunuchs. It is quite possible that Jesus said this on some other occasion, and that Matthew puts it here, because he is collecting Jesus' teaching on marriage, for it was always Matthew's custom to collect together Jesus' teaching on any subject.

A eunuch is a man who is unsexed. Jesus distinguishes three classes of people. There are those who, through some physical imperfection or deformity, can never be capable of sexual intercourse. There are those who have been made eunuchs by men. This represents customs which are quite strange to western civilization. Quite frequently in royal palaces servants, especially those who had to do with the royal harem, were deliberately castrated. And also, quite frequently priests who served in temples were castrated; this, for instance, is true of the priests who served in the Temple of Diana in Ephesus.

Then Jesus talks about those who have made themselves

eunuchs for the sake of the Kingdom of God. We must be quite clear that this is not to be taken literally. One of the tragedies of the early Church was the case of Origen. When he was young he took this text quite literally and castrated himself, although he came to see that he was in error. Clement of Alexandria comes nearer it. He says, " The true eunuch is not he who cannot, but he who will not indulge in fleshly pleasures." By this phrase Jesus meant those who for the sake of the Kingdom deliberately bade farewell to marriage and to parenthood and to human physical love.

How can that be so? It can happen that a man has to choose between some call to which he is challenged and human love. It has been said, " He travels farthest who travels alone." A man may feel that he can only do the work of some terrible slum parish by living in circumstances in which marriage and a home are impossible. He may feel that he must accept some missionary call to a place where he cannot in conscience take a wife and beget children. He may even find that he is in love, and that then he is offered an inescapable call, which the person he loves refuses to share. Then he must choose between human love and the task to which Christ calls him.

Thank God, it is not often that such a choice comes to a man; but there are those who have taken upon themselves the voluntary vows of chastity, celibacy, purity, poverty, abstinence, continence. That will not be the way for the ordinary man, but the world would be a poorer place had there not been those who accepted the challenge to travel alone for the sake of the work of the Kingdom of God.

MARRIAGE AND DIVORCE

Matthew 19: 10-12 (continued)

IT would be wrong to leave this matter without some attempt to see what it actually means for the question of divorce at the present time.

We may at the beginning note one thing. *What Jesus laid down was a principle and not a law.* To fail to remember that, and to turn this saying of Jesus into a law, is gravely to misunderstand it. The Bible does not give us *laws*; it gives *principles* which we must prayerfully and intelligently apply to any given situation. Of the Sabbath the Bible says, " In it thou shalt not do any work " (*Exodus* 20: 10). In point of fact we know that a complete cessation of work was never possible in any civilization. In an agricultural civilization cattle had still to be tended, and cows had to be milked no matter what the day was. In a developed civilization certain public services must go on, or transport will stand still, water, and light, and heat will not be available. In any home, especially where there are children, there has to be a certain amount of work. A principle can never be quoted as a final law; a principle must always be applied to the individual situation, as God Himself would have it to be applied. We cannot therefore settle the question of divorce simply by quoting the words of Jesus. That would be to be guilty of legalism; we must take the words of Jesus as a principle which we will apply to the individual cases as they meet us. If that be so, certain truths emerge.

(i) Beyond all doubt the *ideal* is that marriage should be an indissoluble union between two people, and that marriage should be entered into as a total union of two personalities, not designed to make one act possible, but designed to make all life a satisfying and mutually completing fellowship. That undoubtedly is the essential basis on which we must proceed.

(ii) But life is not, and never can be, a completely tidy and orderly business. Into life there is bound to come sometimes the element of the unpredictable and the unforecastable. Suppose, then, that two people enter into the marriage relationship; suppose they do so with the highest hopes and the highest ideals; and then suppose that something unaccountable goes wrong, and that that relationship which should be life's greatest joy becomes hell upon earth. No one knows that is going to happen until people actually attempt the experiment of living together. Suppose all available help is called in to mend this broken and terrible situation. Suppose the doctor is called in to deal with physical things; the psychiatrist to deal with psychological things; the priest or the minister to deal with spiritual things. Suppose the trouble still to be there; suppose one of the partners to the marriage to be so constituted physically, mentally or spiritually in such a way that he or she is one of these rare persons for whom marriage is an impossibility, and suppose that that discovery could not have been made until the experiment itself had been made—are then these two people to be told that they are for ever fettered together in a situation which cannot do other than bring a lifetime of misery to both? It is extremely difficult to see how such reasoning can be called Christian; it is extremely hard to see Jesus legalistically condemning two people to any such situation. This is not to say that divorce should be made easy, but it is to say that when all the physical and mental and spiritual resources have been brought to bear on such a situation, and the situation remains incurable and even dangerous, then the situation should be ended, and the Church, so far from regarding people who have been involved in such a situation as being beyond the pale, should do everything it can in strength and tenderness to help them. There does not seem to be any other way than that in which to bring the real Spirit of Christ to bear on the situation.

(iii) But in this matter we are face to face with a most tragic situation. It often happens that the things which wreck marriage are in fact the things which the law cannot touch. A man in a moment of passion and failure of control commits adultery, and he may well spend the rest of his life in shame and in sorrow for what he did. That he should ever repeat his sin is the least likely thing in the world

On the other hand a man may be a model of rectitude in public; to commit adultery might well be the last thing that he would do; and yet by a day-to-day sadistic cruelty, a day-to-day selfishness, a day-to-day criticism and sarcasm and mental cruelty, he may make life a hell for those who live with him; and he may do it with callous deliberation. We may well remember that the sins which get into the newspapers, and the sins whose consequences are most glaringly obvious, need not be in the sight of God the greatest sins. Many a man and many a woman wreck the marriage relationship, and yet present to the outer world a front of unimpeachable rectitude.

This whole matter is a matter to which we might well bring more sympathy and less condemnation, for, of all things, the failure of love must least be approached in legalism, and most in love. In such a case it is not a so-called law that must be conserved; it is a human heart and soul. What is wanted is that there should be brought to marriage a prayerful care and thought before the married state is entered upon; that if a marriage is in danger of failure every possible medical, psychological and spiritual resource should be mobilized to save it; but, that if there is something beyond the mending, the situation should be dealt with not with a rigid legalism, but with an understanding love.

JESUS' WELCOME FOR THE CHILDREN
Matthew 19: 13-15

> Children were brought to Him, that He might lay His hands on them, and pray for them. The disciples spoke sternly to them. Jesus said, " Let the little children come to me, and do not hinder them, for the Kingdom of Heaven belongs to such as they are." And after He had laid His hands on them, He went away from there.

IT may well be said that here we have the loveliest incident in the gospel story. The characters in it all stand out clear and plain, although it only takes two verses to tell it.

(i) There are those who brought the children. No doubt these would be the mothers of the children. No wonder they wished Jesus to lay His hands on them. They had seen what these hands could do; they had seen them touch disease and pain away. They had seen them bring sight to the blind eyes, and peace to the distracted mind; and they wanted hands like that to touch their children. There are few stories which show so clearly the sheer loveliness of the life of Jesus. Those who brought the children would not know who Jesus was; they would be well aware that Jesus was anything but popular with the Scribes and the Pharisees, and the Priests and the Sadducees and the leaders of orthodox religion; but there was a loveliness on Him. Premanand, the high-born Indian, in his autobiography, tells of a thing his mother once said to him. When Premanand became a Christian his family cast him off, and the doors were shut against him; but sometimes he used to slip back to see his mother. She was broken-hearted that he had become a Christian, but she did not cease to love him. She told him that when she was carrying him in her womb a missionary used sometimes to come and talk to her. The missionary gave her a copy of one of the gospels. She read it; she still had it. She told Premanand, her son, that she had no desire to become a Christian, but that sometimes, in those days before he was born, she used to long that her unborn son might grow up to be a man like this Jesus. There is a loveliness on Jesus Christ that anyone can see. It is easy to think of these mothers in Palestine feeling that the touch of a man like that on their children's heads would bring a blessing, even if they did not understand why.

(ii) There are the disciples. The disciples sound as they were rough and stern; but, if they were, it was love that made them so. Their one desire was to protect Jesus. They saw how tired He was; they saw what healing cost Him, for every time He healed virtue went out of Him. He was talking to them so often about a cross, and they must have seen on His face the tension of His heart and soul. All that they wanted was to see that Jesus was not bothered. They could only think that at such a time as this the children were a nuisance to the Master. We must not think of the disciples as rough and hard and stern; we must not condemn them; they only wished to save Jesus from another of these insistent demands which were always laying their imperious claims upon His strength.

(iii) There was Jesus Himself. This story tells us much about Him. He was the kind of person children loved. George Macdonald used to say that no man could be a follower of Jesus, if the children were afraid to play at his door. Jesus was certainly no grim ascetic, if the children loved Him. Further, to Jesus no one was unimportant. Someone would say, " It's only a child; don't let him bother you." Jesus would never say that. No one was ever a nuisance to Jesus. He was never too tired, never too busy to give all of Himself to anyone who needed it. There is a strange difference between Jesus and many a famous preacher or evangelist. It is often next door to impossible to get into the presence of one of these famous ones at all. They have a kind of retinue and bodyguard which keep the public away lest the great man be wearied and bothered. Jesus was the opposite of that. The way to the presence of Jesus is open to the humblest person and to the youngest child.

(iv) There were the children; and Jesus said of them that they were nearer God than anyone else there. The child's simplicity is nearer God than anything else. It is life's tragedy that, as we grow older, we so often grow further from God, and not nearer to Him.

THE GREAT REFUSAL

Matthew 19: 16-22

And, look you, a man came to Him and said, " Teacher, what good thing am I to do to possess eternal life? "

He said to him, " Why do you ask me about the good?
There is One who is good. If you wish to enter into
life, keep the commandments." He said to Him,
" What kind of commandments? " Jesus said, " ' You
must not kill; you must not commit adultery; you
must not steal; honour your father and your mother.'
And, ' You must love your neighbour as yourself.' "
The young man said, " I have observed all these
things. What am I still lacking? " Jesus said to
him, " If you wish to be complete, go, sell your
possessions, and give to the poor, and you will have
treasure in heaven; and come, follow me! " When
the young man heard that saying, he went away in
sorrow, for he had many possessions.

HERE is one of the best-known and best-loved stories in the
gospel history. One of the most interesting things about it
is the way in which most of us, quite unconsciously, unite
different details of it from the different gospels in order
to get a complete picture. We usually call this story, the
story of the Rich Young Ruler. All the gospels tell us
that this man was *rich*, for therein is the point of the story.
But only Matthew says that he was *young* (*Matthew* 19: 20);
and only Luke says that he was a *ruler* (*Luke* 18: 18). It is
interesting to see how, quite unconsciously, we have created
for ourselves a composite picture composed of elements
taken from all three gospels (*Matthew* 19: 16-22; *Mark*
10: 17-22; *Luke* 18: 18-23).

There is another interesting point about this story.
Matthew alters the question to Jesus of this man. Both
Mark and Luke say that the question was: " Why callest
thou me good? none is good, save one, that is God " (*Mark*
10: 18; *Luke* 18: 19). Matthew says that the question
was: " Why do you ask me about the good? There is
One who is good " (*Matthew* 19: 17). The text of the Authorized Version is in error here, as reference to any of the
newer and more correct translations will show. Matthew's
is the latest of the first three gospels, and his reverence
for Jesus is such that he cannot bear to show Jesus asking
the question: " Why do you call me good? " That almost

sounds to him as if Jesus was refusing to be called good, so he alters it into: " Why do you ask me about the good? " in order to avoid the seeming irreverence.

Within this story one of the deepest of all lessons is to be learned, for it has within it the whole basis of the difference between the right and the wrong idea of what religion is.

The man who came to Jesus was seeking for what he called *eternal life*. He was seeking for happiness, for satisfaction, for peace with God. But his very way of phrasing his question betrays him. He asks, " What must I *do*? " He is thinking in terms of *actions*. He is like the Pharisees; he is thinking in terms of keeping rules and laws and regulations. He is thinking of piling up a credit balance-sheet with God by keeping the works of the law. He clearly knows nothing of a religion of grace; he thinks in terms of a religion of law, and of earning the approval of God. So Jesus tries to lead him on to a correct view.

Jesus answers him in his own terms. He tells him to keep the commandments. The young man asks what kind of commandments Jesus means. Thereupon Jesus cites five of the ten commandments. Now there are two important things about the commandments which Jesus chooses to cite. First, they are all commandments which deal with *man's duty to man*. They are all from the second half of the decalogue, the half which deals, not with our duty to God, but with our *duty to men*. They are the command ments which govern our *personal relationships*, and our *attitude to our fellow-men*. Second, Jesus cites one commandment, as it were, out of order. He cites the command to honour parents last, when in point of fact it ought to come first. Why? It is clear that Jesus wishes to lay special stress on that commandment. Why? May it not be that this young man had grown rich and successful in his career, and had then forgotten his parents, who may have been very poor. He may well have risen in the world, and have been half-ashamed of the folks in the old home;

and then he may have justified himself perfectly legally by the law of *Korban*, which Jesus had so unsparingly condemned (*Matthew* 15: 1-6; *Mark* 7: 9-13). These passages show that he could well have done that, and still have legally claimed to have obeyed the commandments. In the very commandments which he cites Jesus is asking this young man what his attitude to his fellow-men and to his parents was, what his personal relationships were like.

The young man's answer to Jesus was that he had kept the commandments, and yet there was still something which he knew he ought to have, and which he had not got. So Jesus' commandment came to him to sell all he had and to give it to the poor and follow Him.

Now it so happens that we have another account of this whole incident in the *Gospel according to the Hebrews*, which was one of the very early gospels which failed to be included in the New Testament. Its account gives us certain very valuable additional information. Here it is:

> "The second of the rich men said to Him, 'Master, what good thing can I do and live?' He said unto him, 'O man, fulfil the law and the prophets.' He answered Him, 'I have kept them.' He said unto him, 'Go, sell all that thou ownest, and distribute it unto the poor, and, come, follow me.' But the rich man began to scratch his head, and it pleased him not. And the Lord said unto him, 'How sayest thou, I have kept the law and the prophets? For it is written in the law: Thou shalt love thy neighbour as thyself; and lo, many of thy brethren, sons of Abraham, are clad in filth, dying of hunger, and thine house is full of many good things, and nought at all goeth out of it unto them.' "

Here is the very key to the whole passage. The young man claimed to have kept the law. In the legal sense that might be true; but in the spiritual sense it was not true, because his whole attitude to his fellow-men was wrong. In the last analysis his attitude was utterly selfish. That is why Jesus confronted him with the challenge to sell all and to give to the poor. This man was so shackled to his possessions that nothing less than this surgical excision of them would suffice. If a man looks on his possessions as being given to him for nothing but his own comfort and convenience, then his possessions are a chain which must be broken; if a man looks at his possessions as a means to helping others, then his possessions are his crown.

The great truth of this story lies in the way it illumines the meaning of eternal life. Eternal life is life such as God Himself lives. The word for *eternal* is *aiōnios*, which does not mean *lasting for ever*; it means such as befits God, or such as belongs to God, or such as is characteristic of God. The great characteristic of God is that God so loved and God so gave. Therefore the essence of eternal life is not a carefully calculated keeping of the commandments and the rules and the regulations; eternal life is based on an attitude of loving and sacrificial generosity to our fellow-men. If we would find eternal life, if we would find happiness, joy, satisfaction, peace of mind and serenity of heart, we shall not find it by seeking to pile up a credit balance with God by keeping commandments and observing rules and regulations; we shall find it in reproducing God's attitude of love and care to our fellow-men; for to follow Christ and in grace and generosity to serve the men for whom Christ died are one and the same thing.

In the end the young man turned away in great distress. He refused the challenge, because he had great possessions. And his tragedy was that he loved things more than he loved people; and he loved himself more than he loved others; and any man who puts things before people, and self before others, must of necessity turn his back on Jesus Christ.

THE PERIL OF RICHES

Matthew 19: 23-26

> Jesus said to the disciples, " This is the truth I tell you—it is with difficulty that a rich man shall enter

> into the Kingdom of Heaven. Again I say unto you—it is easier for a camel to pass through the eye of a needle than for a rich man to enter into the Kingdom of Heaven." When the disciples heard this, they were exceedingly astonished. "What rich man, then," they said, "can be saved?" Jesus looked at them, "With men," He said, "this is impossible, but with God all things are possible."

THE case of the Rich Young Ruler shed a vivid and a tragic light on the danger of riches; here was a man who had made the great refusal because he had great possessions. Jesus now goes on to underline that danger. "It is difficult," He said, "for a rich man to enter into the Kingdom of Heaven." To illustrate how difficult that was He used a vivid simile. He said that it is as difficult for a rich man to enter the Kingdom of Heaven as it is for a camel to pass through the eye of a needle. Different interpretations have been given of the picture which Jesus is drawing. The camel was the largest animal which the Jews knew. It is said that sometimes in walled cities there were two gates. There was the great main gate through which all trade and traffic moved. Beside it there was often a little low and narrow gate. When the great main gate was closed and locked and guarded at night, the only way into the city was through the little gate, through which even a man could hardly pass erect. It is said that sometimes that little gate was called "The Needle's Eye." So, on that picture, Jesus is saying that it is just as difficult for a rich man to enter the Kingdom of Heaven as it would be for a huge camel to get through the little gate, through which a man can hardly pass. There is another, and a very attractive, suggestion. The Greek word for *camel* is *kamēlos*; the Greek word for a *ship's hawser* is *kamilos*. Now it was characteristic of later Greek that the vowel sounds tended to lose their sharp distinctions and to approximate to each other. In such Greek there would be hardly any discernible difference between the sound of *i* and *ē*; they would both be pronounced as *ee* is in English.

So, then, what Jesus may have said is that it is just as difficult for a rich man to enter into the Kingdom of Heaven as it would be to thread a darning-needle with a ship's cable or hawser. That indeed is a vivid picture. But the likelihood is that Jesus was using the picture quite literally, and that He was actually saying that it was as hard for a rich man to enter the Kingdom of Heaven as it was for a camel to go through the eye of a needle. Wherein then lies this difficulty? Riches have three main effects on a man's outlook.

(i) *Riches encourage a false independence.* If a man is well-supplied with this world's goods, he is very apt to think that he can well deal with any situation which may arise. There is a vivid instance of this in the letter to the Church of Laodicaea in the *Revelation*. Laodicaea was the richest town in Asia Minor. She was laid waste by an earthquake in A.D. 60. The Roman government offered aid, and a large grant of money to repair her shattered buildings. She refused it, saying that she was well able to handle the situation by herself. " Laodicaea," said Tacitus, the Roman historian, " rose from the ruins entirely by her own resources and with no help from us." The Risen Christ hears Laodicaea say, " I am rich, and increased with goods, and have need of nothing " (*Revelation* 3: 17). It was Walpole who coined the cynical epigram that every man has his price. If a man is wealthy he is apt to think that everything has its price, that if he wants a thing enough he can buy it, that if any difficult situation descends upon him, he can buy his way out of it. He can come to think that he can buy his way into happiness and buy his way out of sorrow. So he comes to think that he can well do without God, that he is quite able to handle life by himself. There comes a time when a man discovers that that is an illusion, that there are things which money cannot buy, and things from which money cannot save him. But always in life there is the danger that great possessions encourage that false independence which thinks

—until it learns better—that it has eliminated the need for God.

(ii) *Riches shackle a man to this earth.* " Where your treasure is," said Jesus, " there will your heart be also " (*Matthew* 6: 21). If everything a man desires is contained within this world, if all his interests are here, he never thinks of another world and of a hereafter. If a man has too big a stake on earth, he is very apt to forget that there is a heaven. After a tour of a certain wealthy and luxurious castle and estate, Dr. Johnson grimly remarked: " These are the things which make it difficult to die." It is perfectly possible for a man to be so interested in earthly things that he forgets heavenly things, to be so involved in the things that are seen that he forgets the things that are unseen—and therein lies tragedy for the things which are seen are temporal, but the things which are unseen are eternal.

(iii) *Riches tend to make a man selfish.* However much a man has, it is human for him to want still more, for, as it has been epigrammatically said, " Enough is always a little more than a man has." Further, once a man has possessed comfort and luxury, he always tends to fear the day when he may lose them. Life becomes a strenuous and worried struggle to retain the things he has. The result is that when a man becomes wealthy, instead of having the impulse to give things away, he very often has the impulse to cling on to them. His instinct is to amass more and more for the sake of the safety and the security which he thinks they will bring. The danger of riches is that they tend to make a man forget that he loses what he keeps, and he gains what he gives away.

But Jesus did not say that it was impossible for a rich man to enter the Kingdom of Heaven. Zacchaeus was one of the richest men in Jericho, yet, all unexpectedly, he found the way in (*Luke* 19: 9). Joseph of Arimathaea was a rich man (*Matthew* 27: 57); Nicodemus must have been very wealthy, for he brought spices to anoint the dead body of Jesus, which were worth a king's ransom (*John* 19: 39). It is not that those who have riches are shut out. It is not that riches are a sin—but they are a danger. The basis of all Christianity is an imperious sense of need; when a man has many things on earth, he is in danger of thinking that he does not need God; when a man has few things on earth, he is often driven to God because he has nowhere else to go.

A WISE ANSWER TO A MISTAKEN QUESTION

Matthew 19: 27-30

> Then Peter said to Him, " Look you, we have left everything and have followed you. What then will we get? " Jesus said to Him, " When all things are reborn, and when the Son of Man shall sit on the throne of His glory, you too, who have followed me, will also sit on twelve thrones, judging the twelve tribes of Israel. Anyone who has left houses, or brothers, or sisters, or father, or mother, or children, or lands for my name, will receive them a hundred times over, and he will enter into possession of eternal life. But many who were first will be last, and many who were last will be first."

IT would have been very easy for Jesus to dismiss Peter's question with an impatient rebuke. In a sense, it was entirely the wrong question to ask. To put it bluntly, Peter was asking, " What do we get out of following you? " Jesus could well have said that anyone who followed Him in that kind of spirit had no idea what following Him meant at all. And yet it was a natural question. True, it would have its implicit rebuke in the parable which was to follow; but Jesus did not roughly rebuke Peter. He took Peter's question, and out of it He laid down three great laws of the Christian life.

(i) It is always true that he who shares Christ's campaign will share Christ's victory. In human warfare it has been too often true that the common soldiers who fought the

242

battles and the campaigns were forgotten once the warfare was ended, and the victory won, and their usefulness past. In human warfare it has been too often true that men who fought to make a country in which heroes might live found that that same country had become a place where heroes might starve. It is not so with Jesus Christ. He who shares Christ's warfare will share Christ's triumph; and he who bears the Cross will wear the crown.

(ii) It is always true that the Christian will receive far more than ever he has to give up; but what he receives is not new material possessions, but a new fellowship, human and divine. When a man becomes a Christian he enters into a new *human* fellowship; so long as there is a Christian Church, it ought to be impossible that a Christian should ever be friendless or lonely. If his Christian decision has meant that he has had to give up friends, it ought also to mean that he has entered into a wider circle of friendship than ever he knew before. It ought to be true that there is hardly a town or village or city anywhere where the Christian can be a stranger. For in every town and village and city there is a Church, and into that fellowship he has a right to enter. It may be that the Christian who is a stranger is too shy to make that entry as he ought; it may be that the Church in the place where he is a stranger has become too much of a private clique to open its arms and its doors to him. But if the Christian ideal is being realized there is no place in the world where there is a Christian Church where the individual Christian should be friendless, lonely or a stranger. Simply to be a Christian ought to be to have entered into a fellowship which goes out to the ends of the earth.

But further, when a man becomes a Christian he enters into a new *divine* fellowship. He enters into possession of eternal life. Eternal life is the life which is the very life of God. From other things a Christian may be separated, but he can never be separated from the love of God in Christ Jesus his Lord.

(iii) Finally, Jesus lays it down that there will be surprises in the final assessment. God's standards of judgment are not men's standards of judgment, if for no other reason than that God sees into the hearts of men. There is a new world to redress the balance of the old; there is eternity to adjust the misjudgments of time. And it may be that those who were humble on earth will be great in heaven, and that those who were great in this world will be humbled in the world to come.

THE MASTER SEEKS HIS WORKERS

Matthew 20: 1-16

" For the situation in the Kingdom of Heaven is like what happened when a householder went out first thing in the morning to hire workers for his vineyard. When he had come to an agreement with them that they would work for ninepence a day, he sent them into his vineyard. He went out again about nine o'clock in the morning, and saw others standing idle in the market-place. He said to them, ' Go you also into the vineyard, and I will pay you whatever is right.' And they went. He went out again about twelve o'clock midday, and about three o'clock in the afternoon, and did the same. About five o'clock in the evening he went out and found others standing there, and said to them, ' Why are you standing here the whole day idle? ' They said to him, ' Because no one has hired us.' He said to them, ' Go you also to the vineyard.' When evening came, the master of the vineyard said to his steward, ' Call the workers, and give them their pay, beginning from the last and going on until you come to the first.' So, when those who had been engaged about five o'clock in the afternoon, came, they received ninepence each. Those who had come first thought that they would receive more; but they too received ninepence each. When they received it, they grumblingly complained against the master. ' These last,' they said, ' have only worked for one hour, and you have made them equal to us, who have borne the burden and the hot wind of the day.' He answered one of them, ' Friend,

I am doing you no wrong. Did you not come to an agreement with me to work for ninepence? Take what is yours and go! It is my will to give to this last man the same as to you. Can I not do what I like with my own money? Or, are you grudging because I am generous? ' Even so the last shall be first, and the first shall be last."

THIS parable may sound to us as if it described a purely imaginary situation, but that is far from being the case. Apart from the method of payment, the parable describes the kind of thing that frequently happened at certain times in Palestine. In Palestine the grape harvest ripens towards the end of September, and then close on its heels the rains come. If the harvest is not ingathered before the rains break, then it is ruined; and so to get the harvest in is a frantic race against time. Any worker is welcome, even if he can only give an hour to the work.

The pay was perfectly normal; a *denarius* or a *drachma* was the normal day's wage for a working man; and, even allowing for the difference in modern standards and in purchasing power, ninepence a day was not a wage which left any margin.

The men who were standing in the market-place were not street-corner idlers, lazing away their time. In Palestine the market-place was the equivalent of the labour exchange. A man came there first thing in the morning, carrying his tools, and he waited there until someone came and hired him. The men who stood in the market-place were not gossiping idlers; they were waiting for work, and the fact that some of them stood on until even five o'clock in the evening is the proof of how desperately they wanted work.

These men were hired labourers; they were the lowest class of workers, and life for them was always desperately precarious. Slaves and servants were regarded as being at least to some extent attached to the family; they were within the group; their fortunes would vary with the fortunes of the family, but they would never be in any imminent danger of starvation in normal times. It was very different with the hired day-labourers. They were not attached to any group; they were entirely at the mercy of chance employment; they were always living on the semi-starvation line. As we have seen, the pay was ninepence a day; and, if they were unemployed for one day, the children would have to go hungry at home, for no man ever saved much out of ninepence a day. With them, to be unemployed for a day was disaster.

The hours in the parable are the normal Jewish hours. The Jewish day began at sunrise, at 6 a.m., and the hours were counted from then until 6 p.m., when officially the next day began. Counting from 6 a.m. therefore, the third hour is 9 a.m., the sixth hour is twelve midday, and the eleventh hour is 5 p.m.

The picture in this parable is a vivid picture of the kind of thing which could happen in the market-place of any Jewish village or town any day, when the grape harvest was being rushed in before the rains should come.

WORK AND WAGES IN THE KINGDOM OF GOD

Matthew 20: 1-16 (*continued*)

C. G. MONTEFIORE calls this parable " one of the greatest and most glorious of all." It may indeed have had a comparatively limited application when it was spoken for the first time; but it contains within it truth which goes to the very heart of the Christian religion. We shall begin with the comparatively limited significance it originally had.

(i) It is in one sense a warning to the disciples. It is as if Jesus said to them, " You have received the great privilege of coming into the Christian Church and fellowship very early and very soon, right at the beginning. The time will come when, in the later days, others will come in. You must not claim a special honour and a special place because you were Christians before they were. All men, no matter when they come, are equally precious and valuable to God." There are people who think that, because they have been members of a Church for a long time, the Church practically belongs to them, and that they can dictate and control its policy; such people resent what seems to them the intrusion of new blood into a Church, or the rise of a new generation who have different plans and different ways. In the Christian Church seniority does not necessarily mean honour.

(ii) There is an equally definite warning to the Jews. The Jews knew that they were the chosen people, nor would they ever willingly forget that choice. As a consequence they looked down on the Gentiles. Usually they hated and despised them, and hoped for nothing but their destruction. If the Gentiles were to be allowed into the fellowship of the Church at all, they must come in as inferiors. " In God's economy," as someone has said, " there is no such thing as a most favoured nation clause." Christianity knows nothing of the conception of a *herrenvolk*, a master race. It may well be that we who have been Christian for so long have much to learn from those younger Churches who are the late-comers to the fellowship of the faith.

(iii) These were the original lessons of this parable, but, as we read it now, centuries after it was written, it has very much more to say to us.

Surely in it there is *the comfort of God*. It means that no matter when a man enters the Kingdom, late or soon, in the first flush of youth, in the strength of the midday, or when the shadows are lengthening, he is equally dear and precious to God. The Rabbis had a saying, " Some enter the Kingdom in an hour; others hardly enter it in a lifetime." In the picture of the holy city in the *Revelation* there are twelve gates. There are gates on the *East* which is the direction of the dawn, and whereby a man may enter in the glad morning of his days; there are gates on the

West which is the direction of the setting sun, and whereby a man may enter in his age. No matter when a man comes to Christ, he is equally dear to Him.

May we not go even further with this thought of comfort? Sometimes a man dies full of years and full of honour, with his day's work ended and his task completed and his labour done. Sometimes a young person is taken away, almost before the door of life and achievement opened at all. From God they will both receive the same welcome, and for both Jesus Christ is waiting, and for neither, in the divine sense, has life ended too soon or too late.

(iv) Here, also, there is the infinite *compassion* of God. There is an element of human tenderness in this parable. There is nothing more tragic in this world than a man who is unemployed, a man whose talents are rusting in idleness because there is nothing for him to do. Hugh Martin reminds us that a great teacher used to say that the saddest words in all Shakespeare's plays are the words: " Othello's occupation's gone." There in the market-place in Palestine stood those men still waiting because no one had hired them; in his compassion the master gave them work to do. He could not bear to see them idle, for his heart was touched by the sight of a man with no work to do. Further, in strict justice the fewer hours a man worked, the less pay he should have received. But the master well knew that ninepence a day was no great wage; he well knew that, if the workman went home with less, there would be a worried wife and hungry children at home; and therefore the master went beyond justice and gave them more than was their due. As it has been put, this parable states implicitly two great truths which are the very charter of the working man—the right of every man to work, and the right of every man to a living wage for his work.

(v) Here also is the *generosity* of God. These men did not all do the same work; but they did receive the same pay. There are two great lessons here. The first is, as it has been said, "All service ranks the same with God." It is not the amount of service given, but the love in which it is given which matters. A man out of his plenty may give us a gift of a hundred pounds, and in truth we are grateful; a child may give us a birthday or a Christmas gift which cost only a few pence but which was laboriously and lovingly saved up for—and that little gift, with no value of its own, touches our heart far more. God does not look on the amount of our service. So long as our service is all we have to give, all service ranks the same with God.

The second lesson is even greater—it is that all God gives is of grace. We cannot earn what God gives us; we cannot deserve it; we cannot put God in our debt; what God gives to us is given out of the goodness of His heart, out of His grace; what God gives is not pay, but a gift; not a reward, but a grace.

(vi) And surely that brings us to the supreme lesson of this parable—*the whole point of work is the spirit in which work is done*. The servants in this parable are clearly divided into two classes. The first came to an agreement with the master; they had a contract; they said, "We work, if you give us so much pay." They worked for pay, and, as their conduct showed, all that they were concerned with was to get as much as possible out of their work. But in the case of those who were engaged later, there is no word of contract or engagement; all that they wanted was the chance to work; they never mentioned a wage or a payment or a contract or an agreement; all they wanted was to work, and they would willingly leave the reward to the master.

There is the basic difference. A man is not a Christian, if his first concern is pay. That is what Peter asked: "What do we get out of it?" The Christian works for the joy of the working and the joy of serving God and his fellow-men. That is why the first will be last and the last will be first. Many a man in this world, who earned great rewards, will have a very low place in the Kingdom, for his sole thought was his rewards; many a man in this world, who, as the world counts reward, is a poor man, will be great in the Kingdom, because he never thought in terms of reward, but worked for the thrill of the working and for the joy of serving. It is the paradox of the Christian life that he who aims at reward loses reward, and he who forgets reward finds reward.

TOWARDS THE CROSS

Matthew 20: 17-19

> As He was going up to Jerusalem, Jesus took the twelve disciples apart, and said to them, while they were on the road, " Look you, we are going up to Jerusalem, and the Son of Man will be delivered to the chief priests and the Scribes, and they will condemn Him to death, and they will hand Him over to the Gentiles to mock, and to scourge, and to crucify; and on the third day He will be raised."

THIS is the third time that Jesus warned His disciples that He was on the way to the Cross (Matthew 16: 21; 17: 22, 23). Both Mark and Luke add their own touches to this story, to show that on this occasion there was in the atmosphere of the apostolic band a certain tenseness and a certain foreboding of tragedy to come. Mark says that Jesus was walking ahead by Himself, and that the disciples were amazed and afraid (Mark 10: 32-34). They did not understand what was happening, but they could see in every line of Jesus' body the struggle of His soul. Luke too tells how Jesus took the disciples to Himself alone that He might try to compel them to understand what lay ahead (Luke 18: 31-34). There is here the first decisive step to the last act of the inescapable tragedy. Here Jesus deliberately and open-eyed sets out for Jerusalem and the Cross.

There is a strange inclusiveness in the suffering to which

Jesus looked forward; it was a suffering in which no pain of heart or mind or body was to be lacking.

He was to be *betrayed* into the hands of the chief priests and Scribes; there we see the suffering of the *heart broken by the disloyalty of friends*. He was to be *condemned to death*. There we see the suffering of *injustice*, which is very hard to bear. He would be *mocked* by the Romans. There we see the suffering of *indignity* and *humiliation* and of *deliberate insult*. He was to be scourged. There were few tortures in the world to compare with the Roman scourge; and there we see the torture of *physical pain*. Finally, He was to be *crucified*; there we see the ultimate suffering of *death*. It is as if Jesus was going to gather in upon Himself every possible kind of physical and emotional and mental suffering that the world could inflict upon Him.

But even at such a time that is not the end of His words, for He finishes with the confident assertion of the Resurrection. Beyond the curtain of suffering there lay the revelation of glory; beyond the Cross there was the Crown; beyond the defeat there was triumph; and beyond death there was life.

THE FALSE AND THE TRUE AMBITION

Matthew 20: 20-28

At that time the mother of Zebedee's sons came to Him with her sons, kneeling before Him, and asking something from Him. He said to her, " What do you wish? " She said to Him, " Speak the word that these two sons of mine may sit, one on your right hand, and one on your left, in your Kingdom." Jesus answered, " You do not know what you are asking. Can you drink the cup which I have to drink? " They said to Him, " We can." He said to them, " My cup you are to drink; but to sit on my right hand and my left is not mine to give, but that belongs to those for whom it has been prepared by my Father." When the ten heard about this, they were angry with the two brothers. Jesus called them to Him and said, " You know that the rulers of the Gentiles lord it over them, and their great ones exercise authority over them. It shall not be so among you, but whoever wishes to prove himself great among you must be your servant; and whoever wishes to occupy the foremost place will be your slave, just as the Son of Man did not come to be served but to serve, and to give His life a ransom for many."

HERE we see the worldly ambition of the disciples in action. There is one very revealing little difference between Matthew's and Mark's account of this incident. In *Mark* 10: 35-45 it is James and John who themselves come to Jesus with this request. In *Matthew* it is their mother. The reason for the change is this—Matthew was writing twenty-five years later than Mark; by that time a kind of halo of sanctity and saintliness had become attached to the disciples. Matthew did not wish to show James and John guilty of worldly ambition, and so he puts the request into the mouth of their mother rather than of themselves.

There may have been a very natural reason for this request. It is very probable that James and John were closely related to Jesus. Matthew, Mark and John all give lists of the women who were at the Cross when Jesus was crucified. Let us set them down.

Matthew's list is:

> Mary Magdalene, Mary the mother of James and Joses, and the mother of Zebedee's children (*Matthew* 27: 56).

Mark's list is:

> Mary Magdalene, Mary the mother of James the Less and of Joses, and Salome (*Mark* 15: 40).

John's list is:

> Jesus' mother, His mother's sister, Mary the wife of Cleophas, and Mary Magdalene.

Mary Magdalene is named in all the lists; Mary the mother of James and Joses must be the same person as Mary the

252

wife of Cleophas; therefore the third woman is described in three different ways. Matthew calls her *the mother of Zebedee's children*; Mark calls her *Salome*; and John calls her *Jesus' mother's sister*. So, then, we learn that the mother of James and John was named Salome, and that she was the sister of Mary the mother of Jesus. That means that James and John were almost certainly full cousins of Jesus; and it may well have been that they felt that their close relationship to Jesus entitled them to a special place in His Kingdom.

This is one of the most revealing passages in the New Testament, and especially in the gospel story. It sheds a light in three directions.

First, it sheds a light on the *disciples*. It tells us three things about them. It tells us of their *ambition*. They were still thinking of things in terms of personal prominence and personal reward and personal distinction; and they were thinking of personal success without personal sacrifice. They wanted Jesus with a royal command and with a wave of His hand to ensure for them a princely life. Every man has to learn that true greatness lies, not in dominance, but in service; and every man has to learn that in every sphere the price of greatness must be paid. That is on the debit side of the account of the disciples; but there is much on the credit side. There is no incident which so demonstrates their *invincible faith in Jesus*. Think of when this request was made. It was made after a series of announcements by Jesus that ahead of Him there lay an inescapable Cross; it was made at a moment when the air was heavy with the atmosphere of tragedy and the sense of foreboding. And yet in spite of that, and in the midst of that, the disciples are thinking of a Kingdom. It is of immense significance to see that, even in a world in which the dark was coming down, the disciples were incapable of thinking of Jesus in terms of ultimate defeat. Somehow, when everything seemed to deny it and to prove it impos-

sible, they would not abandon the conviction that the
victory belonged to this Jesus. In Christianity there
must always be this invincible and eternal optimism in
the moment when all things are conspiring to drive a
man to despair. And still further, here is demonstrated
the *unshakable loyalty* of the disciples. Even when they
were bluntly told that there lay ahead a bitter cup, it
never struck them to turn back; they were determined to
drink it. If to conquer with Christ meant to suffer with
Christ, they were perfectly willing to face that suffering.

It is easy to condem the disciples, but the faith and the
loyalty which lay behind the ambition must never be
forgotten.

THE MIND OF JESUS

Matthew 20: 20-28 (continued)

SECOND, this passage sheds its light upon the Christian
life. Jesus said that those who would share His triumph
must drink His cup. What was that cup? It was to James
and to John that Jesus spoke. Now life treated James and
John very differently. James was the first of the apostolic
band to die a martyr (*Acts* 12: 2). For him the cup was
martyrdom. On the other hand, by far the greater weight
of tradition goes to show that John lived on to a great
old age in Ephesus, and died a natural death when he
must have been close on a hundred years old. For him
the cup was the constant discipline and struggle of the
Christian life throughout the years. It is quite wrong to
think that for the Christian the cup must always mean the
short, sharp, bitter, agonizing struggle of martyrdom; the
cup may well be the long routine of the Christian life,
with all its daily sacrifice, its daily struggle, and its heart-
breaks and its disappointments and its tears. A Roman
coin was once found with the picture of an ox on it; the

ox was facing two things—an altar and a plough; and the inscription read: " Ready for either." The ox had to be ready either for the supreme moment of sacrifice on the altar, or the long labour of the plough on the farm. There is no one cup for the Christian to drink. His cup may be drunk in one great moment; his cup may be drunk throughout a lifetime of Christian living. To drink the cup simply means to follow Christ, wherever Christ may lead, and to be like Christ in any situation life may bring.

Third, this passage sheds its light on *Jesus*. It shows us Jesus' *kindness*. The amazing thing about Jesus is that He never lost patience and became irritated with men. In spite of all He had said, here were these men and their mother still chattering about posts in an earthly government and kingdom. But Jesus does not explode at their obtuseness, or blaze at their blindness, or despair at their unteachableness. In gentleness, in sympathy, and in love, with never an impatient word, He seeks to lead them to the truth. The most amazing thing about Jesus is that He never despaired of men. It shows us Jesus' *honesty*. He was quite clear that there was a bitter cup to be drunk, and He did not hesitate to say so. No man can ever claim that he began to follow Jesus under false pretences. Jesus never failed to tell men that, even if life ends in crown-wearing, it continues in cross-bearing. It shows us Jesus' *trust in men*. He never doubted that James and John would maintain their loyalty. They had their mistaken ambitions; they had their blindness; they had their wrong ideas; but He never dreamed of writing them off as bad debts. He believed that they could and would drink the cup, and that in the end they would still be found at His side. One of the great fundamental facts to which we must hold on, even when we hate and loathe and despise ourselves, is that Jesus Christ believes in us. The Christian is a man upon his honour, and put upon his honour by Jesus Christ.

THE CHRISTIAN REVOLUTION

Matthew 20: 20-28 (*continued*)

THE request of James and John not unnaturally annoyed the other disciples. They did not see why the two brothers should steal a march on them, even if they were the cousins of Jesus. They did not see why they should be allowed to stake their claims to pre-eminence to the exclusion of the others. Jesus knew what was going on in their minds; and He spoke to them words which are the very basis and foundation of the Christian life. Out in the world, said Jesus, it is quite true that the great man is the man who controls others; the man who is master; the man to whose word of command others must leap; the man who with a wave of his hand can command service, and have his slightest need supplied. Out in the world there was the Roman governor with his retinue; the eastern potentate with his slaves; the man of affairs with his staff of attendant slaves. The world counts them great. But in the Christian assessment service alone is the badge of greatness; greatness does not consist in commanding others to do things for us; greatness consists in doing things for others; and the greater the service, the greater the honour. Jesus uses a kind of gradation. " If you wish to be *great*," He says, " be a *servant*; if you wish to be *first of all* be a *slave*." Here is the Christian revolution; here is the complete reversal of all the world's standards. Here a complete new set of values has been brought into life.

The strange thing is that instinctively the world itself has accepted these standards. The world knows quite well that a good man is a man who serves his fellow-men. The world will respect, and admire, and sometimes fear, the man of power; but it will love the man of love. The doctor who will come out at any time of the day or night to serve and save his patients; the parson who is always on the road amongst his people; the employer who takes an active interest in the lives and troubles of his employees; the person to whom we can go and never be made to feel a nuisance—these are the people whom all men love, and in whom instinctively they see Jesus Christ.

When that great modern saint Toyohiko Kagawa first came into contact with Christianity, he felt its fascination, until one day the cry burst from him: " O God, make me like Christ." To be like Christ he went to live in the slums, and when he went he himself was suffering from tuberculosis. He went to the last place on earth to which a man in his condition should have gone. Cecil Northcott in *Famous Life Decisions* tells of what Kagawa did. He went to live in a six foot by six hut in a Tokyo slum. " On his first night he was asked to share his bed with a man suffering from contagious itch. That was a test of his faith. Would he go back on his point of no return? No. He welcomed his bed-fellow. Then a beggar asked for his shirt and got it. Next day he was back for Kagawa's coat and trousers, and got them too. Kagawa was left standing in a ragged old kimono. The slum dwellers of Tokio laughed at him, but they came to respect him. He stood in the driving rain to preach, coughing all the time. ' God is love,' he shouted. ' God is love. Where love is, there is God.' He often fell down exhausted, and the rough men of the slums carried him gently back to his hut."

Kagawa himself wrote: " God dwells among the lowliest of men. He sits on the dust heap among the prison convicts. He stands with the juvenile delinquents. He is there with the beggars. He is among the sick, He stands with the unemployed. Therefore let him who would meet God visit the prison cell before going to the temple. Before he goes to Church let him visit the hospital. Before he reads his Bible let him help the beggar."

Therein is greatness. The world may assess a man's greatness by the number of people whom he controls and who are at his beck and call; or by his intellectual standing and his academic eminence; or by the number of committees of which he is a member; or by the size of his bank balance and the material possessions which he has amassed; but in the assessment of Jesus Christ these things are irrelevant. His assessment is quite simply—how many people have you helped?

THE LORDSHIP OF THE CROSS

Matthew 20: 20-28 (continued)

WHAT Jesus calls upon His followers to do, He Himself did. Jesus came, not to be served, but to serve. He came to occupy, not a throne, but a cross. It was just because of this that the orthodox religious people of His time could not understand Him. All through their history the Jews had dreamed of the Messiah; but the Messiah of whom they had dreamed was always a conquering king, a mighty leader, one who would smash the enemies of Israel, and reign in power over the kingdoms of the earth. They looked for a conqueror; they received one broken on a cross. They looked for the raging Lion of Judah; they received the gentle Lamb of God. Rudolf Bultmann writes: " In the Cross of Christ Jewish standards of judgment and human notions of the splendour of the Messiah are shattered." Here is demonstrated, as never before, the new glory and the new greatness of suffering love and sacrificial service. Here is royalty and kingship restated and remade.

Jesus summed up His whole life in one poignant sentence: " The Son of Man came to give His life a ransom for many." It is worth stopping to see what the crude hands of theology have done that lovely saying. Very early men began to say, " Jesus gave His life a ransom for many. Well, then, to whom was that ransom paid? " Origen has no doubt that the ransom was paid to the devil. " The ransom could not have been paid to God; it was therefore paid to the Evil One, who was holding us fast until the ransom should be given to him, even the life of Jesus." Gregory of Nyssa saw the glaring fault in that theory. It puts the Devil on a level with God; it means that the Devil could dictate his terms to God, before he would let men go. So Gregory of Nyssa has a strange idea. The devil was tricked by God. He was tricked by the seeming helplessness of Jesus; He took Jesus to be a mere man; he tried to retain hold of Jesus, and in trying to do so, he lost his power and was broken for ever. Gregory the Great took the picture even further, and to even more grotesque, and almost revolting, lengths. The Incarnation, he said, was a divine stratagem to catch the great leviathan. The deity of Christ was the hook; His flesh was the bait; the bait was dangled before leviathan; he swallowed it and was taken. The limit of shocking and fantastic grotesqueness was reached by Peter the Lombard. " The cross," he said, " was a mousetrap (*muscipula*) to catch the devil, baited with the blood of Christ."

All this is what happens when men take the poetry of love, and try to turn it into man-made theories. Jesus came to give His life a ransom for many. What does it mean? It means quite simply this. Men were in the grip of a power of evil which they could not break; their sins dragged them down; their sins separated them from God; their sins wrecked life for themselves, and for the world and for God Himself. Now a ransom is simply something paid or given to liberate a man from a situation from which it is impossible for him to free himself. Therefore what this saying means is quite simply—*It cost the life and the death of Jesus Christ to bring men back to God.* There is no question of to whom the ransom was paid. There is simply the great, tremendous truth that without Jesus Christ and His life of service and His death of love, we could never have found our way back to the love of God. Jesus gave everything to bring men back to God; and we too must walk in the steps of Him who loved to the uttermost.

LOVE'S ANSWER TO NEED'S APPEAL

Matthew 20: 29-34

> When they were leaving Jericho, a great crowd
> followed Him. And, look you, two blind men were
> sitting by the roadside, and, when they heard that
> Jesus was passing by, they shouted out, " Lord,
> have pity on us, you Son of David! " The crowd
> rebuked them, so that they might be silent. Jesus
> stood and called them. " What do you want me to do
> for you? " He said. " Lord," they said, " what we
> want is that our eyes should be opened." Jesus was
> moved with compassion to the depths of His being,
> and touched their eyes; and immediately they
> recovered their sight and followed Him.

HERE is the story of two men who found their way to a
miracle; and for that reason it is a very significant story,
for it paints a picture of the spirit, and of the attitude of
mind and heart to which the most precious gifts of God
are open.

(i) These two men were waiting, and when their chance
came they seized it with both hands. No doubt they had
heard of the wondrous power of Jesus; and no doubt
they wondered if that power might be exercised for them.
Jesus was passing by. If they had let Him pass, their
chance would have gone by for ever; but when the chance
came they seized it. There are a great many things which
have to be done at the moment, or they will never be done.
There are a great many decisions which have to be taken
on the spot, or they will never be taken. The moment
to act goes past; the impulse to decide fades; there is a
time to act and a time to decide. After Paul had preached
on Mars Hill, there were those who said, " We will hear
thee again of this matter " (*Acts* 17: 32). They put it
off until a more convenient time, but it so often happens
that the more convenient time never comes.

(ii) These two men were undiscourageable. The crowd
commanded them to stop their shouting. They were
making a nuisance of themselves. It was the custom in

Palestine for a Rabbi to teach as He walked along the road; and no doubt those around Jesus could not hear what Jesus was saying for this clamorous uproar; but nothing would stop these two blind men; for them it was a matter of sight and blindness, and nothing was going to keep them back. It often happens that we are very easily discouraged from seeking the presence of God. It is the man who will not be kept from Christ who in the end finds Christ.

(iii) These two men had an imperfect faith, but they were determined to act on the faith they had. It was as *Son of David* that they addressed Jesus. That meant that they did believe Him to be the Messiah, but it also meant that they were thinking of Messiahship in terms of kingly and of earthly power. It was an imperfect faith, but they acted on it; and Jesus accepted it. However imperfect our faith may be, if faith is there, Jesus accepts it.

(iv) These two blind men were not afraid to bring a great request. They were beggars; but it was not money they asked for, it was nothing less than sight. No request is too great to bring to Jesus Christ.

(v) These two blind men were men of gratitude. When they had received the boon for which they craved, they did not go away and forget; they followed Jesus. So many people, both in things material and in things spiritual, get what they want, and then forget even to say thanks. Ingratitude is the ugliest of all sins. These blind men received their sight from Jesus, and then they gave to Him their grateful loyalty. We can never repay God for what He has done for us, but we can always be grateful to Him.

THE BEGINNING OF THE LAST ACT OF THE DRAMA

Matthew 21: 1-11

When they had come near to Jerusalem, and when they had come to Bethphage, to the Mount of Olives, then Jesus sent on two disciples ahead. " Go into the village which is facing you," He said, " and immediately you will find an ass tethered, and a colt with her. Loose them, and bring them to me. And, if anyone says anything to you, say, ' The Master needs them.' Immediately He will send them on." This was done that there might be fulfilled that which was spoken through the prophet, when he said, " Say to the daughter of Sion, Look you, your king comes to you, gentle, and riding upon an ass, and a colt, the foal of a beast who bears the yoke." So the disciples went, and they carried out Jesus' orders, and they brought the ass and the colt, and put their cloaks upon them; and He took His seat on them. The very large crowd spread their cloaks on the road. Others cut down branches from the trees and strewed them on the road; and the crowds who went in front and followed behind kept shouting, " Hosanna to the Son of David! Blessed in the name of the Lord is He who comes. Hosanna in the highest! " As He entered Jerusalem, the whole city was shaken. " Who is this? " they asked; and the crowds said, " This is the prophet, Jesus, who comes from Nazareth in Galilee."

WITH this passage we embark on the last act in the drama of the life of Jesus; and this indeed is a dramatic moment. It was the Passover time, and Jerusalem and the whole surrounding neighbourhood would be crowded with pilgrims. Thirty years later than this a Roman governor was to take a census of the lambs slain in Jerusalem and to find that the number was not far off a quarter of a million. Now it was the Passover regulation that there must be a party of a minimum of ten for each lamb; and, if these figures are accurate, it means that at the Passover time more than two and a half million people crowded their way into Jerusalem. The law was that every adult male Jew who lived within twenty miles of Jerusalem must come to the Passover; but not only the Jews of Palestine, but Jews from every corner of the world made their way to the greatest of their national festivals. Jesus could not have chosen a more dramatic moment; it was into a city surging with people, who were keyed up with religious expectations, that He came.

Nor was this a sudden decision of Jesus, taken on the moment. It was something which He had prepared in advance. The whole tone of the story shows that He was carrying out plans which He had made ahead. He sent His disciples into the village to collect the ass and her foal. Matthew mentions Bethphage only (the pronunciation is not *Bethphage* with the *age* as in the English word *page*; the *e* at the end is pronounced as *ae*; the word is *Bethphagae*). But Mark also mentions Bethany (*Mark* 11: 1). No doubt the village was Bethany. Jesus had already arranged that the ass and her foal should be waiting for Him, for He must have had many friends in Bethany; and the phrase, " The Master needs them," was a pass-word by which their owner would know that the hour which Jesus had arranged had come.

So Jesus rode into Jerusalem. The fact that the ass had never been ridden before made it specially suitable for sacred purposes. The red heifer which was used in the ceremonies of cleansing must be a beast " upon which never came yoke " (*Numbers* 19: 2; *Deuteronomy* 21: 3); the cart on which the ark of the Lord was carried had to be a vehicle which had never been used for any other purpose (1 *Samuel* 6: 7). The special sacredness of the occasion was underlined by the fact that the ass had never been ridden by any man before.

The crowd received Jesus like a king. They spread their cloaks in front of him. That is what his friends had done when Jehu was proclaimed king (2 *Kings* 9: 13). They cut down and waved the palm branches. That is what they did when Simon Maccabaeus entered Jerusalem after one of his most notable victories (1 *Maccabees* 13: 51).

They greeted Him as they would greet a pilgrim, for the greeting: " Blessed in the name of the Lord is he who comes " (*Psalm* 118: 26) was the greeting which was addressed to pilgrims as they came to the Feast.

They shouted " Hosanna! " We must be careful to
see what this word means. *Hosanna* means *Save now*! and it
was the cry for help which a people in distress addressed
to their king or their god. The cry of the people is really
a kind of quotation from *Psalm* 118: 25: " *Save now*,
I beseech Thee, O Lord." The phrase, " Hosanna in the
highest! " must mean, " Let even the angels in the highest
heights of heaven cry unto God, Save now! "

It may be that the word *hosanna* had lost some of its
original meaning; and that it had become to some extent
only a cry of welcome and of acclamation, like " Hail! ";
but essentially it is a people's cry for deliverance and
for help in the day of their trouble; it is an oppressed
people's cry to their saviour and their king.

THE INTENTION OF JESUS

Matthew 21: 1-11 *(continued)*

WE may then take it that Jesus' actions in this incident
were planned and deliberate. In acting as He did He was
following a method of awakening men's minds which was
deeply interwoven with the methods of the prophets.
Again and again in the religious history of Israel, when a
prophet felt that words were of no avail against a barrier
of indifference or incomprehension, he put his message
into a dramatic act which men could not fail to see and to
understand. Out of many Old Testament instances we
may choose two of the most outstanding. When it became
clear that the kingdom would not stand the excesses and
extravagances of Rehoboam, and that Jeroboam was
marked out as the rising power, the prophet Ahijah the
Shilonite chose a dramatic way of foretelling the future.
Ahijah clad himself in a new garment; he went out and
he met Jeroboam alone; he took the new garment and
tore it into twelve pieces; then of the pieces he gave to

Jeroboam ten and two of the pieces he kept; and by this dramatic action he made it clear that ten of the twelve tribes were about to revolt in support of Jeroboam, while only two would remain faithful to Rehoboam (I *Kings* II: 29-32). Here is the prophetic message delivered in dramatic action. When Jeremiah was convinced that Babylon was about to conquer Palestine in spite of the easy optimism of the people, he made bonds and yokes and sent them to Edom, to Moab, to Ammon, to Tyre and to Sidon; and put a yoke upon his own neck that all might see it. By this dramatic action he made it clear that, as he saw it, nothing but slavery and servitude lay ahead (*Jeremiah* 27: I-6); and when Hananiah, the false prophet with the mistaken optimism, wished to show that he thought Jeremiah's gloomy foreboding altogether wrong, he took the yoke from Jeremiah's neck and broke it (*Jeremiah* 28: I0, II). It was the custom of the prophets to express their message in dramatic action, when they felt that words were not enough. And there is no doubt that that was what Jesus was doing when He entered Jerusalem. There are two pictures behind Jesus' dramatic action.

(i) There is the picture of *Zechariah* 9: 9, in which the prophet saw the king coming to Jerusalem, lowly and riding upon an ass, and upon a colt the foal of an ass. Therefore, in the first instance, Jesus' dramatic action is a deliberate Messianic claim. Jesus was here offering Himself to the people, at a time when Jerusalem was surging with Jews from all over the country and from all over the world, as the Anointed One of God. Just what Jesus meant by that claim we shall go on to see; but that He made the claim there is no doubt.

(ii) There may have been another intention in Jesus' mind. To us this second intention is not obvious, although it would almost certainly have been clear to a Jewish mind; and in the light of events it may well have been there. One of the supreme disasters of Jewish history was the capture of Jerusalem by Antiochus Epiphanes about 175 B.C. Antiochus was determined to stamp out Judaism and to introduce into Palestine Greek ways of life and worship. He deliberately defiled and profaned the Temple, offering swine's flesh on the altar, making sacrifices to Olympian Zeus, and even turning the Temple chambers into public brothels. It was then that the Maccabees rose against him, and ultimately rescued their native land. In due time Jerusalem was retaken and the desecrated Temple was restored and purified and rededicated. In 2 *Maccabees* 10: 7 we read of the rejoicing of that great day: " Therefore they bare branches, and fair boughs, and palms also, and sang psalms unto Him that had given them good success in cleansing His place." On that day the people carried the palm branches and sung their psalms; it is an almost exact description of the actions of the crowd who welcomed Jesus into Jerusalem. It is at least possible that Jesus knew this, and that He entered into Jerusalem with the deliberate intention of cleansing God's house, as Judas Maccabaeus had done two hundred years before. That was in fact what Jesus did. He may well be saying in dramatic symbol, not only that He was the Anointed One of God, but that He had also come to cleanse the House of God from the abuses which defiled it and its worship. Had not Malachi said that the Lord would suddenly come to His Temple (*Malachi* 3: 1)? And, in his vision of judgment had not Ezekiel seen the terrible judgment of God begin at the sanctuary (*Ezekiel* 9: 6)?

THE CLAIM OF THE KING

Matthew 21: 1-11 (*continued*)

To conclude our study of this incident, let us look at Jesus in its setting. It shows us three things about Jesus.

(i) It shows us the *courage* of Jesus. Jesus knew full well that He was entering into a hostile city. However enthusiastic the crowd might be, the authorities hated Him, and had sworn to eliminate Him, and with them there lay the last word. Almost any man in such a case would have considered that discretion was the better part of valour, and, if he had come to Jerusalem at all would have slipped in under cover of night, and would have kept prudently to the back streets until he reached his shelter. But Jesus entered Jerusalem in a way that deliberately set Himself in the centre of the stage, and deliberately riveted every eye upon Himself. All through Jesus' last days there is in His every action a kind of magnificent and sublime defiance; and here He begins the last act with a flinging down of the gauntlet, a deliberate challenge to the authorities to do their worst.

(ii) It shows us the *claim* of Jesus. Certainly it shows us His claim to be God's Messiah, God's Anointed One; very probably it shows us His claim to be the cleanser of the Temple and House of God. If Jesus had consented to claim to be a prophet, the probability is that He need never have died. But Jesus is satisfied with nothing less than the topmost place; with Jesus it is all or nothing. Men must acknowledge Him as king, or not receive Him at all.

(iii) But equally it shows us the *appeal* of Jesus. It was not the kingship of the throne which He claimed; it was the kingship of the heart. He came lowly and riding upon an ass. We must be careful to see the real meaning of that. In western lands the ass is a despised beast; but in eastern lands the ass could be a noble animal. Often a king came riding upon an ass, but when he came upon an ass, it was the sign that *he came in peace*. The horse was the mount of *war*; the ass was the mount of *peace*. So when Jesus claimed to be king, He claimed to be the king of peace. He showed that He came, not to destroy, but to love; not to condemn, but to help; not in the might of arms, but in the strength of love.

So here, at one and the same time, we see the courage

of Christ, the claim of Christ, and the love of Christ.
It was a last appeal to men to open, not their palaces
but their hearts to Him.

THE SCENE IN THE TEMPLE

Matthew 21: 12-14

> And Jesus entered into the precincts of the Temple
> of God, and cast out all who were selling and buying
> in the Temple precincts, and overturned the tables
> of the money-changers, and of those who were selling
> doves. " It is written," He said to them, " My house
> shall be called a house of prayer, but you make it
> ' a robbers' cave.' "
>
> And the blind and the lame came to Him in the
> Temple and He healed them.

IF the entry into Jerusalem had been defiance, here is
defiance added to defiance. To see this scene unfolding
before our eyes we need to visualize the picture of the
Temple. There are in the New Testament two words
which are both translated *Temple*, and rightly so, but
there is a clear distinction between them. The Temple
itself is called the *naos*. It was a comparatively small
building, and contained the Holy Place and the Holy of
Holies into which only the High Priest might enter, and
he only on the great Day of Atonement. But the *naos*
itself was surrounded by a vast space which was occupied
by successive and ascending courtyards. First there was
the *Court of the Gentiles*, into which anyone might come,
and beyond which it was death for a Gentile to penetrate.
Then there came the *Court of the Women*, entered by the
Beautiful Gate of the Temple, into which any Israelite
might come. Next there came the *Court of the Israelites*,
entered by the gate called Nicanor's Gate, a great gate
of Corinthian bronze which needed twenty men to open
and shut it. It was in this court that the people assembled
for the Temple services. Lastly there came the *Court of*

the Priests, into which only the priests might enter; in which there stood the great altar of the burnt-offering, the altar of the incense, the seven-branched lamp-stand, the table of the shewbread, and the great brazen laver; and at the back of which there stood the *naos* itself. This whole area, including all the courts, is also in the Authorized Version called the *Temple*; the Greek is *hieron*. It is better to keep a distinction between the two words; and to retain the word *Temple* for the Temple proper, that is the *naos*, and to use the term the *Temple Precincts*, for the whole area, that is the word *hieron*.

The scene of this incident is the Court of the Gentiles into which anyone might come. It was always crowded and busy; but at the Passover time, with pilgrims there from all over the world, it would be thronged to capacity. There would, even at any time, be many Gentiles there, for the Temple at Jerusalem was famous throughout the world, so that even the Roman writers described it as one of the world's most amazing buildings.

In this Court of the Gentiles two kinds of trading were going on. There was the business of *money-changing*. Every Jew had to pay a temple tax of one half-shekel, and that tax had to be paid near to the Passover time. A month before booths were set up in all the towns and villages, and the money could be paid there, but after a certain date it could only be paid in the Temple itself; and it would be there that the vast majority of pilgrim Jews from other lands paid it. This tax had to be paid in certain currency, although for general purposes all kinds of currencies were equally valid in Palestine. It must not be paid in ingots of silver, but in stamped currency; it must not be paid in coins of inferior alloy or coins which had been clipped, but in coins of high-grade silver. It could be paid in shekels of the sanctuary, in Galilaean half-shekels, and especially in Tyrian currency which was of a very high standard. The function of the money-changers was to change unsuitable currency into the correct currency. That seems on the face of it to be an entirely necessary function; but the trouble was that these money-changers charged the equivalent of twopence for changing the currency at all; and, if the coin was of greater value than a half-shekel, they charged another twopence for giving back the surplus change. That is to say that many a pilgrim had not only to pay his half-shekel—which was about one shilling and sixpence in value—but another fourpence also in changing dues; and this has to be evaluated against a background where a working man's wage was about eightpence a day. This surplus charge was called the *qolbon*. It did not by any means all go into the money-changer's pockets; some of it was classed as freewill offerings; some of it went to the repair of the roads; some of it went to purchase the gold plates with which it was planned entirely to cover the Temple proper; and some of it found its way into the Temple treasury. The whole matter was not necessarily an abuse; but the trouble was that it lent itself to abuse. It lent itself to the exploitation of the pilgrims who had come to worship, and there is no doubt that the Temple money-changers made large profits out of it.

The selling of doves was worse. For most visits to the Temple some kind of offering was necessary. Doves for instance were necessary when a woman came for purification after childbirth, or when a leper came to have his cure attested and certified (*Leviticus* 12: 8; 14: 22; 15: 14, 29). It was easy enough to buy animals for sacrifice outside the Temple; but any animal offered in sacrifice must be without blemish. There were official inspectors of the animals, and it was to all intents and purposes certain that they would reject an animal bought outside and would direct the worshipper to the Temple stalls and booths. No great harm would have been done if the prices had been the same inside and outside the Temple, but a pair of doves could cost as little as ninepence outside the Temple, and as much as fifteen shillings inside the

Temple. This was an old abuse. A certain Rabbi, Simon ben Gamaliel, was remembered with gratitude because " he had caused doves to be sold for silver coins instead of gold." Clearly he had attacked this abuse. Further, these stalls where the victims were sold were called the Bazaars of Annas, and were the private property of the family of the High Priest of that name. Here, again, there was no necessary abuse. There must have been many honest and sympathetic traders. But abuse readily and easily crept in. Burkitt can say that " the Temple had become a meeting place of scamps," the worst kind of commercial monopoly and vested interest. Sir George Adam Smith can write: " In those days every priest must have been a trader." There was every danger of shameless and conscienceless exploitation of poor and humble pilgrims—and it was that exploitation which raised the wrath of Jesus.

THE WRATH AND THE LOVE

Matthew 21: 12-14 (continued)

THERE is hardly any passage in the gospel story where we need to make a more deliberate and more conscious effort to be fair than in this passage. It is easy to use this passage as a basis for a complete condemnation of the whole Temple worship. There are two things to be said. There were many traders and hucksters in the Temple Court, but there were also many whose hearts were set on God. It is never fair to take any system at its worst manifestation and to judge it at that; as Aristotle said long ago, a man and an institution must be judged at their best, and not at their worst. And the other thing to be said is simply this—let Him, and let the Church, which is without sin cast the first stone. Not even the traders were all exploiters, and even those who seized the opportunity of making a quick profit were not all simply money-grabbers. That great Jewish scholar Israel Abrahams has a comment on the too common Christian treatment of this passage in which he speaks with a certain dignity of his nation's faith, and in which he speaks of certain things which to this day happen in the *Christian* Church of the Holy Sepulchre in Jerusalem. " When Jesus overturned the money-changers and ejected the sellers of doves from the Temple, He did a service to Judaism. . . . But were the money-changers and the dove-sellers the only people who visited the Temple? And was everyone who bought or sold a dove a mere formalist? Last Easter I was in Jerusalem, and along the facade of the Church of the Holy Sepulchre I saw the stalls of the vendors of sacred relics, of painted beads and inscribed ribbons, of coloured candles, gilded crucifixes, and bottles of Jordan water. There these Christians babbled and swayed and bargained, a crowd of buyers and sellers in front of the Church sacred to the memory of Jesus. Would, I thought, that Jesus were come again to overthrow these false servants of His, even as He overthrew His false brothers in Israel long ago." In this matter even the Christian Church is not altogether without blame.

But this incident shows us certain things about Jesus.

(i) It shows us that one of the fiercest manifestations of His anger was directed against those who exploited their fellow-men, and especially against those who exploited them in the name of religion. It was Jeremiah who had said that men made the Temple a den of thieves (*Jeremiah* 7: 11). Jesus could not bear to see simple people exploited for profit. Too often the Church has been silent in such a situation; the Church has a duty to protect those who in a highly competitive economic situation cannot protect themselves.

(ii) It shows us that His anger is specially directed against those who make it impossible for simple people to worship in the House of God. It was Isaiah who said that God's House was a House of Prayer for all nations (*Isaiah*

56: 7). It is to be noted that the Court of the Gentiles was, in fact, the only part of the Temple into which Gentiles might come. It is not to be thought that every Gentile came to stare and to sight-see. Some, at least, must have come with haunting longings in their souls to worship and to pray, if haply they might find God. But in that uproar of buying and selling and bargaining and auctioneering prayer was impossible. Those who sought God's presence were being debarred from it by the very people of God's House. God will never hold guiltless those who make it impossible for others to worship God. It can happen yet. A spirit of bitterness, a spirit of argument, a spirit of strife can get into a Church, which makes worship impossible. Men and office-bearers can become so concerned with their rights and their wrongs, and their dignities and their prestiges, and their practice and their procedure that in the end no one can worship God in the atmosphere which is created. Even ministers of God can be more concerned with imposing their practices and their ways of doing things on a congregation than with preaching the gospel, and the end is a service with an atmosphere in which all true worship becomes impossible. The worship of God and the disputes of men can never go together. Let us remember the wrath of Jesus at those who blocked the approach to God for their fellow-men.

(iii) There remains one thing to note. Our passage ends with Jesus healing the blind and the lame in the Temple Court. They were still there; Jesus did not clear everyone out. Only those with guilty consciences fled before the eyes of His wrath. Those who needed Him stayed. Need is never sent empty away by Jesus Christ. And mark this— Jesus' anger was never merely negative; it never stopped with the attack on that which was wrong; it always went on to the positive helping of those who were in need. In the truly great man anger and love go hand in hand. There is anger at those who exploit the simple and bar the seeker; but there is love for those whose need is great.

The destructive force of anger must always go hand in hand with the healing power of love.

THE KNOWLEDGE OF THE SIMPLE IN HEART

Matthew 21: 15-17

> When the chief priests and Scribes saw the wonderful things that He did, and the children shouting in the Temple, " Hosanna to the Son of David! " they were angry. " Do you hear what these are saying? " they said. Jesus said to them, " Yes! Have you never read: ' Out of the mouths of babes and sucklings you have the perfect praise '? " And He left them, and went out of the city to Bethany, and lodged there.

THERE are some scholars who have found difficulty with this passage. It is said that it is unlikely that there would be crowds of children in the Temple Court; and that, if the children were there at all, the Temple police would have dealt swiftly and efficiently with them if they had dared to cry out as this passage says they did. Now earlier in the story *Luke* has an incident where the *disciples* are depicted as shouting their glad cries to Jesus, and where the authorities are described as trying to silence them (*Luke* 19: 39, 40). Very often a Rabbi's disciples were in fact called his *children*. We see for instance the phrase *my little children* occurs in the writings of John. So it is suggested that Luke and Matthew are really telling the same story, and that the *children* are in fact the *disciples* of Jesus, and not real children at all.

No such explanation is necessary. The use that Matthew makes of the quotation from *Psalm* 8: 3 makes it clear that he had real children in mind; and, in any event, things were happening that day in the Temple Court which had never happened before. It was not every day that the traders and the money-changers were sent packing; and it was not every day that the blind and the lame were healed. Maybe ordinarily it would have been impossible for the children to shout like this, but then this was no ordinary day.

When we take this story just as it stands, and when we listen again to the fresh, clear voices of the children shouting their praises, we are faced with one great truth. There are truths which only the simple in heart can see, and which are hidden from the wise and the learned and the sophisticated. There are many times when heaven is nearer the child than it is to the wisest of men.

It is said that Thorwaldsen, the great sculptor, once carved a statue of Jesus. He wished to see if the statue would cause the right reaction of heart in those who saw it. He brought a little child and bade him look at the statue, and asked him: " Who do you think that is? " The child looked, and then answered: " It is a great man." And Thorwaldsen knew that he had failed. So he scrapped his first statue and began again. Again when he had finished, he brought the little child, and again he bade him look at it, and he again asked the same question: " Who do you think that is? " And the child smiled and answered: " That is Jesus who said: ' Let the children come to me.' " And Thorwaldsen knew that this time he had succeeded. He submitted the statue to the test of the eyes of a child.

When all is said and done that is no bad test. George Macdonald once said that he placed no value on the alleged Christianity of a man at whose door, or at whose garden gate, the children were afraid to play. If a child thinks a person good, then all the likelihood is that that person is good; and if a child shrinks away, a man may be great, but very certainly he is not Christlike. Somewhere Barrie draws a picture of a mother putting her little one to bed at night, and looking down on him when he is half asleep, with an unspoken question in her eyes and in her heart: " My child, have I done well today? " The goodness which can meet the clear gaze of a child, and which can stand the test of a child's simplicity, is goodness indeed

It is but natural that the children should recognize Jesus, when the scholars were blind.

THE WAY OF THE FIG TREE

Matthew 21: 18-22

> When Jesus was returning to the city early in the morning, He was hungry. When He saw a fig tree by the roadside, He went up to it, and found nothing but leaves. He said to it, " Let no fruit come from you any more for ever! " And immediately the fig tree withered away. When the disciples saw it, they were astonished. " How did the fig tree immediately wither away? " they said. Jesus answered them: " This is the truth I tell you—if you have faith, and, if you do not doubt, not only will you do what happened to the fig tree, but you will even say to this mountain: ' Be removed and be cast into the sea,' and it will happen. All that you ask in prayer, if you believe, you will receive."

THERE are few honest readers of the Bible who would deny that this is perhaps the most uncomfortably difficult passage in the New Testament. If it be taken with complete and unquestioning literalism, it shows us Jesus in an action which is an acute shock to our whole conception of Him. It is, therefore, a passage which we must approach with a real desire to find out the truth which lies behind it, and with a real courage to think our way through it.

It is first to be noted that Mark also tells this story in *Mark* 11: 12-14, 20, 21. We may note at once that there is one basic difference between the two versions of the story. In Matthew's version the withering of the fig tree is immediate, and takes place at once. The Authorized Version has: " And *presently* the fig tree withered away." In Elizabethan English *presently* meant *immediately, at that present moment.* The Greek is *parachrēma,* which means *immediately,* and which the American Revised Standard Version translates *at once,* and which Moffatt translates *instantly.* On the other hand, in Mark's version of the story, nothing happened to the tree immediately, and it is only next morning, when they are passing on the same road, that the disciples see that the tree has withered away. From the existence of these two versions of the story, it is quite clear that some development has taken place; and, since Mark's is the earliest gospel, it is equally clear that his version must be nearer to the actual historical facts.

In order to understand this story, it is necessary to understand the growing and fruit-bearing habits of fig trees. In Palestine the fig tree was the favourite of all trees. The picture of the Promised Land was the picture of " a land of wheat and barley, vines and fig trees " (*Deuteronomy* 8: 8). Pomegranates and figs were part of the treasures which the spies brought back to show the rich fertility of the land (*Numbers* 13: 23). The picture of peace and prosperity which is common to every part of the old Testament is the picture of a time when every man will sit under his own vine and his own fig tree (I *Kings* 4: 25; *Micah* 4: 4; *Zechariah* 3: 10). The picture of the wrath of God is the picture of a day when He would smite and destroy the fig trees (*Psalm* 105: 33; *Jeremiah* 8: 13; *Hosea* 2: 12). The fig tree is the very symbol of fertility and peace and prosperity. The tree itself is a handsome tree; it can be three feet thick in its trunk. It grows to a height of from fifteen to twenty feet; and the spread of its thick branches can be twenty-five to thirty feet. It was, therefore, much valued for its shade. In Cyprus the cottages have their fig trees at the door, and Tristram, the traveller, tells how often he sheltered under them, and found coolness on the hottest day. Very commonly the fig tree grows overshadowing wells, so that there is shade and water in the one place. Often it was the shade of the fig tree which was a man's private room for meditation and prayer; and that is why Nathanael was amazed that Jesus had marked him under the fig tree (*John* 1: 48).

But it is the fig tree's habit of fruit-bearing which is

relevant for the study of this incident. The fig tree is unique in that it bears two full crops in the year. The first crop is borne on the old wood. Quite early in the year little green knobs appear at the end of the branches. They are called *paggim*, and they will one day be the figs. These fruit buds come in April, but they are quite uneatable. Bit by bit the leaves and the flowers open out, and the unique thing about the fig is that it is in full fruit and full leaf and full flower all at the same time; that happens by June. No fig tree ever bore fruit in April; that was far too early. The process is then repeated with the new wood; and the second crop comes in September. The strangest thing about this story is twofold. First, it tells of a fig tree in full leaf in April. Jesus was at Jerusalem for the Passover; the Passover fell on 15th April; and this incident happened a week before. The second thing is equally clear, Jesus looked for figs on a tree where no figs could possibly be. That Mark saw, for Mark clearly says, " The time of figs was not yet " (*Mark* 11: 13).

The difficulty of this story is not so much the difficulty of possibility; the difficulty is a *moral* difficulty; and it is twofold. First, we see Jesus depicted as blasting a fig tree for not doing that which it was not able to do. The tree could not have borne fruit in the second week of April, and yet we are shown Jesus destroying it for not doing what it was impossible for it to do. Second, we see Jesus using His miraculous powers for His own end. That is precisely what in the temptations in the wilderness He once and for all determined never to do. He would not turn stones into bread to satisfy His own hunger; He would never selfishly use His power. The plain truth is this—if we had read of anyone else blasting a fig tree for not bearing figs in April, we would certainly have said that it was the act of an ill-tempered petulance, springing from personal disappointment. In Jesus that is incredible and inconceivable; therefore there must be some explanation. What is that explanation?

There are some who have found an explanation on the following lines. In *Luke* there is the parable of the fig tree which failed to bear fruit. Twice the gardener pleaded for mercy for it; twice mercy and delay were granted; in the end it was still fruitless and it was therefore destroyed (*Luke* 13: 6-9). Now the curious thing is that Luke has that parable of the barren fig tree, but he has not this incident of the withering of the fig tree. Matthew and Mark have this incident of the withering of the fig tree, but they have not the parable of the barren fig tree. It looks very much as if the gospel writers felt that if they included the one section they did not need to include the other; certainly Luke knew the section of the withering of the fig tree because he knew Mark and used him as the basis of his own gospel. So, then, it is suggested that the parable of the barren fig tree has been misunderstood and has been turned into an actual incident when it should have remained as a parable; that there has been a confusion which changed a *story* Jesus *told* into an *action* Jesus *did*. That is by no means impossible; but it seems to us that the real explanation must be sought elsewhere. And now we must go on to seek it.

PROMISE WITHOUT PERFORMANCE

Matthew 21: 18-22 (*continued*)

LET us remember a Jewish prophetic custom which Jesus knew and used. When we were studying the story of the entry of Jesus into Jerusalem, we saw that frequently the prophets made use of symbolic actions; that when they felt that words would not penetrate, they did something dramatic to drive a lesson home. Now, let us suppose that some such symbolic action is at the back of this story. Jesus, let us suppose, was on His way to Jerusalem. By the wayside He saw a tree in full leaf. It was perfectly legitimate for Him to pluck the figs from it, if there had been any. Jewish law allowed that (*Deuteronomy* 23: 24, 25); and Thomson in *The Land and the Book* tells us that even in modern times the wayside fig tree is open to all. Jesus went up to the fig tree, well knowing that there could be no fruit, and well knowing that there was something radically wrong with this fig tree. One of two things could have happened. The fig tree could have reverted to its wild state, just as roses revert to briars. That did happen. Or, the fig tree could be in some way diseased. A fig tree with full leaf in the first days of April was inevitably a diseased tree. So, then, Jesus said, looking at it: " This tree will never bear fruit; this tree will certainly wither." It was the statement of a man who knew nature, because He had lived with nature. And, indeed, on the next day it was clear that the diagnosis of the expert eye of Jesus was infallibly correct.

Now if this was a symbolic action, it was definitely meant to teach something. What was it meant to teach? It was meant to teach two things about the Jewish nation, for with that nation the head-on clash of Jesus was imminent.

(i) This symbolic action taught that *uselessness invites disaster*. That is the law of life. Anything which is useless is on the way to elimination; any thing and any person can only justify its or his existence by fulfilling the end for which it was meant and created. The fig tree was useless; therefore it was doomed. Now the nation of Israel had been brought into existence for one reason and one reason only—that from it there might come the Son of God, God's Anointed One. He had come; the nation had failed to recognize Him; nay more, they were about to crucify Him. The nation had failed in its function which was to welcome God's Son—and therefore the nation was doomed. Failure to realize the purpose of God brings necessary disaster. Everyone in this world is judged in terms of usefulness. Even if a person is helpless on a bed, they can be of the greatest use by patient example and by prayer. No one need be useless; and he who is useless is heading for disaster.

(ii) This incident teaches that *profession without practice is condemned*. The tree had leaves; the leaves were a claim to have figs; the tree had no figs; its claim was false; it was an empty profession; therefore it was doomed. The Jewish nation professed faith in God; were they not the chosen people and was God not their God? But, in spite of their profession, in practice they were out for the blood of God's Son; therefore they stood condemned.

Profession without practice was not only the curse of the Jews; it has been throughout the ages the curse of the Church. G. T. Bellhouse quotes an amazing example of it from the autobiography of Gandhi. During his early days in South Africa—in Pretoria—Gandhi did inquire into Christianity. For several Sundays he attended a Christian Church, but, he says, "the congregation did not strike me as being particularly religious; they were not an assembly of devout souls, but appeared rather to be worldly-minded people going to Church for recreation and in conformity to custom." He, therefore, concluded that there was nothing in Christianity which he did not already possess—and Gandhi was lost to the Christian Church with incalculable consequences to India and to the British Empire and to the world.

Profession without practice is something of which we are all more or less guilty. It does incalculable harm to the Christian Church; and it is doomed to disaster, for it produces a faith which cannot do anything else but wither away.

We may well believe that Jesus used the lesson of a diseased and degenerate fig tree to say to the Jews—and to us—that uselessness invites disaster, and profession without practice is doomed. That is surely what this story means, for we cannot think of Jesus as literally and physically blasting a fig tree for failing to bear fruit at a season when fruit was impossible.

THE DYNAMIC OF PRAYER

Matthew 21: 18-22 (*continued*)

THIS passage concludes with certain words of Jesus about the dynamic of prayer. They are words which it is absolutely necessary correctly to understand. If they are misunderstood, they can bring nothing by heartbreak; if they are correctly understood, they can bring nothing but power.

In them Jesus says two things. He says that prayer can remove mountains; and He says that, if we ask in belief, we will receive. It is abundantly clear that these promises are not to be taken physically and literally. Neither Jesus Himself nor anyone else ever removed a physical, geographical mountain by the word of prayer. Many and many a person has prayed with a passionate faith that something may happen or that something may not happen, that something may be given or that someone may be spared from death, and in the literal sense of the words that prayer has not been answered. What then is Jesus promising us through prayer?

(i) Jesus promises that prayer gives us *the ability to do*. Prayer is never the easy way out; prayer is never simply pushing things on to God that He may do them for us. *Prayer is power*. Prayer is not asking God to do something; prayer is asking, by His power, to make us able to do it ourselves. Prayer is not taking the easy way; prayer is the way to receive power to take the hard way. Prayer is the channel through which there comes to us power to tackle and to remove mountains of difficulty by ourselves, with the help of God. If prayer were simply a method of getting things done for us, then prayer would be very bad for us, for its result would be to make us flabby and lazy and inefficient. Prayer is the means whereby we receive power to do things for ourselves. And, therefore, no man may pray and then sit and wait; he must pray and then rise and work; but he will find that, when he prays, and then works, a new dynamic has entered into life, and that in truth with God all things are possible, and that with God the impossible has become that which can be done.

(ii) Prayer is *the ability to accept,* and in accepting, *to transform.* Prayer is not meant to bring deliverance from a situation; it is meant to bring the ability to accept the situation, and to transform it. There are two great examples of that in the New Testament. The one is the example of Paul. Desperately he prayed that he might be delivered from the thorn in his flesh, and from the physical pain which his situation brought him. He was not delivered from that situation; he was made able to accept it; and in that very situation he discovered the strength that was made perfect in his weakness and the grace which was sufficient for all things—and in that strength and grace the situation was not only accepted, but also transformed into glory (2 *Corinthians* 12: 1-10). The other instance is Jesus Himself. In Gethsemane He prayed that the cup might pass from Him, that He might be delivered from the agonizing situation in which He found Himself; that request could not be granted; but in that prayer He found the ability to accept the situation; and in being accepted the situation was transformed, for the agony of the Cross lead straight to the glory of the Resurrection. We must always remember that prayer does not bring deliverance from a situation; it brings conquest of it. Prayer is not a means of running away from a situation; it is a means whereby we may gallantly face it.

(iii) Prayer brings *the ability to bear.* It is very natural and inevitable that, in our human need and with our human hearts and our human weakness, there should be things which we feel we cannot bear. We see some situation developing; we see some tragic happening approaching with a grim inevitability; we see some task looming ahead which is obviously going to demand more than we have got to give to it. At such a time our inevitable feeling is that we cannot bear this thing. Prayer does not remove the tragedy; it does not give us escape from the situation; it does not give us exemption from the task; but it does make us able to bear the unbearable, to face the unfaceable, to pass the breaking point and not to break.

So long as we regard prayer as escape, nothing but bewildered disappointment can result; but when we regard prayer as the way to conquest, and the divine dynamic, then things happen indeed.

THE EXPEDIENT IGNORANCE

Matthew 21: 23-27

> When Jesus had come into the Temple precincts, the chief priests and elders of the people came to Him as He was teaching and said, " By what authority do you do these things? And who gave you this authority? " Jesus answered them, " I will ask you one question, and if you give me an answer to it, I too will tell you by what authority I do these things. Whence was the baptism of John? Was it from heaven? Or, was it from men? " They debated within themselves. " If," they said, " we say ' From heaven,' He will say to us, ' Why then did you not believe in Him? ' But, if we say, ' From men,' we fear the crowd, for all regard John as a prophet." So they answered Jesus, " We do not know." So He too said to them, " Neither do I tell you by what authority I do these things."

WHEN we think of the extraordinary things which Jesus had been doing, we cannot be surprised that the Jewish authorities asked Him what right He had to do them. They asked Him what His authority was and where He had received it. At the moment Jesus was not prepared to give them the direct answer that His authority came from the fact that he was the Son of God. To do so would have been to precipitate the end. There were actions still to be done, and teaching still to be given. It sometimes takes more courage to bide one's time, and to await the necessary moment, than it does to throw oneself on the enemy and invite the end. For Jesus everything had to be done in God's time; and the time for the final crisis had not yet come.

So He countered the question of the Jewish authorities with a question of His own, a question which placed them in a dilemma. He asked them whether John's whole ministry came from heaven or from men, whether it was divine or merely human in its origin. Were those who went out to be baptized at the Jordan responding to a merely human impulse, or were they in fact answering a divine challenge? The dilemma of the Jewish authorities was this. If they said that the ministry of John was from God, then they had no alternative to admitting that Jesus was the Messiah, for John had borne definite and unmistakable witness to that fact. If God was speaking through John, then beyond argument Jesus was the Anointed One of God. On the other hand, if these authorities denied outright that John's ministry came from God, then they would have to bear the anger of the people, for the people were convinced that John was the messenger of God. For a moment the Jewish chief priests and elders were silent. And then they gave the lamest of all lame answers. They said, " We do not know." If ever men stood self-condemned, they stood self-condemned; they ought to have known; it was their duty to know. It was part of the duty of the Sanhedrin, of which they were members, to distinguish between true and false prophets; and they were saying that they were quite unable to make that distinction. Their dilemma drove them into a shameful self-humiliation.

There is a grim warning here. There is such a thing as the deliberately assumed ignorance of cowardice. If a man consults *expediency* rather than *principle*, his first question will be, not, " What is the truth? " but, " What is it safe to say? " And again and again his worship of expediency will drive him to a cowardly silence. He will lamely say, " I do not know the answer," when he well knows the answer, but is afraid to give it. The true question is not: " What is it safe to say? " but, " What is it right to say? "

The deliberately assumed ignorance of fear, the cowardly silence of expediency are shameful things. If a man knows the truth, he is under obligation to tell the truth, though the heavens should fall.

THE BETTER OF TWO BAD SONS

Matthew 21: 28-32

> Jesus said: " What do you think? A man had two children. He went to the first and said, ' Child, go and work in my vineyard today.' He answered, ' I will not.' But afterwards he changed his mind and went. He went to the second and spoke to him in the same way. He answered, ' Certainly, sir.' And he did not go. Which of these two did the will of his father? " " The first," they answered. Jesus said to them: " This is the truth I tell you—the tax-collectors and harlots go into the Kingdom of Heaven before you. For John came to you in the way of righteousness, and you did not believe in him; but the tax-gatherers and harlots did believe in him. And when you saw this, you did not even then change your minds, and so come to believe in him."

THE meaning of this parable is crystal clear. The Jewish leaders are the people who said that they would obey God, and then did not. The tax-gatherers and the harlots are those who said that they would go their own way, and then took God's way.

The key to the correct understanding of this parable is that it is not really praising anyone. It is setting before us a picture of two very imperfect sets of people, of whom one set were none the less better than the other. Neither son in the story was the kind of son to bring full joy to his father. Both were unsatisfactory creatures; but the one who in the end obeyed was incalculably better than the other. The ideal son would be the son who accepted the father's orders with obedience and with respect, and who unquestioningly and fully carried them out. But there are truths in this parable which go far beyond the situation in which it was first spoken.

This parable tells us that there are two very common classes of people in this world. First, there are the people whose profession is much better than their practice. They will promise anything; they make great protestations of piety and fidelity; but their practice lags far behind their profession. Second, there are those whose practice is far better than their profession. They claim to be tough, hard-boiled, hard-headed materialists, but somehow they are found out doing kindly and generous things almost in secret, as if they were ashamed of it. They profess to have no interest in the Church and in religion, and yet, when it comes to the bit, they live more Christian lives than many professing Christians. We have all of us met these people, the people whose practice is far away from the almost sanctimonious piety of their profession, and the people whose practice is far ahead of the sometimes cynical, and sometimes almost irreligious, profession which they make. The real point of the parable is that, while the second class are infinitely to be preferred to the first class, neither class is anything like perfect. The really good man is the man in whom profession and practice meet and match.

Still further, this parable teaches us that promises can never take the place of performance, and fine words are never a substitute for fine deeds. The son who said he would go, and did not, had all the outward marks of courtesy. In his answer he called his father " Sir " with all respect. But a courtesy which never gets beyond words is a totally illusory thing. True courtesy is obedience, willingly and graciously given. On the other hand this parable teaches us that a man can easily spoil a good thing by the way in which he does it. He can do a fine thing with a lack of graciousness and a lack of winsomeness which spoils the whole deed. Here we learn that the Christian way is in performance and not promise, and that the mark of a Christian is obedience graciously and courteously given.

THE VINEYARD OF THE LORD

Matthew 21: 33-46

Jesus said, " Listen to another parable. There was a householder who planted a vineyard, and surrounded it with a hedge, and dug a wine press in it, and built a tower, and gave it out to cultivators and went away. When the time of the fruits had come, he dispatches his servants to the cultivators, to receive his fruits; and the cultivators took his servants and beat one of them, and killed another of them, and stoned another of them. Again he dispatched other servants, more than the first; and they did the same to them. Afterwards he dispatched his son to them. ' They will respect my son,' he said. But when the cultivators saw the son, they said to themselves, ' This is the heir. Come, let us kill him, and let us take the inheritance.' And they threw him out of the vineyard and killed him. When the owner of the vineyard comes, what will he do to these cultivators? " They said to Him, " He will bring these evil men to an evil end, and he will give out the vineyard to other cultivators, who will pay him the fruits at their correct time." Jesus said to them, " Have you never read in the Scriptures: ' The stone which the builders rejected, this has become the headstone of the corner. This is the doing of the Lord, and it is amazing in our eyes '? That is why I tell you that the Kingdom of God will be taken from you, and will be given to a nation which produces its fruits. And he who falls against the stone will be broken; and it will shatter to powder him on whom it falls."

When the chief priests and Pharisees heard His parables, they knew that He was speaking about them. They tried to find a way to lay hold on Him, but they were afraid of the crowds, for they regarded Him as a prophet.

IN interpreting a parable it is normally a first principle that every parable has only one point, and that that point has to be seized, and that the details are not to be stressed. Normally to try to find a meaning for every detail is to make the mistake of treating a parable as an allegory. But in the case of this parable it is different. This is a parable so crystal clear that the details do have a meaning, and the chief priests and the Pharisees well knew what Jesus was meaning this parable to say to them.

Every detail of the parable is founded on what, for those who heard it for the first time, was familiar fact. The picture of the Jewish nation as the vineyard of God was a familiar prophetic picture. " The vineyard of the Lord is the house of Israel " (*Isaiah* 5: 7). The hedge was a thick-set thorn hedge, designed to keep out both the wild boars, who might ravage the vineyard, and the thieves who might steal the grapes. Every vineyard had its wine press. The wine press consisted of two troughs either hollowed out of the rock, or built of bricks; the one was a little higher than the other, and was connected with the lower one by a channel. The grapes were pressed in the higher trough and the juice ran off into the lower trough. The tower served a double purpose. It served as a watch-tower, from which to watch for thieves when the grapes were ripening; and it served as a lodging for those who were working in the vineyard.

The actions of the owner of the vineyard were all quite normal. In the time of Jesus, Palestine was a troubled place with little luxury; it was, therefore, very familiar with absentee landlords, who let out their estates, and who were interested only in collecting the rental at the right time. The rent might be paid in any of three ways. It might be a money rent; it might be a fixed amount of the fruit, no matter what the crop might be; and it might be an agreed percentage of the crop.

Even the action of the cultivators was not out of the common. In the time of Jesus Palestine was seething with economic unrest; the working people were discontented and rebellious, and the action of the cultivators in seeking to eliminate the son was not by any means impossible.

As we have said, it would have been easy for those who heard this parable to make the necessary identifications. Before we treat the parable in detail, let us set them down. The vineyard is the nation of Israel, and the owner of the vineyard is God. The cultivators are the religious leaders of Israel, who had charge, as it were, for God of the welfare of the nation. The messengers who were sent successively are the prophets, who were sent by God, and who were so often rejected and killed. The son who came last is none other than Jesus Himself. Here in a vivid story Jesus set out at one and the same time the history and the doom of Israel.

PRIVILEGE AND RESPONSIBILITY

Matthew 21: 33-46 (continued)

THIS parable has much to tell us in three directions.

(i) It has much to tell us about God.

(a) It tell us of God's *trust* in men. The owner of the vineyard entrusted it to the cultivators. He did not even stand over them to exercise a police-like supervision. He went away and left them with their task. God pays men the compliment of entrusting them with His work. Every task we receive is a task given to us to do by God.

(b) It tells us of God's *patience*. The master sent messenger after messenger. He did not come with sudden vengeance when one messenger had been abused and ill-treated. He gave the cultivators chance after chance to respond to his appeal. God bears with men in all their sinning, and will not cast them off.

(c) It tells us of God's *judgment*. In the end the master of the vineyard took the vineyard from the cultivators and gave it to others. God's sternest judgment is when He takes out of our hands the task which He meant us to do. A man has sunk to his lowest level when he has become useless to God.

(ii) It has much to tell us about men.

(a) It tells us of human *privilege*. The vineyard was equipped with everything—the hedge, the wine press, the tower—which would make the task of the cultivators easy, and which would enable them to discharge it well. God does not only give us a task to do; He also gives us the means whereby to do it.

(b) It tells us of human *freedom*. The master left the cultivators to do the task as they liked. God is no tyrannical task-master; He is like a wise commander who allocates a task and then trusts a man to do it.

(c) It tells us of human *answerability*. To all men there comes a day of reckoning. We are answerable for the way in which we have carried out the task which God gave us to do.

(d) It tells us of the *deliberateness of human sin*. In the parable the cultivators carry out a deliberate policy of rebellion and disobedience towards the master. Sin is deliberate opposition to God; it is the deliberate taking of our own way, when we know quite well what the way of God is.

(iii) It has much to tell us about Jesus.

(a) It tells us of the *claim of Jesus*. This parable shows us quite clearly Jesus lifting Himself out of the succession of the prophets. Those who came before Him were the messengers of God; no one could deny them that honour; but they were *servants*; He was the *Son*. This parable contains one of the clearest claims which Jesus ever made to be unique; and to be different from even the greatest of those who went before.

(b) It tells us of the *sacrifice of Jesus*. This parable makes it clear that Jesus knew what lay ahead. In the parable the hands of wicked men killed the son. Jesus was never in any doubt of what lay ahead. He did not die because He was compelled to die; He went willingly and open-eyed to death.

THE SYMBOL OF THE STONE

Matthew 21: 33-46 (*continued*)

THIS parable concludes with the picture of the stone. There are two pictures here.

(i) The first is quite clear. It is the picture of a stone which the builders rejected and which became the most important stone in the whole building. The picture is from *Psalm* 118: 22: " The stone which the builders rejected is become the head-stone of the corner." Originally the Psalmist meant this as a picture of the nation of Israel. Israel was the nation which was despised and rejected. The Jews were hated by all men. They had been servants and slaves of many nations; but none the less the nation which all men despised was the chosen people of God. It may be that men reject Christ, and refuse Him, and seek to eliminate Him, but they will yet find that that Christ whom they rejected is the most important person in the world. It was Julian, the Roman Emperor, who tried to turn the clock back. He tried to banish Christianity, and to bring back the old pagan gods. He failed and failed completely; and at the end of it the dramatist makes him say, " To shoulder Christ from out the topmost niche was not for me." The man upon the Cross has become the Judge and King of all the world.

(ii) But there is here also a more difficult picture, the picture of a stone which breaks a man, if he stumbles against it, and which crushes a man to powder, if it falls upon him. This is a composite picture. There are three pictures of a stone in the Old Testament out of which this passage is woven together. The first is in *Isaiah* 8: 14, 15: " Sanctify the Lord of hosts Himself, and let Him be your fear, and let Him be your dread. And He shall be for a sanctuary; but for a stone of stumbling and a rock of offence to both the houses of Israel, for a gin and for a snare to the inhabitants of Jerusalem. And many among them shall stumble, and fall, and be broken, and be snared, and be taken." The second passage is in *Isaiah* 28: 16: " Behold, I lay in Zion for a foundation a stone, a tried stone, a precious corner stone, a sure foundation." The third passage is in *Daniel* 2: 34, 44, 45 where there is a strange picture of a stone, cut without hands, which brake in pieces the enemies of God.

The idea behind all this is that in the Old Testament there are these pictures of a stone; and all these pictures are summed up in Jesus Christ. Jesus is the foundation stone on which everything is built, and the corner stone which holds everything together. To refuse His way is to batter one's head against the walls of the law of God. To defy Him is in the end to be crushed out of life. However strange these pictures may seem to us, they were pictures familiar to every Jew who knew the prophets.

JOY AND JUDGMENT

Matthew 22: 1-10

Jesus again answered them in parables: " The King-dom of Heaven is like the situation which arose when a man who was a king arranged a wedding for his son. He sent his servants to summon those who had been invited to the wedding, and they refused to come. He again sent other servants. ' Tell those who have been invited,' he said, ' look you, I have my meal all prepared; my oxen and my specially fattened animals have been killed; and everything is ready. Come to the wedding.' But they disregarded the invitation and went away, one to his estate, and another to his business. The rest seized the servants and treated them shamefully and killed them. The king was angry, and sent his armies, and destroyed those murderers, and set fire to their city. Then he said to his servants, ' The wedding is ready. Those who have been invited did not deserve to come. Go, then, to the highways and invite to the wedding all you may find.' So the servants went out to the roads, and collected all whom they found, both bad and good; and the wedding was supplied with guests.''

VERSES 1-14 of this chapter form not one parable, but two; and we will grasp their meaning far more easily and far more fully if we take them separately. The events of this parable were completely in accordance with normal Jewish customs. When the invitations to a great feast, like a wedding feast, were sent out, the time was not stated; and when everything was ready and prepared, then the servants were sent out with a final summons to tell the guests to come. So, then, the king in this parable had long ago sent out his invitations; but it was not till every-thing was ready and prepared that the final summons to attend was issued—and insultingly refused. This parable has two meanings.

(i) It has a purely local meaning. Its local meaning was a driving home of what had already been said in the Parable of the Wicked Husbandmen; once again it was an accusation of the Jews. The guests who had been invited, and who when the time came refused to come, stand for the Jews. Ages ago they had been invited by God to be His chosen people; yet when God's Son came into the world, and they were invited to follow Him and to accept Him, they contemptuously refused the invitation. The result was that the invitation of God went out direct to the highways and the byways; and the people in the highways and the byways stand for the sinners and the Gentiles, who never expected an invitation into the Kingdom of God.

As the writer of the gospel saw it, the consequences of the refusal were terrible. There is one verse of the parable which is strangely out of place; and it is out of place because it is not part of the original parable as Jesus told it, but a comment and an interpretation by the writer of the gospel. That is verse 7, which tells how the king sent his armies against those who refused the invitation, and burned their city. This introduction of armies and the burning of the city seems at first sight completely out of place when taken in connexion with invitations to a wedding feast. But let us remember when Matthew was composing his gospel. He was doing so some time between A.D. 80 and 90. What had happened during the period between the actual life of Jesus, and the composing of the gospel? The answer is—*the destruction of Jerusalem by the armies of Rome.* In A.D. 70 Jerusalem was indeed destroyed. The Temple was sacked and burned; the city was destroyed stone from stone, so that a plough was drawn across it. Complete disaster had come to those who refused to recognize the Son of God when He came. The writer of the gospel adds as his comment the terrible things which did in fact happen to the nation which would not take the way of Christ. And it is indeed the simple historical fact that if the Jews had accepted the way of Christ, and had walked in love, in humility and in sacrifice they would never have been the rebellious, warring people who finally provoked the avenging wrath of Rome, when Rome could stand their political machinations no longer.

(ii) But equally this parable has much to say on a much wider scale.

(a) It reminds us that the invitation of God is the invitation to a feast as joyous as a wedding feast. God's invitation is to joy. To think of Christianity as a gloomy giving up of everything which brings laughter and sunshine and happy fellowship to life is to mistake its whole nature. It is to joy that the Christian is invited; and it is joy he misses, if he refuses the invitation.

(b) It reminds us that the things which make men deaf to the invitation of Christ are not necessarily bad things in themselves. One man went to his estate; the other to his business. They did not go off on a wild carousal or an immoral adventure. They went off on the, in itself, excellent task of efficiently administering their business life. It is very easy for a man to be so busy with the things of time that he forgets the things of eternity, to be so preoccupied with the things which are seen that he forgets the things which are unseen, to hear so insistently the claims of the world that he cannot hear the soft invitation of the voice of Christ. The tragedy of life is that it is so often the second bests which shut out the bests, that it is things which are good in themselves which shut out the things that are supreme. A man can be so busy making a living that he forgets to make a life; he can be so busy with the administration and the organization of life that he forgets life itself.

(c) It reminds us that the appeal of Christ to us is not so much to consider how we will be punished as it is to see what we miss, if we will not take His way of things. Those who would not come were punished, but their real tragedy was that they lost the joy of the wedding feast. If we refuse the invitation of Christ, some day our greatest pain will lie, not in the things we suffer, but in the realization of the precious things which we have missed, and of which we have cheated ourselves.

(d) It reminds us that in the last analysis God's invitation to us is the invitation of grace. Those who were gathered in from the highways and the byways had no claim on the king at all; they could never by any stretch of imagination have ever expected an invitation to the wedding feast, still less could they ever have deserved it. It came to them from nothing other than the wide-armed, open-hearted, generous hospitality of the king. It was grace which offered the invitation, and grace which gathered men in.

THE SCRUTINY OF THE KING

Matthew 22: 11-14

The king came in to see those who were sitting at table, and he saw there a man who was not wearing a wedding garment. " Friend," he said to him, " how did you come here with no wedding garment? " The man was struck silent. Then the king said to the attendants, " Bind him hands and feet, and throw him out into the outer darkness. There shall be weeping and gnashing of teeth there. For many are called, but few are chosen."

THIS is the second of the two parables which are woven together in this passage. As we shall see this is a second parable, but it is also a very close continuation and amplification of the previous parable. The story is the story of a guest who appeared at a royal wedding feast without a wedding garment.

One of the great interests of this parable is that in it we see Jesus taking a story which was already familiar to His hearers, and using it in His own way. The Rabbis had two stories which involved kings and garments. The first tells of a king who invited his guests to a feast, without telling them the exact date and time of it; but he did tell the guests that they must wash, and anoint, and clothe themselves that they might be ready when the summons came. The wise prepared and clothed themselves at once, and took their places waiting at the palace door, for they believed that in a palace a feast could be prepared so quickly that there would be no long warning. The foolish believed that it would take a long time to make the necessary preparations, and that they would see the preparations being made, and would have time to put on their garments and to anoint and array themselves. So they went, the mason to his lime, the potter to his clay, the smith to his furnace, the fuller to his bleaching-ground, and went on with their work. Then, suddenly, the summons to the feast came without any warning. The wise were ready to sit down, and the king rejoiced over them, and they ate and drank. But those who had not arrayed themselves in their wedding garments had to stand outside, sad and hungry, and had to look on at the joy that they had lost. That rabbinic parable tells of the duty of preparedness for the summons of God, and the garments stand for the preparation that must be made.

The second rabbinic parable tells how a king entrusted to his servants royal robes. Those who were wise took the robes, and carefully stored them away, and kept them in all their pristine loveliness. Those who were foolish wore the robes to their work, and so soiled and stained them. The day came when the king demanded the robes back. The wise handed them back fresh and clean; so the king laid up the robes in his treasury and bade them go in peace. The foolish handed them back stained and soiled. The king commanded that the robes should be given to the fuller to cleanse, and that the foolish servants should be cast into prison. This parable teaches that a man must hand back his soul to God in all its original purity; but that the man who has nothing but a stained soul to render back stands condemned. No doubt Jesus had these two parables in His mind, when He told His own story. What, then, was Jesus seeking to teach by this story? As did the previous parable this parable also contains a local and a temporary lesson, and a universal and a permanent lesson.

(i) The local lesson is this. Jesus has just said that the king, to supply his feast with guests, sent his messengers out into the highways and byways to gather all men in. That was the parable of the open door. It told how the Gentiles and the sinners would be gathered in. This parable strikes the necessary balance. It is true that the door is open to all men, but when they come they must bring with them a life which seeks to fit the love which has been given to them. Grace is not only a gift; grace is a grave responsibility. A man cannot go on living the life he lived before he met Jesus Christ. He must be clothed in a new purity and a new holiness and a new goodness. The door is open, but the door is not open that the sinner may come and remain a sinner, but that the sinner may come and become a saint.

(ii) But there is a permanent lesson in this parable. The way in which a man comes to anything demonstrates the spirit in which he comes. If we go to visit in a friend's house, we do not go in the clothes that we wear in the shipyard or the garden. We know very well that it is not the clothes which matter to the friend. It is not that we want to put on a show. It is simply a matter of respect that we should present ourselves in our friend's house as neatly and tidily as we can. The fact that we prepare ourselves to go there is the way in which we outwardly show our affection and our esteem for our friend. It is so with God's house. This parable has nothing to do with the *clothes* in which we go to church; it has everything to do with the *spirit* in which we go to God's house. It is profoundly true that church-going must never be a fashion parade. But there are garments of the mind and of the heart and of the soul—the garment of expectation, the garment of humble penitence, the garment of faith, the garment of reverence—and these are the garments without which we ought not to dare to approach God. It is too often the case that we go to God's house with no preparation at all; if every man and woman in our congregations came to church *prepared to worship*, after a little prayer, a little thought, and a little self-examination, then worship would be worship indeed—the worship in which and through which things happen in men's souls and in the life of the Church and in the affairs of the world.

HUMAN AND DIVINE RIGHT

Matthew 22: 15-22

> Then the Pharisees came, and tried to form a plan to ensnare Him in His speech. So they sent their disciples to Him, along with the Herodians. " Teacher," they said, " we know that you are true, and that you teach the way of God in truth, and that you never allow yourself to be swayed by any man, for you are no respecter of persons. Tell us, then, your opinion—is it right to pay tribute to Caesar, or not? "

Jesus was well aware of their malice. " Hypocrites,"
He said, " why do you try to test me? Show me the
tribute coin." They brought Him a denarius. " Whose
image is this," He said to them, " and whose inscription? " " Caesar's," they said to Him. " Well then,"
He said to them, " render to Caesar the things which
are Caesar's, and to God the things which are God's."
When they heard this answer, they were amazed,
and left Him and went away.

Up to this point we have seen Jesus, as it were, on the
attack. He had spoken three parables in which He had
plainly indicted the orthodox Jewish leaders. In the
parable of the two sons (*Matthew* 21: 28-32) the Jewish
leaders appear under the guise of the unsatisfactory son
who did not do his father's will. In the parable of the
wicked husbandmen (*Matthew* 21: 33-46) they are the
wicked husbandmen. In the parable of the king's feast
(*Matthew* 22: 1-14) they are the condemned guests, who
refused the invitation. Now we see the Jewish leaders
launching their counter-attack; and they do so by directing
at Jesus carefully formulated questions. They ask these
questions in public, while the crowd look on and listen,
and their aim is to make Jesus discredit Himself by His
own words in the presence of the people. Here, then, we
have the question of the Pharisees, and it was indeed
subtly and cleverly framed. Palestine was an occupied
country, and the Jews were subject to the Roman Empire;
and the question was: " Is it, or is it not, lawful to pay
tribute to Rome? " There were, in fact, three regular
taxes which the Roman government exacted. There was a
ground tax; a man must pay to the government one tenth of
the grain, and one fifth of the oil and wine which he produced; this tax was paid partly in kind, and partly in a
money equivalent. There was *income tax*, which was
one per cent of a man's income. There was a *poll tax*;
this tax had to be paid by every male person from the
age of fourteen to the age of sixty-five, and by every female

person from the age of twelve to sixty-five; it amounted to one *denarius*—that is what Jesus called *the tribute coin*—and was the equivalent of about ninepence, a sum which is to be evaluated in the memory that eightpence was the usual day's wage for a working-man. The tax in question here is the poll tax.

The question which the Pharisees asked set Jesus a very real dilemma. If He said that it was unlawful to pay the tax, they would promptly report Him to the Roman government officials as a seditious person, and His arrest would certainly follow. If He said that it was lawful to pay the tax, He would stand discredited in the eyes of many of the people. Not only did the people resent the tax as everyone resents taxation; they resented it even more for religious reasons. To a Jew God was the only king; their nation was a theocracy; to pay tax to an earthly king was to admit the validity of his kingship and thereby to insult God. Therefore the more fanatical of the Jews insisted that any tax paid to any foreign king was necessarily wrong. Whichever way Jesus answered—so His questioners thought—He laid Himself open to trouble. The seriousness of this attack is shown by the fact that the *Pharisees* and the *Herodians* combined to make it, for normally these two parties would have been in bitter opposition. The Pharisees were the supremely orthodox, who would resent the payment of the tax to a foreign king as an infringement of the divine right of God. The Herodians were the party of Herod, king of Galilee, who owed his power to the Romans, and who worked hand in glove with them. The Pharisees and the Herodians were strange bed-fellows indeed; their differences were for the moment forgotten in a common hatred of Jesus, and a common desire to eliminate Him. Any man who insists on his own way, no matter what that way is, will hate Jesus.

Nor was this question of tax-paying of merely historical interest. Matthew was writing between A.D. 80 and 90,

The Temple had been destroyed in A.D. 70. So long as the Temple stood every Jew had been bound to pay the half-shekel Temple tax. After the destruction of the Temple the Roman government demanded that that Temple tax should be paid to the temple of Jupiter Capitolinus in Rome. It is obvious how bitter a regulation that was for a Jew to stomach. The matter of taxes was a real problem in the actual ministry of Jesus; and it was still a real problem in the days of the early Church.

But Jesus was wise. He asked to see a denarius, which was stamped with the Emperor's head. In the ancient days coinage was the sign of kingship. As soon as a king came to the throne he struck his own coinage; even a pretender would produce a coinage to show the reality of his kingship; and that coinage was held to be the property of the king whose image it bore. Jesus asked whose image was on the coin. The answer was that it was Caesar's head which was on it. " Well then," said Jesus, " give it back to Caesar; it is his. Give to Caesar what belongs to him; and give to God what belongs to Him."

With His unique wisdom Jesus never laid down laws and rules and regulations; that is why His teaching is timeless, and never goes out of date; He always lays down principles. Here He lays down a very great and very important principle.

Any Christian man has a double citizenship. He is a citizen of the country of the world in which he happens to live. To that country he owes many things. He owes the safety against lawless men which only settled government can give; he owes all public services to the state. To take a simple example, few men are wealthy enough to have a lighting system or a cleansing system or a water system of their own. These are public services. In a welfare state the citizen owes still more to the state—education, medical services, provision for unemployment and old age. This places him under an obligatory debt.

Because the Christian is a man of honour, he must be a responsible citizen; and failure in good citizenship is also failure in Christian duty. Untold troubles can descend upon a country or an industry when Christians refuse to take their part in the administration of the country, and leave that administration to selfish, self-seeking, partisan, and unchristian men. The Christian has a duty to Caesar in return for the privileges which the rule of Caesar brings to him.

But the Christian is also a citizen of heaven. There are matters of conscience and of religion and of principle in which the responsibility of the Christian is to God. It may well be that the two citizenships will never clash; they do not need to. But when the Christian is convinced that it is God's will that something should be done, it must be done; or, if he is convinced that something is against the will of God, it must be resisted, and he can take no part in it. Where the boundaries between the two duties lie Jesus does not say. That is for a man's own conscience to test. But a real Christian—and this is the permanent truth which Jesus here lays down—is at one and the same time a good citizen of his country, and a good citizen of the Kingdom of Heaven. He will fail in his duty neither to God nor to man. He will, as Peter said, " Fear God and honour the king " (1 *Peter* 2: 17).

THE LIVING GOD OF LIVING MEN

Matthew 22: 23-33

On that day the Sadducees, who deny that there is any resurrection, came to Him, and questioned Him. " Teacher," they said, " Moses said, ' If anyone dies without children, his brother shall marry his wife, and shall raise up a family for his brother.' Amongst us there were seven brothers. The first married and died, and, since he had no children, he left his wife to his brother. The same thing happened with the second and the third, right to the end of the seven of them. Last of all the woman died. Of which of the seven will she be the wife in the resurrection? For they all had her." Jesus answered: " You are in error, because you do not know the Scriptures or the power of God. In the resurrection they neither marry nor are married, but they are as the angels in heaven. Now, in regard to the resurrection of the dead, have you never read what God said, ' I am the God of Abraham, the God of Isaac, and the God of Jacob.' God is not the God of dead men, but of those who live." When the crowds heard this answer, they were amazed at His teaching.

WHEN the Pharisees had made their counter-attack on Jesus, and had been routed, the Sadducees took up the battle. Beyond doubt the Sadducees were delighted at the rout of the Pharisees, for the Pharisees and the Sadducees held antithetically opposite views.

The Sadducees were not many in number; but they were the wealthy, the aristocratic, and the governing class. The chief priests, for instance, were Sadducees. In politics they were collaborationist; they were quite ready to co-operate with the Roman government, if co-operation was the price of the retention of their own privileges. In thought they were quite ready to open their minds to Greek ideas. In their Jewish belief they were traditionalists. They refused to accept the oral and scribal law, which to the Pharisees was of such paramount importance. They went even further; the only part of scripture which they regarded as binding was the Pentateuch, the Law *par excellence*, the first five books of the Old Testament. They did not accept the prophets or the poetical books as scripture at all. In particular they were at variance with the Pharisees in that they completely denied any life after death, a belief on which the Pharisees insisted. The Pharisees indeed laid it down that any man who denied the resurrection of the dead was shut out from God.

The Sadducees insisted that the doctrine of life after death could not be proved from the Pentateuch. The Pharisees said that it could be so proved. It is interesting to look at the proofs which the Pharisees adduced. The Pharisees cited *Numbers* 18: 28 which says, " Ye shall give thereof the Lord's heave-offering to Aaron the priest." That is a permanent regulation; the verb is in the present tense; therefore Aaron is still alive! They cited *Deuteronomy* 31: 16: " This people shall rise up," a peculiarly unconvincing citation for the second half of the verse goes on, " and go a-whoring after the gods of the strangers of the land "! They cited *Deuteronomy* 32: 39: " I kill and I make alive." Outside the Pentateuch they cited *Isaiah* 26: 19: " Thy dead men shall live." They cited *The Song of Solomon* 7: 9 which speaks of " causing the lips of those that are asleep to speak." It cannot be said that any of the citations of the Pharisees are really convincing; and no real argument for the resurrection of the dead had ever been produced from the Pentateuch.

The Pharisees were very definite about the resurrection of *the body*. They discussed recondite points—Would a man rise clothed or unclothed? If clothed, would he rise with the clothes in which he died, or other clothes? They used I *Samuel* 28: 14 (the witch of Endor's raising of the spirit of Samuel at the request of Saul) to prove that after death men retain the appearance they had in this world. They even argued that men rose with the physical defects with which, and from which they died—otherwise they would not be the same persons! All Jews would be resurrected in Palestine, the Holy Land, so, they said, that under the earth there were cavities, and, when a Jew was buried in a foreign land, his body rolled through those cavities until it reached Palestine! The Pharisees then held as a primary doctrine the bodily resurrection of the dead; the Sadducees completely denied it.

The Sadducees produced a question which, they believed, reduced the doctrine of the resurrection of the body to an absurdity. There was a Jewish custom called Levirate Marriage. How far it was ever carried out in practice is very doubtful. If a man died childless, his brother was under obligation to marry the widow, and to beget children for his brother; such children were legally regarded as the brother's children. If the man utterly refused to marry the widow, they must both go to the elders. The woman must loosen the man's shoe, spit in his face, and curse him; and the man was thereafter under a stigma of refusal (*Deuteronomy* 25: 5-10). The Sadducees cited a case of Levirate Marriage in which seven brothers one after another married the same woman, each successive brother having died childless; and then asked, " When the resurrection takes place, whose wife will this much-married woman be? " Here indeed was a catch question.

Jesus began by laying down one principle—the whole question starts from a basic error, the error of thinking of heaven in terms of earth, and of thinking of eternity in terms of time. Jesus' answer is that anyone who reads scripture must see that that question is irrelevant, for heaven is not going to be simply a continuation or an extension of this world. There will be new and greater relationships which will far transcend the physical relationships of time.

Then Jesus went on to demolish the whole Sadducean position. They had always held that there was no text in the Pentateuch which could be used to prove the resurrection of the dead. Now, what is one of the commonest titles of God in the Pentateuch? " The God of Abraham, and of Isaac, and of Jacob." God cannot be the God of dead men, and of mouldering corpses. The living God must be the God of living men. The Sadducean case was shattered. Jesus had done what the wisest Rabbis had never been able to do. Out of Scripture itself He had confuted the Sadducees, and routed them, and had shown them that there is a life after death, and that life after death must not be thought of in earthly terms. The crowds were amazed at a man who was a master of argument like this, and even the Pharisees can hardly have forborne to cheer.

DUTY TO GOD AND DUTY TO MAN

Matthew 22: 34-40

> When the Pharisees heard that He had silenced the Sadducees, they gathered together. One of them, who was an expert in the Law, asked Him a question as a test: " What commandment in the Law is greatest? " He said to him, " ' You must love the Lord your God with your whole heart, and your whole soul, and your whole mind.' This is the great and the chief commandment; and the second is like it, ' You must love your neighbour as yourself.' On these two commandments the whole Law and the prophets depend."

IN *Matthew* this scribe's question looks like a return to the attack on the part of the Pharisees; but in *Mark* the atmosphere is different. As Mark tells the story (*Mark* 12: 28-34) the scribe did not ask Jesus this question to trip Him up. He asked it in gratitude that Jesus had confuted the Sadducees, and to enable Jesus to demonstrate how well He could answer; and the passage ends with the scribe and Jesus very close to each other.

We may well say that here Jesus laid down the complete definition of religion.

(i) Religion consists in loving God. The verse which Jesus quotes is *Deuteronomy* 6: 5. That verse was part of the *Shema*, the basic and essential creed of Judaism, the sentence with which every Jewish service still opens, and the first text which every Jewish child commits to memory. It means that to God we must give a total love, a love which dominates our emotions, a love which directs our thoughts, and a love which is the dynamic of our actions. All religion starts with the love which is total commitment of life to God.

(ii) The second commandment which Jesus quotes comes from *Leviticus* 19: 18. Our love for God must issue in love for men. The only way in which a man can prove that he loves God is in fact by loving his fellow-men. But it is to be noted in which order the commandments

come; it is love of God first, and love of man second.
It is only when we love God that man becomes lovable.
The Biblical teaching about man is not that man is a
collection of chemical elements, not that man is part of
the brute creation, but that man is made in the image
of God (*Genesis* 1: 26, 27). It is for that reason that man
is lovable. The true basis of all democracy is in fact the
love of God. Take away the love of God and we can become
angry at man the unteachable; we can become pessimistic
about man the unimprovable; we can become callous
to man the machine-minder. The basis of the love of man
is firmly grounded in the love of God.

To be truly religious is to love God, and to love the
men whom God made in His own image; and to love God
and man, not with a nebulous sentimentality, but with
that total commitment which issues in devotion to God
and practical service of men.

NEW HORIZONS

Matthew 22: 41-46

> When the Pharisees had come together, Jesus asked
> them a question: "What is your opinion about
> The Anointed One? Whose son is He?" "David's
> son," they said. He said to them, "How, then, does
> David in the Spirit call Him *Lord*, when he says,
> 'The Lord said to my Lord, Sit on my right hand
> till I put your enemies beneath your feet.' If David
> calls Him *Lord*, how is He his son?" And no one was
> able to give Him any answer. And from that day
> no one any longer dared to ask Him a question.

To us this may seem one of the most obscure things which
Jesus ever said. It may be so, but none the less it is one
of the most important statements He ever made. Even if,
at first sight, we do not fully grasp its meaning, we can
still see the air of awe and astonishment and mystery
which it has about it.

We have seen again and again that Jesus refused to
allow His followers to proclaim Him as the Messiah until

He had taught them what Messiahship meant. Their ideas of Messiahship needed the most radical change.

The commonest title of the Messiah was *Son of David*. Behind it there lay the expectation that there would one day come a great prince of the line of David, who would shatter Israel's enemies, and lead the people to the conquest of all nations. The Messiah was most commonly thought of in nationalistic, political, military terms of power and glory. This is another attempt by Jesus to alter that conception.

Jesus asked the Pharisees whose son they understood the Messiah to be: they answered, as He knew they would, "David's son." Jesus then quotes *Psalm* 110: 1: "The Lord said to my Lord, sit Thou at my right hand." All accepted that as a Messianic text. In it the first *Lord* is God; the second *Lord* is the Messiah. That is to say that David calls the Messiah *Lord*. But, if the Messiah is David's son, how could David call his own son *Lord*? How could that be?

The clear result of the argument is that *it is not adequate to call the Messiah Son of David*. He is not David's son; He is David's Lord. When Jesus healed the blind men, they called Him Son of David (*Matthew* 20: 30). When He entered Jerusalem the crowds hailed Him as Son of David (*Matthew* 21: 9). Jesus is here saying, "It is not enough to call the Messiah Son of David. It is not enough to think of Him as a Prince of David's line and an earthly conqueror and a leader of earthly armies. You must go beyond that, for the Messiah is David's *Lord*." What did Jesus mean? He can only have meant one thing—that the only true description of Him is *Son of God*. *Son of David* is not an adequate title; only *Son of God* will do. And, if that be so, Messiahship is not to be thought of in terms of Davidic conquest, but in terms of divine and sacrificial love. Here, then, Jesus makes His greatest claim. In Him there came, not the earthly conqueror who would repeat the military triumphs of David, but the Son of God who would demonstrate the love of God upon His Cross.

There would be few that day who caught anything like all that Jesus meant; but when Jesus said that, even the densest of them felt the shiver in the presence of the eternal mystery. They had the awed and the uncomfortable feeling that they had heard the voice of God, and for a moment, in this man Jesus, they glimpsed the very face of God.

SCRIBES AND PHARISEES

IF a man is characteristically and temperamentally an irritable, ill-tempered and irascible creature, notoriously given to uncontrolled outbursts of passionate anger, then his anger is neither effective nor impressive. Nobody pays any attention to the anger of a bad-tempered man. But when a person who is characteristically meek and lowly, gentle and loving, suddenly erupts into blazing wrath, then even the most thoughtless person must be shocked into taking thought. That is why the anger of Jesus is so awe-inspiring a sight. It is seldom in literature that we find so unsparing and sustained an indictment as we find in this chapter. This wrath of Jesus is directed against the Scribes and Pharisees. Before we begin to study this chapter in detail, it will be well briefly to see what these Scribes and Pharisees stood for.

The Jews had a deep and lasting sense of the continuity of their religion; and we can see best what the Pharisees and Scribes stood for by seeing where they came into this scheme of Jewish religion. The Jews had a saying, " Moses received the Law and delivered it to Joshua; and Joshua to the elders; and the elders to the prophets; and the prophets to the men of the Great Synagogue." All Jewish religion is based first on the Ten Commandments, and then on the Pentateuch, the Law, the first five books of the Old Testament. The history of the Jews was designed to make them a people of the Law. As every nation has, they had had their dream of greatness. But the experiences of history had made that dream take a special direction. They had been conquered by the Assyrians, the Babylonians, the Persians, and Jerusalem had been left desolate. It was clear that they could not be pre-eminent in political power. But although political power was an obvious impossibility, they none the less possessed the Law, and to them the Law was the very word of God, the greatest thing, and the most precious possession in the world. There came a day in their history when that pre-eminence of the Law was, as it were, publicly admitted; and there came what one can only call a deliberate act of decision, whereby the people of Israel became in the most unique sense the people of the Law. Under Ezra and Nehemiah the people were allowed to come back to Jerusalem, and to rebuild their shattered city, and to take up their national life again. When that happened, there came a day when Ezra, the Scribe, took the book of the Law, and read it to them, and there happened something that was nothing less than a national dedication of a people to the keeping of the Law (*Nehemiah* 8: 1-8).

From that day the study of the Law became the greatest of all professions; and that study of the Law was committed to the men of the Great Synagogue. The men whose business it was to study the Law were the *Scribes*.

We have already seen how the great principles of the Law were broken up into thousands upon thousands of little rules and regulations (see section on *Matthew* 5: 17-20). We have seen, for instance, how the Law said that a man must not work on the Sabbath day; and we have seen how the Scribes laboured to define work, how they laid it down how many paces a man might walk on the Sabbath, how heavy a burden he might carry, the things he might and might not do. By the time this Scribal interpretation of the Law was finished, it took more than fifty volumes to hold the mass of regulations which resulted.

The return of the people to Jerusalem and the first dedication of the Law took place about 450 B.C. But it is not till long after that that the Pharisees emerge. About 175 B.C. Antiochus Epiphanes of Syria made a deliberate attempt to stamp out the Jewish religion, and to introduce Greek religion and Greek customs and practices. It was then that the Pharisees arose as a separate sect. The name means *The Separated Ones*; and they were the men who dedicated their whole life to the careful and meticulous observance of every rule and regulation which the Scribes had worked out. In face of the threat directed against Judaism they determined to spend their whole lives in one long observance of Judaism in its most elaborate and ceremonial and legal form. They were men who accepted the mass and the ever-increasing number of religious rules and regulations extracted from the Law.

There were never very many of them; at most there were not more than six thousand of them; for the plain fact is that, if a man was going to accept and carry out every little regulation of the Law, he would have time for nothing else; he had to withdraw himself, to separate himself, from ordinary life in order to keep the Law.

The Pharisees then were two things. First, they were dedicated legalists; religion to them was the observance of every detail of the Law. But second—and this is never to be forgotten—they were men in desperate earnest about their religion, for no one would have accepted the impossibly demanding task of living a life like that unless they had been in the most deadly earnest. They could, therefore, develop at one and the same time all the faults of legalism, and all the virtues of complete self-dedication. A Pharisee might either be a dessicated or an arrogant legalist, or a man of burning and consuming devotion to God.

To say this is not to pass a particularly Christian verdict on the Pharisees, for the Jews themselves passed that very verdict. The *Talmud* distinguishes seven different kinds of Pharisees.

(i) There was the *Shoulder Pharisee*. He was meticulous in his observance of the Law; but he wore his good deeds upon his shoulder. He was out for a reputation for purity and goodness. True, he obeyed the Law, but he did so in order to be seen of men.

(ii) There was the *Wait-a-little Pharisee*. He was the Pharisee who could always produce an entirely valid excuse for putting off a good deed. He professed the creed of the strictest Pharisees but he could always find an excuse for allowing practice to lag behind creed. He spoke, but he did not do.

(iii) There was the *Bruised* or *Bleeding Pharisee*. The Talmud speaks of the plague of *self-afflicting Pharisees*. These Pharisees received their name for this reason. Women had a very low status in Palestine. No really strict, orthodox teacher could be seen talking to a woman in public, even if that woman was his own wife or sister. These Pharisees went even further; they would not even allow themselves to look at a woman on the street. In order to avoid doing so they would shut their eyes, and so bump into walls and buildings and obstructions. They thus bruised and wounded themselves, and their wounds and bruises gained them a special reputation for exceeding piety.

(iv) There was the Pharisee who was variously described as the *Pestle and Mortar Pharisee*, or the *Hump-backed Pharisee*, or the *Tumbling Pharisee*. Such men walked in such an ostentatious humility that they were bent like a pestle in a mortar, or like a hunch-back. They were so humble that they would not even lift their feet from the ground and so tripped over any obstruction they met. Their humility was in fact a self-advertising ostentation.

(v) There was the *Ever-reckoning* or *Compounding Pharisee*. This kind of Pharisee was for ever reckoning up his good deeds; he was for ever striking a balance sheet between himself and God, and he believed that every good deed he did put God a little further in his debt.

To him religion was always to be reckoned in terms of a profit and loss account.

(vi) There was the *Timid* or *Fearing Pharisee*. He was always in dread of divine punishment. He was, therefore, always cleansing the outside of the cup and the platter, so that he might seem to be good. He saw religion in terms of judgment, and life in terms of a terror-stricken evasion of this judgment.

(vii) Finally, there was the *God-fearing Pharisee*; he was the Pharisee who really and truly loved God, and who found his delight in obedience to the Law of God, however difficult that Law might be.

That was the Jew's own classification of the Pharisees; and it is to be noted that there were six bad types to one good one. There would be not a few listening to Jesus' denunciation of the Pharisees who agreed with every word of it.

MAKING RELIGION A BURDEN

Matthew 23: 1-4

> Then Jesus said to the crowds and to His disciples, " The Scribes and Pharisees sit on Moses' seat. Therefore do and observe everything they tell you; but do not act as they act; for they speak, but they do not do. They bind burdens that are heavy and hard to bear, and place them on men's shoulders; but they themselves refuse to lift a finger to remove them."

HERE we already see the lineaments of the Pharisees beginning to appear. Here we see the Jewish conviction of the continuity of the faith. God gave the Law to Moses; Moses handed it to Joshua; Joshua transmitted it to the elders; the elders passed it down to the prophets; and the prophets gave it to the Scribes and Pharisees.

It must not for a moment be thought that Jesus is commending the Scribes and Pharisees with all their rules and regulations. What He is saying is this, " In so far as these Scribes and Pharisees have taught you the great principles of the Law which Moses received from God, you must obey them." When we were studying Matthew 5: 17-20 we saw what these principles were. The whole of the Ten Commandments are based on two great principles. They are based on *reverence*, reverence for God, for God's name, for God's day, for the parents God has given to us. They are based on *respect*, respect for a man's life, and possessions, and personality, and good name, and for oneself. These principles are eternal; and, in so far as the Scribes and Pharisees teach reverence for God and respect for men, their teaching is eternally binding and eternally valid.

But their whole outlook on religion has had one fundamental effect. It has made religion a thing of thousands upon thousands of rules and regulations; and therefore *it has made religion an intolerable burden*. Here is the test of any presentation of religion. Does it make religion wings to lift a man up, or a deadweight to drag him down? Does it make religion a joy or a depression? Is a man helped by his religion or is he haunted by it? Does his religion carry him, or has he to carry it? Whenever religion becomes a depressing affair of burdens and prohibitions and thou shalt nots, it has ceased to be true religion.

Nor would the Pharisees allow the slightest relaxation. Their whole self-confessed purpose was to " build a fence around the Law." Not one regulation would they relax or remove. Whenever religion becomes a burden, it may be some kind of religion, but it is certainly not the Christian religion.

THE RELIGION OF OSTENTATION

Matthew 23: 5-12

" They perform all their actions to be seen by men. They broaden their phylacteries; they wear outsize tassels. They love the highest places at meals, and the front seats in the synagogues, and greetings in the market-place, and to be called Rabbi by men. You must not be called Rabbi; for you have only one teacher, and you are all brothers. Call no one upon earth father; you have one Father—your Father in Heaven. Nor must you be called leaders; you have one leader—Christ. He who is greatest among you will be your servant. Anyone who will exalt himself will be humbled; and whoever will humble himself will be exalted.

THE religion of the Pharisees became almost inevitably a religion of ostentation. If religion consists in obeying countless rules and regulations, then it will be easy for a man to see to it that everyone is aware how well he fulfils the regulations, and how perfect his piety is. Jesus selects certain actions and customs in which the Pharisees showed their ostentation.

They made broad their *phylacteries*. It is said of the commandments of God in *Exodus* 13: 9: " It shall be a sign unto thee upon thine hand, and for a memorial between thine eyes." The same saying is repeated, " It shall be for a token upon thine hand, and for frontlets between thine eyes " (*Exodus* 13: 16; cp. *Deuteronomy* 6: 8; 11: 18). In order to fulfil these commandments the Jew wore, and still wears, at prayer what are called *tephillin* or *phylacteries*; they are worn on every day except the Sabbath and special holy days. They are like little leather boxes, strapped one on the wrist and one on the forehead. The one on the wrist is a little leather box of one compartment, and inside it there is a parchment roll with the following four passages of scripture written on it—*Exodus* 13: 1-10; 13: 11-16; *Deuteronomy* 6: 4-9; 11: 13-21. The one worn on the forehead is the same except that in it there are four little compartments, and in each compartment there is a little scroll inscribed with one of these four passages. The Pharisees, in order to draw attention to himself, not only wore phylacteries, but wore specially big ones, so that he might demonstrate his exemplary obedience to the Law, and his exemplary piety.

They wear outsize *tassels*; the tassels are in Greek *kraspeda* and in Hebrew *zizith*. In *Numbers* 15: 37-41 and in *Deuteronomy* 22: 12 we read that God commanded His people to make *fringes* on the borders of their garments, so that when they looked on them they might remember the commandments of God. These fringes were like tassels worn on the four corners of the outer garment. Later they were worn on the inner garment, and today they are perpetuated in the tassels of the prayer-shawl which the devout Jew wears at prayer. It was easy to make these tassels of specially large size, so that they became an ostentatious display of piety, worn, not to remind a man of the commandments, but to draw attention to himself.

Still further, the Pharisees liked to be given the principal places at meals, on the left and on the right of the host. They liked the front seats in the synagogues; in Palestine the back seats were occupied by the children and the most unimportant people; the further forward the seat, the greater the honour. The most honoured seats of all were the seats of the elders which *faced* the congregation. If a man was seated there, everyone would see that he was present, and he could conduct himself throughout the service with a pose of piety which the congregation could not fail to see. Still further, the Pharisees liked to be addressed as Rabbi, and to be treated with the greatest respect. They claimed, in point of fact, greater respect than that which was given to parents, for, they said, a man's parents give him ordinary, physical life, but a man's teacher gives him eternal life. They even liked to be called *father* as Elisha called Elijah (2 *Kings* 2: 12) and as the fathers of the faith were known.

It is Jesus' insistence that the Christian should remember that he has one teacher only—and that teacher is Christ; and only one Father in the faith—and that Father is God.

The whole design of the Pharisees was to dress and act in such a way as to draw attention to themselves; the whole design of the Christian is to obliterate himself, so that if men see his good deeds, they may glorify not him, but his Father in Heaven. Any religion which begets ostentation in action and pride in the heart is a false religion.

SHUTTING THE DOOR

Matthew 23: 13

" Alas for you, Scribes and Pharisees, hypocrites, for you shut the door to the Kingdom of Heaven in the face of men! You yourselves are not going into it; nor do you allow those who are trying to get into it to enter it."

VERSES 13-26 of this chapter form the most terrible and the most sustained denunciation in the New Testament. Here we hear what A. T. Robertson called " the rolling thunder of Christ's wrath." As Plummer has written, these *woes* are " like thunder in their unanswerable severity, and like lightning in their unsparing exposure. . . . They illuminate while they strike." Here Jesus directs a series of seven *woes* against the Scribes and Pharisees. The Authorized Version begins every one of them: " Woe unto you! " The Greek word for *woe* is *ouai*; it is hard to translate for it includes not only *wrath*, but also *sorrow*. There is righteous anger here, but it is the anger of the heart of love, broken by the stubborn blindness of men. Here there is not only an air of savage denunciation; there is also an atmosphere of poignant tragedy.

The word *hypocrite* occurs here again and again. Originally the Greek word *hupokritēs* meant *one who answers*; it then came to be specially connected with the statement and answer, the dialogue of the stage; and it is the regular and normal Greek word for an *actor*. It then came to mean an actor in the worse sense of the term, a *pretender*, one who acts a part, one who wears a mask to cover his true feelings, one who puts on an external show while inwardly his thoughts and feelings are very different. To Jesus the Scribes and Pharisees were men who were acting a part. What He meant was this. Their whole idea of religion consisted in outward observances, the wearing of elaborate phylacteries and tassels, the meticulous observance of the rules and regulations of the Law. But in their hearts there was bitterness and envy and pride and arrogance. To Jesus these Scribes and Pharisees were men who, under a mask of elaborate godliness, concealed hearts in which the most godless feelings and emotions held sway. And that accusation holds good in a greater or lesser degree of any man who lives life on the assumption that religion consists in external observances and external acts of any kind.

There is an unwritten saying of Jesus which says, " The key of the Kingdom they hid." Jesus' condemnation of these Scribes, and Pharisees is that they have not themselves entered the Kingdom, and they have shut the door in the faces of those who are seeking an entry to the Kingdom. What did Jesus mean by this accusation?

We must remember what the Kingdom is. We have already seen (Matthew 6: 10) that the best way to think of the Kingdom is to think of it as a society on earth where God's will is as perfectly done as it is in heaven. To be a citizen of the Kingdom, and to do God's will, are one and the same thing. The Pharisees believed that to do God's will was to observe their thousands of petty rules and regulations; and nothing could be further from that Kingdom whose basic idea is love. When people tried to find entry into the Kingdom the Pharisees presented them with these rules and regulations, which was as good as shutting the door of the Kingdom in their faces. The Pharisees preferred their ideas of religion to God's idea of religion. They had forgotten the basic truth that, if a man would teach others, he must himself first listen to

God. The gravest danger which any teacher or preacher encounters is that he should erect his own prejudices into universal principles, and that he should substitute his own ideas for the truth of God. When he does that he is not a guide, but a barrier, to the Kingdom, for, misled himself, he misleads others.

MISSIONARIES OF EVIL

Matthew 23: 15

> " Alas for you, Scribes and Pharisees, for you range over the sea and the dry land to make one proselyte, and, when that happens, you make him twice as much a son of hell as yourselves! "

ONE of the strange features of the ancient world was the repulsion and the attraction which Judaism exercised over men at one and the same time. There was no more hated people than the Jews. Their separatism and their isolation and their contempt of other nations gained them hatred. It was, in fact, believed that a basic part of their religion was an oath that they would never under any circumstances give help to a Gentile, even to the extent of giving him directions if he asked the way to anywhere. Their observance of the Sabbath gained them a reputation for laziness; their refusal of swine's flesh gained them mockery, even to the extent of the rumour that they worshipped the pig as their god. Anti-semitism was a real and universal force in the ancient world.

And yet there was an attraction. The idea of one God came as a wonderful thing to a world which believed in a multitude of gods. Jewish ethical purity and standards exercised a fascination on a world steeped in immorality, especially for women. The result was that there were many who were attracted to Judaism. But their attraction was on two levels. There were those who were called the *god-fearers*. These accepted the conception of one God;

they accepted the Jewish moral law; but they took no part in the ceremonial law, and they did not become circumcised. Such people existed in large numbers, and were to be found listening and worshipping in every synagogue, and indeed provided Paul with his most fruitful field for evangelization. They are, for instance, the *devout Greeks* of Thessalonica (*Acts* 17: 4). It was the aim of the Pharisees to turn these *god-fearers* into *proselytes*; the word *proselyte* is an English transliteration of a Greek word *prosēlutos*, which means *one who has approached* or *drawn near*. The *proselyte* was the full convert who had accepted the ceremonial law and circumcision and who had become in the fullest sense a Jew. As so often happens, as someone has put it, " the most converted were the most perverted." A convert often becomes the most fanatical devotee of the religion to which he has gone over; and many of these proselytes were more fanatically devoted to the Jewish Law than even the Jews themselves.

Jesus accused these Pharisees of being missionaries of evil. It was true that very few became proselytes, but when these few did become proselytes, they went the whole way: The sin of the Pharisees was that they were not really seeking to lead men to God, they were seeking to lead men to Pharisaism. One of the gravest dangers which any missionary runs is that he should try to convert people to a sect rather than to a religion, and that he should be more concerned in bringing people to a Church than to Jesus Christ.

The great Indian Christian mystic, Premanand, in his autobiography, has certain things to say about this sectarianism which so often disfigures so-called Christianity. " I speak as a Christian, God is my Father, the Church is my Mother. Christian is my name; Catholic is my surname. Catholic, because we belong to nothing less than the Church Universal. So do we need any other names? Why go on to add Anglican, Episcopalian, Protestant, Presbyterian, Methodist, Congregational, Baptist, and so on, and so on? These terms are divisive, sectarian, narrow. They shrivel up one's soul." It was not to God the Pharisees sought to lead men; it was to their own sect of Pharisaism. That in fact was their sin. And is that sin even yet gone from the world, when it would still be insisted in certain quarters that a man must leave one Church and become a member of another before he can be allowed a place at the Table of the Lord? The greatest of all heresies is the sinful conviction that any Church has a monopoly of God, or of the truth of God, or that any Church is the only gateway to the presence of God and to His Kingdom.

THE SCIENCE OF EVASION

Matthew 23: 16-22

" Alas for you, Scribes and Pharisees! Blind guides! You who say, ' If any one swears by the Temple, it is nothing; but whoever swears by the gold of the Temple is bound by his oath.' Foolish ones and blind! Which is the greater? The gold? Or the Temple which hallows the gold? You say, ' If anyone swears by the altar, it is nothing; but if anyone swears by the gift that is on it, he is bound by his oath.' Blind ones! Which is greater? The gift? Or the altar which hallows the gift? He who swears by the altar, swears by it and all that is on it. He who swears by the Temple, swears by it, and by Him who inhabits it. And he who swears by heaven, swears by the throne of God, and by Him who sits upon it.'

WE have already seen that in matters of oaths the Jewish legalists were masters of evasion (*Matthew* 5: 33-37). The general principle of evasion was this. To the Jew an oath was absolutely binding, *so long as it was a binding oath.* Broadly speaking, a binding oath was an oath which definitely and without equivocation employed the name of God; such an oath must be kept, no matter what the cost. Any other oath might be legitimately broken. The idea was that, if God's name was actually used, then God was introduced as a partner into the transaction, and to break the oath was, not only to break faith with men, but to insult God.

In any event the science of evasion had been brought to a high degree. It is most probable that in this passage Jesus is presenting a caricature of Jewish legalistic methods. He is saying, " You have brought the science of evasion to such a fine art that it is possible to regard an oath by the Temple as not binding, while an oath by the gold of the Temple is binding; and an oath by the altar as not binding, while an oath by the gift that is on the altar is binding." This is most likely to be regarded as a *reductio ad absurdum* of Jewish methods than as a literal description of them.

The idea behind this passage is just this. The whole idea of treating oaths in this way, the whole conception of a kind of technique of evasion, is born of a fundamental deceitfulness. The truly religious man will never make a promise with the deliberate intention of evading it; he will never, as he makes it, provide himself with a series of escape routes, which he may use if he finds it hard to keep his promise.

We need not with conscious superiority condemn the Pharisaic science of evasion. The time is not yet ended when a man will seek to evade some duty on a technicality, or when he will call in the strict letter of the law to avoid doing what the spirit of the law clearly means he ought to do.

For Jesus the binding principle was twofold. God hears every word we speak, and God sees every secret thought of our hearts; therefore every word is heard by God, and every intention is seen by God. In view of that the fine art of evasion is an art of which a Christian must be completely ignorant. The technique of evasion may suit the sharp practice of the world; but it can never suit the open honesty of the mind of the Christian.

THE LOST SENSE OF PROPORTION

Matthew 23: 23, 24

> " Alas for you, Scribes and Pharisees, hypocrites! for you tithe the mint, and dill, and cummin, and let go the weightier matters of the Law—justice and mercy and fidelity. These you ought to have done without neglecting the others. Blind guides who strain out a gnat and swallow a camel! "

THE tithe was an essential part of Jewish religious regulations. " Thou shalt truly tithe all the increase of thy seed, that the field bringeth forth every year " (*Deuteronomy* 14: 22). " All the tithe of the land, whether of the seed of the land, or of the fruit of the tree, is the Lord's; it is holy unto the Lord " (*Leviticus* 27: 30). This tithe was specially for the support of the Levites, whose task it was to do the material work of the Temple. The things which had to be tithed were further defined by the Law—" Everything which is eatable, and is preserved, and has its nourishment from the soil, is liable to be tithed." It is laid down: " Of dill one must tithe the seeds, the leaves and the stalks." So, then, it was laid down that every man must lay aside one-tenth of his produce for God.

Now the point of this saying of Jesus is this. It was universally accepted that tithes of the main crops must be given. But mint and dill and cummin are herbs of the kitchen garden, and would not be grown in any quantity. A man would have only a little patch of them in his garden; all three were used in cooking, and dill and cummin had medicinal uses. To tithe them would be to tithe an infinitesimally small crop, maybe not much more than the produce of one plant. Only those who were superlatively meticulous would tithe the single plants of the kitchen garden. That is precisely what the Pharisees were like. They were so absolutely meticulous about tithes that they would tithe even one clump of mint; and yet these same men might be guilty of injustice; they were hard and arrogant and cruel, and forgot the claims of mercy; they would take oaths and pledges and promises with the deliberate intention of evading them, and so forget fidelity. In other words, they kept the trifles of the Law, and forgot the things which really matter.

That spirit is not dead; it never will be dead until Christ rules in the hearts of men. There is many a man who wears the right clothes to church, carefully hands in his offering to the Church, adopts the right attitude at prayer, is never absent from the celebration of the sacrament, and who, at his day's work, is not doing an honest day's work, and who is irritable and bad-tempered and mean with his money. There are women who are full of good works, and who serve on all kinds of committees, and whose children are lonely for them at night. There is nothing easier than to observe all the outward actions of religion and yet to be completely irreligious.

There is nothing more necessary than a sense of proportion in order to save us from confusing religious observances with real devotion.

Jesus uses a vivid illustration. In verse 24 a curious thing has happened in the Authorized Version. It should not be to strain *at* a gnat, but to strain *out* a gnat. Originally that mistake was simply a misprint and it has been perpetuated for centuries in the Authorized Version. In point of fact the older versions—Tyndale, Coverdale, and the Geneva Bible—all correctly have to strain *out* a gnat. The picture is this. A gnat was an insect and therefore unclean; and so was a camel. In order to avoid the risk of drinking anything unclean wine was strained through muslin gauze so that any possible impurity might be strained *out* of it. This is one of the instances of humour which must have raised a laugh. For it is the picture of a man carefully straining his wine through gauze to avoid swallowing a microscopic insect, and yet cheerfully swallowing a camel. It is the picture of a man who has completely lost his sense of proportion.

THE REAL CLEANNESS

Matthew 23: 25, 26

> " Alas for you, Scribes and Pharisees, hypocrites! for
> you cleanse the outside of the cup and the plate, but
> inside they are full of rapacity and lust. Blind Pharisee!
> cleanse the inside of the cup and the plate first, that
> the outside of it also may be clean."

THE idea of uncleanness is continually arising in the Jewish
Law. Now it must be remembered that this uncleanness
was not physical uncleanness. An unclean vessel was
not in our sense of the term a dirty vessel. For a person
to be ceremonially unclean meant that he could not enter
the Temple or the synagogue; he was debarred from the
worship of God. A man was unclean if, for instance, he
touched a dead body, or came into contact with a Gentile.
A woman was unclean if she had an issue of blood, even
if that issue of blood was perfectly normal and healthy. If
a person who was himself unclean touched any vessel,
then that vessel became unclean; and, thereafter, any
other person who touched or handled the vessel became
in turn unclean. It was, therefore, of paramount importance
to have vessels cleansed; and the law for cleansing them
is fantastically complicated. We can only quote certain
basic examples of it.

An *earthen* vessel which is *hollow* becomes unclean only
on the inside and not on the outside; and it can only be
cleansed by being broken. The following earthen vessels
cannot become unclean at all—a flat plate without a rim,
an open coal-shovel, a grid-iron with holes in it for parching
grains of wheat. On the other hand, a plate with a rim,
or an earthen spice-box, or a writing-case can become
unclean. Of vessels made of leather, bone, wood and glass,
flat ones do not become unclean; deep ones do. If they
are broken, they become clean. Any metal vessel which
is at once smooth and hollow can become unclean; but
a door, a bolt, a lock, a hinge, a knocker cannot become
unclean. If a thing is made of wood *and* metal, then the

wood can become unclean, but the metal cannot. These regulations seem to us fantastic, and yet these are the very regulations the Pharisees religiously and meticulously kept.

The food or drink inside a vessel might have been obtained by cheating or extortion or theft; it might be luxurious and gluttonous; that did not matter, so long as the vessel itself was ceremonially clean. Here is another example of fussing about trifles, and letting the weightier matters go.

Grotesque as the whole thing may seem, it can happen yet. A church can be torn in two about the colour of a carpet, or a pulpit-fall, or about the shape or metal of the cups which are to be used in the Sacrament. The last thing that men and women seem to learn in matters of religion is a relative sense of values; and the tragedy is that it is so often dispute and magnification of matters of no importance which wreck the peace.

DISGUISED DECAY

Matthew 23: 27, 28

> " Alas for you, Scribes and Pharisees! for you are like white-washed tombs, which look beautiful on the outside, but inside are full of the bones of dead men, and of all corruption. So you, too, outwardly look righteous to men, but inwardly you are full of hypocrisy and lawlessness."

HERE again is a picture which any Jew would understand. One of the commonest places for tombs was by the wayside. Now we have already seen that anyone who touched a dead body became unclean (*Numbers* 19: 16). Therefore, anyone who came into contact with a tomb automatically became unclean. At one time in particular the roads of Palestine were crowded with pilgrims—at the time of the Passover Feast. For a man to become unclean on his way to the Passover Feast would have been a disaster, for that meant that he would have been debarred from sharing in it. So, then, it was Jewish practice in the month of Adar to whitewash all wayside tombs, so that no pilgrims might accidentally come into contact with one of them, and so be rendered unclean. So, as a man journeyed the roads of Palestine in the sunshine of a spring day, these tombs would glint white, and almost lovely, in the sunshine; but within they were full of the bones and the bodies the touch of which would defile. That, said Jesus, was a precise picture of what the Pharisees were. Their outward actions were the actions of intensely religious men; their inward hearts were foul and putrid with sin.

It can still happen. As Shakespeare had it, a man may smile and smile and be a villain. A man may walk with bowed head, and reverent steps, and folded hands in the posture of humility, but all the time he may be looking down with cold contempt on those whom he regards as sinners; his very humility may be the pose of pride; and, as he walks so humbly, he may be thinking with relish of the picture of piety which he presents to those who are watching him. There is nothing harder than for a good man not to know that he is good; and once he knows he is good, his goodness is gone, however he may appear to men from the outside.

THE TAINT OF MURDER

Matthew 23: 29-36

" Alas for you, Scribes and Pharisees, hypocrites! for you erect the tombs of the prophets, and adorn the memorials of the righteous, and say, ' If we had lived in the days of our fathers, we would not have been partners with them in the murder of the prophets.' Thus you witness against yourselves that you are the sons of those who slew the prophets. Fill up the measure of your fathers. Serpents, brood of vipers, how are you to escape being condemned to hell fire? For this reason, look you, I send you the prophets and the wise men and the scribes. Some of them you will kill and crucify; and some of them you will scourge in your synagogues, and pursue them with persecution from city to city, that on you there may fall the responsibility for all the righteous blood shed upon the earth from the blood of Abel, the righteous, to the blood of Zacharias, the son of Barachios, whom you murdered between the Temple and the altar. This is the truth I tell you—the responsibility for all these crimes shall fall on this generation.'

HERE Jesus is charging the Jews with the accusation that the taint of murder is in their history, and that that taint has not even yet worked itself out. The Scribes and Pharisees tend the tombs of the martyrs and beautify their memorials, and claim that, if they had lived in the old days, they would not have slain the prophets and the men of God. But that is precisely what they would have done, and that is precisely what they are going to do.

Jesus' charge is that the history of Israel is the history of the murder of the men of God. He says that the righteous men from Abel to Zacharias were murdered. Why are these two chosen? The murder of Abel by Cain is a murder of which everyone knows; but the murder of Zacharias is a murder which is not nearly so well known. The story is told in a grim little cameo in 2 *Chronicles* 24: 20-22. It happened in the days of Joash. Zacharias rebuked the nation for their sin, and Joash stirred up the people to stone him to death in the very Temple court; and Zacharias died saying, " The Lord look upon it, and require it." By a mistake Zacharias is called the son of Barachios, whereas, in fact, he was the son of Jehoiada. That is no doubt simply a slip of the gospel writer in retelling the story. But why should Zacharias be chosen? In the Hebrew Bible *Genesis* is the first book, as it is in ours; but, unlike our order of the books, 2 *Chronicles* is the last book in the Hebrew Bible. That is to say, we could say that the murder of Abel is the first murder in the Bible story, and the murder of Zacharias is the last murder in

the Bible story. From beginning to end, the history of
Israel is the rejection, and often the slaughter, of the
men of God.

And Jesus is quite clear that that murder taint is still
there. He knows that now He must die, and that in the
days to come His messengers will be persecuted and ill-
treated and rejected and slain.

Here indeed is tragedy; the nation which God chose
and loved had turned their hands against God; and the
day of reckoning was to come.

It makes us think. When history judges us, will its
verdict be that we were the hinderers or the helpers of
God? That is a question which every individual, and every
nation, must answer.

THE REJECTION OF LOVE'S APPEAL

Matthew 23: 37-39

" Jerusalem, Jerusalem, killer of the prophets, stoner
of those sent to you, how often have I wished to gather
your children together, as a bird gathers her nestlings
under her wings—and you refused. Look you, your
house is left to you desolate, for I tell you from now you
will not see me until you will say, ' Blessed in the
name of the Lord is he that comes.' "

HERE is all the poignant tragedy of rejected love. Here
Jesus speaks, not so much as the stern judge of all the
earth, as the lover of the souls of men.

There is one curious light that this passage throws on
the life of Jesus which we may note in the passing. According to the story of the Synoptic Gospels Jesus was never
in Jerusalem, after His public ministry began, until He
came to it to this last Passover Feast. We can see here
how much the gospel story leaves out, for Jesus could not
have said this unless He had paid repeated visits to Jerusalem, and issued to the people repeated appeals. A
passage like this shows us that in the gospels we have the

merest sketch and outline of the life of Jesus. This passage shows us four great truths.

(i) It shows us *the patience of God.* Jerusalem had killed the prophets and had stoned the messengers of God; yet God did not cast her off; and in the end He sent His Son. There is a limitless patience in the love of God which bears with men's sinning and which will not cast them off.

(ii) It shows us *the appeal of Jesus.* Here Jesus speaks as the lover. He will not force an entry; the only weapon he can use is the appeal of love. He stands with outstretched hands of appeal, an appeal which men have the awful responsibility of being able to accept or to refuse.

(iii) It shows us *the deliberation of the sin of man.* Men looked on Christ in all the splendour of His appeal—and refused Him. There is no handle on the outside of the door of the human heart; it must be opened from the inside; and sin is the open-eyed deliberate refusal of the appeal of God in Jesus Christ.

(iv) It shows us *the consequences of rejecting Christ.* Only forty years were to pass, and in A.D. 70 Jerusalem would be a heap of ruins. That disaster was the direct consequence of the rejection of Jesus Christ. Had the Jews accepted the Christian way of love, and had they abandoned the way of power politics, Rome would never have descended on them with its avenging might. It is the fact of history—even in time—that the nation which rejects God is doomed to disaster.

THE VISION OF THINGS TO COME

WE have already seen that it is one of the great characteristics of Matthew that he gathers together in large blocks the teaching of Jesus about different subjects. Matthew is the great systematizer of the words of Jesus. In chapter 24 Matthew gathers together things that Jesus said about the future; in it he gives us the vision of things to come. But in this chapter Matthew weaves together sayings of Jesus about different aspects of the future; and it will make this difficult chapter very much easier to understand if we can disentangle these various strands and if we can separate the different pieces of the pattern and look at them one by one. Matthew's interweaving of the sayings of Jesus lasts throughout the first 31 verses of the chapter. It will be best if, first of all, we set down these verses as a whole; if, next, we set down the various aspects of the future with which they deal; and if, last, we try to assign each section of these first 31 verses to its place in the pattern. It must be understood that we cannot claim certainty or finality for the pattern which we obtain; but, even if certain details must still be left uncertain, the general picture will become clear. First then we set down these verses, and, in this case we shall number them to make easier the assignment of them to their place in the pattern.

THE VISION OF THE FUTURE

Matthew 24: 1-31

1. When Jesus had left the precincts of the Temple, He was going away; and His disciples came to Him to point out to Him the buildings of the
2. Temple area. He said to them, " Do you not see all these things? This is the truth I tell you —one stone will not be left here upon another that will not be thrown down."
3. His disciples came to Him privately when He was sitting on the Mount of Olives. " Tell us," they said, " when these things shall be. And tell us what will be the sign of your coming, and of
4. the consummation of the age." Jesus answered, " Be on the look-out lest anyone lead you astray,
5. for many will come in my name saying, ' I am God's Anointed One,' and they will lead many astray.
6. You will hear of wars and reports of wars. See that you are not disturbed; for these things

7. must happen; but the end is not yet. For nation shall rise against nation, and kingdom against kingdom, and there will be famines and earth-
8. quakes in various places. All these things are
9. the beginning of the agonies. Then they will deliver you to affliction, and they will kill you, and you will be hated by all nations be-
10. cause of my name. And then many will stumble, and will betray each other, and will hate each
11. other. And many false prophets will arise, and
12. they will lead many astray. And the love of many will grow cold, because lawlessness will
13. be multiplied. But it is he who endures to
14. the end who will be saved. And the gospel will be proclaimed to the whole inhabited world, for a testimony to all nations—and then
15. the end will come. When you see the desolat-ing abomination, which was spoken of by the prophet Daniel, standing in the Holy Place
16. (let him who reads understand), then let him
17. who is in Judaea flee to the mountains. Let him who is on the housetop not come down to remove
18. his goods from his house; and let him who is in the field not come back to remove his cloak.
19. Alas for those who in those days are carrying children in the womb, and who are suckling
20. children. Pray that your flight may not be
21. in the winter time, nor on a Sabbath. For at that time there will be great affliction, such as has never happened from the beginning of the world until now, and such as never will
22. happen. And, if the days had not been shorten-ed, no human being would have survived. But the days will be shortened for the sake of the
23. elect. At that time, if anyone says to you, ' Look you, here, or here, is the Anointed One of
24. God,' do not believe him. For false Messiahs and false prophets will arise, and they will
25. produce great signs and wonders, the conse-quences of which will be, if possible, to lead
26. astray the elect. Look you, I have told you about these things before they happen. If anyone says to you, ' Look you, he is in the wilderness,' do not go out. ' Look you, he is in the inner chamb-
27. ers,' do not believe him. For as the lightning comes from the east and shines as far as the west, so shall

28. be the coming of the Son of Man. Where the body is,
29. there the vultures will be gathered together. Immediately after the affliction of these days the sun
will be darkened, and the moon will not give her
light, and the stars will fall from heaven, and the
30. powers of heaven will be shaken. Then there will
appear the sign of the Son of Man in heaven. And
then all the tribes of the earth will lament, and
they will see the Son of Man coming on the clouds
31. of heaven with power and much glory. And He will
send His angels with a great trumpet call, and they
will gather the elect from the four winds, from one
boundary of heaven to the other."

THE INTERWEAVING OF THE STRANDS

THERE then we have the composite vision of the future
which Matthew collects for us; we must now try to disentangle the various strands in it; and to assign each section
to the strand to which it belongs. At this stage we shall
only indicate the strands, and make the assignments, and
we shall leave fuller explanation for the detailed commentary.

(i) There are here sections which foretell the terrible
days of *the siege of Jerusalem* by Titus, the Roman general,
a siege which was one of the most terrible sieges in all
history. To that strand belong verses 15-22.

(ii) There are sections which tell of the ultimate complete
destruction of Jerusalem, and its reduction to a heap of
ruins. To that strand belong verses 1 and 2.

(iii) There are pictures which are taken from the Jewish
conception of the *Day of the Lord*. We have spoken about
that conception before, but we must briefly outline it
again. The Jews divided all time into two ages—this
present age, and the age to come. This present age is
wholly bad, and beyond all hope of human reformation.
It can only be mended by the direct intervention of God.
When God does intervene the golden age, the age to come,
will arrive. But in between the two ages there will come the

Day of the Lord, which will be a time of terrible and fearful upheaval, like the birth-pangs of a new age. In the Old Testament itself there is many a picture of the Day of the Lord; and in the Jewish books written between the Old and the New Testaments these pictures are still further developed and made still more vivid and still more terrible. It would be a time of *terror*. " That day is a day of wrath, a day of trouble and distress, a day of wasteness and desolation, a day of darkness and gloominess, a day of clouds and thick darkness " (*Zephaniah* 1: 14-18). The pictures of that terror became ever more terrible and lurid. It would come *suddenly*. " The Day of the Lord cometh as a thief in the night " (1 *Thessalonians* 5: 2). " Three things," said the Rabbis, " are sudden—the coming of the Messiah, a discovery, and a scorpion." The universe would be *shattered to pieces*. The sun would be turned into darkness and the moon into blood (*Joel* 2: 30, 31; *Isaiah* 13: 10, 13). It would be a time of *moral chaos*, when moral standards would be turned upside down, and when even nature would act contrary to herself, and when wars and violence and hatred would be the common atmosphere of life. Schürer (*The Jewish People in the Time of Christ* ii, 154) sums up the Jewish ideas of the day of the Lord, ideas with which Jewish literature was full, and ideas which everyone knew in the time of Jesus. " The sun and moon will be darkened, swords appear in heaven, trains of horses and foot march through the clouds. Everything in nature falls into commotion and confusion. The sun appears by night, the moon by day. Blood trickles from wood, the stone gives forth a voice, and salt is found in fresh water. Places that have been sown will appear as unsown, full barns be found empty, and the springs of wells be stopped. Among men all restraints of order will be dissolved, sin and ungodliness rule upon earth. And men will fight against each other as if stricken with madness, the friend against the friend, the son against the father, the daughter against the mother. Nation will rise against nation, and to war shall be added earthquake, fire and famine, whereby men shall be carried off." Such were the terrible pictures of the day of the Lord. To this strand belong verses 6-8 and 29-31 of our passage.

(iv) There are verses which deal with the *persecution* which the followers of Christ will have to endure. To this strand belong verses 9 and 10.

(v) There are verses which deal with the *threats* which will develop against the life and purity of the Church. To this strand belong verses 4 and 5, 11-13, 23-26.

(vi) Finally there are verses which speak directly of the *Second Coming* of Christ. To this strand belong verses 3, 14, 27 and 28.

So, in this amazing and difficult chapter of *Matthew*, we have in the first 31 verses a kind of sixfold vision of the future. We shall now go on to look at this vision, taking the verses of the chapter, not consecutively, but taking together in turn those which deal with each strand. And let us begin with the verses in which Jesus foretells the doom of the city of Jerusalem.

THE DOOM OF THE HOLY CITY

Matthew 24: 1, 2

> When Jesus had left the precincts of the Temple, He was going away; and His disciples came to Him to point out to Him the buildings of the Temple area. He said to them, " Do you not see all these things? This is the truth I tell you—one stone will not be left here upon another that will not be thrown down."

IT may well be that at least some of the disciples had not been very often to Jerusalem. They were Galilaeans, men of the highlands and of the country, fishermen who knew the lakeside far better than they knew the city. Some of them at least would be like country folk come up to London for a visit, and they were staggered by what

336

they saw; and well they might be, for there was nothing
quite like the Temple in the ancient world. The summit
of Mount Sion had been dug away to leave a plateau of
1,000 feet square. At the far end of it there was the Temple
itself (the *naos*). It was built of white marble plated with
gold, and it shone and glinted in the sun so that a man
could scarcely bear to look at it. Between the lower city
and the Temple mount there lay the valley of the Tyropoeon,
and across this valley there stretched a colossal bridge.
Its arches had a span of 41½ feet, and its spring stones
were 24 feet long by 6 inches thick. The Temple area
was surrounded by great porches, Solomon's Porch and
the Royal Porch. These porches were upheld by pillars,
cut out of solid blocks of marble in one piece. They were
37½ feet high, and of such a thickness that three men
linked together could scarcely put their arms round them.
At the corners of the Temple angle stones have been found
which measure from 20 to 40 feet in length, and which
weigh more than 100 tons. How they were ever cut and
placed in position is one of the mysteries of ancient engin-
eering. Little wonder that the Galilaean fishermen looked
with awe on these vast stones, and these amazing buildings,
and called Jesus' attention to them.

It was Jesus' answer that the day would come when not
one of these stones would be left standing upon the other—
and Jesus was right. For in A.D. 70 the Romans, finally
exasperated by the rebellious intransigence of the Jews,
gave up all attempt at pacification and turned to destruction, and Jerusalem and the Temple were laid waste and
devastated, so that Jesus' prophecy literally came true.

Here speaks Jesus the prophet. Jesus knew that the
way of power politics can only end in doom. The man and
the nation which will not take the way of God are heading
for disaster—even in material things. The man and the
nation which refuse the dream of God will find their own
dreams shattered also.

THE GOSPEL OF MATTHEW

THE GRIM TERROR OF THE SIEGE

Matthew 24: 15-22

" When you see the desolating abomination, which was spoken of by the prophet Daniel, standing in the Holy Place (let him who reads understand), then let him who is in Judaea flee to the mountains. Let him who is on the housetop not come down to remove his goods from his house; and let him who is in the field not come back to remove his cloak. Alas for those who in those days are carrying children in the womb, and who are suckling children. Pray that your flight may not be in the winter time, nor on a Sabbath. For at that time there will be great affliction, such as has never happened from the beginning of the world until now, and such as never will happen. And, if the days had not been shortened, no human being would have survived. But the days will be shortened for the sake of the elect."

THE siege of Jerusalem was one of the most terrible sieges in all history. Jerusalem was obviously a difficult city to take, for it is the city that is set upon an hill, and it was defended by religious fanatics; so Titus determined to starve the city out.

No one quite knows what the *desolating abomination* is. The phrase itself comes from *Daniel* 12: 11. There it is said that the *abomination which maketh desolate* is set up in the Temple. The *Daniel* reference is quite clear. About 170 B.C. Antiochus Epiphanes, the king of Syria, determined to stamp out Judaism and to introduce into Judaea Greek religion and Greek practices. He captured Jerusalem, and desecrated the Temple by erecting an altar to Olympian Zeus in the Temple Court and by sacrificing swines' flesh upon it, and by turning the priests' rooms and the Temple chambers into public brothels. It was a deliberate attempt to stamp out and to obliterate Jewish religion. It was the prophecy of Jesus that the same thing would happen again, and that once again the Holy Place would be desecrated, as indeed it was. Jesus saw coming upon Jerusalem a repetition of the terrible things which had happened

200 years ago; only this time there would arise no Judas Maccabaeus; this time there would be no deliverance, and no purification; there would be nothing but ultimate destruction.

Jesus foretold of that siege that unless the days of it had been shortened, no human being could survive it. It is strange to see how Jesus gave practical advice, advice which was not taken, and the disregarding of which redoubled the disaster. It was Jesus' advice that when that day came men ought to flee to the mountains; they did not; they crammed themselves into the city and into the walls of Jerusalem from all over the country, and that very folly redoubled the grim horror of the famine of the siege a hundredfold.

When we go to the history of Josephus, the Jewish historian, we see how right Jesus was about that terrible future. Josephus writes of these terrible days of siege and famine: " Then did the famine widen its progress, and devoured the people by whole houses and families; the upper rooms were full of women and children that were dying of famine; and the lanes of the city were full of the dead bodies of the aged; the children also and the young men wandered about the market-places like shadows, all swelled with famine, and fell down dead wheresoever their misery seized them. As for burying them, those that were sick themselves were not able to do it; and those that were hearty and well were deterred from doing it by the great multitude of those dead bodies, and by the uncertainty there was how soon they should die themselves, for many died as they were burying others, and many went to their coffins before the fatal hour was come. Nor was there any lamentation made under these calamities, nor were heard any mournful complaints; but the famine confounded all natural passions; for those who were just going to die looked upon those who were gone to their rest before them with dry eyes and open mouths. A deep silence, also, and a kind of deadly night had seized upon the city. . . . And every one of them died with their eyes fixed upon the Temple " (Josephus, *Wars of the Jews*, 5. 12. 3). Josephus tells a dreadful story of a woman who in those days actually killed and roasted and ate her suckling child (6. 3. 4). He tells us that even the Romans, when they had taken the city and were going through it to plunder it, were so stricken with horror at the sights of it that they could not but stay their hands. " When the Romans were come to the houses to plunder them, they found in them entire families of dead men, and the upper rooms full of dead corpses. . . . They then stood on a horror of this sight, and went out without touching anything " (6. 8. 5). We have already seen how this horror was intensified because people flocked into the city instead of making for the mountains. Josephus himself shared in the horrors of this siege, and he tells us that 97,000 were taken captive and enslaved, and 1,100,000 died.

That is what Jesus foresaw; these are the things of which He forewarned. We must never forget that not only men but nations need the wisdom of Christ. Unless the leaders of the nations are themselves led by Christ, they cannot do other than lead men, not only to spiritual but also to physical disaster. Jesus was no impractical dreamer; He laid down the laws by which alone a nation can prosper, and by disregard of which it cannot do other than miserably perish.

THE DAY OF THE LORD

Matthew 24: 6-8, 29-31

> " You will hear of wars and reports of wars. See that you are not disturbed; for these things must happen; for the end is not yet. For nation shall rise against nation, and kingdom against kingdom, and there will be famines and earthquakes in various places.

. . . .

340

Immediately after the affliction of these days the sun will be darkened, and the moon will not give her light, and the stars will fall from heaven, and the powers of heaven will be shaken. Then there will appear the sign of the Son of Man in heaven. And then all the tribes of the earth will lament, and they will see the Son of Man coming in the clouds of heaven with power and much glory. And He will send His angels with a great trumpet call, and they will gather the elect from the four winds, from one boundary of heaven to the other."

WE have already seen that an essential part of the Jewish thought of the future was the *Day of the Lord*. That was the day when God was going to intervene directly in history; and when the present age, with all its incurable evil, would begin to be transformed and recreated into the age which is to come.

Very naturally the New Testament writers, to a very great extent, identified the Second Coming of Jesus and the Day of the Lord; and they took over all the imagery and all the pictures which had to do with the Day of the Lord and applied them to the Second Coming. When we remember that, we will remember one essential thing—none of these pictures are to be taken literally; they *are* pictures, and they *are* visions; they are attempts to put the indescribable into human words, and to find some kind of picture for happenings for which human language has no picture.

But from all these pictures there emerge certain great truths.

(i) They tell us that God has not abandoned the world; for all its wickedness, the world is still the scene in which God's purpose is being worked out. It is not abandonment that God contemplates; it is intervention.

(ii) They tell us that even a very crescendo of evil must not discourage us. An essential part of the Jewish picture of the Day of the Lord is that a complete breakdown of all moral standards, and an apparent complete disintegration of the world must precede it. But, for all that, this is not the prelude to destruction; it is the prelude to recreation.

(iii) They tell us that both judgment and a new creation are certain. They tell us that God contemplates the world both in justice and in mercy. And that God's plan is not the obliteration of the world, but the creation of a world which is nearer to His heart's desire.

We must always remember that the value of these pictures is not in their details, which at best are only symbolic, and which use the only pictures which the minds of men could conceive, but in the eternal truths which they conserve; and the basic truth in them is that, whatever the world is like, God has not abandoned it.

THE PERSECUTION TO COME

Matthew 24: 9, 10

> " Then they will deliver you to affliction, and they will kill you, and you will be hated by all nations because of my name. And then many will stumble and will betray each other, and will hate each other."

HERE is one of these passages which show the uncompromising honesty of Jesus. He never promised His disciples an easy way; He promised them death and suffering and persecution. There is a sense in which a real Church will always be a persecuted Church, so long as it exists in a world which is not a Christian world. Whence comes that persecution?

(i) Christ offers a *new loyalty*; and again and again He declared that that new loyalty must surpass all earthly ties. The greatest ground of hatred in the days of the early Church was the fact that Christianity did split homes and families, when one member decided for Christ and the others did not. The Christian is one who is pledged to give Jesus Christ the first place in his life—and many a human clash is liable to result from that.

(ii) Christ offers a *new standard*. There are customs and practices and ways of life which may be all right for the world, but which are far from being all right when they are judged by the new standard of Christianity. For many people the difficulty about Christianity is that in fact Christianity is a judgment upon themselves, and upon their way of life in their business or in their personal relationships. The awkward thing about Christianity is that anyone who does not wish to be changed is bound to hate it and to resent it.

(iii) The Christian, if he is a true Christian, introduces into the world a *new example*. There is a daily beauty in his life which makes the life of others ugly. The Christian is the light of the world, not in the sense that he criticizes and condemns others, but in the sense that he demonstrates in his own life the beauty of the Christ-filled life, and therefore the ugliness of the Christless life.

(iv) This is all to say that Christianity brings a *new conscience* into life. Neither the individual Christian nor the Christian Church can ever know anything of a cowardly concealment or a cowardly silence. The Church and the individual Christian must at all times constitute the conscience of Christianity—and it is characteristic of men that there are many times when they would wish to silence conscience.

THREATS TO THE FAITH

Matthew 24: 4, 5, 11-13, 23-26

> Jesus answered, " Be on the look-out lest anyone lead you astray, for many will come in my name saying, ' I am God's Anointed One,' and they will lead many astray.
>
> . . . .
>
> And many false prophets will arise, and they will lead many astray. And the love of many will grow cold, because lawlessness will be multiplied. But it is he who endures to the end who will be saved.
>
> . . . .

At that time, if anyone says to you, ' Look you, here, or here, is the Anointed One of God,' do not believe him. For false Messiahs and false prophets will arise, and they will produce great signs and wonders, the consequence of which will be, if possible, to lead astray the elect. Look you, I have told you about these things before they happen. If anyone says to you, " Look you, he is in the wilderness," do not go out. ' Look you, he is in the inner chambers,' do not believe him."

IN the days to come Jesus saw that two dangers would threaten the Church.

(i) There would be the dangers of *false leaders*. A false leader is a man who seeks to propagate his own version of the truth rather than the truth as it is in Jesus Christ. He is a man who is out to spread his own ideas, rather than the truth of God. And, above all, he is a man who tries to attach other men to himself rather than to Jesus Christ. The inevitable result is that a false leader is a man who spreads division instead of building up unity. The test of any leader is likeness to Christ.

(ii) The second threat is the threat of *discouragement*. There are those whose love will grow cold because of the increasing lawlessness of the world. The true Christian is the man who holds to his belief, when belief is at its most difficult; and who, in the most discouraging circumstances, refuses to believe that God's arm is shortened or His power grown less.

THE COMING OF THE KING

Matthew 24: 3, 14, 27, 28

His disciples came to Him privately, when He was sitting on the Mount of Olives. " Tell us," they said, " when these things shall be. And tell us what will be the sign of your coming, and of the consummation of the age."

.   .   .   .

The gospel will be proclaimed to the whole inhabited world, for a testimony to all nations—and then the end will come.

. . . .

For as the lightning comes from the east and shines as far as the west, so shall be the coming of the Son of Man. Where the body is, there the vultures will be gathered together."

HERE Jesus speaks of His Second Coming directly. The New Testament does not ever use the phrase *the Second Coming*. The word which it uses to describe the return of Christ in glory is an interesting word. It is the word *Parousia*; this word has come into English as a description of the Second Coming. It is quite common in the rest of the New Testament, but in the gospels this is the only chapter in which it occurs (verses 3, 27, 37, 39). The interesting thing about it is that it is the regular word for the arrival of a governor into his province, or for the coming of a king to his subjects. It regularly describes a coming in authority and in power.

The remainder of this chapter will have much to tell us about the Second Coming of Christ, but at the moment we may note that, whatever else is true about the doctrine of the Second Coming, it certainly conserves two great facts.

(i) It conserves the fact of the ultimate triumph of Christ. He whom men crucified on a cross will one day be the Lord of all men. For Jesus Christ the end is sure—and the end is the universal kingship of the world.

(ii) It conserves the fact that history is going somewhere. Sometimes men have felt that history was plunging to an ever wilder and wilder chaos, that history is nothing more than " the record of the sins and follies of men." Sometimes men have felt that history was cyclic and that the same weary round of things would happen over and over again. The Stoics believed that there are certain fixed periods, that at the end of such a period the world is destroyed in a great conflagration; and that then the same story in every littlest detail takes place all over again. As Chrysippus had it: " Then again the world is restored anew in a precisely similar arrangement as before. The stars again move in their orbits, each performing its revolution in the former period, without any variation. Socrates and Plato and each individual man will live again, with the same friends and fellow-citizens. They will go through the same experiences and the same activities. Every city and village and field will be restored, just as it was. And this restoration of the universe takes place, not once, but over and over again—indeed to all eternity, without end." That is a grim thought, the idea that men are bound to an eternal tread-mill in which there is no progress, and from which there is no escape.

But the Second Coming has in it this essential truth—that there is " one divine far-off event, to which the whole creation moves," and that event is not dissolution, it is nothing other than the universal and eternal rule of God.

THE COMING OF THE KING

Matthew 24: 32-41

" Learn the lesson which comes from the fig tree. Whenever the branch has become tender, and puts forth its leaves, you know that summer is near. Even so, when you too see these things, know that He is near at the doors. This is the truth I tell you—this generation shall not pass away, until these things have happened. Heaven and earth will pass away, but my words will not pass away.

No one knows about that day and hour, not even the angels of heaven, not even the Son, but only the Father. As were the days of Noah, so will be the coming of the Son of Man. For, as in those days before the flood they spent their time eating and drinking, marrying and giving in marriage, until the day that Noah entered into the ark, and were quite unaware of what was to happen until the flood came and swept them all away, so will be the coming of the Son of Man. At that time there will be two men in the field; one is taken, and the other is left. There will be two women grinding with the mill; one is taken, and the other is left."

THERE are few passages which confront us with greater difficulties than this passage does. It is in two sections, and the two sections seem to contradict each other. The first section (verses 32-35) seem to indicate that, as a man can tell by the signs of nature when summer is on the way, so he can tell by the signs of the world when the Second Coming is on the way. And then it seems to go on to say that the Second Coming will happen within the lifetime of the generation who were listening to Jesus at the moment at which He was speaking.

The second section (verses 36-41) says quite definitely that no one knows the time of the Second Coming, not the angels, not even Jesus Himself, but only God; and that it will come upon men with the suddenness of a rainstorm out of a blue sky.

There is a very real difficulty here, a difficulty which, even if we cannot completely solve it, we must nevertheless boldly face.

Let us take as our starting-point verse 34: "This is the truth I tell you—this generation shall not pass away, until these things have happened." When we consider that saying, three possibilities emerge. (a) If Jesus said it in reference to the Second Coming, He was mistaken, for He did not return within the lifetime of the generation which was listening to His words. There are many who accept that point of view, believing that Jesus in His humanity had limitations of knowledge, and that He did believe that within that generation He would return. We can readily accept the fact that in His humanity Jesus had limitations of knowledge; but it is difficult to believe that He was in error regarding so great a spiritual truth as this. (b) It is possible to hold that Jesus said something like this, and that it was changed in the transmitting. In *Mark* 9: 1 Jesus is reported as saying, " Verily I say unto you, that there be some of them that stand here which shall not taste of death till they have seen the Kingdom of God come with power." That was gloriously and triumphantly true. Within that generation the Kingdom of God did spread mightily until there were Christians throughout the known world. Now the early Christians did look for the Second Coming immediately. In their situation of suffering and persecution they looked and longed for the release that the coming of their Lord would bring, and sometimes they took sayings which were intended to speak of the *Kingdom* and attached them to the *Second Coming* which is a very different thing. Something like that may have happened here. What Jesus may have said was that His *Kingdom* would come mightily before that generation had passed away. (c) But there is a third possibility. What if Jesus did not say this with reference to the Second Coming at all? What if the phrase *until these things have happened* has no reference to the Second Coming? What if their reference is, in fact, to the prophecy with which the chapter began? What if they refer to the siege and the fall of Jerusalem? If we accept that, then there is no difficulty. What Jesus is saying is that these grim warnings of His regarding the doom of Jerusalem will be fulfilled within that very generation—and they were fulfilled forty years later. It seems by far the best course to take verses 32-35 as referring, not to the Second Coming, but to the doom of Jerusalem, for then all the difficulties in them are removed.

Then verses 36-41 do refer to the Second Coming; and about it they tell us certain most important truths.

(i) They tell us that the hour of that event is known to God and to God alone. It is, therefore, clear that speculation regarding the time of the Second Coming is nothing less than blasphemy, for the man who so speculates is seeking to wrest from God secrets which belong to God alone. It is not any man's duty to speculate; it is his duty to prepare himself, and to watch.

(ii) They tell us that that time will come with shattering suddenness on those who are immersed in material things. In the old story Noah prepared himself in the calm weather for the flood which was to come, and when it came he was ready. But the rest of mankind were lost in their eating and drinking and marrying and giving in marriage, and were caught completely unawares, and were therefore swept away. These verses are a warning never to become so immersed in time that we forget eternity, never to let our concern with worldly affairs, however necessary, completely distract us from remembering that there is a God, that the issues of life and death are in His hands, and that whenever His call comes, at morning, at midday, or at evening, it must find us ready.

(iii) They tell us that the coming of Christ will be a time of separation and of judgment, when Jesus Christ will gather to Himself those who are His own.

Beyond these things we cannot go—for God has kept the ultimate knowledge to Himself and to His wisdom.

READY FOR THE COMING OF THE KING

Matthew 24: 42-51

" Watch, therefore, for you do not know on what day your Lord comes. Understand this—that if the householder had known at what watch of the night the thief was coming, he would have been awake, and he would not have allowed him to break into his house. That is why you, too, must show yourselves ready; for the Son of Man is coming at an hour you do not expect.

Who, then, is the dependable and wise servant whom his master put in charge over his household staff, to give them their food at the right time? Happy is the servant whom his master, when he has come, will find acting thus. This is the truth I tell you— he will put him in charge of all his belongings. But if that bad servant says to himself, ' My master will not be back for a long time yet,' and if he begins to beat his fellow-servants, and if he eats and drinks with drunkards, then the master of that servant will come on a day when he is not expecting him, and at an hour which he does not know, and will cut him in pieces, and assign him a place with the hypocrites. There will be weeping and gnashing of teeth there."

HERE is the practical outcome of all that has gone before. If the day and the hour of the coming of Christ is known to none save God, then all life must be a constant preparation for that coming. And, if that is so, there are certain basic and fundamental sins.

(i) To live without watchfulness invites disaster. A thief does not send a letter saying when he is going to burgle a house; his principal weapon in his nefarious undertakings is surprise; therefore a householder who has valuables in his house must maintain a constant guard. But to get this picture right, we must remember that the watching of the Christian for the coming of Christ is not the watching of terror-stricken fear and shivering apprehension; it is the watching of eager expectation for the coming of the glory and the joy.

(ii) The spirit which leads to disaster is the spirit which says that there is plenty of time. It is the comfortable delusion of the servant in the second parable that he will have plenty time to put things to rights before his master returns. For him there was no need to think of his master's return for a long time yet. There is a fable which tells of three apprentice devils who were coming to this earth to finish their apprenticeship. They were talking to Satan the chief of the devils, about their plans to tempt and to ruin men. The first said, " I will tell them that there it no God." Satan said, " That will not delude many, for they know that there is a God." The second said, " I will tell men that there is no hell." Satan answered, " You will deceive no one that way; men know even now that there is a hell for sin." The third said, " I will tell men that there is no hurry." " Go," said Satan, " and you will ruin men by the thousand." The most dangerous of all delusions is that there is plenty of time. The most dangerous day in a man's life is when he learns that there is such a word as *tomorrow*. There are things which cannot be put off, for no man knows if for him tomorrow will ever come.

(iii) Rejection is based on failure in duty, and reward is based on fidelity in duty. The servant who fulfilled his duty faithfully was given a still greater place; and the servant who failed in his duty was dealt with in severity. The inevitable conclusion of that is that, when he comes, Jesus Christ can find us employed in no better and greater task than in doing our duty.

A negro poet writes:

" There's a king and a captain high,
    And he's coming by and by,
    And he'll find me hoeing cotton when he comes.
    You can hear his legions charging in the regions of the
        sky,
    And he'll find me hoeing cotton when he comes.
    There's a man they thrust aside,
    Who was tortured till he died,
    And he'll find me hoeing cotton when he comes.
    He was hated and rejected,
    He was scorned and crucified,
    And he'll find me hoeing cotton when he comes.
    When he comes! When he comes!
    He'll be crowned by saints and angels when he comes.
    They'll be shouting out Hosanna! to the man that
        men denied,
    And I'll kneel among my cotton when he comes."

If a man is doing his duty, however simple that duty may be, on the day Christ comes, there will be joy for him.

THE FATE OF THE UNPREPARED

Matthew 25: 1-13

" What will happen in the Kingdom of Heaven is like the situation which arose when ten virgins took their lamps and went out to meet the bridegroom. Five of them were foolish and five were wise. The foolish took their lamps, but did not take oil with them; but the wise took oil in their vessels together with their lamps. When the bridegroom was long in coming, all of them settled down to rest and slept. In the middle of the night the cry went up, ' Look you, the bridegroom! Go out to meet him! ' Then all these virgins awoke, and they prepared their lamps. The foolish ones said to the wise ones, ' Give us some of your oil, for our lamps have gone out.' But the wise answered, ' No; we cannot do that in case there is not enough for us and for you. Go rather to those who sell oil, and buy it for yourselves.' While they went away to buy oil, the bridegroom came; and those who were ready entered with him into the marriage celebrations, and the door was shut. Later the rest of the virgins came too. ' Sir, sir,' they said, ' open the door to us.' But he answered, ' This is the truth I tell you—I do not know you.' Be on the watch then, for you do not know the day and the hour."

IF we look at this parable with western eyes, it may seem to us to tell an unnatural and a " made-up " story. But, in point of fact, it tells a story which could have happened at any time in a Palestinian village, and which could still happen today.

In a village in Palestine a wedding was a great occasion. The whole village turned out to accompany the couple to their new home, and they went by the longest possible road, in order that they might receive the glad good wishes of as many as possible. " Everyone," runs the Jewish saying, " from six to sixty will follow the marriage drum." The Rabbis agreed that a man might even abandon the study of the law to share in the joy of a wedding feast.

Now the point of this story lies in a Jewish custom which is very different from anything which we know. When a couple married in Palestine, they did not go away for a honeymoon; they stayed at home; and for a week they kept open house; they were treated, and even addressed, as a prince and princess; it was the gladdest week in all their lives. To the festivities of that week their chosen friends were admitted; and it was not only the marriage cermony, it was also that joyous week that the foolish virgins missed, because they were unprepared.

The story of how they missed it all is perfectly true to life. Dr. J. Alexander Findlay tells of what he himself saw in Palestine. " When we were approaching the gates of a Galilaean town," he writes, " I caught a sight of ten maidens gaily clad and playing some kind of musical instrument, as they danced along the road in front of our car; when I asked what they were doing, the dragoman told me that they were going to keep the bride company till her bridegroom arrived. I asked him if there was any chance of seeing the wedding, but he shook his head, saying in effect: ' It might be tonight, or tomorrow night, or in a fortnight's time; nobody ever knows for certain.' Then he went on to explain that one of the great things to do, if you could, at a middle-class wedding in Palestine, was to catch the bridal party napping. So the bridegroom comes unexpectedly, and sometimes in the middle of the night; it is true that he is required by public opinion to send a man along the street to shout: ' Behold! the bridegroom is coming! ' but that may happen at any time; so the bridal party have to be ready to go out into the street at any time to meet him, whenever he chooses to come. . . . Other important points are that no one is allowed on the streets after dark without a lighted lamp, and also that, when the bridegroom has once arrived, and the door has been shut, late-comers to the ceremony are not admitted." There the whole drama of Jesus' parable is re-enacted in the twentieth century. Here is no synthetic story, but a slice of life from village life in Palestine.

Like so many of Jesus' parables, this parable has an immediate and a local meaning, and a wider and a universal meaning.

In its immediate significance it was directed against the Jews. They were the chosen people; their whole history should have been a preparation for the coming of the Son of God; they ought to have been prepared for Him when He came. Instead of that they were quite unprepared to receive Him, and therefore they were shut out. Here in dramatic form there is the tragedy of the unpreparedness of the Jews.

But this parable has at least two universal warnings.

(i) It warns us that there are certain things which cannot be got at the last minute. It is far too late for a student to be preparing when the day of the examination has come. It is too late for a man to acquire a skill, or a character, if he has not already got it, when some task offers itself to him. It is so with us and God. It is easy to leave things so late that we can no longer prepare ourselves to meet with God. When Mary of Orange was dying, her chaplain sought to tell her of the way of salvation. Her answer was: " I have not left this matter to this hour." To be too late is always tragedy.

(ii) It warns us that there are certain things which cannot be borrowed. The foolish virgins found it impossible to borrow oil, when they discovered they needed it. A man cannot borrow a relationship with God; he must possess it. A man cannot borrow a character; he must be clothed with it. We cannot always be living on the spiritual capital which others have amassed. There are certain things which we must win or possess for ourselves, for we cannot borrow them from others.

Tennyson took this parable and turned it into verse in the song the little novice sang to Guinevere the queen, when Guinevere had too late discovered the cost of sin:

" Late, late so late! and dark the night and chill!
Late, late so late! but we can enter still.
Too late, too late! ye cannot enter now.

No light had we; for that we do repent;
And learning this, the bridegroom will relent.
Too late, too late! ye cannot enter now.

354

No light: so late! and dark and chill the night!
O let us in, that we may find the light!
Too late, too late: ye cannot enter now.

Have we not heard the bridegroom is so sweet?
O let us in, tho' late, to kiss his feet!
No, no, too late! ye cannot enter now."

There is no knell so laden with the tears of regret as the sound of the words *too late.*

THE CONDEMNATION OF THE BURIED TALENT

Matthew 25: 14-30

" Even so, a man who was going abroad called his servants, and handed over his belongings to them. To one he gave a thousand pounds; to another five hundred pounds; to another two hundred and fifty pounds; to each according to his individual ability. So he went away. Straightway the man who had received the thousand pounds went and worked with them, and made another thousand pounds. In the same way the man who had received the five hundred pounds made another five hundred pounds of profit. But the man who had received the two hundred and fifty pounds went away and dug up the earth, and hid his master's money. After a long time the master of those servants came, and struck a reckoning with them. The one who had received the thousand pounds came and brought another thousand pounds. ' Sir,' he said, ' you gave me a thousand pounds. Look! I have made a profit of another thousand pounds.' His master said to him, ' Well done! good and faithfu servant. You have been faithful in a few things; I will put you in charge over many things; enter into the joy of your master.' The one who had received the five hundred pounds came and said, ' Sir, you handed over to me five hundred pounds. Look! I have made a profit of another five hundred pounds.' His master said to him, ' Well done! good and faithful servant. You have been faithful in a few things. I will put you in charge over many things.' The one who had received the two hundred and fifty pounds came also. ' Sir,' he said, ' I knew that you are a harsh man, reaping where you did not sow, and gathering where you did not winnow. So I was afraid, and I went away and hid your two hundred and fifty pounds in the earth. Look! you have what is yours.' The master answered him, ' Evil and timid servant! You were well aware that I reap where I have not sowed, and that I gather where I have not winnowed. You ought to have put my money out to the bankers, and when I came I would have received back what is my own with interest. Take, then, the two hundred and fifty pounds from him, and give it to him who has the two thousand pounds. For to everyone who has, it will be given, and he will have abundance; but from him who has not, even what he has will be taken away from him. And cast the useless servant into the outer darkness. There shall be weeping and gnashing of teeth there.' "

LIKE the preceding parable this parable also had an immediate lesson for those who heard it for the first time, and a whole series of permanent lessons for us today. This parable is always known as the Parable of the Talents; in our translation we have changed the talents into modern currency. In Palestine the *talent* was not a *coin*, it was a *weight*; and therefore the value of the talent obviously depended on whether the coinage involved was copper, gold or silver. The commonest metal involved was silver; and the value of a talent of silver was about £240. It is on that basis that we have made the translations of the various sums involved in the parable.

There can be no doubt that originally in this parable the whole attention is riveted on the useless servant, who received the one talent. For whom then does he stand? And who is it that Jesus is specially warning and rebuking? There can be little doubt that the useless servant stands for the Scribes and the Pharisees, and for their attitude to the Law and to the truth of God. The useless servant took and buried his talent in the ground, in order that he might hand it back to his master exactly as it was. The whole aim of the Scribes and Pharisees was to keep the Law exactly as it was. In their own phrase, they sought

" to build a fence around the Law." Any change, any development, any alteration, anything new was to them anathema. Their method involved the paralysis of religious truth, and the hatred of everything that was new. Like the man with the talent, they desired to keep things exactly as they were—and it is for that that they are condemned. In this parable Jesus tells us that there can be no religion without adventure, and that God can find no use for the shut mind. But there is much more in this parable than that.

(i) It tells us that God gives men differing gifts. One man received five talents, another two, and another one. It is not a man's talent which matters; what matters is how he uses it. God never demands from a man abilities which he has not got; but God does demand from a man that he should use to the full the abilities which he does possess. Men are not equal in talent; but men can be equal in effort. The parable tells us that whatever talent we have, little be it or great, we must lay it at the service of God.

(ii) It tells us that the reward of work well done is still more work to do. The two servants who had done well are not told to lean back and to rest on their oars, because they have done well. They are given greater tasks, and greater responsibilities in the work of the master. The reward of work is not rest, but more work.

(iii) It tells us that the man who is punished is the man who will not try. The man with the one talent did not lose his talent; he simply did nothing with it. Even if he had adventured with it and lost it, it would have been better than to do nothing with it at all. It is always a temptation for the one talent man to say, " I have so small a talent, and I can do so little with it, that it is not worth while to try, for all the contribution that I can make." But the condemnation is for the man who, having even one talent, will not try to use it, and who will not risk it for the common good.

(iv) It lays down a rule of life which is universally true. It tells us that to him that hath shall be given, and from him that hath not shall be taken away that which he has. The meaning of that saying is this. If a man has a talent, and exercises it, he is progressively able to do more with it. But, if he has a talent, and fails to exercise it, he will inevitably lose it. If we have some proficiency at a game or an art, if we have some gift for doing something, the more we exercise that proficiency and that gift, the harder the work and the bigger the task we will be able to tackle. Whereas, if we fail to use it, we lose it. That is equally true of playing golf or playing the piano, of singing songs or writing sermons, of carving wood or thinking out ideas. It is the lesson of life that the only way to keep a gift is to use it in the service of God and in the service of our fellow-men.

GOD'S STANDARD OF JUDGMENT

Matthew 25: 31-46

" When the Son of Man shall come in His glory, and all the angels with Him, then He will take His seat upon the throne of His glory, and all nations will be assembled before Him, and He will separate them from each other, as a shepherd separates the sheep from the goats, and He will place the sheep on His right hand and the goats on His left. Then the King will say to those on his right hand, ' Come, you who are blessed by my Father, enter into possession of the Kingdom which has been prepared for you since the creation of the world. For I was hungry, and you gave me to eat; I was thirsty, and you gave me to drink; I was a stranger, and you gathered me in; naked, and you clothed me; I was sick, and you came to visit me; in prison, and you came to me.' Then the righteous will answer Him, ' Lord, when did we see you hungry, and nourish you? Or thirsty, and gave you to drink? When did we see you a stranger, and gather you to us? Or naked, and clothed you? When did we see you sick, or in prison, and come to you?' And the King will answer them, ' This is the truth I tell you—insomuch as you did it to one of the least of these my brothers, you did it to me.' Then He will say to those on the left, ' Go from me, you cursed ones, to the eternal fire prepared for the devil and his angels. For I was hungry, and you did not give me to eat; I was thirsty, and you did not give me to drink; I was a stranger, and you did not gather me to you; naked, and you did not clothe me; sick and in prison, and you did not come to visit me.' Then these too will answer, ' Lord, when did we see you hungry, or thirsty, or a stranger, or naked, or sick, or in prison, and did not render service to you?' Then He will answer them, ' This is the truth I tell you—in so far as you did not do it to one of the least of these, you did not do it to me.' And these will go away to eternal punishment, but the righteous will go away to eternal life."

THIS is one of the most vivid parables which Jesus ever spoke, and the lesson of it is crystal clear. The lesson is this—that God will judge us in accordance with our reaction to human need. God's judgment does not depend on the knowledge we have amassed, or the fame that we have acquired, or the fortune that we have gained, but on the help that we have given. But there are certain things which this parable teaches us about the help which we must give.

(i) It must be help in simple things. The things which Jesus picks out—giving a hungry man a meal, or a thirsty man a drink, welcoming a stranger, cheering the sick, visiting the prisoner—are things which anyone can do. It is not a question of giving away thousands of pounds, or of writing our names in the annals of history; it is a case of giving simple, human help to the people we meet every day. There never was a parable which so opened the way to glory to the simplest people.

(ii) It must be help which is quite uncalculating. Those who helped did not think that they were helping Christ, and thus piling up eternal merit; they helped because they could not stop themselves helping. It was the natural, instinctive, quite uncalculating reaction of the loving heart. Whereas, on the other hand, the whole attitude of those who failed to help was: ' If we had known it was *you* we would gladly have helped; but we thought it was only some common man who was not worth helping,'' It is still true that there are those who will help if they are given praise and thanks and publicity; but to help like that is not to help, it is simply to pander to self-esteem. Such help is not generosity; it is simply disguised selfishness. The help which wins the approval of God is the help which is given for nothing but the sake of helping.

(iii) Jesus confronts us with the wonderful truth that all such help which is given is given to Himself, and all such help which is withheld is withheld from Himself. How can that be? If we really wish to delight a parent's heart, if we really wish to move him to gratitude indeed, then the best way to do it is to help his child. God is the great Father; and the way to delight the heart of God is to help His children, who are our fellow-men.

There were two men who found this parable blessedly true. The one was Francis of Asissi; he was rich and he was wealthy and he was high-born and high-spirited. But he was not happy. He felt that life was incomplete. Then one day he was out riding and he met a leper, loathsome and repulsive in the ugliness of his disease. Something moved Francis to dismount and fling his arms around this wretched sufferer; and, lo, in his arms the face of the leper changed to the face of the Christ.

The other was Martin of Tours. He was a Roman soldier, and a Christian. One cold winter day, as he was entering a city, a beggar stopped him and asked him for alms. Martin had no money; but the beggar was blue and shivering with cold, and Martin gave what he had. He took off his soldier's coat, worn and frayed as it was; he cut it in two and gave half of it to the beggar man. That night he had a dream. In it he saw the heavenly places and all the angels and Jesus in the midst of them;

and Jesus was wearing half of a Roman soldier's cloak. One of the angels said to Him, " Master, why are you wearing that battered old cloak? Who gave it to you ? " And Jesus answered softly, " My servant Martin gave it to me."

When we learn the generosity which without calculation helps men in the simplest things, then we too will know the joy of helping Jesus Christ Himself.

THE BEGINNING OF THE LAST ACT OF THE TRAGEDY

Matthew 26: 1-5

> When Jesus had completed all these sayings, He said to His disciples, " You know that in two days time it is the Passover Feast, and the Son of Man is going to be delivered to be crucified." At that time the chief priests and the elders of the people gathered in the courtyard of the High Priest, who was called Caiaphas, and took counsel together to seize Jesus by guile and to kill Him. They said, " Not at the time of the Feast, lest a tumult arise among the people."

HERE then is the final and the definite beginning of the last act of the divine tragedy. Once again Jesus warned His disciples of that which was to come. For the last few days He had been acting with such magnificent defiance that they might have thought that He proposed to defy the Jewish authorities; but here once again He makes it clear that His aim is the Cross.

And at the same time the Jewish authorities were laying their plots and stratagems. Joseph Caiaphas, to give him his full name, was High Priest. We know very little about Caiaphas, but we do know one most suggestive fact about him. In the old days the office of High Priest had been hereditary and it had been for life; but when the Romans took over in Palestine High Priests came and went in a rapid series, for the Romans erected and deposed High Priests to suit their own purposes. Between 37 B.C. and A.D. 67, when the last of the High Priests was appointed before the destruction of the Temple, there were no fewer than twenty-eight High Priests. The suggestive thing is that Caiaphas was High Priest from A.D. 18 to A.D. 36. This was an extraordinarily long time for a High Priest to last, and Caiaphas must have brought the technique of co-operating with the Romans to a fine art. And therein precisely there lay his problem. The one thing the Romans would not stand was civil disorder. Let there be any rioting and very certainly Caiaphas would lose his position. At the Passover time the atmosphere in Jerusalem was always explosive. The city was packed tight with people. Josephus tells us of an occasion when an actual census of the people was taken (Josephus, *Wars of the Jews*, 6. 9. 3). It happened in this way. The governor at the time was Cestius; Cestius felt that Nero did not understand the number of the Jews and the problems which they posed to any governor. So Cestius asked the High Priests to take a census of the lambs slain for sacrifice at a certain Passover time. Josephus goes on to say, " A company of not less than ten must belong to every sacrifice (for it is not lawful for them to feast singly by themselves), and many of us are twenty in a company." It was found that on this occasion the number of lambs slain was 256,500. It is Josephus' estimate that there were in the city for that Passover some two and three-quarter million people. It is little wonder that Caiaphas sought some stratagem to take Jesus secretly and quietly, for many of these pilgrims were Galilaeans, and to them Jesus was a prophet. It was in fact the plan of Caiaphas to leave the whole thing over until after the Passover Feast had ended, and the city was quieter; but Judas was to provide him with a solution to his problem. Caiaphas was ready to adopt any ruse to rid himself of this disturbing Jesus.

LOVE'S EXTRAVAGANCE

Matthew 26: 6-13

> When Jesus was in Bethany, in the house of Simon the leper, a woman came to Him with an alabaster phial of very costly perfume, and poured it over His head as He reclined at table. When the disciples saw it, they were vexed. " What is the good of this waste? " they said. " For this could have been sold for much money, and the proceeds given to the poor." When Jesus knew what they were saying, He said to them, " Why do you distress the woman? It is a lovely thing that she has done to me. For you always have the poor with you, but you have not me always. When she poured this perfume on my body, she did it to prepare me beforehand for burial. This is the truth I tell you—wherever the gospel is preached throughout the whole world, this too that she has done shall be spoken of so that all will remember her."

IN the gospel record this story of the anointing at Bethany is told also by Mark and by John. Mark's story is almost exactly the same; but John adds the information that the woman who anointed Jesus was none other than Mary, the sister of Martha and of Lazarus. Now Luke does not tell this story; but he does tell the story of an anointing in the house of Simon the Pharisee (*Luke* 7: 36-50), but in Luke's story the woman who anointed Jesus' feet and wiped them with the hair of her head was a notorious sinner. It must always remain a most interesting question whether the story Luke tells is, in fact, the same story as is told by Matthew and Mark and John. In both cases the name of the host is Simon, although in *Luke* he is Simon the Pharisee, and in *Matthew* and *Mark* he is Simon the leper; and in *John* the host is not named at all, although the narrative reads as if it took place in the house of Martha and Mary and Lazarus. Simon was a very common name; there are at least ten Simons in the New Testament, and more than twenty in the history of Josephus. The greatest difficulty in identifying the stories of Luke and of the other three gospel writers is that in Luke's story the woman was notorious sinner; and there is no indication that that is true of Mary of Bethany; and yet the very intensity with which Mary loved Jesus may well be the result of the depths from which He had rescued her. It must always remain uncertain whether Luke's story is the same story as the other three; we can only say that it is not impossible that it is.

However that may be, the story is indeed what Jesus called it—the story of a lovely thing; and in it there are enshrined certain very precious truths.

(i) It shows us love's *extravagance*. The woman took the most precious thing that she had and poured it out on Jesus. Jewish women were very fond of perfume; and often they carried a little alabaster phial of it round their necks. Such perfume was very precious. Both Mark and John make the disciples say that this perfume could have been sold for three hundred *denarii* (*Mark* 14: 5; *John* 12: 5). A *denarius* was a silver coin worth about ninepence; but when we try to evaluate it we must remember that a working man's wage was eightpence a day; and, therefore, this phial of perfume represented very nearly a whole year's wages. Or we may think of it this way. When Jesus and His disciples were discussing how the multitude were to be fed, Philip's answer was that two hundred *denarii* would scarcely be enough to feed them. This phial of perfume would cost as much money as it would to feed a crowd of five thousand people. It was something as precious as that that this woman gave to Jesus, and she gave it to Him because it was the most precious thing she had. Love never calculates; love never thinks how little it can decently give; love's one desire is to give to the uttermost limits; and, when it has given all it has to give, it still thinks the gift too little. We have not even begun to be Christian if we think of giving to Christ and to His Church in terms of as little as we respectably can.

(ii) It shows us that there are times when the common-sense view of things fails. On this occasion the voice of common sense said, " What waste! " and no doubt it was right. But there is a world of difference between the economics of common sense and the economics of love. Common sense obeys the dictates of prudence; but love obeys the dictates of the heart. There is in life a large place for common sense; but there are times when only love's extravagance can meet love's demands. A gift is never really a gift when we can easily afford it; a gift only becomes a gift when there is sacrifice behind it, and when we give far more than we can afford.

(iii) It shows us that there are certain things which must be done when the opportunity arises, or they can never be done at all. The disciples were anxious to help the poor; but the Rabbis themselves said, " God allows the poor to be with us always, that the opportunities for doing good may never fail." There are some things which we can do at any time; there are some things which can only be done once; and to miss the opportunity to do them then is to miss the opportunity for ever. Often we are moved by some generous impulse; and so very often we do not act upon it; and, if we do not act upon it, all the chances are that the circumstances, the person, the time, and the impulse, will never return. For so many of us the tragedy of life is that life is the history of the lost opportunities to do the lovely thing.

(iv) It tells us that the fragrance of a lovely deed lasts for ever. There are so few lovely things that when one is done it shines like a light in a dark world. At the end of Jesus' life there was so much bitterness, so much treachery, so much intrigue, so much tragedy that this story shines like an oasis of light in a darkening world in these last days. In this world there are few greater things that a man may do than to leave the memory of a lovely deed.

THE LAST HOURS IN THE LIFE OF THE TRAITOR

INSTEAD of taking the story of Judas piece-meal as it occurs in the gospel record, we shall take it as a whole, reading one after another the last incidents, and the final suicide of the traitor.

THE TRAITOR'S BARGAIN

Matthew 26: 14-16

> Then one of the Twelve, called Judas Iscariot, went to the chief priests and said, " What are you willing to give me, if I hand Him over to you? " They settled with him for a sum of thirty shekels; and from that time he sought for an opportunity to betray Him.

WE have seen that the Jewish authorities wished to find a way in which to arrest Jesus without provoking riotous disturbances, and now that way was presented to them by the approach of Judas. There can only be three real basic reasons why Judas betrayed Jesus. All other suggested reasons are variations of these three.

(i) It may have been because of greed and avarice. According to Matthew and Mark it was immediately after the anointing at Bethany that Judas struck his dreadful bargain; and when John tells his story of that same event, he says that Judas made his protest against the anointing because he was a thief and pilfered from the money that was in the bag (*John* 12: 6). If that is so, Judas struck one of the most dreadful bargains in history. The sum for which he agreed to betray Jesus was thirty *arguria*. An *argurion* was a *shekel*, and was worth about three shillings. If, then, this is true, Judas sold Jesus for less than five pounds. If avarice was the cause of Judas' act of treachery, then this is the most terrible example in history of the depths which love of money can reach.

(ii) It may have been because of bitter hatred, based on complete disillusionment. The Jews always had their dream of power; therefore they had their violent nationalists who were prepared to go to any lengths of murder and violence to drive the Romans from Palestine. These nationalists were called the *sicarii*, the dagger-bearers, because they followed a deliberate policy of assassination. It may be that Judas was such, that he had looked on Jesus as the divinely sent leader, who, with His miraculous powers, could lead the great rebellion. Then he may have seen that Jesus had deliberately taken another way, the way that led to a cross. And in his bitter disappointment, Judas' devotion may have turned, first to disillusionment, and then to hatred, a hatred which drove him to seek the death of the man from whom he had expected so much. Judas may have hated Jesus Christ because Jesus Christ was not the Christ he wished him to be.

(iii) It may be that Judas never intended Jesus to die. It may be that, as we have seen, Judas saw in Jesus the divine leader. He may have thought that Jesus was proceeding far too slowly; and he may have wished for nothing else than to force Jesus' hand. He may have betrayed Jesus with the intention of compelling Jesus to act. That is in fact the view which best suits all the facts. And that explains why Judas was shattered into suicide when his plan went wrong.

However we look at it, the tragedy of Judas is that he refused to accept Jesus as He was, and tried to make Jesus what he wanted Him to be. It is not Jesus who can be changed by us, but we who must be changed by Jesus. We can never use Jesus for our purposes; we must submit to Him to be used for His. The tragedy of Judas is the tragedy of the man who thought that he knew better than God.

LOVE'S LAST APPEAL

Matthew 26: 20-25

When evening had come, Jesus was reclining at table with the twelve disciples. While they were eating

He said, " This is the truth I tell you—one of you
will betray me." They were greatly distressed and
began one by one to say to Him, " Lord, can it be
I? " He answered, " He who dips his hand with me
in the dish, it is he who will betray me. The Son of
Man is going to go away, as it stands written concerning
Him, but alas for that man through whom the Son
of Man is betrayed! It had been good for that man if
he had not been born." Judas, who betrayed Him,
said, " Master, can it be I? " He said to him, " It is
you who have said it."

THERE are times in these last scenes of the gospel story
when Jesus and Judas seem to be in a world where they
are alone together, and where there is none other present
except themselves. One thing is certain—Judas must have
gone about his grim business with complete secrecy. He
must have kept his comings and goings completely hidden,
for, if the rest of the disciples had known what Judas was
doing, he would never have escaped with his life. Judas
had concealed his plans from his fellow-disciples—but
he could not conceal them from Christ. It is always the
same; a man can hide his sins from his fellow-men, but
he can never hide them from the eyes of Jesus Christ,
who sees the secrets of the heart. Jesus knew, although
no other knew, what Judas was about.

And now we can see Jesus' methods with the sinner.
Jesus could have used His power to blast Judas, to paralyse
him, to render him helpless, even to kill him. But the only
weapon that Jesus will use is the weapon of love's appeal.
One of the great mysteries of life is the respect that God
has for the free will of man. God does not force; God does
not coerce; God can only appeal.

When Jesus seeks to stop a man from sinning, He does
two things. First, He confronts a man with his sin. He
tries to make a man stop and see and think what he is
doing. He, as it were, says to him, " Look at what you are
contemplating doing—can you really do a thing like that? "
It has been said that our greatest security against sin lies
in our being shocked by it. And again and again Jesus

bids a man pause and look and realize, that the man may be shocked into sanity. Second, He confronts a man with Himself. He bids a man look at Him, as if to say, " Can you look at me, can you meet my eyes, and go out to do the thing you purpose doing? " The appeal of Jesus is to seek to make a man realize the horror of the thing he seeks to do, and the love which yearns to stop him doing it.

And it is just therein that we see the real awfulness of sin. The real awfulness of sin lies in its terrible deliberation. In spite of love's last appeal Judas went on. Even when he was confronted with his sin and confronted with the face of Christ, Judas would not turn back. There is sin and sin. There is the sin of the passionate heart, and of the man who, on the impulse of the moment, is swept into sin before he knows what has happened. Let no man belittle such a sin; its consequences can be very terrible. But far worse is the cold, calculated, callous sin of deliberation, which in cold blood knows what it is doing, which is confronted with the bleak awfulness of the deed, and with the love in the eyes of Jesus, and still takes its own way. Our hearts revolt against the son or daughter who cold-bloodedly breaks a parent's heart—and that is what Judas did to Jesus—and the tragedy is that that is what we ourselves so often do.

THE TRAITOR'S KISS

Matthew 26: 47-50

> While Jesus was still speaking, there came Judas, one of the Twelve, and a great crowd with swords and cudgels, from the chief priests and the elders of the people. The traitor had given them a sign. " Whom I shall kiss," he said, " that is the man. Lay hold on Him! " Immediately he went up to Jesus and said, " Greetings, Master! " and kissed Him lovingly. Jesus said to him, " Comrade, get on with the deed for which you have come! " Then they came forward, and laid hands on Jesus, and held Him.

As we have already seen, the actions of Judas may spring from one of two motives. He may really, either from avarice or from disillusionment, have wished to see Jesus killed; or he may have been trying to force Jesus' hand, and may not have wished to see Him killed, but may have wished to compel Him to act.

There is, therefore, a double way of interpreting this incident. If in Judas' heart there was nothing but black hatred, and a kind of maniacal avarice, then this is simply the most terrible kiss in history, a kiss which was a sign of betrayal. If that is so, then there is nothing too terrible to be said about this Judas.

But there are signs that there is more than that here. When Judas told the armed mob that he would indicate the man whom they had come to arrest by a kiss, the word he uses is the Greek word *philein*, which is the normal word for a kiss; but when it is said that Judas actually did kiss Jesus, the word that is used is *kataphilein*, which is the word for a lover's kiss, and which means to kiss repeatedly, passionately, fervently. Why should Judas do that?

Further, why should any identification of Jesus have been necessary? It was not the identification of Jesus which the authorities required; it was a convenient opportunity to arrest Him. The people who came to arrest Jesus were from the chief priests and the elders of the people; these people must have been the Temple police; that is the only force the chief priests had at their disposal. And it is incredible that the Temple police did not already know only too well the man who only days before had already cleansed the Temple, and who had driven the money-changers and the sellers of doves from the Temple court. It is incredible that they should not have known the man who had taught daily in the Temple cloisters. They needed no identification. Having been led to the garden, they well knew the man whom they had come to arrest.

It is much more likely that, when Judas stepped up

to kiss Jesus, he kissed Him as a disciple kissed a master, and that he meant it; and that then he stood back with expectant pride waiting on Jesus to blast these people and at last to act. The curious thing is that from the moment of the kiss Judas vanishes from the scene in the garden, not to reappear until he is bent on suicide. He does not even appear as a witness at the trial of Jesus. It is far more likely that in one stunning, blinding, staggering, searing moment Judas saw how he had miscalculated and staggered away into the night a for ever broken and for ever haunted man. If this be true, at that moment Judas entered the hell which he had created for himself, for the worst kind of hell is the full realization of the terrible consequences of sin.

THE TRAITOR'S END

Matthew 27: 3-10

> When Judas the traitor saw that Jesus had been condemned, he repented, and he brought the thirty shekels back to the chief priests and the elders. " I have sinned," he said, " for I have betrayed an innocent man." " What has that got to do with us? " they said. " It is you who must see to that." He threw the money into the Temple and went away. And when he had gone away, he hanged himself. The chief priests took the money. " We cannot," they said, " put these into the treasury, for they are the price of blood." They took counsel, and bought with them the potter's field, to be a burying place for strangers. That is why to this day that field is called The Field of Blood. Then there was fulfilled that which was spoken through Jeremiah the prophet, when he said: " And they took the thirty shekels, the price of him on whom a price had been set by the sons of Israel, and they gave them for the field of the potter, as the Lord instructed me."

HERE in all its stark grimness is the last act of the tragedy of Judas. However we interpret the mind of Judas, one thing is clear—Judas now saw the horror of the thing that he had done. Matthew tells us that Judas took the money and flung it into the Temple, and the interesting thing is that the word he uses is not the word for the Temple precincts in general (*hieron*), it is the word for the actual Temple itself (*naos*). It will be remembered that the Temple consisted of a series of courts each opening off the other. Judas in his blind despair came into the Court of the Gentiles; he passed through it into the Court of the Women; he passed through that into the Court of the Israelites; beyond that he could not go; now he had come to the barrier which shut off the Court of the Priests with the Temple itself at the far end of it. He called on them to take the money; but they would not; and he took it and flung it at them and went away and hanged himself. And so the priests took the money, so tainted that it could not be put into the Temple treasury, and with it they bought a field to bury the unclean bodies of Gentiles who died within the city.

The suicide of Judas is surely the final indication that his plan had gone wrong. He had meant to make Jesus blaze forth as a conqueror; he had driven Jesus to the Cross; and life for Judas was shattered. There are two great truths about sin here.

(i) The most terrible thing about sin is that we cannot put the clock back. We cannot undo what we have done. Once a thing is done nothing can alter it or bring it back.

> " The Moving Finger writes; and having writ,
>   Moves on: nor all thy Piety nor Wit
>   Shall lure it back to cancel half a Line,
>   Nor all thy Tears wash out a Word of it."

No one needs to be very old to have that terrible and haunting longing that some hour could only be lived over again. When we remember that no action can ever be recalled, it should make us doubly careful how we act.

(ii) The strange thing about sin is that a man can come to hate the very thing he gained by sin. The very prize he won by sinning can come to disgust and to revolt and

to repel him, until his one desire is to fling it from him
Most people sin because they think that if they can only
possess the forbidden thing it will make them happy.
But the thing which sin desired and took can become
the thing that a man above all would rid himself of—
and so often he cannot.

As we have seen, Matthew finds forecasts of the events
of the life of Jesus in the most unlikely places. Here there
is, in fact, an actual mistake. In this case Matthew is
quoting from memory; and the quotation which he makes
is, in fact, not from *Jeremiah*; it is from *Zechariah*. It is
from a strange passage (*Zechariah* 11: 10-14) in which the
prophet tells us how he received an unworthy reward
and flung it to the potter. In that old picture Matthew
saw a symbolic resemblance to the thing that Judas did.

It might have been that, if Judas had been true to
Jesus, he would have died a martyr's death; but, because
he wanted his own way too much, he died a suicide's
death by his own hand. He missed the glory of the martyr's
crown to find that life was intolerable because he had
sinned.

THE LAST SUPPER

As we took together the passages which tell the story of
Judas so now we take the passages which tell the story
of the Last Supper.

THE ANCESTRAL FEAST

Matthew 26: 17-19

> On the first day of the Feast of Unleavened Bread
> the disciples came to Jesus. " Where," they said,
> " do you wish that we should make the necessary
> preparations for you to eat the Passover? " He said
> " Go into the city to such and such a man, and say
> to him, ' The Teacher says, my time is near. I will
> keep the Passover with my disciples at your house.' "
> And the disciples did as Jesus instructed them, and
> made the preparations for the Passover.

It was for the Passover Feast that Jesus had come to Jerusalem. We have already seen how crowded the city was at such a time. During the Passover Feast all Jews were supposed to stay within the boundaries of the city, but the numbers made that impossible; and for official purposes of a lodging-place villages like Bethany, where Jesus was staying, ranked as the city. But the Feast itself had to be celebrated within the city. The disciples wished to know what preparation they must make. Clearly Jesus had not left the matter to the last moment; He had already made His arrangements with a friend in Jerusalem, and He had already arranged a password—" The Teacher says, my time is near." So the disciples were sent on to give the password and to make all the necessary preparations.

The whole week of which the Passover Feast occupied the first evening was called The Feast of Unleavened Bread. In following the events we must remember that for the Jew the next day began at 6 o'clock in the evening. In this case the Feast of Unleavened Bread began on Thursday morning. On the Thursday morning every particle of leaven was destroyed, after a ceremonial search throughout the house. There was a double reason for that. The whole Feast commemorated the greatest event in the history of Israel, the deliverance from slavery in Egypt. And when the Israelites had fled from Egypt, they had to flee in such haste that they had not time to bake their bread leavened (*Exodus* 12: 34). Leaven is fermented dough and, when a little bit of it is put into the dough which is being baked, the resulting bread is like an ordinary loaf, but an ordinary loaf takes time to bake. Dough without leaven cooks very quickly, but produces a substance more like a water biscuit than like a loaf; and that is what unleavened bread was like. The leaven was banished and the bread was unleavened to repeat the acts of the night on which they left the land of Egypt and its slavery behind them. Second, in Jewish thought leaven is the symbol of corruption. As we have said, leaven is fermented dough, and the Jews identified fermentation and putrefaction; so leaven stood for all that was rotten and corrupt, and was, therefore, as the sign of purification, cleansed away.

What then were the preparations which the disciples would make?

On the Thursday morning, they would prepare the unleavened bread, and rid the house of every scrap of leaven. The other staple ingredient of the Feast was the Passover Lamb. It was indeed from the lamb that the Feast took its name. The last terrible plague which fell on the Egyptians, and which compelled them to let the people go, was that the Angel of Death was to walk throughout the land of Egypt and slay the firstborn son in every house. To identify their houses, the Israelites were to take a lamb and kill it and smear the lintel and the side posts of their doors with the blood of the lamb, so that the avenging angel would see that sign and *pass over* that house (*Exodus* 12: 21-23). On the Thursday afternoon the lamb had to be taken to the Temple and slain, and its blood—which was the life—had to be offered to God in sacrifice.

So, then, the unleavened bread and the lamb would be prepared. There were four other items necessary for the Feast.

(i) A bowl of *salt water* had to be set upon the table, to remind them of the tears they had shed while they were slaves in Egypt, and of the salt waters of the Red Sea through which God's hand had wondrously brought them.

(ii) A collection of *bitter herbs* had to be prepared, composed of horse-radish, chicory, endive, lettuce, horehound and the like. This was again to remind them of the bitterness of slavery, and of the bunch of hyssop with which the blood of the lamb had been smeared on the lintel and the door-posts.

(iii) There was a paste called the *Charosheth*. It was a mixture of apples, dates, pomegranates and nuts. It was to remind them of the clay with which they had been compelled to make bricks in Egypt, and through it there were sticks of cinnamon to remind them of the straw with which the bricks had been made.

(iv) Lastly, there were *four cups of wine*. The four cups were to remind them of the four promises of *Exodus* 6: 6, 7: " I will bring you out from under the burdens of the Egyptians; I will rid you of their bondage; I will redeem you with an outstretched arm; I will take you to me for a people, and I will be your God."

Such then were the preparations of the Thursday morning and afternoon. These were the things that the disciples prepared; and at any time after 6 p.m., that is when Friday, the 15th Nisan, had begun, the guests might gather at the table.

HIS BODY AND HIS BLOOD

Matthew 26: 26-30

> While they were eating, Jesus took bread and blessed it and broke it, and gave it to His disciples and said, " Take, eat; this is my body." Then He took a cup, and when He had given thanks, He gave it to them. " Drink all of you from it," He said, " for this is my blood, the blood of the covenant, which is poured out for many, that their sins may be forgiven. I tell you that from now on I will not drink of this fruit of the vine until that day when I drink it new with you in the Kingdom of my Father." And when they had sung a hymn, they went out to the Mount of Olives.

WE have already seen how the prophets, when they wished to say something in a way that people could not fail to see and to understand, made use of symbolic actions. We have already seen Jesus using that method both in His Triumphal Entry and in the incident of the fig tree. That is what Jesus is doing here. All the symbolism and all the ritual action of the Passover Feast was a picture of what He wished to say to men, for it was a picture of what He had done for men. What then was the picture which Jesus was using, and what is the truth which lies behind it?

(i) The whole Passover Feast was a *commemoration of deliverance*; its whole intention was to remind the people of Israel of how God had liberated them from slavery in Egypt. First and foremost then, Jesus claimed to be *the great liberator*. He came to liberate men from fear and from sin. Jesus Christ liberates men from the fears which haunt them, and from the sins which will not let them go.

(ii) In particular the Passover Lamb was *the symbol of safety*. On that night of destruction it was the blood of the Passover Lamb which kept Israel safe. So, then, *Jesus was claiming to be Saviour*. He had come to save men from their sins and from the consequences of their sins. He had come to give men safety on earth and safety in heaven, safety in time and safety in eternity.

Now there is one word here which is a key word, a word in which the whole of Jesus' work and intention is enshrined. It is the word *covenant*. Jesus spoke of His blood being the blood of the covenant. What did He mean by that? A covenant is a relationship between two people; when two people enter into a covenant, they enter into a relationship with each other. But the covenant of which Jesus spoke was not a covenant between man and man; it was a covenant between God and man. That is to say, it was a new relationship between God and man. What Jesus was saying at the Last Supper was this: "Because of my life, and above all because of my death, a new relationship has become possible between you and God." It is as if He said, "You have seen me; and in me you have seen God; I have told you, I have shown you, how much God loves you; He loves you even enough to suffer this that I am going through; that is what God is like." Because of what Jesus did for men, the way for men is open to all the loveliness of this new relationship with God.

This passage concludes by saying that when the company of Jesus and the disciples had sung a hymn, they went out to the Mount of Olives. An essential part of the Passover ritual was the singing of the *Hallel*. *Hallel* means *Praise God!* And the *Hallel* consisted of Psalms 113-118, which are all praising psalms. At different points of the Passover Feast these psalms were sung in sections; and at the very end of the Passover Feast there was sung *The Great Hallel*, which is Psalm 136. So, then, that psalm was the hymn they sang before they went out to the Mount of Olives.

There remains another thing to note. There was one basic difference between the Last Supper and the Sacrament which we observe. The Last Supper was a real meal; it was, in fact, the law that the whole lamb and everything else must be eaten and that nothing must be left. This was no eating of a cube of bread and drinking of a sip of wine. It was a meal for hungry men. We might well say that what Jesus is teaching men is not only to assemble in church and to eat a ritual and symbolic Feast; He is telling them that every time they sit down to satisfy their hunger and to eat a meal, that meal is in memory of Him. For Jesus is not only Lord of the Communion Table; He must be Lord of the dinner table too.

There remains one final thing to note. This passage concludes with Jesus' last words at the Last Supper; and in them He says that He will not feast with them again until He does so in His Father's Kingdom. Here, indeed, is divine faith and divine optimism. Jesus was going out to Gethsemane, out to trial before the Sanhedrin, out to the Cross—and yet *He is still thinking in terms of a Kingdom.* To Jesus the Cross was never defeat; it was the way to glory. Jesus was on His way to Calvary, but He was also on His way to the throne of the Kingdom of God.

THE COLLAPSE OF PETER

As we gathered together the passages which had to do with Judas in the last days, so we now gather together the passages which tell the story of Peter.

THE MASTER'S WARNING

Matthew 26: 31-35

> Then Jesus said to them, " Every one of you will be made to stumble because of me during this night; for it stands written, ' I will smite the shepherd, and the sheep of the flock shall be scattered abroad.' But after I have been raised, I will go before you into Galilee." Peter answered Him, " If all are made to stumble because of you, I will never be made to stumble." Jesus said to him, " This is the truth I tell you—during this night, before the cock crows, you will deny me three times." Peter said to Him, " Even if I have to die with you, I will not deny you." So also spoke all the disciples.

In this passage certain characteristics of Jesus are clear.

(i) Here we see the *realism* of Jesus. Jesus knew what lay ahead. Matthew actually sees the flight of the disciples foretold in the Old Testament in *Zechariah* 13: 7. Jesus was no easy optimist, who could comfortably shut his eyes to the facts. He foresaw what would inevitably happen, and yet He went on.

(ii) Here also we see the *confidence* of Jesus. " After I have been raised," He says, " I will go before you into Galilee." Always Jesus saw beyond the Cross. He was every bit as certain of the glory as He was of the suffering.

(iii) Here we see the *sympathy* of Jesus. He knew that His men were going to flee for their lives and abandon Him in the moment of His deepest need; but He does not upbraid them, and He does not condemn them, and He does not heap reproaches on them, or call them useless creatures and broken reeds. So far from that, He tells them that when that terrible time will be past, He will meet them again. It is the greatness of Jesus that He knew men at their worst and still loved them. He knows our human weakness; He knows how certain we are to make mistakes and to fail in loyalty; but that knowledge does not turn His love to bitterness or contempt. Jesus has nothing but sympathy for the man who in his weakness is driven to sin.

But, further, this passage shows us something about Peter. Surely Peter's fault is clear; Peter's fault was *over-confidence in himself*. He knew that he loved Jesus—that was never in doubt—and he thought that all by himself he could face any situation which might arise. Peter thought that he was stronger than Jesus knew him to be. We shall only be safe when we replace the confidence which boasts by the humility which knows its weakness and which depends not on itself, but seeks the help of Christ.

The Romans and the Jews divided the night into four watches—6 p.m. to 9 p.m.; 9 p.m. to midnight; midnight to 3 a.m.; 3 a.m. to 6 a.m. It was between the third and the fourth watch that the cock was supposed to crow. What Jesus is saying to Peter is that before the dawn comes Peter will deny Him three times.

THE FAILURE OF COURAGE
Matthew 26: 57, 58, 69-75

Those who had laid hold of Jesus led Him away to the house of Caiaphas the High Priest, where the Scribes and the elders were assembled. Peter followed Him at a distance, right into the courtyard of the High Priest's house, and he went inside and sat down with the servants to see the end.

. . . .

Peter was sitting outside in the courtyard. A maid-servant came up to him and said, " You, too, were with Jesus the Galilaean." He denied it in the presence

of them all. " I do not know," he said, " what you are
saying." When he went out to the porch, another
maid-servant saw him, and said to those who were
there, " This man too was with Jesus of Nazareth."
And again he denied it with an oath: " I do not
know the man." A little later those who were standing
there said to Peter, " Truly you too were one of them;
for your accent gives you away." Then he began to
curse and to swear: " I do not know the man."
And immediately the cock crew. And Peter remembered the saying of Jesus, when He said, " Before
the cock crows, you will deny me three times." And
he went out and wept bitterly.

No one can read this passage without being struck with the
staggering honesty of the New Testament. If ever there
was an incident which one might have expected to be
hushed up, this was it—and yet here it is told in all its
stark shame. We know that Matthew very closely followed
the narrative of Mark; and in Mark's gospel this story is
told in even more vivid detail (*Mark* 14: 66-72). We also
know, as Papias tells us, that Mark's gospel is nothing
other than the preaching material of Peter written down.
And so we arrive at the amazing fact that we possess the
story of Peter's denial because Peter himself was the man
who told it to others. So far from suppressing this story,
Peter made it an essential part of his gospel. And Peter
did so for the very best of reasons; every time he told
the story, Peter could say, " That is the way that this
Jesus can forgive. He forgave me when I failed Him in
His bitterest hour of need. That is what Jesus can do.
He took me, Peter the coward, and used even me." We
must never read this story without remembering that it
is Peter himself who is telling of the shame of his own sin
that all men may know the glory of the forgiving love and
cleansing power of Jesus Christ.

And yet it is quite wrong to regard Peter with nothing
but unsympathetic condemnation. The great blazing
fact is that the disaster which happened to Peter is a
disaster which could only have happened to a man of the

most heroic courage. All the other disciples ran away:
Peter alone did not. In Palestine the houses of the well-to-do
were built in a hollow square around an open courtyard,
off which the various rooms opened. For Peter to enter
that courtyard in the centre of the High Priest's house
was to walk into the lions' den—and yet Peter did it.
However this story ends, it begins with the story of Peter
the one brave man.

The first denial happened in the courtyard; no doubt
the maid-servant had marked Peter as one of the most
prominent followers of Jesus and had recognized him.
Now after that recognition anyone would have thought
that Peter would have fled for his life; a coward would
certainly have been gone into the night as quickly as he
could go. But not Peter; he did retire as far as the porch.
Peter was torn between two feelings. In his heart there
was a fear that made him want to run away; but in his
heart there was a love which kept him there. Again,
in the porch he was recognized; and this time he swore
he did not know Jesus. And still Peter did not go. Here
there is the most dogged courage. But Peter's second
denial had given him away. From his speech it was clear
that he was a Galilaean. The Galilaeans spoke with a burr;
so ugly an accent had the Galilaeans that no Galilaean
was allowed to pronounce the benediction at a synagogue
service. And, once again, he was accused of being a follower
of the Galilaean. Peter went further this time; not only
did he swear that he did not know Jesus; he actually
cursed his Master's name. But still it is clear that Peter
had no intention of leaving that courtyard. And then the
cock crew. There is a distinct possibility here, which
provides us with a vivid picture. It may well be that the
cock-crow was not the voice of a bird; and that from the
beginning it was not meant to mean that. After all the
house of the High Priest was right in the centre of Jerusalem,
and there would not likely be poultry in the centre of
the city. There is, in fact, a regulation in the Jewish law

that it was illegal to keep cocks and hens in the Holy
City, because they defiled the holy things. But it was
the hour of 3 a.m. which was called cock-crow, and for
this reason. It was at that hour that the Roman guard was
changed in the Castle of Antonia; and the sign of the
changing of the guard was a *trumpet call*. The Latin for
that trumpet call was *gallicinium*, which means *cock-crow*.
It is at least possible that just as Peter made his third
denial the voice of the trumpet from the castle battlements
rang out over the sleeping city—the *gallicinium*, the cock-
crow—and Peter remembered; and thereupon he went
out and wept his heart out.

What happened to Peter after that we do not know,
for the gospel story draws a kindly veil over the agony
of his shame. But before we condemn Peter, we must
remember very clearly that there are few of us who would
ever have had the courage to be in that courtyard at all.
And there is one last thing to be said—it was love which
gave Peter that courage; it was love which riveted him
there in spite of the fact that he had been recognized
three times; it was love which made him remember the
words of Jesus; it was love which sent him out into the
night to weep his heart out—and it is love which covers a
multitude of sins. The basic and lasting impression of this
whole story is not that of Peter's cowardice, but that of
Peter's love.

THE SOUL'S BATTLE IN THE GARDEN

Matthew 26: 36-46

> Then Jesus went with them to a place called Gethse-
> mane, and He said to His disciples, " Sit here, while I go
> away and pray in this place." So He took Peter and
> the two sons of Zebedee, and began to be distressed and
> in sore trouble. Then He said to them, " My soul is
> much distressed with a distress like death. Stay here,
> and watch with me." He went a little way forward and

fell on His face in prayer. " My Father," He said, " if it is possible, let this cup pass from me. But let it be not as I will, but as you will." He came to His disciples, and He found them sleeping, and He said to Peter, " Could you not stay awake with me for this for one hour? Watch and pray lest you enter into testing. The spirit is eager, but the flesh is weak." He went away a second time and prayed. " My Father," He said, " if it is not possible for this to pass from me unless I drink it, your will be done." He came again and found them sleeping, for their eyes were weighted down. He left them, and went away again, and prayed the third time, saying the same words over again. Then He came to His disciples and said to them, " Sleep on now and take your rest. Look you, the hour is near, and the Son of Man is being delivered into the hands of sinners. Rise; let us go; look you, he who betrays me is near."

SURELY this is a passage which we must approach upon our knees. In a passage like this surely the demand is that study should pass into wondering adoration.

In Jerusalem itself there were no gardens of any size, for a city that is set on the top of an hill has no room for open spaces, and every inch is of value for building. So, then, it came about that wealthy citizens had their private gardens out on the slopes of the Mount of Olives. The word *Gethsemane* very probably means an *olive-vat*, or an *olive-press*; and no doubt it was a garden of olives to which Jesus had the right of entry. It is a strange and a lovely thing to think of the nameless friends who rallied round Jesus in the last days. There was the man who gave Him the ass on which He rode into Jerusalem; there was the man who gave Him the Upper Room wherein the Last Supper was eaten; and now there is the man who gave Him the right of entry o the garden on the slopes of the Mount of Olives. In a desert of hatred, there were still oases of love.

Into the garden He took the three who had been with Him on the Mount of Transfiguration; and there He prayed; nay more, there He wrestled in prayer. As we look with awed reverence on the battle of Jesus' soul in the garden we see certain things.

(i) We see the *agony* of Jesus. He was now quite sure that death lay ahead. Its very breath was on Him. No one wants to die at thirty-three; and least of all does any man want to die in the agony of a cross. Here Jesus had His supreme struggle to submit His will to the will of God. No one can read this story without seeing the intense reality of that struggle. This is no play-acting; this was a struggle in which the outcome swayed in the balance. The salvation of the world hung in the balance in the Garden of Gethsemane, for even then Jesus might have turnea back, and God's purpose would have been frustrated. At this moment all that Jesus knew was that He must go on, and ahead there lay a cross. In all reverence we may say that here we see Jesus learning the lesson that everyone must some day learn—learning how to accept what He could not understand. All He knew was that the will of God imperiously summoned Him on. Things happen to every one of us in this world that we cannot understand; it is then that faith is tried to its utmost limits; and at such a time it is sweetness to the soul that in Gethsemane Jesus went through that too. Tertullian (*De Bapt.* 20) tells us of a saying of Jesus, which was handed down, although it is not in any of the gospels: " No one who has not been tempted can enter the Kingdom of Heaven." That is to say, every man has his private Gethsemane, and every man has to learn to say, " Thy will be done."

(ii) We see the *loneliness* of Jesus. He took with Him His three chosen disciples; but they were so exhausted with the drama of these last days and hours that they could not stay awake. And Jesus had to fight His battle all alone. That also is true of every man. There are certain things a man must face, and certain decisions a man must make in the awful loneliness of his own soul; there are times when other helpers fail and comforts flee; but in that loneliness there is for us the presence of One who, in Gethsemane, experienced it and came through it.

(iii) Here we see the *trust* of Jesus. We see that trust even better in Mark's account. As Mark has it, Jesus began His prayer: " *Abba*, Father " (Mark 14: 36). There is a world of loveliness in this word *Abba*, which to our western ears is altogether hidden, unless we know the facts about it. Joachim Jeremias, in his book *The Parables of Jesus*, writes thus about this word *Abba*: " Jesus' use of the word *Abba* in addressing God is unparalleled in the whole of Jewish literature. The explanation of this fact is to be found in the statement of the fathers Chrysostom, Theodore, and Theodoret that *Abba* (as *jaba* is still used today in Arabic) was the word used by a young child to its father; it was an everyday family word, which no one had ventured to use in addressing God. Jesus did. He spoke to his heavenly Father in as childlike, trustful, and intimate a way as a little child to its father." We know how our children speak to us, and what they call us who are fathers. That is the way in which Jesus spoke to God. Even when He did not fully understand, even when His one conviction was that God was urging Him to a cross, He called *Abba*, as a little child might speak. Here indeed is trust, a trust which we must also have in that God whom Jesus taught us to know as Father, as He knew Him Himself.

(iv) Finally, here we see the *courage* of Jesus. " Rise," said Jesus, " let us be going. He who betrays me is near." Celsus, the pagan philosopher who attacked Christianity, used that sentence as an argument that Jesus tried to run away. It is the very opposite. " Rise," He said. " The time for prayer, and the time for the garden is past. Now is the time for action. Let us face life at its grimmest and men at their worst." Jesus rose from His knees to go out to the battle of life. That is what prayer is for. In prayer a man kneels before God that he may stand erect in face of men. In prayer a man enters heaven that he may face the battles of earth.

THE ARREST IN THE GARDEN

Matthew 26: 50-56

> Then they came forward and laid hands on Jesus and
> held Him. And, look you, one of these who was with
> Jesus stretched out his hand, and drew his sword,
> and struck the servant of the High Priest, and cut
> off his ear. Then Jesus said to him, " Put back your
> sword in its place; for all who take the sword shall
> perish by the sword. Or, do you not think that I
> am able to call on my Father, and He will on the
> spot send to my aid more than twelve regiments of
> angels? How then are the Scriptures to be fulfilled
> that it must happen so? " At that hour Jesus said
> to the crowds, " Have you come out with swords
> and cudgels to arrest me, as against a brigand? Daily
> I sat teaching in the Temple, and you did not lay
> hold on me. All this has happened that the writings
> of the prophets might be fulfilled." Then all His
> disciples forsook Him and fled.

IT was Judas who had given the authorities the information
which enabled them to find Jesus in the privacy of the
Garden of Gethsemane. The forces at the disposal of the
Jewish authorities were the Temple police, under the
command of the Sagan, or Captain of the Temple. But
the mob which surged after Judas to the Garden was more
like a mob for a lynching than a detachment for an orderly
arrest.

Jesus would allow no resistance. Matthew simply tells
us that one of the disciples drew a knife and prepared to
resist to the death and to sell his life dearly, and wounded
a servant of the High Priest. When John tells the same
story (*John* 18: 10), he tells us that the disciple was Peter,
and the servant was Malchus. The reason why John names
Peter and Matthew does not may very simply be that
John was writing much later, and that when Matthew was
writing it was still not safe to name the disciple who had
sprung so quickly to his Master's defence. Here we have
still another instance of the almost fantastic courage of

387

Peter. He was willing to take on the mob alone; and let us always remember that it was after that, when he was a marked man, that Peter followed Jesus right into the courtyard of the High Priest's house. But in all these incidents of the last hours it is on Jesus that our attention is fastened; and here we learn two things of Jesus.

(i) Jesus' death was *by His own choice*. He need never have come to Jerusalem for the last Passover Feast. Having come, He need never have followed His deliberate policy of magnificent defiance. Even in the Garden He could have slipped away, and saved Himself, for it was night, and there were many who would have smuggled Him out of the city. Even here He could have called down the might of God, and blasted His enemies. Every step of these last days makes it clearer and clearer that Jesus laid down His life, and that His life was not taken from Him. Jesus died, not because men killed Him, but because He chose to die.

(ii) Jesus chose to die because He knew that His death was *the purpose of God*. He took this way because this was the very thing that had been foretold by the prophets. He took it because love is the only way. " He who takes the sword will perish by the sword." Violence can beget nothing but violence; one drawn sword can produce only another drawn sword to meet it. Jesus knew that power and war and force and might settle nothing, that they only produce a train of evil, and beget a grim horde of children worse than themselves. He knew that God's purpose can only be worked out by sacrificial love. And history proved Him right; for these Jews who took Him with violence, and who gloried in violence, and who would gladly have dipped their swords in Roman blood, saw forty years later their city destroyed for ever, while the man who would not fight is enthroned fo ever in the hearts of men.

THE TRIAL BEFORE THE JEWS

Matthew 26: 57, 59-68

Those who had laid hold of Jesus led Him away to the house of Caiaphas the High Priest, where the Scribes and the elders were assembled.

. . . .

The chief priests and the whole Sanhedrin tried to find false witness against Him, in order to put Him to death; but they could not find it, although many false witnesses came forward. Later two came forward and said, " This fellow said, ' I can destroy the Temple of God, and in three days I can build it again.' " The High Priest rose and said, " Do you make no answer? What is it that these witness against you? " But Jesus kept silent. So the High Priest said to Him, " I adjure you by the living God, that you tell us, whether you are the Anointed One of God, the Son of God." Jesus said to him, " It is you who have said it. But I tell you that from now on you will see the Son of Man seated on the right hand of the Power and coming on the clouds of Heaven." Then the High Priest rent his garments, saying, " He has blasphemed. What further need have we of witnesses? Look you, you have now heard His blasphemy. What is your opinion? " They answered, " He has made Himself liable to the death penalty." Then they spat upon His face, and buffeted Him. And some struck Him on the cheek saying, " Prophesy to us, you Anointed One of God! Who is he who struck you? "

THE process of the trial of Jesus is not altogether easy to follow. It seems to have fallen into three parts. First, there is the part which took place after the arrest in the Garden, during the night, and in the High Priest's house, the part which is described in this section. Second, there is the part which took place first thing in the morning, and which is briefly described in *Matthew* 27: 1, 2. Third, there is the part which took place before Pilate and which is described in *Matthew* 28: 3-26. The salient question is this—was the meeting during the night an official meeting of the Sanhedrin, hastily summoned, or was it merely a preliminary examination, in order to formulate a charge, and was the meeting in the morning the official meeting of the Sanhedrin? However that question is answered, the Jews completely violated their own laws in the trial of Jesus; but if the meeting in the night was a meeting of the Sanhedrin, the violation was even more extreme. On the whole it seems that Matthew took the night meeting to be a meeting of the Sanhedrin, for in verse 59 he says that the whole Sanhedrin sought for false witness to put Jesus to death. Let us then first look at this process from the Jewish legal point of view.

The Sanhedrin was the supreme court of the Jews. It was composed of Scribes, Pharisees, Sadducees and elders of the people; it numbered seventy-one members; and it was presided over by the High Priest. For a trial such as this a quorum was twenty-three. It had certain regulations. All criminal cases must be tried during the daytime and must be completed during the daytime. Criminal cases could not be transacted during the Passover season at all. Only if the verdict was Not Guilty could a case be finished on the day it was begun; otherwise a night must elapse before the pronouncement of the verdict, so that feelings of mercy might have time to arise. Further, no decision of the Sanhedrin was valid unless it met in its own meeting place, the Hall of Hewn Stone in the Temple precincts. In regard to witnesses, all evidence had to be guaranteed by two witnesses separately examined, and having no contact with each other. And false witness was punishable by death. The seriousness of the occasion was impressed upon any witness in a case where life was at stake: " Forget not, O witness, that it is one thing to give evidence in a trial for money, and another in a trial for life. In a money suit, if thy witness-bearing shall do wrong, money may repair that wrong; but in this trial for life, if thou sinnest, the blood of the accused and the blood of his seed unto the end of time shall be imputed unto thee." Still further, in any trial the process began by the laying before the court of all the evidence for the *innocence* of the accused, before the evidence for his guilt was adduced.

These were the Sanhedrin's own rules, and it is abundantly clear that, in their eagerness to get rid of Jesus, the Sanhedrin broke their own rules. The Jews had reached such a peak of hatred that any means were justified to put an end to Jesus.

THE CRIME OF CHRIST

Matthew 26: 57, 59-68 (*continued*)

THE main business of the night meeting of the Jewish authorities was to formulate a charge against Jesus. As we have seen, all evidence had to be guaranteed by two witnesses, separately examined. For long not even two false witnesses could be found to agree. And then a charge was found, the charge that Jesus had said that He would destroy the Temple and that He would rebuild it in three days. It is clear that this charge is a twisting of certain things which Jesus did actually say. We have already seen that He did foretell—and rightly foretell—the destruction of the Temple; and this had been twisted into a charge that He had said that He Himself would destroy the Temple. We have seen that He did foretell that He Himself would be killed and would rise on the third day; and this had been twisted into a charge that He had said that He would rebuilt the Temple in three days. This charge was formulated by deliberately and maliciously misrepeating and misinterpreting certain things which Jesus had said. To that charge Jesus utterly refused to reply. Therein the law was on His side, for no person on trial could either be asked, or compelled to answer, any question which would incriminate him.

It was then that the High Priest launched his vital question. We have seen that repeatedly Jesus warned and enjoined and commanded His disciples to tell no man that He was the Messiah. How then did the High Priest know to ask the question, the answer to which Jesus could not escape? It may well be that when Judas laid information against Jesus, he had also told the Jewish authorities about Jesus' revelation of His own Messiahship. It may well be that Judas had deliberately broken the bond of secrecy which Jesus had laid upon His disciples.

In any event, the High Priest asked the question, and asked it upon oath: " Are you the Messiah? " he demanded. " Do you claim to be the Son of God? " Here was the crucial moment in the trial of Jesus. We might well say that all the universe held its breath as it waited for Jesus' answer. If Jesus said, " No," then the bottom fell out of the trial; there was no possible charge against Him. He had only to say, " No," and to walk out a free man, and to escape before the Sanhedrin could think out another way of entrapping Him. On the other hand, if He said, " Yes," then He signed His own death warrant. Nothing more than a simple " Yes " was needed to make the Cross a complete and inescapable certainty. It may be that Jesus paused for a moment once again to count the cost before He made the great decision; and then He said, " Yes." He went further. He quoted *Daniel* 7: 13 with its vivid account of the ultimate triumph and kingship of God's chosen one. He well knew what He was doing. Immediately there went up the cry of blasphemy. Garments were rent in a kind of synthetic and hysterical horror; and Jesus was condemned to death.

Then there followed the spitting on Him, the buffeting Him, the slapping of His face, the mockery of Him. Even the externals of justice were forgotten, and the venomous hatred of the Jewish authorities broke through. That meeting in the night began as a court of justice and ended in a frenzied display of hatred, in which there was no attempt to maintain even the superficialities of impartial justice.

To this day the fact remains that when a man is brought
face to face with Jesus Christ, he must either hate Him
or love Him; he must either submit to Him, or desire to
destroy Him. No man who realizes what Jesus Christ
demands can possibly be neutral. He must either be His
lover or His foe.

THE MAN WHO SENTENCED JESUS TO DEATH

Matthew 27: 1, 2, 11-26

When the morning came, all the chief priests and
elders of the people took counsel against Jesus, to
put Him to death; so they bound Him, and led
Him away, and handed Him over to Pilate the
governor.

. . . .

Jesus stood before the governor, and the governor
put the question to Him, " Are you the King of the
Jews? " Jesus said to Him, " You say so." While
He was being accused by the chief priests and the
elders, He returned no answer. Then Pilate said to
Him, " Do you not hear the evidence which they are
stating against you? " Jesus answered not a single
word, so that the governor was much amazed. At
the time of the Feast the governor was in the habit
of releasing one prisoner to the crowd, a prisoner
whom they wished. At that time he was holding a
very well-known prisoner called Barabbas. So, when
they were assembled, Pilate said to them, " Whom do
you wish me to release to you? Barabbas? Or, Jesus
who is called Christ? " For he was well aware that
they had delivered Jesus to him because of malice.
While he was sitting on his judgment seat, his wife
sent a message to him. " Have nothing to do with
this just man," she said, " for today I have had an
extraordinary experience in a dream because of Him."
The chief priests and the elders persuaded the crowds
to ask for the release of Barabbas, and the destruction
of Jesus. " Which of the two," said the governor,
" am I to release to you? " " Barabbas," they said.
" What then," said Pilate to them, " am I to do with
Jesus who is called Christ." " Let Him be crucified,"

they all said. " What evil has He done? " he said. They kept shouting all the more: " Let Him be crucified." When Pilate saw that it was hopeless to do anything, and that rather a disturbance was liable to arise, he took water, and washed his hands in presence of the crowd. " I am innocent of the blood of this just man," he said. " You must see to it." All the people answered, " Let the responsibility for His blood be on us and on our children." Then he released Barabbas to them; but he had Jesus scourged, and handed Him over to be crucified.

THE first two verses of this passage describe what must have been a very brief meeting of the Sanhedrin, held early in the morning, with a view to formulating finally an official charge against Jesus. The necessity for this lay in the fact that, while the Jews could themselves deal with an ordinary charge, they could not inflict the death penalty. That was a sentence which could only be pronounced by the Roman governor, and carried out by the Roman authorities. The Sanhedrin had therefore to formulate a charge with which they could go to Pilate and demand the death of Jesus. Matthew does not tell us what that charge was; but Luke does. In the Sanhedrin the charge which was levelled against Jesus was a charge of blasphemy (*Matthew* 26: 65, 66). But no one knew better than the Jewish authorities that that was a charge to which Pilate would not listen. He would tell them to go away and settle their own religious quarrels. So, as Luke tells us, they appeared before Pilate with a threefold charge, every item in which was a lie, and a deliberate lie. They charged Jesus with, first, being a revolutionary, second, with inciting the people not to pay their taxes, and third, with claiming to be a king (*Luke* 23: 2). They fabricated three *political* charges, all of them conscious lies, because they knew that only on such charges would Pilate act. So, then, everything hung on the attitude of Pilate. What kind of man was this Roman governor?

Pilate was officially *procurator* of the province; and he was directly responsible, not to the Roman senate, but to the Roman Emperor. He must have been at least twenty-seven years of age. for that was the minimum age for entering on the office of procurator. He must have been a man of considerable experience, for there was a ladder of offices, including military command, up which a man must climb until he became qualified to become a governor. Pilate must have been a tried and tested soldier and administrator. He became procurator of Judaea in A.D. 26 and held office for ten years, until he was recalled from his post.

When Pilate came to Judaea, he found trouble in plenty, and much of it was of his own making. Pilate's trouble was that he was completely out of sympathy with the Jews. More, he was contemptuous of what he would have called their irrational and fanatical prejudices, and what they would have called their principles. The Romans knew the intensity of Jewish religion, and the unbreakable character of Jewish belief, and they very wisely had always dealt with the Jews with kid gloves. Pilate arrogantly proposed to use the mailed fist.

He began with trouble. The Roman headquarters were in Caesarea. The Roman standards were not flags; they were poles with the Roman eagle, or the image of the reigning emperor, on the top of them. In deference to the Jewish hatred of graven images, every previous governor had removed the eagles and the images from the standards before he marched into Jerusalem on his state visits. Pilate refused to do so. The result was such bitter opposition and such intransigeance that Pilate in the end was forced to yield, for it is not possible either to arrest or to slaughter a whole nation. Further, Pilate wisely decided that Jerusalem needed a better water supply. To that end he constructed a new aqueduct—but he took money from the Temple treasury to pay for it. Pilate had built up an evil reputation among the Jews.

Philo, the great Jewish Alexandrian scholar, has in fact a character study of Pilate—and remember that Philo was not a Christian, but was speaking from the Jewish point of view. The Jews, Philo tells us, had threatened to exercise their right to report Pilate to the Emperor for his misdeeds. This threat " exasperated Pilate to the greatest possible degree, as he feared lest they might go on an embassy to the emperor, and might impeach him with respect to other particulars of his government— his corruption, his acts of insolence, his rapine, his habit of insulting people, his cruelty, his continual murders of people untried and uncondemned, and his never-ending gratuitous and most grievous inhumanity." Pilate's reputation with the Jews stank; and the fact that they could report him made his position entirely insecure.

We may follow the career of Pilate to the end. In the end he was recalled to Rome. His recall was due to his savagery in a certain incident in Samaria. A certain impostor had summoned the people to Mount Gerizim with the claim that he would show them the sacred vessels which Moses had hidden there. Unfortunately many of the crowd came armed, and assembled in a village called Tirabatha. Pilate fell on them and slaughtered them with quite unnecessary savagery, for it was a harmless enough movement. The Samaritans lodged a complaint with Vitellius, the legate of Syria, who was Pilate's immediate superior, and Vitellius ordered him to return to Rome to answer for his conduct.

When Pilate was on his way to Rome, Tiberius the Emperor died; and it appears that Pilate never came to trial. Legend has it that Pilate in the end committed suicide; his body was flung into the Tiber, but the evil spirits so troubled the river that the Romans took the body to Gaul and threw it into the Rhone. Pilate's so-called tomb is still shown in Vienne. The same thing happened there; and the body was finally taken to a place near Lausanne and buried in a pit in the mountains. Opposite Lucerne there is a hill called Mount Pilatus. Originally the mountain was called *Pileatus*, which means *wearing*

THE GOSPEL OF MATTHEW

a cap of clouds, but because it was connected with Pilate the name was changed to *Pilatus*.

Later Christian legend was very sympathetic to Pilate, and tended to place all the blame for the death of Jesus on the Jews, and to exonerate Pilate completely. Not unnaturally, legend came to say that Pilate's wife, who it is said was a Jewish proselyte, and was called Claudia Procula, became a Christian. It was even held that Pilate himself became a Christian; and to this day the Coptic Church ranks both Pilate and his wife as saints.

We may conclude this study of Pilate with one very interesting document. It is certain that Pilate must have sent a report of the trial and death of Jesus to Rome; that would happen in the normal course of administration. An apocryphal book called *The Acts of Peter and Paul* contains an alleged copy of that report. This report is actually referred to by Tertullian and Justin Martyr and Eusebius. The report as we have it can hardly be genuine, but it is interesting to read it:

> *Pontius Pilate unto Claudius greeting.*
>
> There befell of late a matter of which I myself made trial; for the Jews through envy have punished themselves and their posterity with fearful judgments of their own fault; for whereas their fathers had promises that their God would send them out of heaven his Holy One, who should of right be called king, and did promise he would send him on earth by a virgin; he then came when I was governor of Judaea, and they beheld him enlightening the blind, cleansing lepers, healing the palsied, driving devils out of men, raising the dead, rebuking the winds, walking on the waves of the sea dry-shod, and doing many other wonders, and all the people of the Jews calling him the Son of God; the chief priests therefore moved with envy against him, took him and delivered him unto me and brought against him one false accusation after another, saying that he was a sorcerer and that he did things contrary to the law.
>
> But I, believing that these things were so, having scourged him, delivered him to their will; and they

crucified him, and, when he was buried, they set
their guards upon him. But while my soldiers watched
him, he rose again on the third day; yet so much
was the malice of the Jews kindled, that they gave
money to the soldiers saying: Say ye that his disciples
stole away his body. But they, though they took
the money, were not able to keep silence concerning
that which had come to pass, for they also have
testified that they saw him arisen, and that they
received money from the Jews. And these things
have I reported unto thy mightiness for this cause,
lest some other should lie unto thee, and thou shouldest
deem right to believe the false tales of the Jews.

No doubt that report is mere legend, but one thing is
certain, Pilate knew that Jesus was innocent, but his past
misdeeds gave the Jews a lever to compel him to do their
will against his better judgment and his sense of justice.

PILATE'S LOSING STRUGGLE

Matthew 27: 1, 2, 11-26 (*continued*)

THIS whole passage gives us the impression of a man
fighting a losing battle. It is clear that Pilate did not wish
to condemn Jesus. Certain things emerge.

(i) Pilate was clearly impressed with Jesus. It is clear
that he did not take the claim to be the King of the Jews
seriously. Pilate knew a revolutionary when he saw one,
and Jesus was no revolutionary. The dignified silence of
Jesus made Pilate feel that it was not Jesus but he himself
who was on trial. Pilate was a man who felt the power of
Jesus—and who was afraid to submit to it. There are
still those who are afraid to be as Christian as they know
they ought to be.

(ii) Pilate sought some way of escape. It appears to
have been the custom at the time of the Feast for a prisoner
to be released. In gaol there was a certain Barabbas.
Barabbas was no sneak thief; he was most probably
either a brigand or a political revolutionary. There are

two interesting speculations about him. His name *Barabbas* means *Son of the Father*; *father* was a title by which the greatest Rabbis were known; it may well be that Barabbas was the son of an ancient and a distinguished family who had kicked over the traces and had embarked on a career of magnificent crime. Such a man would make crime glamorous and would appeal to the people. Still more interesting is the near certainty that Barabbas was also called Jesus. Some of the very oldest versions of the New Testament, for example the ancient Syriac and Armenian versions, call him *Jesus Barabbas*; and both Origen and Jerome knew of that reading, and felt it might be correct. It is a curious thing that twice Pilate refers to *Jesus who is called Christ* (verses 17 and 22), as if to distinguish Him from some other Jesus. Jesus was a common name; it is the same name as Joshua. And the dramatic shout of the crowd most likely was: " Not Jesus Christ, but Jesus Barabbas." Pilate sought an escape, but the crowd chose the violent criminal and rejected the gentle Christ. They preferred the man of violence to the man of love.

(iii) Pilate sought to unshoulder the responsibility for condemning Jesus. There is that strange and tragic picture of him washing his hands. That was a Jewish custom. There is a strange regulation in *Deuteronomy* 21: 1-9. If a dead body was found, and it was not known who the killer was, measurements were to be taken to find what was the nearest town or village. The elders of that town or village had to sacrifice a heifer and to wash their hands to rid them of the guilt. Pilate was warned by his sense of justice, he was warned by his conscience, he was warned by the dream of his troubled wife; but Pilate could not stand against the mob; and Pilate made the futile gesture of washing his hands. Legend has it that to this day there are times when Pilate's shade emerges from its tomb and goes through the action of the hand-washing once again. There is one thing of which a man can never rid himself—

and that is responsibility. It is never possible for Pilate or anyone else to say, " I wash my hands of all responsibility," for responsibility is something that no one and nothing can take away.

The picture of Pilate provokes in our minds pity rather than loathing; for here was a man so emmeshed in his past, and so rendered helpless by it, that he was unable to take the stand he ought to take. Pilate is a figure of tragedy rather than a figure of villainy.

THE SOLDIERS' MOCKERY

Matthew 27: 27-31

Then the governor's soldiers took Jesus to the military headquarters, and collected to Him the whole of the detachment. They stripped Him of His clothes and put a soldier's purple cloak upon Him; and they wove a crown of thorns and put it on His head, and they put a reed in His right hand; and they knelt in front of Him, and mocked Him by saying, " Hail! King of the Jews! " And they spat on Him, and took the reed and hit Him on His head. And when they had mocked Him, they took off the cloak, and clothed Him in His own clothes, and led Him away to crucify Him.

THE dreadful routine of crucifixion had now begun. The last section ended by telling us that Pilate had Jesus scourged. Roman scourging was a terrible torture. The victim was stripped; his hands were tied behind him, and he was tied to a post with his back bent double and conveniently exposed to the lash. The lash itself was a long leather thong, studded at intervals with sharpened pieces of bone and pellets of lead. Such scourging always preceded crucifixion and " it reduced the naked body to strips of raw flesh, and inflamed and bleeding weals." Men died under it, and men lost their reason under it, and few remained conscious to the end of it.

After that Jesus was handed over to the soldiers, while

the last details of crucifixion were arranged, and while the cross itself was prepared. They took him to their barracks in the governor's headquarters; and they called the rest of the detachment. The detachment is called a *speira*; in a full *speira* there were six hundred men. It is not likely that there were as many as that there in Jerusalem. These soldiers were Pilate's bodyguard who had accompanied him from Caesarea, where his permanent headquarters were.

We may shudder at what the soldiers did; but of all the parties involved in the crucifixion these soldiers were least to be blamed. They were not even stationed in Jerusalem; they had no idea who Jesus was; they certainly were not Jews, for the Jews were the only nation in the Roman Empire who were exempt from military service. These soldiers were conscripts who may well have come from the ends of the earth, and they indulged in their rough horse-play; but, unlike the Jews, and unlike Pilate, they did it in ignorance. Maybe for Jesus of all things this was the easiest to bear, for, although they made a sham king of Him, there was no hatred in their eyes. To them He was nothing more than a deluded Galilaean going to a cross. It is not without significance that Philo tells us that in Alexandria a Jewish mob did exactly the same to an imbecile boy: " They spread a strip of linen and placed it on his head instead of a diadem . . . and for a sceptre they handed up to him a small piece of native papyrus bulrush which they found thrown on the roadside. And because he was adorned as a king . . . some came up as though to greet him, others as though to plead a cause." So they mocked a half-idiot lad; and that is what the soldiers took Jesus to be.

Then they prepared to lead Him away to crucifixion. We are sometimes told that we should not dwell on the physical aspect of the Cross; but that is not so; we cannot possibly have too vivid a picture of what Jesus did and suffered for us. Klausner, the Jewish writer, writing of crucifixion says, " Crucifixion is the most terrible and cruel death which man has ever devised for taking vengeance on his fellow-men." Cicero called it " the most cruel and the most horrible torture." Tacitus called it " a torture only fit for slaves." It originated in Persia; and its origin came from the fact that the earth was considered to be sacred to Ormuzd the god, and the criminal was lifted up from it that he might not defile the earth, which was the god's property. From Persia crucifixion passed to Carthage in North Africa; and it was from Carthage that Rome learned it, although the Romans kept it exclusively for rebels, runaway slaves, and the lowest type of criminal. It was indeed a punishment which it was illegal to inflict on a Roman citizen. Klausner goes on to describe crucifixion. The criminal was fastened to his cross, already a bleeding mass from the scourging. There he hung to die of hunger and thirst and exposure, unable even to defend himself from the torture of the gnats and flies which settled on his naked body and on his bleeding wounds. It is not a pretty picture—but that is what Jesus Christ suffered—willingly, for us.

THE CROSS AND THE SHAME

Matthew 27: 32-44

As they were going out, they found a Cyrenian man, Simon by name, and they impressed him into their service, to bear Jesus' Cross. When they had come to the place which is called Golgotha (which means the Place of a Skull), they offered Him wine mingled with gall to drink, and, when He had tasted it, He refused to drink it. When they had crucified Him, they divided His garments among them by casting lots for them; and as they sat there, they watched Him. Above His head they placed a written copy of the charge on which He was being executed: " This is Jesus, the King of the Jews." Then they crucified along with Him two brigands, one on the right hand and one on the left. Those who were passing by kept flinging their insults at Him. They kept shaking their heads and saying, " Destroyer of the Temple, and builder of it in three days, save yourself. If you are really the Son of God, come down from the Cross." In the same way the chief priests also with the Scribes and the elders jeered at Him, " He saved others," they kept saying, " He cannot save Himself. He is King of Israel. Let Him come down from the Cross now, and we will believe on Him. He trusted in God. Let Him rescue Him now, if He wants Him; for He said, ' I am the Son of God.' " The brigands too who were crucified with Him hurled the same reproaches at Him.

THE story of the Crucifixion does not need commentary; it has its power in the telling by itself. All that we can do is simply to paint in the background in order that the picture may be as clear as it can be made.

When a criminal had been condemned, he was led away to crucifixion. He was placed in the centre of a hollow square of four Roman soldiers. It was the custom that he should carry the cross beam of his own cross; the upright was already waiting at the scene of crucifixion. The charge on which he was being executed was written on a board; it was then either hung round his own neck, or carried by an officer in front of the procession; and it was later affixed to the cross itself. The criminal was led to the scene of crucifixion by as long a route as possible, so that as many as possible might see him, and take warning from the grim sight. Jesus had undergone the terrible scourging; after that he had undergone the mockery of the soldiers; before all that He had been under examination for most of the night; and Jesus was physically exhausted, and staggering under His Cross. The Roman soldiers well knew what to do under such circumstances. Palestine was an occupied country; all that a Roman officer had to do was to tap a Jew on the shoulder with the flat of his spear, and the man had to carry out any task, however menial and distasteful, that was laid upon him. Into the city, from one of the surrounding villages, there was coming a man from far off Cyrene in North Africa, called Simon. It may be that for years he had scraped and saved to attend this one Passover—and now this terrible indignity and shame fell upon him; for Simon was compelled to carry the Cross of Jesus. When Mark tells the story, he identifies Simon as "the father of Alexander and Rufus" (*Mark* 15: 21). Such an identification can only mean that Alexander and Rufus were well known in the Church. And it must be that on that terrible day Jesus laid hold on Simon's heart. That which to Simon had seemed his day of shame became his day of glory.

The place of crucifixion was a hill called Golgotha, so called because it was shaped like a skull. When the place was reached the criminal had to be impaled upon his cross. The nails had to be driven through his hands, but commonly the feet were only loosely bound to the cross. At that moment, in order to deaden the pain, the criminal was given a drink of drugged wine, prepared by a group of wealthy women of Jerusalem as an act of mercy. A Jewish writing says, "When a man is going out to be killed, they allow him to drink a grain of frankincense in a cup of wine to deaden his senses. . . . Wealthy women of Jerusalem used to contribute these things and bring them." The drugged cup was offered to Jesus, but He would not drink it, for He was determined to accept death at its bitterest and at its grimmest, and to avoid no particle of pain.

We have already seen that the criminal was led to execution in the middle of a square of four Roman soldiers, criminals were crucified naked, except for a loin cloth; and the criminal's clothes became the property of the soldiers as their perquisite. Every Jew wore five articles of clothing—his shoes, his turban, his girdle, his inner garment, and his outer cloak. There were thus five articles of clothing and four soldiers. The first four articles were all of equal value; but the outer cloak was more valuable than all the others. It was for Jesus' outer cloak that the soldiers drew lots, as John tells us (*John* 19: 23, 24). So when the soldiers had divided the clothes, they sat down on guard until the end should come. So there were there on Golgotha that group of three crosses, in the midst the Son of God, and on either side a brigand. Truly, He was with sinners in His death.

The final verses of this section describe the taunts and the mockery which were flung at Jesus by the passers-by, by the Jewish authorities, and by the brigands who were crucified with Him. The taunts all centred round one thing—the claims that Jesus had made and His apparent helplessness on the Cross. It was precisely there that the Jews were so wrong. They were using the glory of Christ as a means of mocking Him. " Come down," they said, " and we will believe on you." But as General Booth once said, " It is precisely because He would not come down that we believe in Him." The Jews could only see God in power; but Jesus showed men that God is sacrificial love.

THE TRIUMPH OF THE END

Matthew 27: 45-50

> From twelve o'clock midday darkness came over the earth until three o'clock in the afternoon. About three o'clock in the afternoon Jesus cried with a loud voice, " Eli, Eli, lama sabachthani? " (that is, " My God, my God, why have you forsaken me? ") Some of those who were standing there heard this, and said, " This man is calling for Elias." And immediately one of them ran and took a sponge and filled it with vinegar and put it on a reed, and gave Him to drink. The rest said, " Let be! Let us see if Elias will come to save Him." When Jesus had again shouted with a great voice, He gave up His spirit.

As we have been reading the story of the Crucifixion, everything seems to have been happening very quickly; but in reality the hours were slipping past. It is Mark who is most precise in his note of time. He tells us that

But now here is the point. It would have been a terrible thing, if Jesus had died with a cry like that upon His lips—but He did not. The narrative goes on to tell us that, when He shouted with a great shout, He gave up His spirit. That great shout left its mark upon men's minds. It is in every one of the gospels (*Matthew* 27: 50; *Mark* 15: 37; *Luke* 23: 46). But there is one gospel which goes further. John tells us that Jesus died with a shout: " It is finished " (*John* 19: 30). It is finished is in English three words; but in Greek it is one—*Tetelestai*—as it would also be in Aramaic. And *tetelestai* is the victor's shout; it is the cry of the man who has completed his task; it is the cry of the man who has won through the struggle; it is the cry of the man who has come out of the dark into the glory of the light, and who has grasped the crown. So, then, Jesus died a victor and a conqueror with a shout of triumph on His lips.

Here, then, there is the precious thing. Jesus passed through the uttermost abyss, and then the light broke. If we too cling to God, even when there seems to be no God, desperately and invincibly clutching the remnants of our faith, then quite certainly the dawn will break, and we will win through. The victor is the man who refuses to believe that God has forgotten him, even when every fibre of his being feels that God has forsaken him. The victor is the man who will never let go his faith, even when he feels that the last grounds of faith are gone. The victor is the man who has been beaten to the depths, and who still holds on to God, for that is what Jesus did.

THE BLAZING REVELATION

Matthew 27: 51-56

And, look you, the veil of the Temple was rent in two from top to bottom, and the earth was shaken, and the rocks were split, and the tombs were opened, and the bodies of many of God's dedicated ones were raised,

and they came out of the tombs after His resurrection and came into the holy city and appeared to many. The centurion and those who were watching Jesus with him saw the earthquake and the things that had happened, and they were exceedingly afraid. " Truly," they said, " this man was the Son of God."

Many women were there watching from a distance. They were the women who had followed Jesus from Galilee, giving their service to Him. Among them were Mary from Magdala, and Mary the mother of James and Joses, and the mother of the sons of Zebedee.

THIS passage falls into three sections.

(i) There is the story of the amazing things which happened as Jesus died. Whether or not we are meant to take these things literally, they teach us two great truths. (a) The Temple veil was rent from top to bottom. That was the veil which covered the Holy of Holies; that was the veil beyond which no man could penetrate, save only the High Priest on the Day of Atonement; that was the veil behind which the Spirit of God dwelt. There is symbolism here. Up to this time God had been hidden and remote, and no man knew what He was like. But in the death of Jesus we see the hidden love of God, and the way which once was barred to all men is now opened to all men to the presence of God. The life and the death of Jesus show us what God is like, and remove for ever the veil which hid God from men. (b) The tombs were opened. The symbolism of this is that Jesus conquered death. In dying and in rising again Jesus destroyed the power of death. Because of His life, His death and His resurrection the tomb has lost its power, and the grave has lost its terror, and death has lost its tragedy, because now we are certain that because He lives we shall live also.

(ii) There is the story of the adoration of the centurion. There is only one thing to be said about this. Jesus had said, " I, if I be lifted up from the earth, will draw all men unto me " (*John* 12: 32). Jesus foretold the magnetic power of the Cross; and the centurion was the first fruits

Jesus was only a lad. That is what William Blake was thinking of when he wrote his famous poem:

> " And did those feet in ancient time
>   Walk upon England's mountains green?
> And was the Holy Lamb of God
>   In England's pleasant pastures seen?
> And did the Countenance Divine
>   Shine forth upon our clouded hills?
> And was Jerusalem builded here,
>   Among those dark Satanic mills? "

The dark Satanic mills were the tin mines of Cornwall. That is one of those lovely legends of which we can only say that we would like it to be true, for there would be a thrill in the thought that the feet of the boy Jesus once touched English earth.

It is often said that Joseph gave to Jesus a tomb after He was dead, but did not support Him during His life. Joseph was a member of the Sanhedrin (*Luke* 23: 50); and Luke tells us that " he had not consented to the counsel and deed of them " (*Luke* 23: 51). Is it possible that that meeting of the Sanhedrin called in the house of Caiaphas in the middle of the night was a meeting selectively called? It hardly seems likely that the whole Sanhedrin could have been there. It may well be that Caiaphas summoned those whom he wished to be present, and packed the meeting with his supporters, and that Joseph never even got a chance to be there.

It is certainly true that in the end Joseph displayed the greatest courage. He came out on the side of a crucified criminal. He braved the possible resentment of Pilate; and he faced the certain hatred and mockery of the Jews. It may well be that Joseph of Arimathaea did everything that it was possible for him to do.

One obscure point remains. The woman who is called *the other Mary* is identified as Mary, the mother of Joses by *Mark* 15: 47. We have already seen that these women were present at the Cross; their love made them follow Jesus in life and in death.

and they came out of the tombs after His resurrection
and came into the holy city and appeared to many.
The centurion and those who were watching Jesus
with him saw the earthquake and the things that had
happened, and they were exceedingly afraid. " Truly,"
they said, " this man was the Son of God."

Many women were there watching from a distance.
They were the women who had followed Jesus from
Galilee, giving their service to Him.   Among them
were Mary from Magdala, and Mary the mother of
James and Joses, and the mother of the sons of
Zebedee.

THIS passage falls into three sections.

(i) There is the story of the amazing things which
happened as Jesus died. Whether or not we are meant to
take these things literally, they teach us two great truths.
(a) The Temple veil was rent from top to bottom. That
was the veil which covered the Holy of Holies; that was
the veil beyond which no man could penetrate, save only
the High Priest on the Day of Atonement; that was the
veil behind which the Spirit of God dwelt. There is symbolism here. Up to this time God had been hidden and
remote, and no man knew what He was like. But in the
death of Jesus we see the hidden love of God, and the way
which once was barred to all men is now opened to all
men to the presence of God. The life and the death of
Jesus show us what God is like, and remove for ever the
veil which hid God from men. (b) The tombs were opened.
The symbolism of this is that Jesus conquered death.
In dying and in rising again Jesus destroyed the power of
death. Because of His life, His death and His resurrection
the tomb has lost its power, and the grave has lost its
terror, and death has lost its tragedy, because now we
are certain that because He lives we shall live also.

(ii) There is the story of the adoration of the centurion.
There is only one thing to be said about this. Jesus had
said, " I, if I be lifted up from the earth, will draw all
men unto me " (*John* 12: 32). Jesus foretold the magnetic
power of the Cross; and the centurion was the first fruits

Jesus was only a lad. That is what William Blake was thinking of when he wrote his famous poem:

" And did those feet in ancient time
  Walk upon England's mountains green?
And was the Holy Lamb of God
  In England's pleasant pastures seen?
And did the Countenance Divine
  Shine forth upon our clouded hills?
And was Jerusalem builded here,
  Among those dark Satanic mills? "

The dark Satanic mills were the tin mines of Cornwall. That is one of those lovely legends of which we can only say that we would like it to be true, for there would be a thrill in the thought that the feet of the boy Jesus once touched English earth.

It is often said that Joseph gave to Jesus a tomb after He was dead, but did not support Him during His life. Joseph was a member of the Sanhedrin (*Luke* 23: 50); and Luke tells us that " he had not consented to the counsel and deed of them " (*Luke* 23: 51). Is it possible that that meeting of the Sanhedrin called in the house of Caiaphas in the middle of the night was a meeting selectively called? It hardly seems likely that the whole Sanhedrin could have been there. It may well be that Caiaphas summoned those whom he wished to be present, and packed the meeting with his supporters, and that Joseph never even got a chance to be there.

It is certainly true that in the end Joseph displayed the greatest courage. He came out on the side of a crucified criminal. He braved the possible resentment of Pilate; and he faced the certain hatred and mockery of the Jews. It may well be that Joseph of Arimathaea did everything that it was possible for him to do.

One obscure point remains. The woman who is called *the other Mary* is identified as Mary, the mother of Joses by *Mark* 15: 47. We have already seen that these women were present at the Cross; their love made them follow Jesus in life and in death.

AN IMPOSSIBLE ASSIGNMENT

Matthew 27: 62-66

On the next day, which is the day after the Preparation, the chief priests and Pharisees came to Pilate in a body. " Sir," they said, " we remember that, while He was still alive, that deceiver said, ' After three days I will rise again.' Give orders therefore that the tomb should be kept secure until the three days are ended, in case His disciples come and steal Him, and say to the people, ' He has been raised from among the dead.' If that happens, the final deception will be worse than the first." Pilate said, " You have a guard. Go, and make it as secure as you can." They went and secured the tomb by setting a seal upon it as well as by placing a guard.

THIS passage begins in the most curious way. It says that the chief priests and Pharisees went to Pilate on the next day, which is the day after the Preparation. Now Jesus was crucified on the Friday. Saturday is the Jewish Sabbath. The hours from 3 p.m. to 6 p.m. on Friday were called The Eve, or The Preparation. We have seen that, according to Jewish reckoning, the new day began at 6 p.m. Therefore, the Sabbath began at 6 p.m. on Friday; and the last hours of Friday were The Preparation. If this is accurate, it can only mean one thing—it must mean that the chief priests and Pharisees actually approached Pilate *on the Sabbath* with their request. If they did that, it is clear to see how radically they broke the Sabbath Law. If this is accurate, there is hardly any other incident in the gospel story which shows how desperately eager the Jewish authorities were finally to eliminate Jesus. In order to make certain that He was finally out of the way they were willing to break even their own most sacred laws.

There is a grim irony here. These Jews came to Pilate saying that Jesus had said that he would rise after three days. They did not admit that they envisaged the possibility that that might be true, but they thought that the disciples might seek to steal away the body and to say of money to the soldiers. " Say," they said, ' ' His disciples came by night, and stole Him away while we slept.' And if this comes to the governor's ears, we will use our influence, and we will see to it that you have nothing to worry about." They took the money and followed their instructions. And this is the story which is repeated amongst the Jews to this day.

WHEN some of the guard came to the chief priests and told them the story of the empty tomb, the Jewish authorities were desperately worried men. Was it possible that all their planning had come to nothing? So they formed a simple plan; they bribed the members of the guard to say that Jesus' disciples had come while they slept and had stolen His body.

It is interesting to see the means that the Jewish authorities had used in their desperate attempts to eliminate Jesus. They had used treachery to lay hold on Him. They had used illegality to try Him. They had used slander to charge Him to Pilate. And now they were using bribery to silence the truth about Him. *And they failed. Magna est veritas et praevalebit*, ran the Roman proverb; great is the truth and it will prevail. It is the fact of history that not all men's evil machinations can in the end stop the truth. The gospel of goodness is greater than the plots of wickedness.

THE GLORY OF THE FINAL PROMISE

Matthew 28: 16-20

So the eleven disciples went into Galilee, to the mountain where Jesus had instructed them to go. And they saw Him and worshipped Him; but some were not sure. Jesus came and spoke to them. " All power," He said, " is given me in heaven and upon earth. Go, therefore, and make all nations my disciples, baptizing them in the name of the Father and of the Son and of the Holy Spirit, and teaching them to keep all the

AN IMPOSSIBLE ASSIGNMENT

Matthew 27: 62-66

On the next day, which is the day after the Preparation, the chief priests and Pharisees came to Pilate in a body. " Sir," they said, " we remember that, while He was still alive, that deceiver said, ' After three days I will rise again.' Give orders therefore that the tomb should be kept secure until the three days are ended, in case His disciples come and steal Him, and say to the people, ' He has been raised from among the dead.' If that happens, the final deception will be worse than the first." Pilate said, " You have a guard. Go, and make it as secure as you can." They went and secured the tomb by setting a seal upon it as well as by placing a guard.

THIS passage begins in the most curious way. It says that the chief priests and Pharisees went to Pilate on the next day, which is the day after the Preparation. Now Jesus was crucified on the Friday. Saturday is the Jewish Sabbath. The hours from 3 p.m. to 6 p.m. on Friday were called The Eve, or The Preparation. We have seen that, according to Jewish reckoning, the new day began at 6 p.m. Therefore, the Sabbath began at 6 p.m. on Friday; and the last hours of Friday were The Preparation. If this is accurate, it can only mean one thing—it must mean that the chief priests and Pharisees actually approached Pilate *on the Sabbath* with their request. If they did that, it is clear to see how radically they broke the Sabbath Law. If this is accurate, there is hardly any other incident in the gospel story which shows how desperately eager the Jewish authorities were finally to eliminate Jesus. In order to make certain that He was finally out of the way they were willing to break even their own most sacred laws.

There is a grim irony here. These Jews came to Pilate saying that Jesus had said that he would rise after three days. They did not admit that they envisaged the possibility that that might be true, but they thought that the disciples might seek to steal away the body and to say

of money to the soldiers. " Say," they said, ' ' His
disciples came by night, and stole Him away while
we slept.' And if this comes to the governor's ears,
we will use our influence, and we will see to it that
you have nothing to worry about." They took the
money and followed their instructions. And this is
the story which is repeated amongst the Jews to this
day.

WHEN some of the guard came to the chief priests and
told them the story of the empty tomb, the Jewish authorities were desperately worried men. Was it possible that
all their planning had come to nothing? So they formed
a simple plan; they bribed the members of the guard to
say that Jesus' disciples had come while they slept and
had stolen His body.

It is interesting to see the means that the Jewish authorities had used in their desperate attempts to eliminate
Jesus. They had used treachery to lay hold on Him. They
had used illegality to try Him. They had used slander to
charge Him to Pilate. And now they were using bribery
to silence the truth about Him. *And they failed. Magna est
veritas et praevalebit,* ran the Roman proverb; great is the
truth and it will prevail. It is the fact of history that not
all men's evil machinations can in the end stop the truth.
The gospel of goodness is greater than the plots of wickedness.

THE GLORY OF THE FINAL PROMISE

Matthew 28: 16-20

So the eleven disciples went into Galilee, to the
mountain where Jesus had instructed them to go. And
they saw Him and worshipped Him; but some were not
sure. Jesus came and spoke to them. " All power," He
said, " is given me in heaven and upon earth. Go,
therefore, and make all nations my disciples, baptizing
them in the name of the Father and of the Son and of
the Holy Spirit, and teaching them to keep all the

commandments I have given you. And, look you, I am with you throughout all days until the end of the world."

HERE we are come to the end of the gospel story; and here we listen to the last words of Jesus to His men. And in this last meeting Jesus did three things.

(i) *He assured them of His power.* Surely nothing was outside the power of Him who had died and conquered death. Now they were the servants of a Master whose authority upon earth and in heaven was beyond all question.

(ii) *He gave them a commission.* He sent them out to make all the world His disciples. It may well be that the instruction to baptize is something which is, in fact, a development of the actual words of Jesus. That may be argued about; the one salient fact remains that the commission of Jesus is to win all men for Himself.

(iii) *He promised them a presence.* It must have been a staggering thing for eleven humble Galilaeans to be sent forth to the conquest of the world. Even as they heard it their hearts must have failed them. But no sooner was the command given than the promise followed. They were sent out—as we are—on the greatest task in the world, but with them there was the greatest presence in the world.

> " Though few and small and weak your bands,
>   Strong in your Captain's strength,
> Go to the conquest of all lands;
>   All must be His at length."

commandments I have given you. And, look you, I am with you throughout all days until the end of the world."

HERE we are come to the end of the gospel story; and here we listen to the last words of Jesus to His men. And in this last meeting Jesus did three things.

(i) *He assured them of His power.* Surely nothing was outside the power of Him who had died and conquered death. Now they were the servants of a Master whose authority upon earth and in heaven was beyond all question.

(ii) *He gave them a commission.* He sent them out to make all the world His disciples. It may well be that the instruction to baptize is something which is, in fact, a development of the actual words of Jesus. That may be argued about; the one salient fact remains that the commission of Jesus is to win all men for Himself.

(iii) *He promised them a presence.* It must have been a staggering thing for eleven humble Galilaeans to be sent forth to the conquest of the world. Even as they heard it their hearts must have failed them. But no sooner was the command given than the promise followed. They were sent out—as we are—on the greatest task in the world, but with them there was the greatest presence in the world.

" Though few and small and weak your bands,
    Strong in your Captain's strength,
  Go to the conquest of all lands;
    All must be His at length."